AF846112

The Library | UNIVERSITY OF BATH

Bath BA2 7AY · United Kingdom

24 NOV 1988
26 JAN 1989
04 MAY 1992
CANCELLED FEB 1989
12 MAY 1992
FEB 1993
26 FEB 91
-6 MAR 91
15 MAR 91

Ownership, Control, and the Firm

HAROLD DEMSETZ

Ownership, Control, and the Firm

The Organization of Economic Activity
Volume I

UNIVERSITY OF BATH
LIBRARY
0 2 AUG 2022
Withdrawn

Basil Blackwell

UNIVERSITY OF BATH LIBRARY
12 -7 OCT 1988 7
338.68

S019394

Copyright © Harold Demsetz, 1988

First published 1988

Basil Blackwell Ltd
109 Cowley Road, Oxford, OX4 1JF, UK

Basil Blackwell Inc.
432 Park Avenue South, Suite 1503
New York, NY 10016, USA

All rights reserved. Except for the quotation of short passages for the purposes of criticism and review, no part of this publication may be reproduced, stored in a retrieval system, or transmitted, in any form or by any means, electronic, mechanical, photocopying, recording or otherwise, without the prior permission of the publisher.

Except in the United States of America, this book is sold subject to the condition that it shall not, by way of trade or otherwise, be lent, re-sold, hired out, or otherwise circulated without the publisher's prior consent in any form of binding or cover other than that in which it is published and without a similar condition including this condition being imposed on the subsequent purchaser.

British Library Cataloguing in Publication Data

Demsetz, Harold, 1930–
Ownership, control, and the firm. – (The Organization of economic activity; Vol. 1).
1. Companies, Ownership
I. Title II. Series
338.7′4

ISBN 0-631-16175-9

Library of Congress Cataloging in Publication Data

Demsetz, Harold, 1930–
The organization of economic activity.

Includes bibliographies and index.
Contents: v. 1. Ownership, control, and the firm.
1. Industrial organization. I. Title.
HD2328.D46 1988 338.6 88-6366
ISBN 0-631-16175-9 (v. 1)

Typeset in 10 on 12pt Baskerville
by Dobbie Typesetting Service, Plymouth, Devon
Printed in Great Britain by
T. J. Press Ltd, Padstow, Cornwall

Contents

To Rita, Laura, Sid,
Eliz., and Becky

PART I
Introduction

1
Autobiographical Sketch

My mother and her family came to this country from Austria when she was a young child, soon after the turn of the century. My father's family, with German and Russian origins, arrived about the same time. I was born in 1930, the youngest of five children. An apartment on the West Side of Chicago, near to what was then the world headquarters of Sears, was home to me for the first 25 years of my life. The neighborhood offered ample access to the bustling city and security enough in its narrower boundaries. Italian and Jewish families with memories of Europe still strong made up most of its population. The mood was upbeat for most of these families during the last part of the decade of the 1930s. Hard work, cleverness, and investment in one's self were expected to yield significant returns. Education was valued highly, but this value derived mainly from its instrumental use in improving living standards. The emphasis on doing well created little psychological stress for the young. It was easy to progress beyond the status of families lacking wealth and command over English in a world just emerging from the Great Depression. In retrospect, it was a good place and a good time in which to grow to adulthood in America.

No large reservoir of knowledge about American educational institutions was possessed by most of these families. Mine, at least, lacked it. This made for unimaginative and uninformed decisions about higher education. I began college by seeking education that would lead to employment, and I sought it at the nearest and cheapest source. The study of engineering at a free City Junior College within walking distance from home was my choice. By the time I received my undergraduate degree in economics from the University of Illinois in 1953, I had experimented with engineering, forestry, and philosophy at four schools while working a variety of part-time jobs diverse enough to include ushering at Chicago's opera house and driving a taxi.

Graduated from Illinois, I began a tour of duty in the Army that was greatly shortened by the winding down of the Korean War. I entered graduate school at Northwestern University and received a Ph.D. in economics in 1959. On the way to this degree, at a time when I was not sure I would be able to continue graduate education, I took an MBA degree from Northwestern's business school. Part of my dissertation, that which dealt with brand loyalty and competition between highly advertised and "non-advertised" brands, was published in *Econometrica*. That, my second article, is undoubtedly the only contribution I will make to this distinguished journal. My first publication, "The Nature of Equilibrium in Monopolistic Competition," written before I had completed my Ph.D., was accepted by the *Journal of Political Economy* shortly after I arrived at my first academic post at the University of Michigan. At a time when not many graduate students published, these papers constituted an unexpected start for someone whose career objective did not then include active publishing.

In 1955, when I was still at Northwestern, Rita Coleman and I were married. It was my good fortune to meet Rita when I was a young teenager on Chicago's West Side. Her parents had immigrated from Poland and Russia. Our meeting and marriage were "substantively arranged" by the similarity in needs and interests that brought our parents to live within one block of each other. We became neighborhood friends early in our lives. When I returned from the army and began working on my MBA, she had finished her undergraduate work at the University of Chicago, and was then employed at a publishing house in Chicago while contemplating her next move. Our friendship ripened into more, and before the year was out we had fallen in love. After marrying, we settled into an efficiency apartment on Chicago's North Side close to Northwestern. Rita worked full time and, with a research assistantship I received from Northwestern, we kept the family ledger in black ink. With her help, I was able to continue graduate work. She has been a wonderful partner in life, creating conditions that leave me no excuse for whatever failings I may have. Four children and 33 years later, we remain married and in love.

I began teaching at the University of Michigan in 1958, but remained there only two years. My decision to move to UCLA, in fact, turned out to be a good one, but at the time it was made it was not. UCLA had offered me $400 more per year than my Michigan salary, which must have been about $6,500 in 1960. Michigan wanted me to stay, and argued that $400 was not an important sum. I responded that if this sum was not important, Michigan ought to be willing to increase my salary by $400. I was informed by the absence of a counter-offer that what Michigan meant was that $400 was not important to *me*; and so Rita, our new daughter, and I rode off in the sunset to California. This little story, of course, is true, but I suspect that behind my decision was a preference for city life, acquired during the preceding 28 years in Chicago. Two years in lovely, quiet Ann Arbor had not been long enough to offset this preference.

Most of my career has been in association with the University of California at Los Angeles (from 1960 to 1963 and again from 1971 to date) and the University of Chicago from (1963 to 1971). I also have been a Senior Research

Fellow of the Hoover Institution and a Senior Analyst of the Center for Naval Analyses. In 1986 I became the first holder of the Arthur Andersen Alumni Chair at UCLA.

Economics fascinated me when I was first exposed to it as an undergraduate. The existence of the problem of explaining the functioning of an economic system was new to me. My enthusiasm waxed when I learned about the coordinating role of prices. That there existed theory to explain how a decentralized economy works, and that this theory seemed rigorous and yielding of surprises, powerfully impressed me. I am still impressed by the demonstration of the socially beneficial power of self-interest disciplined by competition (itself an expression of self-interest). I did not know then that it was Adam Smith's central problem – coordination in a decentralized social system – that had caught my interest. It continues to hold my interest, and, without much planning to this end, my work mainly treats subjects that are corollaries of it (the functioning of markets, the general nature of firms in these markets, and the legal system that gives content to the way coordination works out in practice).

My approach to this subject, and my style in dealing with it, are fully revealed in these two volumes. My work is mainly a blend of positive theorizing and evidence-gathering, but I have not hesitated to debate normative questions. I rely more heavily on verbal and geometric exposition than is typical today. This reflects no prejudice against mathematical techniques, which, on occasion, I have used. It simply signifies that I experience greater confidence in my understanding of what I am writing about if I can state my thoughts in carefully chosen words or simple geometry. This propensity probably leads to the avoidance of some topics. It also encourages me to search deeply for the essence of a problem; once the central issue has been isolated, it usually can be stated and analyzed with simple techniques. The style has advantages and disadvantages. One of its chief advantages is the contribution it makes to communicating with larger audiences. For me, its advantages outweigh its disadvantages, but this apparently is not true for many other economists.

Although much of my writing is in the area of economics known as industrial organization, the reader must soon realize that I have avoided two approaches that have been popular tools for other economists working in this field. These are the industry study and game theory. This is not happenstance but derives from a belief that, for the topics that interest me, these tools (in my hands, at least) would not be very productive. These topics concern the principles of coordination in a decentralized economy. Industry studies undertaken about the time I was learning economics were rich in details, but poor in generalizing power. They were to the study of decentralizing as studies of the European family are to the study of Western culture. Some guidance may be obtained from the details that can be mastered through a narrower focus, but not so much as to make it a desirable methodology for someone interested in theorizing at a broader level of generality. However, more recent uses of the industry study, in testing theories, seem to me to be highly productive. The industry study used to assess the consequences of regulation is a considerably more useful tool than one designed to reveal a theory of regulation.

Game-theoretic constructs have, or will have, things to say about the interactions of decision-makers when their numbers are small. It is the interest in such situations that gave birth to game theory, and this remains the context in which it does best. My interest, however, is in system-wide forces that render this context less useful. The decentralized, competitive *system* functions to overwhelm tactical moves that may have been stimulated by interactions between small numbers of decision-makers. The analytical usefulness of the concept of decentralization derives precisely from the fact that it allows the analyst to ignore the behavior of a single individual or a small group of individuals. It implicitly asserts that the tactical measures taken by incumbent firms to bar entrants from an industry cannot long hold at bay the continuous onslaught of more efficient organizations and techniques of production. The analysis of tactical decisions is not likely to be very useful in studying the general and central tendencies of decentralized economic systems, especially when these result from repeated "plays" in contexts that are not zero-sum in nature. Future developments may convince me of my error in holding this belief; I state it not to persuade readers of its truth, but to give them a better understanding of my interests and perspectives.

Although I embraced economics quickly once exposed to it, I did not similarly embrace a professional life devoted largely to research and publishing. I began graduate school expecting to live the life of a teacher, which I took to be nine months of teaching preparations and class meetings and three months of fun, travel, and relaxation. Until graduate school, I had thought economics a subject that had reached a high state of completion. It was to be learned, enjoyed, and taught. I wonder how many students enter our graduate programs with notions similar to this? Whatever this number may be, such notions do predict the behavior of a considerable number of professional economists, the overwhelming percentage of whom neither publish nor perish. This vision of my future proved quite wrong. I give considerable time to research and writing; never yet have I taken more than two or three weeks' vacation; and traveling has lost much of its attraction. I hope I am not as dull as this makes me seem, but I enjoy my work and my home.

I held for some time to this erroneous vision of what my life was going to be, even after I had experienced publishing success early in my career. The change that has come about has not been due to greater awareness of the sources of professional stature. The conscious design of a stature-improving career has not kept me awake nights. I simply have found enjoyment in ideas and in writing about and discussing them. Moreover, for reasons not known to me, I have never been shy about putting my thoughts on paper, nor have I been fearful of someone uncovering faults with them. More than anything else, these two traits – the enjoyment of ideas and the lack of fear in being wrong – have altered my career.

The transition to becoming a ''player'' in the publishing game might not have been so easy had I not taken up company with some truly outstanding economists, but it would have happened anyway. An able group of young economists taught in Northwestern's economics department when I studied for my Ph.D., including Bob Basmann, Meyer Burstein, Bob Clower, Robert Eisner, Charles Tiebout, and Robert Strotz. It was a good department in which to learn what professional economists do. But I was most influenced by persons who were to become colleagues. Most important among these are Armen A. Alchian, whose unorthodox approaches to economics have fascinated me for years now; R. H. Coase, whose work on the firm and on social cost have been important in motivating several of my papers; Frank H. Knight, whose views on human nature and whose book *Risk, Uncertainty, and Profit* still give me much food for thought; Aaron Director, who freely gave of his scholarly knowledge and thoughtful insights; and George J. Stigler, whose help and support warrant a few additional words.

Stigler has been a diligent critic of my ideas and a careful reader of my manuscripts for 25 years. The questions he raises generally have been the most penetrating. Although he has focused his attention in recent years on the economics of politics, and I have not, we share similar interests in economics, and, I believe, we hold similar judgments about the importance of different types of work. This may partly account for his willingness to comment on my work. Stigler also has been a catalyst by virtue of the energy and enthusiasm he shows for pushing the frontiers of our knowledge out a bit farther. In these respects, he has been a superb colleague and a thoroughly enjoyable and entertaining friend. It is his work, however, that has been of paramount importance. He has a rare talent for giving content to a topic when he touches it, and for leaving it in a more enticing state than when he came to it. Had I never met the man, I would have come under his influence through his work; it has always been a source of encouragement for me to get on with my own.

During my years at Chicago, a uniquely large number of economists were discussing and writing about problems that interested me. The Economics Department, the Law School, and the Business School all housed economists (and some non-economists, too) with these interests. In addition to Coase, Director, and Stigler, there were Reuben Kessel, Lester Telser, and Peter Pashigian. Richard Posner and Gary Becker arrived on the scene somewhat later in my stay. Milton Friedman loomed in the background, but his professional attention was not then on these issues. Frank Knight had retired well before I came to Chicago, but he was still in residence. Stigler, who had been a student when Knight actively taught at Chicago, occasionally brought him to lunch. He was then struggling against age to remain professionally active. His feistiness still showed. That was an exciting time for me, as I think it must have been for all who were there.

The industrial organization workshop directed by Stigler was the central discussion arena, although lunches at the Quadrangle Club were not models of quiet dining either. The workshop became famous for the lively and open debate with which it enveloped presentations made by outsiders and insiders alike. My first exposure to the University of Chicago, and of the university to me, was as a visitor to this workshop in 1963. The invitation came, I think, as a result of Alchian's good words about me to Kessel. Kessel and I met at the 1963 meeting of the American Economics Association. He asked me if I was happy at UCLA. I did not know it at the time, but the answer I gave him – "Make me unhappy" – was just to his taste, and I received the invitation.

I was then working on a sequel to my first paper on monopolistic competition, one that discussed welfare problems and dynamics to a greater extent, and this is what I presented. Many people were in attendance because the workshop was serving as a recruiting seminar. Only one person kept my adrenaline running by mounting a constant barrage of pertinent questions. He was taller than the rest and sat at the back of the room. It was George Stigler, of course. Partly as a result of this workshop, Chicago invited me to join the tenured faculty of its Business School. I accepted. Stigler told me years later that it was not the content of my paper so much as the way I handled myself that won me the invitation. (He never has had much use for monopolistic competition.)

I completed several papers while at Chicago. The most successful of these, measured by subsequent impact, were "Why Regulate Utilities?," "Toward a Theory of Property Rights," "Information and Efficiency: Another Viewpoint," and "The Cost of Transacting." At Chicago, I also began work (with Alchian who was visiting Chicago) on "Production, Information Costs, and Economic Organization," which we completed after I had rejoined UCLA's faculty; this paper also has had a discernible impact.

My return to UCLA came about for several reasons, of which two may be of interest to readers. One was strictly professional. That there could be such a reason at the time of my move will surprise some people, most of whom are still at Chicago. I wanted more access to Ph.D. students in economics than it was possible to obtain in a business school at that time. Most business students, even at the Ph.D. level, majored in finance, accounting, or marketing. Economics, even in a business school so noted for emphasizing economics, served students whose main interests were in other areas. (There is no necessity for economics to play such a limited role in the education of students bound for a career in business. One of the tasks I have undertaken over the last four years has been that of innovating a new program in business economics for undergraduates at UCLA.)

The courses I taught, price theory and industrial organization, were pitched to MBAs at a level not much different than upper-level undergraduate. Doctoral students in economics wrote their dissertations and did most of their studying in the Economics department. I was gaining little experience in dissertation supervision or in teaching graduate-level economics courses. These activities seemed important to me if I was to maintain my professional capability, enlarge my influence, and mature into the full role of professor of economics. To some degree, the absence of Ph.D. students in economics accelerated the rate at which the technical tooling I had received at Northwestern depreciated. (It will surprise some readers to learn that I was capable enough in such tools that when I joined UCLA's department the first time around I had sole responsibility for the graduate course in econometrics.)

The situation would not have been an easy one to remedy at Chicago without moving to the Economics department. I was too proud to solicit an invitation to joint the department, and none ever came. Coase was soon to retire, and my friends and colleagues had planned on my taking his position in the Law School, where I already taught part-time. It would have been an honor to succeed Henry Simons, Aaron Director, and R. H. Coase, and it was a reasonable fit of position and man; indeed, in several respects it was an ideal fit. The respect in which it was not was my age. It would have been unwise to isolate myself even more from Ph.D. work in economics at that early stage in my career.

I did not follow R. H. Coase into this position, but neither did I abandon my interest in law and economics. I continued to do some writing in this field, but I refer here to my participation as a major lecturer (with Alchian) in two long-running programs to teach economics to law professors and federal judges. These programs were entrepreneured and organized by Henry G. Manne, and I believe that they have had more to do with bringing economics to law schools in the United States than any other teaching effort of which I am aware.

The second reason for moving to UCLA was financial. I had joined a small group of business school colleagues in the purchase of long-term treasuries. We were speculating heavily, having put up only 5 percent of the price of the bonds. The rate of growth of the money supply had turned down. Being strong believers in monetary theory, we expected the economy and interest rates to turn down also. Interest rates did not fall immediately, or for a very long time after our purchase. I found myself sending margin to my broker as frequently as one feeds a pet dog. My proverbial "shirt" was lost. Reuben Kessel dryly observed that we still have a lot to learn about interest rates. Were Reuben still alive, he would be pleased to learn that my understanding of interest rates has improved considerably. Now, I lose a much smaller fraction of my wealth speculating on changes in these rates (which are sure to come).

At this time, the chairman of UCLA's Economics department, Clay LaForce, made me a financially attractive offer merely to visit for one year. It was an offer I could not afford to turn down, and I did not. Simultaneously, UCLA's department recruited Robert Clower and Phoebus Dhrymes. With

Alchian, Jack Hirshleifer, Axel Leijonhufvud, and Sam Peltzman already there, the department seemed to me to have a bright future and to warrant closer examination.

My ties to Chicago, and especially to Coase and Stigler, were quite strong, however, and I was in a genuine quandary about whether to stay at UCLA after my year's visit. I vacillated, took much too long to decide, and thereby imposed costs on my friends at both places. They did derive some compensation for this at my expense, for my indecision had become the butt of humor at many luncheons, some of which I had to attend. De facto, I remained at UCLA, but I do not know whether I really *decided* to remain. Things have worked out well at UCLA. I have had the pleasure of good colleagues and the opportunity to influence and be influenced by many fine graduate students. My appetite for interaction with students in a quality graduate program has been more than fully satisfied. One of my few complaints now is about the excessive number of dissertations I chair!

My work product is different as a result of being at UCLA. I have little doubt that legal issues in property, contracts, and antitrust, discussed mainly in terms of formal logic, would have been more important to me had I returned to Chicago. At UCLA I have given mainstream industrial organization more attention. When I returned to UCLA, there were no continuing workshops in the Economics department. I began one in Law and Economics, but its content was mainly industrial organization because this offered an easier route by which to bring empirical work to the students. I had been disappointed in the dissertations that were then being done at UCLA. Very little empirical work was involved. I tried to change this through the workshop and, in anticipation of a demonstration effect, through empirical work of my own. Industrial organization offered better targets for such work at that time. One important project, the first I took up after completing the theory of the firm paper with Alchian at UCLA, was to review the market concentration doctrine and to bring new views and data to bear on it. This work, summarized in "Two Systems of Belief About Monopoly," began an important antitrust policy debate. Although antitrust frequently was discussed at Chicago at that time, and Stigler had published serious work on this topic, the "structuralists," led by Joe Bain, had convinced most industrial organization economists of the validity of the market concentration doctrine. The debate was rekindled at an important conference held at the Airlie House in Virginia in 1974 (and since published as *Industrial Concentration: The New Learning*).

I continued to blend theory and empirical work at UCLA, writing mostly about firms, markets, and public policy. Barriers to entry, the nature of the firm, and the economics of the modern corporation have received the bulk of my attention in recent years, except for a block of time I gave to the preparation of a series of invited lectures delivered in Rotterdam under the auspices of the De Vries Institute. These have been published as a small book titled

Economic, Legal, and Political Dimensions of Competition. They contain a reinterpretation of the perfect competition model and a discussion of the similarities and differences between competition in the three arenas named in the title.

Curiously, my work on the firm and on barriers to entry has brought me full circle back to topics in the law that I touched on at Chicago, and that I might have focused on had I returned to the Law School there. My writings about the nature of the firm, virtually all of which are included in the first volume of this book, have become increasingly concerned with the problem of explaining ownership. Ownership inevitably leads to notions about the underlying system of property rights. Reapproaching the subject from the perspective offered by the theory of the firm has made it easier to give it an empirical bent that is lacking in earlier work. (Especially see, in volume I, "The Structure of Corporate Ownership: Causes and Consequences," co-authored with Lehn.)

A person who has not planned his writing program comes to the task of organizing a sample of his published and unpublished papers with some trepidation, especially for a book titled *The Organization of Economic Activity.* I am therefore surprised to discover one central theme – ownership – and a few secondary themes – market structure, ethics, policy, and politics. The papers in volume I deal (more rather than less) with the topic of ownership. The sequel to this volume deals much more with the secondary themes. Both volumes contain several new papers.

2
A Framework for the Study of Ownership

Ownership is a topic that has a long history in the social sciences and philosophy, but the discussion remains unintegrated in its economic dimension to this date. This is true even for writings as recent as those dating from R. H. Coase's publication of "The Problem of Social Cost" (1960). The main objective of this chapter is to bring some order to the discussion, with special reference to the place in this order of several of the papers in this volume. A general peculiarity of recent literature is that its focus often is not on ownership itself. Nowhere is this more true than in Coase's famous paper on social cost. His topic is externalities, not ownership. His objective is to demonstrate that the received doctrine on externalities is wrong, not to draw conclusions bearing on a theory of ownership. The study of regulation is another example. Price controls, minimum wages, profit constraints, and so on are discussed quite properly in the context of regulation. Yet, the essence of effective regulation is to truncate the bundle of rights that defines ownership. Without recognizing the fact, the authors of this vast literature have been writing about the economics of ownership.

Because ownership is treated neither explicitly nor centrally in much of this writing, no clear framework for the economics of ownership has emerged. This chapter adopts the following simple framework:

- A Ownership as an exogenous phenomenon
  - 1 The identity of owners (or the assignment of rights)
  - 2 The truncation of ownership rights
  - 3 Normative and ethical dimensions of ownership
- B Ownership as an endogenous phenomenon
  - 1 Allocation by individual action
  - 2 Allocation by cooperative action
    - (a) Management of the business firm (the corporation)
    - (b) The distribution of wealth and efficient control

OWNERSHIP AS AN EXOGENOUS PHENOMENON

The approach taken here is to accept a bundle of ownership rights as given fact and to examine the consequences that flow from hypothetically altering certain characteristics of the legal framework that defines ownership. No attempt is made to rationalize the existence of a particular bundle of rights or to examine actual changes in the legal framework. Two major hypothetical changes are considered. The first asks about the consequences that flow from altering the identity of owners of entitlements. What difference does it make whether farmers or ranchers own the right to control the wandering of cattle? The second asks about the consequences of altering the content of the bundle of rights. What difference does it make if owners are barred by regulation from exercising the right to offer entitlements for sale at all possible prices?

The identity-of-owner problem

This problem derives from Coase's (1960) work on social cost, in which he asks how market negotiations work to eliminate or reduce divergences between private and social cost. Coase analyzes the role of negotiations in two contexts, which, in today's jargon, may be called 'models.' One model assumes zero transaction cost, the other assumes positive transaction cost. He concludes that externalities are eliminated by market negotiations if transaction cost is zero. Something akin to externalities remains if transaction cost is positive; however, in this case, Coase finds error in the prescription put forward by the traditional externality doctrine. Taken together, these models constitute a refutation of this doctrine.

Coase's paper led to controversy, much of it having to do with the unrealism of the first model. Not only does this model utilize zero transaction cost, but it also assumes that income effects are absent (and that competition constrains all negotiations). Coase himself views the first model as a stepping stone to the more realistic one in which transaction cost is positive (but in which income effects still are ignored). He and his critics are too quick to undermine the significance of the zero transaction cost model. It is no mere stepping stone. To the contrary, it is central to the debate.

The intellectual position attacked by Coase had nothing to do with differences in income or with positive transaction cost. The soot that descends from a steel mill's smokestack onto a nearby laundry is an externality from the perspective of neoclassical economics because it raises the *cost* of laundering – not because it makes the owner of the laundry poorer, and not because interacting parties face insurmountable transaction cost. In the context of the intellectual position he challenges, Coase is quite correct to assume away complications that have nothing to do with the traditional doctrine's basic allegation. If his first model describes an irrelevant world, so does that of the traditional doctrine. This doctrine focuses on the cost that arises out of an interaction between two activities. Its conclusion in regard to this interaction is that inefficient resource utilization arises from the presence of the interaction, but it pays no attention to the role of negotiation in resolving or ameliorating this inefficiency.

Coase does not put his criticism this way, but the traditional position ignores the crucial role played by implicit cost in guiding people's decisions. The central point in his analysis is that implicit cost motivates behavior that ameliorates potential externality problems. How better to demonstrate this than by conjuring a world in which implicit cost is given full reign? This is a world with no barriers to negotiation, since implicit cost is brought to bear through negotiation.

Coase's first model is essential to demonstrate the fallacy in the traditional view. The best that Coase can do with the traditional view when he appeals to the more realistic world of positive transaction cost is to point to a dilemma that it fails to see: that there is more than one policy option available to ameliorate a problem of externalities. The owner of the factory may be held liable or the laundry owner can be left to bear the soot cost that has befallen him. Contrary to the traditional view, Coase shows through the use of his second model that it is not clear from theory alone which alternative is better. This conclusion hardly constitutes an attack so basic as that which is drawn from the first model. It is the first model that lays bare the failure to recognize the important role to be played by implicit cost.

Coase's incidental contribution to a theory of ownership derives from the technique he uses to demonstrate the importance of implicit cost. To set up his analysis, he assumes that property (ownership) rights are fully specified and respected. This assumption, when added to zero transaction cost and zero income effects (and competitive conditions), completes the specification of his model. He then asks what difference it makes (to the existence of externalities) if farmers or, alternatively, ranchers control where cattle may walk. What difference does it make if farmers or owners of railroads control the spark content of airspace? As a by-product of considering these questions, we can begin to understand when the identity of owners makes a difference to resource allocation and when it does not. In the zero-transaction-cost, zero-income-effects model, the same mix of output, a mix that is efficient, results from the negotiated solution no matter who owns the relevant entitlement.

The conclusion that production would be efficient should not have stimulated the controversy that in fact arose; for it is a particular application of the standard deduction of price theory that competitive markets allocate resources efficiently, a deduction that is made without reference to the identity of owners. However, to this efficiency conclusion Coase adds the proposition that the efficient mix of output is *identical* under the stipulated assumptions no matter which person, or class of persons, is designated as owner of the entitlement. The assumption that income effects are absent helps one to reach this supplementary conclusion. If a farmer is made richer, and a rancher poorer, under one assignment of entitlements than under another, the absence of income effects assures us that each person's marginal rate of substitution between the relevant goods is no different under one ownership assignment than under the other. Although ownership is wealth, and altering the identity of owners necessarily changes the distribution of wealth, the change one ordinarily would expect in the marginal rates of substitution between goods is partly negated by assuming that income effects are absent.

However, this negation is insufficient to carry the analysis to the supplementary conclusion. Persons who are wealthier under one assignment of entitlements spends more than under the alternative assignment. If they do not purchase more corn, they purchase more beef, or they save more. If the persons made wealthier purchase these goods in different proportions than do persons made poorer, then, even though *each* person spends in the same proportion on all relevant goods at different income levels, the total mix of outputs in the economy must change if the distribution of wealth changes. As long as those who are made wealthier and those who are made poorer, taken as two groups, have different marginal rates of substitution, alternative distributions of wealth imply different efficient mixes of output. The choice of different owners of rights changes the weights given by market negotiations to the different tastes that must be presumed to exist in any large population.

This anticipated alteration in the product mix contained in the efficient solution is not discussed by Coase. If one reads his work in a spirit of trying to understand what was going through his mind, the reason for this omission becomes clear. Simply put, he views the interacting parties as producers, not consumers. His discussion is of farmers, ranchers, and owners of railroads in the context of their being producers. He takes the market prices of the relevant goods as given because he does not consider alterations in the wealth of producers important to patterns of consumption, and what he means by the absence of income effects is that the demands for the relevant commodities are unaffected by a redistribution of wealth between farmers and ranchers as producers. Implicitly, the consumption of these goods is by third parties not involved in the costly interaction; or, alternatively, the households of farmers and ranchers, taken in the large, are assumed to exhibit no predictably different preferences between consumption goods.

This is quite appropriate to the effort in which Coase is engaged. The traditional position on externalities does *not* claim there is too small an output of corn (if ranchers are left without liability for damage done by straying cattle) *because* farmers *consume* less corn if their wealth is adversely impacted by the damage done. The traditional position alleges that less corn is *produced* because the *cost* of growing corn is raised (too much) by a failure to discourage appropriately the straying of cattle. The tastes of farmers as between corn and beef, relative to the tastes of ranchers, simply are irrelevant to the conclusions drawn by the traditional intellectual position on externalities. Readers would have been distracted by the extraneous issue of taste differences if Coase had discussed this problem. The correct issue is the failure of the traditional doctrine to take account of implicit cost.

From the perspective of the present essay, it is important to note that Coase, incidental to discussing the externality issue, has introduced and partially analyzed a different issue, one dealing with the *identity of owners*. One may conclude from Coase's reasoning that the identity of owners has no impact on resource allocation in a competitive setting in the absence of transaction costs if the affected parties play no significant role in the overall pattern of demands for goods. With positive transaction costs or with affected parties significantly impacting the pattern of demands for goods, the identity of owners affects the mix of output that is efficient, but does not alter the conclusion that each resulting mix of output is efficient when judged by the demands emanating from the wealth distribution associated with a particular specification of ownership.

It is important to realize that Coase is not considering a *change* in the assignment of rights. He is discussing hypothetical *alternative* assignments of rights. The distinction may be seen clearly by way of example. Assume that land is about to be settled. Parcels are to be distributed through some random selection device that matches potential owners to parcels of land. Does it affect the uses to be made of this land if the people about to settle it are told that the use of a parcel of land for farming (or, alternatively, for ranching) entitles its owner to determine also whether and where cattle may walk across the land? This question is different from one that asks whether successive changes in the assignment of rights affect the use to which land is put, and it is different from one that asks what the consequences will be if those who have a personal comparative advantage in farming (and in ranching) have different marginal rates of substitution between corn and beef. Changes in ownership identities through time, as when slaves are 'set' free or when land use is unexpectedly re-zoned, are situations in which it is difficult to believe that resource use will be unaffected. This is not to argue that Coase is wrong, but that information and transaction costs are plausibly significant in dealings over time. Unless all *prospective* owners are known, the cost of their negotiating with present owners is necessarily large.

If Coase's interest in the traditional externality doctrine is kept clearly in mind, much of the criticism associated with income distribution, transaction cost, and the altering of rights through time disappears. It is in this spirit that I wrote "When Does the Rule of Liability Matter?" (chapter 4 below). It addresses questions bearing on the problem of blackmail, or extortion, and on the relevance or irrelevance of the distinction between the short run and long run – issues that concerned critics of Coase's paper.

However, in "The Exchange and Enforcement of Property Rights" (chapter 3 below), I raise a criticism of my own bearing on a different aspect of the problem: the problem of demand revelation in the presence of a property right that is collectively owned. If a railroad is to be induced by farmers to reduce the number of trains run, so as to reduce spark output and, thereby, the quantity of crops burned, why would any one farmer find it in his interest fully to reveal his demand for a reduction in sparks?

"The Cost of Transacting" (chapter 5) attempts, in a limited way, to begin remedying our ignorance about the determinants of transaction cost. This paper took on a life of its own, influencing work in the finance field that has little direct concern with the issues raised by Coase. Although some headway is made in this paper in the context of security markets, we still do not have an empirically implementable theory of transaction cost. My concern about this resurfaces in "The Theory of the Firm Revisited" (chapter 9), since transaction cost has been taken by many to be the cornerstone of the theory of the firm.

The truncation of ownership

This aspect of the economics of ownership was developed outside the context of ownership (except possibly in regard to not-for-profit firms) as part of the economics of regulation. How is behavior affected by setting price floors and ceilings? By capping allowable profit rates? By barring certain forms of competition? Our understanding of the answers to such questions is quite good, but because the economics of shortages and surpluses began its development before and outside the context of property rights it is not generally thought of as part of the economics of ownership. Surely, it is, dealing as it does with the consequences of restricting the bundle of rights that defines ownership. An enforced legal price restriction denies to owners the right to ask for and to offer certain prices.

Early work on such problems stops short at recognizing that truncating rights in this fashion creates shortages and surpluses. More recent work seeks to understand how people react to the implied queuing that results. Alchian and Kessel (1962) recognize the relationship between the truncation of rights and the behavior that is likely to follow. I follow their lead in a provocative paper, "Minorities in the Market Place" (chapter 6 below). Central to our argument is the heightened emphasis that is given to modes of competing other than through prices when restrictions on property rights bar outright payments. Restricting one's freedom to use pecuniary wealth to influence others, say by offering higher prices to win agreements to sell, results in greater emphasis on "personal characteristics competition." Rent control makes people depend in greater degree on the basis of color, religion, family size, and so on when competing to secure living space. Prevented from maximizing fully on the margin of pecuniary returns by regulations that truncate ownership rights, owners seek to maximize utility by indulging their preferences for certain personal characteristics more intensely.

Reactions to restrictions on price need not be reflected only in more intense use of personal characteristics competition. The important paper by Averch and Johnson (1962) argues persuasively that owners seek to maximize utility through increased investment in enlarging firm size when regulators bar higher rates of return on capital. The truncation of ownership rights issue is also at the heart of the notion of barriers to entry, although the topic is not often approached from this perspective. Because it is not, the literature on barriers presupposes too much objectivity. The value judgments concerning what owners may or may not do, implicit in barriers to entry, are discussed in the paper "Barriers to Entry," reprinted in the second volume.

The lesson to be learned here cannot be as specific as that which may be derived from Coase's discussion of the assignment of rights problem. The substitute avenues of adjustment to which people turn in reacting to restrictions on the content of their ownership entitlements are too many, yet much depends on the particular case. The general conclusion is that constraining the ability of persons to exercise specific rights of ownership causes tham to rely in greater degree on substitute margins of adjustment in their attempt to maximize utility. The result is a different allocation of goods and a different implicit distribution of wealth. Those most able to compete in allowed ways and least able to compete in disallowed ways (had they not become disallowed) enjoy the equivalent of an increase in real wealth.

It may be noted that this conclusion refers to the consequences that flow from an ad hoc legal action affecting the condition of ownership, one that truncates the bundle of ownership rights. No such truncation is involved in Coase's problem, where the issue involves the assignment of a "complete" bundle of rights as between alternative owners. However, the different problem of reassigning ownership rights to different persons *over time* does involve truncation, and, consistent with the above general conclusion, behavior is affected. The more insecure is tenure on the land, the greater the degree to which utility maximization requires under-investment in capital improvements. This under-investment would be eliminated via Coase's analysis if future owners could be known and could transact costlessly with present owners; but because the stream of future owners, even if known, has a *collective* interest in capital improvements, a demand revelation problem might arise that would prevent the complete avoidance of under-investment.

A deeper inquiry into the truncation issue could make it appear formally more like the identity-of-owner problem raised by Coase. Rights that become truncated often do so because some agent, such as the state, has acquired the right to alter the ownership arrangements allowed to others. The control of the abrogated portion of the *private* right bundle has been assigned to, or has been taken by, the state. From this perspective the identity-of-owner problem is reintroduced, but with an important change. Instead of alternative private owners of an entitlement, as discussed by Coase, private individuals (and their institutions) and the state (an alternative institution) are the potential owners.

The conclusions derived by Coase cannot be applied directly to these new alternatives because the considerations that go into the state's use of what it owns are not necessarily the same as those that govern private use. Private owners as producers, for example, largely follow the dictates of profit maximization, but the state is motivated by political considerations. This difference may undermine an attempt to apply Coase's analysis. The economic theory of democracy has not developed sufficiently to allow us to understand enough about the behavior of "the state," or its members, to draw hard and fast conclusions about the consequences of alternative owners in this case. The notion that political democracy works like market capitalism is, I believe, wrong. Some thoughts about a few of the differences between the market and political arenas are given in "Business Firms and Political Parties: How Good an Analogy?" and in "The Growth of Government," appearing in volume II.

The truncation of ownership rights is perceived as the deletion of some private rights from an implicit bundle of rights that define "full" private ownership. Coase's identity-of-owners problem also refers to well defined private rights. The meaning of full private ownership, however, is vague. In one sense it must always remain so, for there is an infinity of potential rights of actions that can be owned privately, communally, or by the state. It is impossible to describe the complete set of rights that are potentially ownable, and to discuss these as being owned privately or by the state. However, certain rights of action loom more important than others. Exclusivity and alienability are among them. These can be discussed explicitly in relation to the truncation issue; but the more one probes into matters of definition and meaning, the more complex the matter becomes.

Exclusivity in use can refer to the use of some physical resource, such as land, or to the use of some conceptual resource, such as an idea or an identity. But, why stop at these conceptual resources? Why not contemplate the private right to exclusively sell in a specified market such as sometimes was purchased from the English Crown or Parliament? In this fashion, the economics of ownership can be extended to include the question of monopoly. It is clear that full private rights, full state rights, full communal rights are notions that are very elastic with respect to the substantive bundle of entitlements involved. The *private* enterprise economy, *public* ownership, *socialism*, are implicitly different specifications of ownership arrangements; but the full contents of these arrangements are vague and ill-specified in some respects, making it difficult to give a clear definition of each social arrangement. Does the fully private social system include within it a private right to vote collective solutions to social problems? If voters are barred from voting socialism into being, has their private right to vote been violated?

The situation is made more complex once it is recognized that the extension of a private right of action often (always?) curtails another private right of action. Barring the owners of firms from establishing an exclusive entitlement to sell to a given market, perhaps by invoking a constitutional prohibition on the state's ability to grant monopoly, truncates some private rights while simultaneously extending the private right to enter any and all markets. Does this constitutional prohibition make a society more or less private? The problems being raised here come to the fore in discussions of normative issues, some of which are taken up in the last part of this first volume.

OWNERSHIP AS AN ENDOGENOUS PHENOMENON

Since ownership always exists in one form or another, an inquiry into the development and content of ownership really seeks to examine the sources of change in the bundle of rights that define ownership. From this perspective, ownership itself is viewed as responsive to underlying benefits and costs. A positive theory of ownership requires a systematic treatment of these determinants of the structure of ownership rights. By implication, this structure has consequences. In the Coasian world of fully developed rights and zero transaction costs, the identity of owners has no resource allocation consequences; in the world of changing and evolving rights, in which information and transaction costs cannot be zero, the identity of owners, the content of the bundle of ownership rights, and the structure of ownership all have consequences. This is why some bundles of rights are more appropriate to one set of underlying conditions than to another.

Two different contexts arise in the literature that treats ownership endogenously. The first bears on what may be called allocation by *individual action*. It emphasizes a context in which decisions by owners are assumed to be fully carried out, as if no other individuals need cooperate in executing these decisions. Although agency problems cannot be dismissed completely here (internalizing an externality can be viewed as reducing the severity of an agency problem), no attempt is made to deal with them explicitly in this literature. The owner of a herd of cattle decides on the size of the herd, and, it is assumed, this decision actually brings the desired herd into being. Resources are allocated by *decision*. The second context explicitly considers how ownership bears on the probability that a team of individuals actually executes the desired allocation of resources. *Cooperative action* is required to implement owner decisions, and agency problems (shirking, opportunism) occupy center-stage.

Allocation by individual action

"Toward a Theory of Property Rights" (chapter 7), considers potential externalities as an important source of variation in the costs and benefits associated with particular bundles of ownership rights. The case that is highlighted is that in which communal rights of ownership in land gave way to private rights among Indians of the American North-east. The externalities at issue are those associated with land use, with special emphasis given to the problem of conserving animal stocks. Two conditions are treated: the market value of animals, and their migratory habits. Market value may be taken to index the benefit to avoiding waste, and migratory habit to index the cost of conserving inventories of these animals. The coming of the fur trade to America altered the benefit/cost ratio in a way that increased the advantage of privatizing land. This advantage was easier to realize in the case of forest animals than in that of grazing animals. The difference is used to explain the development of private rights in Indian land and in the American North-east and the failure of such rights to develop in the Great Plains states.

The issue raised here is the changing content of the bundle of rights that defines ownership, and how this change is predictably related to changes in underlying circumstances. The content of the bundle of rights may be categorized in many different ways, but one useful way is to consider two important components of the bundle of rights: exclusivity and alienability. Exclusivity refers to the right to determine who may use a scarce resource in a particular way. The notion of exclusivity, of course, derives from the right to insist that no one other than the "owner" use the resource, but this notion is extended here to include the right of the owner to determine who else may use a resource. Alienability refers to the right to reassign ownership to someone else. It includes the right to offer for sale at any price.

Exclusivity and alienability are both absent when the ownership of scarce resources is communal. No one may be kept from using a communal resource and no one owns the right to assign ownership of the resource to others. Strictly speaking, and as a practical matter, neither attribute can be completely absent if a resource is truly scarce. Exclusivity obtains through actual use of the resource when ownership is communal. Occupying a freeway (on which all are entitled to drive) conveys a right to use a "moving" space on the road. It does not, however, convey a right to determine who, or how many, may use other spaces on the freeway. Alienability also obtains in principle. Political processes exist by which it can be decided that a freeway is to be sold to a private party, or is to be operated as a toll way. The comparative advantages of one set of ownership rights over another (communal *v.* private) turns on a comparison of the consequences of relying on "full" private ownership, which permits exclusivity and alienability by private decision, or on exclusivity obtained through actual use and alienability obtained through political processes. The benefit/cost calculation associated with these consequences surely varies from context to context. Communal use of land is less likely when prices of wool and other agricultural products are relatively high, when population growth increases congestion, and so on, because *use* as a method of determining "temporary ownership" and *politics* as a method of alienating ownership become more wasteful in these circumstances.

Between communal and "full" private ownership lies a vast terrain. Truncation of ownership rights in a manner that restrains alienability while retaining exclusivity occupies a half-way position between these extremes. Rent control, for example, eliminates the right to offer and receive rent exceeding legal limits, an issue in alienability. However, the right to determine who occupies rental space generally remains with its "owner," an issue in exclusivity. If, now, the allowed rent is placed hypothetically at successively lower levels, finally approaching zero, the alienability feature of apartment ownership approaches that of communal ownership, where no money price need be paid to use a resource. A queue forms, the size of which is determined partly by the quantity of rental space demanded at a zero rent. On a city freeway during rush hours, the queue to use this communally owned resource (at a zero price) is resolved by early arrival time, waiting, and slow driving. Practically speaking, no one exercises a right of exclusivity in regard to entering the freeway. In the apartment case, unlike full communal ownership, permission from a private owner is still required (at least in the absence of legalized "squatting") before an apartment can be occupied. This allows the owner to emphasize different criteria (such as personal characteristics) in lieu of positive financial compensation in deciding on occupancy. Whereas full communal ownership rewards the ability to occupy or to use a resource before others do, the quasi-communal/private arrangement, exemplified by rent control, rewards desired personal characteristics. In comparison to full and quasi-communal ownership, full private ownership gives greater emphasis to willingness and ability to pay.

The consequences of these rationing systems may be compared, and their relative advantages and disadvantages should be found to vary with underlying circumstances (as in "Minorities in the Market Place"). For example, if the circumstance is such that augmentation of supply has become a more important and valued option, the rationing system offered by full private ownership should become more attractive because of its practical reliance on self-interest to increase supply when price exceeds unit cost. If, on the other hand, augmentation of supply becomes less important, perhaps because wartime priorities "dictate" that resources not be diverted to, say, housing construction, the advantage offered by this rationing system is lessened.

Another example involves the heterogeneity of the population in characteristics that are preferred by the "society." A society whose population is very homogeneous in these personal characteristics is one in which personal traits will not count for much in resolving the queues wrought by effective price controls. A population that is heterogeneous with respect to color, religion, language, and so on is one in which price control will give rise to considerable personal characteristics discrimination in the determination of resource use in the face of price controls. The benefits and costs that flow from price control, as these are judged politically by a society's population, will not be the same in these two contexts, and a change in the heterogeneity of a nation's population must alter its readiness to adopt one form of rationing over another. Whether price control is as likely, and whether "anti-discrimination" controls will augment price control, as population heterogeneity increases are complex questions whose resolution depends on the fraction of a society's population endowed with "non-preferred" personal characteristics and on the political rights of this fraction.

Ownership is more productive in some circumstances than in others. Little benefit is obtained from enforcing private ownership of resources that are not scarce, and there may be a cost for doing so. Such resources need not be husbanded because they are ample enough in supply to satisfy all potentially competing uses. Legal ownership of the right to use sunshine or to use the *open* seas as a roadway for international commerce serve little allocative function under normal conditions. Private or state ownership could create potential monopoly problems, and attendant policing costs, only if enforcement of entitlements were possible. Communal rights serve the productive function of barring such monopolies, but communal rights become increasingly counter-productive as conditions of "natural" scarcity become more prevalent.

More relevant to the practical problem of resource allocation, the productivity of full ownership increases as the number of alternative uses to which scarce resources can be put increases. Private ownership of resources held in "liquid" condition (before being committed to some specific task) is more productive than private ownership of an already-in-place sewer system constructed to carry waste liquid away. Private ownership may improve on the operation and maintenance of such a system, but it no longer can improve easily on the uses to which the resources embodied in the sewer system can be put. The longer-run the perspective taken, the more productive is full private ownership, precisely because the long-run view is that in which maximum resource fungibility exists. In addition, the more certain are the values to be obtained from alternative deployments of resources, the less useful are the opinions and risk-taking preferences of private entrepreneurs, and the easier it is to substitute state ownership for private ownership without incurring as great a penalty.

My reference here is only to the direction of change in ownership rights that is likely to occur when underlying determinants of costs and benefits change, not to the "level" of the bundle of rights that defines ownership. The bases from which these changes take place are determined by a much broader set of considerations related to the history, religion, and culture of societies. Within the narrower context of changes in ownership arrangements, consideration of conditions such as those discussed above suggests that full private ownership increases in productivity as does the scarcity value of a resource, the ease with which its use can be monitored, the competitiveness of its production, the variety of the uses to which it can be put, the uncertainty of its values in these uses, and the longer the perspective taken.

Allocation by cooperative action

The larger the size of a society, the more likely it is that underlying conditions favor private ownership. The attempt to run a society on a centralized, state-controlled basis is more difficult in a larger society. The bureaucratic costs of obtaining desired cooperative action surely rise steeply once a society breaches rather modest size limits. Societies as large as those of China and Russia simply cannot function well enough to raise per capita living standards relative to those obtained by other large economies organized on a decentralized basis. Isolated from the outside world, and under threat from outside intervention, centralization can be maintained for lengthy periods in spite of low living standards, but in peaceful competition with other large decentralized societies it cannot. As societies grow in size, so must their dependency on private ownership. Effective decentralization cannot be achieved without de facto movement toward private ownership because privatization means that controllers of resources (their "owners") bear more of the consequences of their actions than do controllers (the bureaucracy) when "the state" is owner. It is precisely this "bearing of consequences" that is prerequisite to an effective incentive system once bureaucratic costs undermine the effectiveness of non-market incentives. Hence, the larger a society becomes, the more it will institute private ownership arrangements (or the more it will isolate itself from international competition and social interaction). The shift from individual to family, from family to clan, from clan to small nation, and from small nation to large nation requires ever greater reliance on private ownership.

Only World War II, a period of imposed isolation, and propagandized ideological preference (in the name of a grand social experiment) have slowed Russia's move toward capitalistic institutions, a move that began prior to the Russian revolution and will inevitably continue. Similarly, China cannot long retain the degree of centralized control that has existed since World War II. The state ownership base from which these movements start are those set in place by the revolutions in Russia and China (and by the post-World War II realignment of control over East Europe). These may be interpreted as violent reorganizations of ownership rights, constituting huge redistributions in wealth, in which the state takes entitlements away from previous private owners. (Presumably, the success of these revolutions derives from prior institutionalized rigidities that had produced too few avenues for the private progress of large fractions of the populations of these countries. The lack of such rigidities in the United States and Western European nations compares favorably with the rigidities that characterized Russian and Chinese society prior to their communist revolutions.) Once this forced taking of entitlements has been accomplished, once the old distribution of wealth has been altered, it becomes imperative for the state to relinquish control again to private individuals through some more preferred redistribution of wealth. If a large society is to succeed in raising living standards, the state cannot persist in owning the wealth of a nation. Effective, well directed control of resources (directed to increase per capita wealth) cannot be obtained through bureaucratic incentives in a large society. Self-interest must be harnessed to the task. The economics of control requires decentralization, and effective decentralization requires considerable privatization if self-interest is to be marshaled in wealth-enhancing ways.

The problem of control, of course, persists in capitalistic societies, mainly for three reasons. First, it persists because the desires of owners must be translated into cooperative action by employees (the agency problem). Second, it persists because the optimum-size firm sometimes requires a commitment of equity capital, to establish effective control, that exceeds the capabilities of a single individual private owner (the diffuse ownership problem). Third, it persists because private interests sometimes diverge from social interests (the monopoly and externality problems). As to the externality aspect of the third of these problems, reference has already been made to the ownership literature deriving from Coase's paper on social cost; the monopoly aspect is discussed mainly outside the context of ownership (see volume II). Recent developments in the economics of ownership have come to grips with the agency and diffuse-ownership problems.

The agency problem, in the form of shirking, is the theme in "Production, Information Cost, and Economic Organization" (chapter 8 – with A. Alchian). The internal organization of the firm, the role of monitoring, and particular compensation methods are explained by the interplay between underlying conditions and the need to cope with shirking. There is special reference to the productivity of a two-fold compensation system, one component being the "wages" that accrue to employees, which is largely independent of the firm's performance, and the other being the "residual" or "profit" that accrues to the owner(s), and which is highly dependent on performance. Compensation methods are specifications of entitlements to flows of income. The bundles of rights that define these compensation methods, the ownership rights in these flows, reflect the desire of all cooperating parties to cope with private incentives to shirk. This approach is different from that taken by Coase in his important paper on "The Nature of the Firm," in which he relies on positive transaction cost to explain the existence and organization of the firm; and it is different from that taken by Knight, in which he relies on efficient risk distribution to rationalize the traditional theoretical firm's compensation structure. [At the time our paper was written, we did not recognize Knight's discussion of moral hazard, which appears as a minor theme in *Risk, Uncertainty, and Profit* (Knight, 1965), but which anticipates Alchian and Demsetz.]

The agency problem, especially in conjunction with asset specificity, has become a popular explanation of the scope of activities controlled by one ownership interest (i.e., the degree of vertical integration within a single firm). Recent views on vertical integration see the vertical scope of ownership as importantly determined by whether asset specificity is a source of production economies (Riordan and Williamson, 1985). "The Theory of the Firm Revisited" and "Vertical Integration: Theories and Evidence," also included here (chapters 9 and 10), discuss my mounting concern with the tendency to attribute more explanatory power than is deserved to transaction cost, asset specificity, and agency problems when explaining the varying substance of the firm. However, the general direction of inquiry, which looks to underlying conditions that vary from situation to situation to explain the organization of the firm, is a very healthy one.

The main issues examined in this literature deal with compensation and vertical integration. Both issues tend to be analyzed without reference to, or by taking as exogenous, the ownership structure of the firm. Ownership structure in the present context refers to the degree to which the ownership of a single firm is diffuse or concentrated. Standard price theory implicitly assumes that a single person owns and manages the theoretical firm, costlessly combining inputs to maximize profit. The structure of ownership varies, of course, and it is important in understanding the organization of economic activity to understand how and why it does vary. This problem is explored in "The Structure of Ownership and the Theory of the Firm" (chapter 11) and "The Structure of Corporate Ownership: Causes and Consequences" (chapter 12 – with Kenneth Lehn). The analysis of this problem has generated derivative papers on three topics: insider trading, the distribution of wealth, and the amenity potential of a firm's output. Included in this volume are "Corporate Control, Insider Trading, and Rates of Return" (chapter 13) and "The Control Function of Private Wealth" (chapter 14). "Newspaper Publishing and the Fairness Doctrine" and "Business Firms and Political Parties: How Good An Analogy?", which focus on the role of amenity potential, appear in volume II.

"The Control Function of Private Wealth" is a short paper, but I believe it introduces a very important, neglected issue. It extends the discussion of the ownership and control of firms to the broader topic of wealth and its distribution, arguing that effective control of enterprise and the distribution of wealth are not independent when large size is efficient. If we are to have effective control, we cannot have wealth equality. If we have wealth equality, we cannot have effective control of enterprise. The linkage between wealth distribution and effective control derives from the need to concentrate the ownership of enterprise in the hands of a few owners if control is to be effective.

If large-scale enterprise is efficient, an equal distribution of wealth undermines our ability to concentrate ownership in this fashion. The control function of ownership thus provides a logical linkage to macro questions that are usually discussed without reference to the efficiency of enterprise.

REFERENCES

Alchian, A. and Kessel, R. (1962). "Competition, Monopoly, and the Pursuit of Pecuniary Gain," *Aspects of Labor Economics*, 157.

Averch, H. and Johnson, L. (1962). "The Firm under Regulatory Constraint," *American Economic Review*, 52.

Coase, R. H. (1937). "The Nature of The Firm," *Economica*, 4.

—— (1960). "The Problem of Social Cost," *Journal of Law and Economics*, 3.

Knight, Frank H. (1965). *Risk, Uncertainty, and Profit*. New York: Harper & Row (1st edn, Hart Schaffner and Marx, 1921).

Riordan, M. H. and Williamson, O. E. (1985). "Asset Specificity And Economic Organization," *International Journal of Industrial Organization*, 3.

PART II

Private Rights: Externalities, Content, and Development

3
The Exchange and Enforcement of Property Rights

Our economic system, with its specialization of economic activities into separate ownership and decision units, requires both control over goods and exchange of goods if it is to cope with the diversity of wants of specialist producers. This paper is concerned with the fact that the exchange of goods and the maintenance of control over the use of goods impose costs on traders and owners. It is also concerned with the cost of government alternatives to the market place. I seek to establish both the importance and the wide role of these costs in economic life.

A large part of my argument will be illustrated by two important controversies in welfare economics in which I will show, on the one hand, that zero pricing of scarce goods need not result in inefficiency, and, on the other, that zero pricing of "public" goods may result in inefficiency. The standard criticisms of resource allocation by the market, which turn on the market's failure to price "external" effects and on its tendency to price "public" goods, are shown to be invalid. To do this I extend the well-known axiom that there is no such thing as a free scarce good by including such goods as markets, government bureaus, and policing devices.

Throughout this paper, my attention is confined to the problem of efficiency within the framework of smoothly running markets and governments, in the sense that I assume that persons, whether in their capacity as civil servants or as private citizens, do not make arithmetic errors in calculating, or, at least, that they do not tend to make more errors in one role than in another. I do not concern myself with problems of monopoly by either a firm or the government, but the problem of imperfect knowledge is treated.

Instead of "external effects" or "neighborhood effects," I will use the phrase "side-effects" to identify those for which no account *seems* to be taken in the market place. This avoids the flavor of location and of being *necessarily* outside

The author thanks Armen A. Alchian, Gary S. Becker, William H. Meckling, Peter Pashigian, and George J. Stigler for comments. Reprinted with permission from *Journal of Law and Economics*, Oct., 1964.

of the market place that seem to be associated with the more common names for these effects.

EXCHANGE COST

Recent developments

R. H. Coase,[1] in an important article written recently for this Journal, demonstrates that there is, in general, nothing special about side-effects that rules out the possibility of their being taken account of by the market. These effects can be taken into account by market transactions between the parties affected once the courts have established who has what right of action. Under competitive conditions and assuming zero exchange costs, these transactions will result in an efficient solution to the scarcity problem. Thus, if ranchers are given the right to allow their cattle to roam and the cattle stray accidentally onto unfenced farm land, it will be in the farmer's interest to bring the damage they cause to the rancher's attention by offering to pay the rancher to reduce the number of cattle foraging nearby. If the rancher disregards this offer, he sacrifices a potential receipt equal to the crop damage. Thus, the crop damage becomes a private cost to the rancher of raising additional cattle and will be taken account of in his calculations. Moreover, Coase points out the efficiency of the solution with respect to the number of cattle and the size of the crops in the absence of exchange costs is independent of whether the farmer or the rancher is legally liable for the damage. The party not held liable, of course, acquires the right to act in ways that may have harmful side-effects. The assignment of the liability for crop damage to the rancher would lead to a direct accounting for this cost in his operations, and he would need to decide whether to reduce his herd or pay the farmer to reduce the crop he plants. Whether the farmer will find it worthwhile to pay enough to the rancher to reduce his herd or whether the rancher can pay enough to the farmer to reduce the area he cultivates depends on whether the value lost because of the crop reduction is greater or less than the value lost because the size of the herd is reduced. Whichever way the rights are initially assigned, the outcome of the subsequent bargaining will be that which maximizes the value of output.

Coase has advanced the analysis of the roles that can be played by the market and the government a step beyond its previous position. For now Coase has shown that, if exchange costs are positive, it is necessary to ask whether government can take the harmful effects of an action into account at less cost than can the market or, indeed, if the resulting resource realignment is worth the cost of taking the side-effects into account at all.

Misapplication of optimality theorems

The question that asks whether or not realignment is worthwhile brings to light an improper usage to which we frequently have put our optimality theorems. The cost of using the market relative to the cost of using a political mechanism has seldom been considered explicitly or in detail in the bulk of the theory of welfare economics. This has led to an improper usage of those theorems. As a consequence of the conventional approach to these problems, it has not been recognized that the very conditions under which side-effects are believed to lead to inefficiency are those conditions for which the welfare theorems used are inapplicable.

The usual analysis of market inefficiency in such cases attributes the difficulty to the absence of markets in which ''appropriate'' prices for measuring side-effects can be revealed.[2] But absence of a market or of a price can be consistent with efficiency when optimality theorems are appropriately interpreted. *For produced goods*, the optimality theorems require equalities among various marginal rates of substitution. These same optimality conditions, however, do not require such equalities for goods and services that are *not produced* in the final efficient equilibrium; for these we have corner solutions involving inequalities. Thus, a basic premise in requiring equalities is that we are talking about goods which we require to be produced in positive quantities.

We then turn to the competitive model and observe that market prices will often bring about the equalities required for produced commodities and services. But, we ask, what if some goods produce side-effects that are not exchanged over a market? We answer that the market fails to provide us with incentives that will guide behavior to take account of the side-effects and that, therefore, the required equalities will be absent. The allegation is that even perfectly competitive markets fail to achieve efficiency. But this reasoning generally fails to take account of the fact that the provision of a market (for the side-effect) is itself a valuable and costly service. Where a market, or the political action that would be its counterpart, does not exist, this service is not being produced. If this service is not being produced, some *in*equalities (instead of the equalities required for produced goods) among our marginal rates of substitution and marginal rates of transformation may be consistent with efficiency, as will be the case if the cost of taking account of side-effects through either the market or the government exceeds the value of realigning resources. In such cases zero amounts of market pricing or the government equivalent will be efficient. In asking the implications of the non-existence of some markets, we seem to have forgotten the cost of providing market services or their government equivalent. The existence of prices to facilitate exchange between affected parties has been too much taken for granted. A price for every produced good or service is not a necessary condition for efficiency, so that the absence of a price does not imply that either market transactions or substitute government services are desirable. If we insist either that all actions (services or commodities) be priced in the market or that the government intervene, we are insisting that we do not economize on the cost of producing exchanges or government services. Thus, most welfare propositions concerned with side-effects are based on an invalid use of the standard optimality theorems; i.e., they ignore the cost of some of the goods.

Some examples

We shall consider two examples to illustrate this point. In the first rights of action are clearly defined; in the second they are not.

Our first example is zero-priced parking at shopping plazas in which unpaid-for benefits exist insofar as shoppers, in the prices they pay, confer benefits on non-shopping parkers. Most economists, regardless of their philosophical persuasion, would probably argue that the number of spaces is non-optimal. But when we say non-optimal, we must have some idea of what is the optimal number of spaces. Assuming the absence of increasing returns, the less careful of us are apt to reply that the proper number of spaces is the number that would clear the market when a charge is levied to cover construction cost. A more careful reply would include exchange costs in the charge. *Neither* answer is necessarily correct.

It is true that the setting and collecting of appropriate shares of construction and exchange costs from each parker will reduce the number of parking spaces needed to allow ease of entry and exit. But while we have reduced the resources committed to constructing parking spaces, we have increased resources devoted to market exchange. We may end up by allocating more resources to the provision and control of parking than had we allowed free parking because of the resources needed to conduct transactions. By insisting that the commodity be priced, we may become less efficient than had we allowed persons to ration spaces on a first-come, first-served basis. Similarly, rationing by government involves its own costs and may be no better. Those who purchase merchandise and indirectly pay for parking spaces may prefer to substitute the smaller total cost of constructing additional spaces to accommodate free-loaders rather than ration out the non-buying parkers by paying the required exchange cost minus the savings of constructing fewer parking spaces. Since the cost of providing additional parking spaces depends largely on the price of land, it follows that we should expect to observe free parking allowed more frequently in suburbs than in the center of towns because of the differential prices of land. Given this differential, both methods of allocating parking may be efficient.

Is this example consistent with competition? Will not competing stores open nearby and charge lower prices because their customers use a free parking lot supplied by a competitor? Will they, thereby, force their competitor out of business? The desirability of providing parking spaces implies that we are dealing with a world of finite dimension in which all cars cannot be parked at zero cost on a dimensionless point. For this reason, differential land rent will be taken into account. Owners of land surrounding the free parking lot will enjoy windfall profits, a question of wealth redistribution; but potential competitors will have the advantages of the nearby lot capitalized and included in the rent they pay; they will enjoy no competitive advantage. The equilibrium is a stable competitive one although it gives rise to differential land rent. If the windfall is expected to be large enough to warrant the additional transactions required to purchase surrounding land, the (prospective) owners of the shopping plaza could take account of these gains in their calculations by purchasing the surrounding land before free parking is allowed. This option, which Coase refers to as extending the role of the firm, is alternative to both exchange and government action.[3]

In this particular example, the efficiency of producing this costly but zero-priced parking depends on the supplier being able to recoup the cost by other means, namely in the prices of his merchandise. This method of financing the parking lot becomes economically superior *only* if demand interrelations are such that a sale-in-combination arrangement reduces exchange costs sufficiently. Both the loose combination sale (not all parkers need to buy merchandise) and the tighter tie-ins may, in fact, be methods that reduce the cost of allocating and lead to optimal quantities of goods. I shall have more to say on the relevance of this for the problems posed by public goods.

For contrast, our next example, one that has become a favorite, involves neither tie-in arrangements nor defined rights of action. It is the case in which market transactions do not take place in the use of nectar by bees, so that prices do not arise that reflect the beneficial effects of apple blossoms on the productivity of bees. Clearly, as Coase would probably point out, it is possible for beekeepers and apple growers to strike a bargain over how many trees are to be planted, the bargain taking account of an apple tree's contribution to honey production and a bee's contribution to cross-fertilization of trees. Further, were there significant predictable benefits from the interaction, significant enough to offset any diseconomies of underspecialization, beekeeping and apple growing would be carried on by the same farmer. However, the benefits may be small relative to the costs of forsaking specialization. Merger will not then be the solution. Suppose, also, that estimates of benefits are small relative to estimates of the cost of developing the science of the apple–bee interaction and to the costs of either transacting in the market or providing substitute government services. Then efficiency requires that bees be allowed to "help themselves" on a first-come, first-served basis, which is, after all, an alternative arrangement for settling scarcity problems.

Here no combination sales are directly involved. A valuable and costly good, nectar, is provided free of charge because it would be too costly to take account of the indirect benefits to beekeepers. In contrast to the parking and merchandising example, the separate marketing of the two products, apples and blossoms, is costly. Hence a zero-priced good may be efficient even though no combination sale is used. Since no low-cost combination sale seems possible, the good (nectar) will be provided free if apples, per se, are worth producing. If apples are not worth producing, our recognition of the existence of a benefit to beekeepers will not make the production of apples desirable, for the cost of inducing the apple grower to take this benefit into account is too high to make it worthwhile.

POLICE COST

Up to now we have largely limited our attention to situations in which direct bargaining between individuals requires an exchange cost that is larger than the benefits derived from the exchange. To take account of these side-effects, therefore, the interested parties resort to combination sales, or to extensions of the firm, or else they find it expedient not to modify these effects. All of these alternatives are consistent with efficiency, and yet all fail to exhibit a market in the side-effect. There are situations, however, which are somewhat different in that the cost of *policing* the effects of actions, rather than the cost of exchange, may be so high as to cause additional complications. The following discussion of these situations is designed to reveal the roles played by police cost and private property and to help clear up some public good problems.

Property rights and the valuation problem

There are two tasks that must be handled well by any acceptable allocative mechanism. These are, first, that information must be generated about all the benefits of employing resources in alternative uses, and, second, that persons be motivated to take account of this information. To the extent that both these tasks are solved by the allocative mechanism, the problem of attaining an efficient allocation of resources reduces to arithmetic. Setting aside the second problem, we turn to the first, and in particular to the necessity for protecting the right to use economically valuable resources if we are to obtain accurate information about benefits.

It is well known that prices can serve as guideposts to where resources are wanted most, and in addition, that exchangeability of goods at these prices can provide incentives for people to follow these guideposts. However, analytical concentration on the price mechanism has kept us from closely examining what it is that is being traded. The value of what is being traded depends crucially on the rights of action over the physical commodity and on how economically these rights are enforced. The enforcement of the accompanying property rights has an important impact on the ability of prices to measure benefits. An emphasis on this aspect or view of the problem, in conjunction with our emphasis on exchange cost, will allow us to unify our treatment of what is now largely a collection of special cases in which our measures of benefits diverge from actual benefits. The petroleum and fishery "pool" problems are good examples of problems created by treating economic goods as free goods. The general conclusion reached by the analysis of pool problems is that a resource, be it petroleum, fish, or game, is too rapidly worked. This conclusion is correct, and if we think in terms of producible inventories, the absence of property right enforcement also can be shown to result in too little production of the good, or in too small an increment to the pool or inventory of the good. This is because the prices, which reflect private benefits, fail to measure the whole of the social benefit derived from the good. As a special case of this general proposition, if we assume that it costs nothing to police property rights, it follows that there exists a direct relationship between the degree to which private benefits approach social benefits and the degree to which the conveyed property rights are enforced. This relationship can be illustrated with two examples.

Given any definition of the rights that accompany ownership in an automobile, the price mechanism will ration the existing stock of automobiles. But the total private value of this stock will depend on the degree to which auto theft is reduced by our laws and police. If we pass a law *prohibiting* the arrest and prosecution of auto thieves, and also prohibiting the use of private protection devices, the bids that persons subsequently offer for the purchase of automobiles will fall below the social value of automobiles. The lower bids will result from the reduction in control that a purchaser can expect to exercise over the use of a purchased auto and, in addition, from his ability to "borrow" at no charge those autos that are purchased by others. The bids submitted after the passage of such a law will underestimate the social value of autos, for we can assume for our purposes that the usefulness of an auto remains the same whether it is used by the purchaser or by the legal thief. This is true even though the existing stock of autos is efficiently distributed among owners. The total value of autos will fall below social value and the subsequent increase in the stock of autos will be less than it should.

The lowering of bids that results from our law is similar to the lowering of bids that will take place when high police cost reduces the degree of private control that it is economical to guarantee owners. The provision of national defense provides us with a classic example of the impact of high police cost. Voluntarily submitted bids for defense will be lower than the social value of defense because the bidder can count on being able to enjoy (some of) the defense bought and also enjoyed by his fellow citizen. The effect on bidding is similar to that which takes place in our example of legalized auto theft except that the reason for lack of control is not merely the absence of an appropriate law but, rather, the high cost of defending a purchaser from a foreign aggressor while at the same time preventing his neighbors from enjoying protection. The cost of excluding those who have not contracted for benefits from the enjoyment of some of these benefits is so high that a general attitude of letting others bear the cost of defense can be expected. Consequently, voluntarily submitted bids will underestimate the social value of defense.

If a low-cost method is available and is used to prevent those who do not contract for defense from benefiting from the defense bought by others, the market would reveal accurate information about the social value of defense. Such information would be extremely useful if the market or the planner is to allocate resources efficiently.

The institution of private property, which attempts to exclude non-purchasers from the use of that which others have purchased, should, therefore, not be looked upon as either accidental or undesirable. On the contrary, its existence is probably due in part to its great practicality in revealing the social values upon which to base solutions to scarcity problems. This is precisely why we do not worry that bids for, say, candy will fail to reveal the social value of candy. The price of candy is accurate in its measure of social value because reflected in it is the ability of each purchaser to control the use of his purchase, whether that use be for resale or for charity, for his children or for his own consumption. This valuation function is related to but distinct from the incentives to work provided by a property system; for even in a society where work is viewed as a pleasurable activity, and, hence, where incentives to work are not needed, it would still be necessary to properly value the varieties of alternative output that can be produced.

We have already observed that the value of what is being traded depends upon the allowed rights of action over the physical good and upon the degree to which these rights are enforced. This statement at once raises the question of which rights and which degrees of enforcement are efficient. If changing the mix of property rights that accompany ownership increases the value of property, such a change will be desirable from the viewpoint of wealth-maximizing. For example, if the problem is whether to allow automobile owners to increase the speed at which they travel on side streets, one could assess whether there would result an increase in the total value of affected property. Would people be willing to pay higher prices for automobiles? It is by no means clear that they would, for some prospective owners may fear high speed more than they value it. And, if there would result an increase in the price of automobiles, would it be large enough to offset any increase in the cost of insuring life, limb, and home (i.e., the resulting decline in the value of other property)? If a net increase in the total value of property follows a change in the mix of rights, the change should be allowed if we seek to maximize wealth. Not to allow the change would be to refuse to generate a surplus of value sufficient to compensate those harmed by the change. The process of calculating the net change in value will, of course, involve the taking into account of side-effects, and this is a problem that we have already discussed. The enforcement of rights can be viewed in the same way. Indeed, we can insist that a proper definition of a right of action include the degree to which the owner or the community is allowed to enforce the right. Enforcement thus becomes the specification of additional rights and can be included in the above analytical framework. The conclusion we have reached depends, of course, upon the existence of competitive entry in the exercise of particular rights. It is therefore necessary to exclude rights which confer monopoly by restricting entry and to insist that all owners have the same rights of action. There are some difficult problems which we do not take up here. For example, since everyone has the right to take out a patent or a copyright on "newly created" goods or ideas, does the granting of this right involve the granting of monopoly power?

It is, of course, necessary to economize on police cost, so that we will not always want to guarantee full control to the purchaser; more will be said below about this aspect of the problem. But, this aspect aside, it is essential to note that the valuation power of the institution of property is most effective when it is most *private*. It is ironic, therefore, that one of the strongest intellectual arguments for expanding the role of government has been based on the alleged necessity for eliminating exclusivity and for allowing free access to the use of certain types of resources. These resources have been given the name "public goods," and they are characterized by their alleged ability to confer benefits on additional persons without thereby reducing the benefits conferred on others. The provision of national defense is a well-known example.

The public goods problem

The relevance of what we have been discussing for public goods is that, if the cost of policing the benefits derived from the use of these goods is low, there is an excellent reason for excluding those who do not pay from using these goods. By such exclusion we, or the market, can estimate accurately the value of diverting resources from other uses to the production of the public good. Thus, even though extending the use of an existing bridge to additional persons adds nothing to the direct cost of operating the bridge, there is good reason for charging persons for the right to cross the bridge. Excluding those who do not pay for the use of the bridge allows us to know whether a new bridge is likely to generate more benefit than it is likely to cost.[4] Why should we desire information about a new bridge if the direct marginal cost of using the existing bridge is zero? First, the bridge may depreciate with time rather than with traffic, so that the question of replacement remains relevant even though the marginal cost of use is zero. Second, there is a private marginal benefit to users of the bridge, at least in lessening their driving costs, and this benefit can be measured by pricing the use of the bridge. Such information would allow us to ascertain whether it is economic to have a new bridge closer to some persons than is the present bridge.

For some goods, air for example, the supply is so plentiful that diversion from some uses is not required to increase the intensity with which they are used elsewhere. Only where scarcity is absent is it *a priori* reasonable to charge a zero price. Superabundance is the only true *a priori* case for a zero-priced public good. All other goods are such that their provision forces us into resource allocation problems. To solve these problems efficiently, we need information which is obtained by excluding non-purchasers, *provided that the additional information is worth more than the exchange and police costs necessitated.* In cases where the costs are greater, a zero price can be reconciled with efficiency requirements. If we must distinguish among goods, we had best do away with the "public goods" *v.* private goods dichotomy and instead classify goods according to whether they are truly free or economic, and classify economic goods according to whether marketing costs are too high relative to the benefits of using markets and to the costs of substituting non-market allocation devices.

Alternative devices

The use of taxation for the provision of scarce goods must be defended on grounds other than the usual rationale of their being public goods. As we have seen, insofar as efficiency is concerned, the fact that side benefits can be derived by non-purchasers from the acquisition by others of these goods is inconclusive. If the planner's or the market's calculation of benefits can be improved by a small expenditure to protect or to confer property rights, the use of price rationing to measure these benefits may be justified. The problem can be viewed as that of determining the degree to which it is desirable to purchase valuation information through the competitive pricing process. A purchase of valuation information reduces the utilization of a public good below the levels that seem to be warranted by the direct cost of extending utilization. If the direct cost of, say, increasing the volume of traffic carried by an existing bridge is zero, it may nonetheless be *un*desirable to charge a zero price because of the indirect costs implied by zero pricing. These indirect costs are of two kinds.

First, and obviously, valuation information about the bridge is sacrificed. (Is not valuation information one of the most important public goods?) Second, the alternative methods of financing the building of bridges may also lead to inefficiency, especially by degrading valuation information elsewhere. This is most easily seen by supposing that an excise tax is levied on other goods to finance bridges. Such a tax will lead to inefficiently small rates of production of these other goods (assuming competitive markets). Alternatively, the levying of an income tax will inefficiently reduce the quantities of income-generating activities undertaken by those taxed. A tax on property values, even one on rent, would tend to discourage the seeking out of more valuable uses of property. A head tax would have the least effect because it is not concentrated on particular activities. Even a head tax, one could argue, would alter a person's choice of community; and, moreover, a resident who refused to pay the tax might be excluded from use of the bridge. Taxes exclude just as do prices, so that on grounds of exclusion there is not much principle to guide us. Given these indirect costs of alternative methods of financing the provision of public goods, the desirability of zero pricing is not at all clear, especially if the cost of policing is low.

For some goods, however, it must be recognized that police cost may seem too high to allow the market to generate accurate information on social benefits economically. In these cases taxation *may* be the most practical method of finance and zoning the most practical way of establishing rights, just as subsidies, excise taxes, and government nonprice rationing may be the most practical way of coping with high exchange costs. But it must be remembered that all these devices are "exclusionary" and have costs of their own. At best, they would be second-best alternatives to a market in which police and exchange costs are small and in which there is no bias in arithmetic mistakes as between civil servants and others, for these devices are not as likely to turn up correct estimates of the social values of alternative goods.

In a world in which exchange and police cost and the cost of providing alternative political devices are all zero, reliance on the political mechanism of a smoothly run democracy will result in less efficiency than will reliance on the market. Aside from problems of monopoly in government or of errors in calculation, in a one-man, one-vote democracy, where votes are not for sale, the polling place will generate information that is based on majoritarian principles rather than on maximum benefit principles. Thus, suppose that some citizens prefer a stronger national defense but that a majority prefer a weaker defense. Left to a vote, the weaker defense will be our chosen policy even though the minority is willing to pay more than the additional cost required to bring defense up to the level they desire. (And so, if possible, they may hire private police services.) An error in the opposite direction is also possible. The majority of voters may approve of a large space effort even though they would not be able to bid high enough to acquire these resources for space in the absence of forced tax contributions. (Here, however, the minority cannot privately adjust.)

Although taxation is sometimes the most practical way of dealing with the provision of high-police-cost goods, there are other methods which are likely to arise in the market and which will lower the required police cost. As we have seen, extending the firm and the practice of sale-in-combination may overcome many instances of high exchange cost. These devices can also be used to reduce high police cost.

In the famous railway example, sparks from passing trains destroy some crops. The damage caused was believed to be adequate grounds for the government to take action through one or more of the political devices we have already mentioned. Direct contracting between the farmers and the railroad might take account of this side-effect were it not that a bargain struck between a farmer and the railway would automatically confer benefits on all surrounding farmers by reducing spark fall-out on their land. Police costs are too high to allow benefits to be conferred on the contracting farmer without at the same time conferring them on non-contracting farmers. Therefore, it is believed that each farmer will wait for someone else to buy a reduction in spark output. (This conclusion requires two preliminary assumptions. The exchange cost of farmers getting together to submit a joint bid must be high relative to the benefits they will receive so that it is blocked by the expense it entails, and the exchange cost of their getting together to submit a joint bid must be higher than the cost of their organizing politically to lobby for anti-spark legislation.)

However, once the spatial aspects of the problem are admitted, we must again consider the phenomenon of differential land rent. Presumably, land rents on property adjacent to railways have been suitably depressed to allow farmers to compete with those not affected by sparks. The landowners, who find it in their interest to reduce the railroad's output of sparks, also find themselves not willing to enter into contracts through which other landowners will benefit. To some extent each would wait for the other to transact with the railway for a reduction in spark output. However, the analysis is not yet finished. The railway may realize a profit by purchasing the surrounding land at its depressed price. The purchase of a parcel of land does not confer benefits on neighbors to the same degree as would a purchase of spark curtailment, so that this action would not hamper the concluding of similar contracts with other landowners as much as would the sale of a reduction in sparks. After the railroad purchases title to enough land to make it worthwhile, it could take into account the effect of its output of sparks on land values and profitably bring about an adjustment of this output to the socially optimal amount – that which maximizes the joint value of railroading and landowning. The land must, of course, be rented or resold with a contractual agreement requiring a continuance of reduced spark output. The low police cost asociated with the purchase of land is substituted for the very high police cost that would be required to eliminate sparks on some land but not on other nearby land. The necessity for purchasing a reduction in spark output is obviated by substituting a purchase of land.

The extension of the firm together with the combination-sale devices that are associated with differential land rent are extremely important alternatives to government action. These devices can extend considerably the usefulness of markets for revealing and measuring the value of many side-effects. The sale of land may entail much less exchange and policing cost than the direct exchange of whatever is producing the side-effect. The smoke emitted from a nearby factory would, in principle, be subject to solution in the same manner. Now, of course, in many of these cases we do not observe such solutions taking place because exchange and police costs are not reduced sufficiently and because they may require too much underspecialization cost. Governmental devices, say, zoning laws, may help take account of such benefits, however inaccurately, at a lower cost (in which case we should include those costs imposed by the rigidities of zoning laws). It may be, however, that both governmental and market solutions are too costly and that the most efficient alternative is not to attempt to take account of some side-effects.[5]

There are other indirect devices for internalizing via combination sales. The activities of labeling, branding, and advertising allow for internalization of side-effects by tying in the sale of information with other goods. Suppose that persons would like their tuna boiled longer before canning. Each canner would find it in his interest to prepare the tuna more carefully except that, in a world without labels, all competitors would enjoy at no cost some of the benefits of the resulting increase in demand. Some, therefore, wait for competitors to act. Under-investment in tuna boiling (or over-investment in boiling tuna at home) takes place and government regulations governing canning procedures are instituted.

Suppose we allow each canner to state on the label both his name and the minimum boiling time. The name is required to establish responsibility and thereby to reduce policing cost, which is another way of saying that the cost of exercising the rights acquired by purchasers by reason of the purchase contract is reduced for the buyer. The sale of knowledge jointly with that of tuna allows the value of longer boiling to be taken into account by producers and buyers. Structural market imperfections of the monopolistic competition variety can be ruled out if both longer boiled and less boiled tuna have numerous producers. The demand for each producer's tuna will then be the going market price of the particular quality he produces.[6]

Still other institutional arrangements have been devised to combine extensions of the firm with the sale-in-combination device. Department stores and shopping plazas are organizational devices for overcoming high police cost. The owner of the department store or shopping plaza can provide a general environment that is conducive for shopping, such as pleasant plantings, escalators, and other customer services that merchants who owned their own land might hesitate to pay for, hoping instead that neighboring landowners would incur the necessary expenses from which all would benefit. The enclosing of the land into a single ownership entity which often undertakes to provide services usually provided by government from tax revenues, such as streets, sidewalks, refuse collection, and even police protection, allows the owner to exclude those who refuse to pay rentals which cover the cost of these services. The competition of various plazas and department stores will provide ample opportunity for merchants to select the services that they wish to buy without fearing or counting on free-loading. Apartment buildings can also be viewed in the same light, and especially the modern apartment building which combines office and recreational space with living space. The development of these institutional arrangements provides an interesting challenge to political institutions for the provision of many of the services generally presumed to be within the scope of the polling place.

The preceding discussion has taken as given the state of technical arts. The levels of exchange and police costs that are required for effective marketing and the costs of government substitute services depend on how well we master the technology of operating markets and governments. Attention is sometimes called to the fact that emerging technical developments will make the use of markets or governments more economic than they now are. There are surely many instances where this is true. However, our analysis suggests that technological developments can operate in the opposite direction. At the same time that technology is reducing the cost of using these alternative institutional arrangements for economizing, it is also reducing the cost of constructing parking spaces, of developing fire-resistant corn, and of mass-producing automobiles. Whether or not it pays to increase the extent to which we exchange via markets, protect private property rights, or use alternative government devices depends on how much we will thereby reduce production cost and crop damage. Markets or their government alternatives should come into greater prominence only if technical developments lower the costs of these institutional arrangements more than they reduce the costs of producing parking spaces and cars and the cost of crop damage.

Essentially, I have argued in this paper that there exist no qualitative differences between side-effects and what we may call "primary" effects. The only differences are those that are implicitly based on quantitative differences in exchange and police cost. Suppose a factory invents a new more efficient furnace which can burn a cheaper grade of coal than can existing furnaces. The burning of cheap coal, we will assume, dirties homes in the neighborhood. We label this effect as side or neighborhood or external, but its real economic implication is to reduce the wealth of nearby homeowners. If this same factory, by virtue of its new furnace, successfully forces a nearby competing firm out of business, and if the resulting decline in demand for housing reduces the wealth of neighborhood homeowners, we do not become concerned. Why the difference in our attitudes toward these two situations, which have the same effect on homeowners?

The decline in wealth that results from the fall in demand for housing is more than offset by an increase in wealth elsewhere. This increase accrues primarily to other homeowners and to persons purchasing the lower-priced product produced by the factory. We accept the reallocation, I conjecture, because we feel that the existence of a smoothly operating market will insure that wealth is maximized. In the smoke case, exchange and police costs are high relative to the benefits of marketing smoke, and, therefore, we do not have an existing market to rely on for the reallocation, although a potential one always stands ready. If the costs of exchanging and policing smoke contracts were zero (and if the cost of exchanging houses were zero) there would be no reason for distinguishing between the two cases insofar as "remedial" action is concerned. I have already argued that the most efficient arrangement may, in fact, require that nothing be done to prohibit smoke, and I will not go into these matters again. My present purpose is merely to emphasize that there is nothing special or qualitatively different about any of these effects, including the effects that stem from what we ineptly call public goods, and that any special treatment accorded to them cannot be justified merely by observing their presence.

NOTES

1 Coase (1960).

2 Cf. Arrow (1963, pp. 941, 944–5):

> An individual who fails to be immunized not only risks his own health, a disutility which presumably he has weighed against the utility of avoiding the procedure, but also that of others. In an ideal price system, there would be a price which he would have to pay to anyone whose health is endangered, a price sufficiently high so that the others would feel compensated; or, alternatively, there would be a price which would be paid to him by others to induce him to undergo the immunization procedure. . . . It is, of course, not hard to see that such price systems could not, in fact, be practical; to approximate an optimal state it would be necessary to have collective intervention in the form of subsidy or tax or compulsion.

and Bator (1958), pp. 351, 353–4):

> Pareto-efficient . . . points . . . are characterized by a complete set of marginal-rate-of-substitution . . . equalities (or limiting inequalities) which, in turn, yield a set of price-like constants. Where no such constants exist, reference will be to *failure of existence* [of prices, and hence, of efficiency].

3 The existence of unique locations does not necessarily imply the inefficiency usually associated with monopolistic competition. Cf. Demsetz (1964). It should also be noted that, if the landowners could know of the differential land rents that would result from the superior technology offered by free parking, they would be inclined to enter into an agreement sharing the differential rent accruing to land adjacent to the shopping plaza. If they did not enter into such an agreement there would be an inclination to let the free parking facility be built on the other man's property.

4 See Coase (1946), for an early application of this point in reference to the use of multipart pricing in natural monopoly situations. See also Minasian (1964, p. 71).

5 The ability of combination sales to take account of side benefits depends on how closely the value of the tied-in good reflects the value of the public good. There is a direct and exact correspondence between the value of land and the (negative to farmers) value of spark output. A less exact correspondence between the values of the tied goods, while not a perfect device, can nonetheless be useful for taking account of the value of public goods.

Even the stubborn classic case of providing for the national defense is amenable to some usable tie-in arrangements. The provision of defense again presents us with a situation in which it is in the interest of a beneficiary to let others buy defense since he will benefit from their purchases. Suppose, however, that, instead of financing defense with taxes, the government resorts to the sale of insurance to citizens which covers their lives and property in the event of loss arising from war. The tied goods, insurance and defense, are substitutes, but they do not fully correspond in value fluctuations. For a stated premium per $1,000 of insurance and a stated maximum, citizens would buy more insurance the more likely they thought war and the less able they thought our defense. Those having more at stake would buy more insurance. The premiums could then be used to finance the defense establishment. The side-effect is not fully captured, however, because your purchase of insurance, although it fully internalizes your losses in the event of war, also decreases the likelihood of war, and, hence, reduces the amount of insurance others would volunteer to buy. This smaller remaining public aspect of the good could be accounted for by offering the insurance for premiums that are believed to be subsidized.

War, as well as other events, can topple governments, so that to make the insurance credible, the government might need to offer citizens the option of cancelling their insurance and receiving all or some of the premiums they have paid. This cancellation option need be effective only up to the date before a war starts. The insurance device is not without dangers. By raising the maximum purchasable insurance (and lowering premiums), the government could induce a more aggressive attitude among the citizens than is warranted by actuarial fair insurance.

6 It is not really necessary for efficiency to obtain to require that producers take the product price as given and beyond their control. See Demsetz (1964).

REFERENCES

Arrow, K. J. (1963). "Uncertainty and the Welfare Economics of Medical Care." *American Economic Review*, 53.

Bator, F. M. (1958). "The Anatomy of Market Failure." *Quarterly Journal of Economics*, 72.

Coase, R. H. (1946). "The Marginal Cost Controversy." *Economica*, 13.

—— (1960). "The Problem of Social Cost." *Journal of Law and Economics*, 3.

Demsetz, H. (1964). "The Welfare and Empirical Implications of Monopolistic Competition." *Economic Journal*, 74.

Minasian, J. R. (1964). "Television Pricing and the Theory of Public Goods." *Journal of Law and Economics*, 7.

4
When Does the Rule of Liability Matter?

The active interface between law and economics has been limited largely to antitrust and regulation, but recent work, primarily in economics, has revealed a much wider area of common interest. The new development, which deals with the definition and structure of property rights, has implications for central areas of the law, such as real property, torts, and contracts, although it originated in an economic analysis of the divergence between private and social cost. While still in its embryonic stage, the analysis has proceeded far enough for it to be called to the attention of a wider audience.

The questions with which we shall be concerned are whether and under what conditions a legal decision about liability affects the uses to which resources will be put and the distribution of wealth between owners of resources. If ranchers are held liable for the damage done by their cattle to corn fields, how will the outputs of meat and corn be affected? If drivers or pedestrians, alternatively, are held liable for automobile–pedestrian accidents, how will the accident rate be affected? What implications for extortion (an extreme form of wealth redistribution) are found in the decision about who is liable for damages?

I

Recent developments in this area began with an article by Professor R. H. Coase.[1] Coase's work presented a penetrating criticism of the conventional treatment by economists of divergences between private and social cost. The social cost of furthering an economic activity is the resulting reduction in the value of production that is obtainable from other activities. Such reductions

The author thanks the Charles R. Walgreen Foundation for financial aid through its grant to the University of Chicago, and the Lilly Endowment through its grant to the University of California. Reprinted with permission from *Journal of Legal Studies*, University of Chicago Law School, 1(1) 1972.

occur because the resources required to further an activity are scarce and must be diverted from other possible uses. According to the view that Coase challenged, social cost, being the sum total of the costs incurred to carry on any activity, might very well differ from private cost. For example, the social cost of running steam locomotives properly includes the fire damage done to surrounding farm crops by sparks from the locomotive. If the railroad is not required to pay for these damages, perhaps through a tax per train, then, according to the conventional analysis, the railroad will not take account of crop damage costs in deciding how many trains to run. In the absence of a specific public policy to intervene, the rate at which an activity is carried forth, which is determined solely by private cost, will diverge from the optimum rate, which is determined by social cost. In the present example, the private cost of running additional trains, being less than the social cost because crop damage is not taken into account, will encourage the railroad to run too many trains per day. The conventional economic analysis called for the levy of a tax per train, equivalent to the damages, in order to bring social cost and private cost into equality.

Coase demonstrated that the imposition of such a tax could, in some circumstances, aggravate the difficulty, but two other aspects of his work are of more concern to us: (1) he showed that powerful market forces exist that tend to bring private and social cost into equality without the use of a tax; and (2) he discussed the conditions under which the legal position toward liability for damages would and would not alter the allocation of resources. Coase discusses an interaction between two productive activities, ranching and farming, in the context of a competitive regime in which the cost of transacting (or negotiating) is assumed to be zero.[2] His analysis concludes that social cost and private cost will be brought into equality through market negotiations – and this regardless of which party is assigned the responsibility for bearing the cost that results from the proximity of ranching and farming.

The law, reasoning that crops *stand in the way* of a neighbor's cattle, can leave the farmer to bear the cost of crop damage; alternatively, reasoning that cattle *stray errrantly* across farm fields, the law can assign liability for crop damages to ranchers. Coase's work demonstrates that either legal position will result in the same resource allocation – i.e., in the same quantities of corn and meat – and also that negotiations between the parties to the damage will, with either legal position, eliminate any divergence between private and social cost. If the law favors ranchers by leaving farmers to bear the cost of crop damage, then there exist incentives for farmers to pay ranchers to reduce the sizes of the herds, or to take other measures that will reduce the amount of damage. A summary arithmetic example reveals how such market transactions lead to Coase's results.

Suppose that the net return to an owner of ranchland would be increased by $50 if herd size were increased by one head of cattle but that the additional head of cattle would impose corn damage on the owner of neighboring farmland that reduced his net return by $60. If the law did *not* require the rancher to compensate the farmer, the farmer would offer to pay the rancher a sum up to $60, the damage he would suffer if the rancher increased his herd by one head. The rancher would accept the offer since any amount above $50 would be more than ample compensation for the reduction in net returns associated with the smaller herd size.

Negotiations would continue until the net return to the rancher of a head of cattle exceeded the reduction in net return to the farmer associated with the damage done by that head of cattle. Such negotiations would bring the total value of corn and beef produced to a maximum since herd size would be reduced only when the consequent increase in the net value of corn output ($60 in the above example) exceeded the decrease in the net value of beef output ($50 in the example) required to reduce crop damage.

If the rule of liability were the reverse, requiring the owner of ranchland to compensate the farmer for the crop damage, the same equilibrium would be reached. Since the rancher earns a net return of only $50 and must pay damages of $60 if he raises an additional head of cattle, he would find it in his interest not to increase the size of his herd. Moreover, he would reduce the size of his herd as long as the net return forgone was smaller than the resulting increase in the net return to farming, since this would be the liability to him if he did not reduce herd size by another unit. He would be led to settle upon the same herd size, with the same consequence for crop size, as he would have chosen in the absence of liability. The mix of output is not changed[3] because negotiations between the parties eliminate all divergence between private and social cost.

The resulting equality between social and private cost is important enough to warrant a few more words. The conventional analysis of the farmer-rancher interaction would have concluded that in the absence of liability for damage (or of an appropriate tax per head of cattle) the social cost of increasing herd size would have exceeded the rancher's private cost by the $60 damage done to the neighboring farmer's crops. The rancher, if he were neither held liable nor taxed, would have no reason to take account of this damage and would therefore be led to raise too many cattle and impose too much damage on farm crops. It is the supposed existence of this gap between private and social cost that seems to call for a tax per head of cattle or for an assignment of liability to the rancher. Coase's reasoning shows this logic to be in error. Even in the absence of a tax or liability for damage, the harmful effects of his activities on surrounding crops would be brought to bear on the private calculations of the owner of ranchland, for he must reckon as a true (but implicit) cost of increasing herd size the payment from the farmer that he must forgo if he refuses to agree to the farmer's request for a reduction in herd size. Market negotiations bring the full cost of his decision to bear on him through the offers made by the farmer and thereby eliminate any difference between private and social cost. This, as Coase recognized, would not be true if the cost of negotiating could not be assumed to be negligible. We shall return to this problem later.

It is not generally appreciated that Coase's reasoning has legal applications that extend beyond problems of the divergence between social and private cost as these typically are conceived. What is at issue in the farmer–rancher case is which party has a particular property right. In the one case the farmer has the right to allow or prohibit cattle grazing on certain specified lands, while in the other case it is the rancher who has the right. Private property takes the form of a bundle of rights, of which different components may be held by different persons. In the absence of significant negotiating cost, the use to which these property rights is put is independent of the identities of the owners since each owner will be given market incentives to use his property right in the most valuable way. Just what is the most valuable way depends on market conditions and not owner identities.

The analysis can be extended to many types of property right problems. One that is of current interest to lawyers is the continuing litigation about the legal status of the reserve clause in organized baseball. An important defense of the reserve clause has been the assertion that it prevents wealthy baseball clubs from acquiring too large a share of the good players. By applying the above analysis to this problem it is possible to refute the assertion, especially since the cost of negotiations would seem to be negligible in this case. For what is at issue is whether the identity of the owner of a player's baseball services will alter the location of his playing activities. An application of Coase's analysis to this problem suggests that the reserve clause should have no effect on the identity of the team for which a player plays.

When signing initially with a major league organization, a player owns his baseball talent in the sense that he has the right to offer his services for sale to any ball club. But once he signs with a major league club, he can no longer negotiate with other clubs for the sale of his services, although he retains the right to refuse to play. The reserve clause, which is written into every major league contract, requires major league clubs who wish to acquire the services of a player who is already under contract to purchase his contract from the club currently owning it. Thus, once a player signs with a major league organization, part of the bundle of property rights to his services are transferred from the player to the club with which he signs. The right to play on various teams passes via the reserve clause from the player to the club owning his contract, and his club can reserve the player for its own use even though other teams might be willing to pay the player more than he is receiving.

The question considered here is *not* whether there exists a correlation between the wealth of a club and the quality of its players. The relevant question is whether the distribution of players among teams would change were the reserve clause to be declared illegal. Would wealthier clubs acquire more good players if the right to negotiate with other teams always resided with the player?[4]

In the absence of the reserve clause, a player would change clubs only if he found it in his interest to do so. With the reserve clause, a player will change clubs only if the club that owns his contract finds it in its interest. It appears that a different pattern of player migration between clubs might exist with the reserve clause than without it. But the appearance is deceptive. No matter who owns the right to sell the contract for the services of a baseball player, the distribution of players among teams will remain the same.

To see why this is so, assume that a player *not* subject to the reserve clause receives a $15,000 per annum wage from club A for which he currently plays. Club B offers him $16,000 to play for them. If this amount exceeds the value of the player to club A, the club will not find it in its interest to make a counter-offer large enough to retain the player's services and he will join club B. However, if his services are worth more than $16,000 to club A, the club will find it in its interest to make a counter-offer large enough to retain his services. With no reserve clause, the player plays for the club that most highly values his services.[5]

Let us now suppose that the reserve clause is effective and, as before, that the player is currently paid $15,000 by club A. Club B now offers club A $1,000 per annum (or its present value equivalent) for the player's contract, so that if the negotiations succeed club B will pay $16,000 for the player's services of which $15,000 is paid to the player under the terms of the purchased contract and $1,000 is paid to club A. If $1,000 per annum exceeds the player's net value to club A after it pays his $15,000 annual salary, then it will be in club A's interest to sell his contract to club B, but if the player is worth more to club A than $16,000 (equal to the $1,000 offer from club B plus the player's $15,000 salary), it will refuse to sell his contract.

The condition under which the player is transferred to club B when he is subject to the reserve clause is precisely the condition under which he will elect to transfer to club B when he is not subject to the reserve clause. He transfers to club B if club B finds his services more valuable than does club A whether or not the reserve clause is in effect. The reserve clause, therefore, cannot be expected to result in a different distribution of players among teams than would prevail in its absence.

The reader may object, suggesting that non-pecuniary considerations might make the distribution of players different depending on the legal status of the reserve clause. But this objection also would be in error. Suppose that the player presently owned by a California club, has developed a preference for working in California. If there were no reserve clause, his preference would lead him to ask at least $1,000 more to play ball with a Chicago club than he earns playing for a California club; and, in the absence of a reserve clause, a Chicago club would need to bid $1,000 more than a California club to obtain his services. But this is also true with the reserve clause. Under reserve clause arrangements, suppose that the Chicago club offers the California club only $500 more than the player's net value to the California club. The California club, indeed, will be tempted to sell the player's contract to Chicago. It appears that the $500 increment, which would be too small to move the player were there no reserve clause, is large enough to move him if there is a reserve clause. This is incorrect, because the player, when working under the reserve clause arrangement, would be willing to offer a sum of up to $1,000 (the value of the non-pecuniary amenities to him of California) to the California club to induce it to refuse to sell his contract to Chicago. Any amount above $500 would be sufficient to make the California club reject Chicago's offer since Chicago is offering only $500 more than the player is worth to the California club. (The player can 'offer' such an amount by accepting a pay reduction.) With or without the reserve clause, then, the player will locate where the value he places on amenities plus the value of his baseball talent is greatest.

II

The significance of Coase's work quickly led to critical responses by Wellisz,[6] Calabresi,[7] and others, although Calabresi withdrew his criticism in a later paper.[8] The criticism centered around two allegations – that the Coase theorem neglects long-run considerations that negate it, and that the spirit of the work endorses the use of resources for the undesirable purpose of "extortion." The long-run issue is discussed here and the "extortion" problem in section III. In section IV, I discuss the problems introduced when the assumption of negligible transaction cost is dropped.

The question of long-run considerations has been raised because it would seem that different liability rules would alter the profitability of remaining inside or outside each industry. It is alleged that, if farmers are left to bear the cost that arises from proximity to cattle, the rate of return to farming will fall and resources will therefore leave the farming industry. Alternatively, if ranchers are left to bear the cost, the resulting reduction in rate of return to ranching will lead to the exit of resources from that industry. Hence, even if transaction cost is zero, the market will allocate resources differently in the long run depending upon which rule of liability is chosen.

But short-run *v.* long-run considerations should have no bearing on the Coase theorem, which is based on the proposition that an implicit cost (the forgone payment from the farmer) is just as much a cost as is an explicit cost (the liability damage), and this proposition surely must hold in the long run as well as in the short run. One way of demonstrating this is by allowing the two activities to be merged under a common owner. A detailed example of this is given by G. Warren Nutter.[9] If there is no special cost to operating a multi-product firm, the costly interaction between farming and ranching will be fully brought to the owner's attention in his operation of a farming–ranching enterprise. The mix of output that he produces will be that which maximizes his earnings. The rule of liability that is chosen can have no effect on his decisions because the owner of such a firm must bear the interaction cost whichever legal rule is adopted. The cost interdependence is a technical–economic interdependence, not a legal one. Since such merged operations are possible, the rule of liability is rendered irrelevant to the choice of output mix. But a refutation of the criticism that is based on the use of the joint product enterprise gives rise to the (incorrect) suspicion that the basic problem has been begged, since the rule of liability that is chosen cannot in this case alter the wealth of the owner of a farming–ranching enterprise. The spirit of the argument can be preserved, while the suspicion is allayed, by assuming that the advantages offered by specialization of ownership are so great that it is uneconomic to merge the two activities into a single ranching–farming firm.

If owners of farmland bear the cost of crop damage, what must be the cost conditions that are associated with an equilibrium allocation of land to farming, ranching, and other uses? For such damage to arise there must be a sufficient scarcity of land to force farms and ranches into proximity. Marginal farm acreage (acreage that just ''breaks even'') must earn revenue sufficient to cover all cost, including the cost of crop damage done by straying cattle. Suppose the proximity of ranching and farming reduces the net return to the owner of farmland by $100 as compared with what could be earned were there no neighboring ranch. If ranching continues on the neighboring acres, it must be true that the net return to the owner of the ranchland exceeds $100, for otherwise the farmer would have been able to purchase the removal of cattle from neighboring land by offering $100 to the neighboring ranchers. The reduction in net return to farming brought about because of crop damage is thus implicitly taken into account by the owner of the ranchland when he refuses the offer of the owner of the neighboring farmland. The money offered by the farmer is refused by the rancher precisely because the continued use of the land for grazing brings in additional net revenue in excess of $100.

Land that is submarginal as farm or ranchland (land that cannot be profitably farmed or ranched) is unable to earn revenue sufficient to cover the explicit $100 damage cost if it is put to the plough or the $100 implicit cost if it is employed in ranching. Were this land to be employed in farming, its owner would suffer losses attributable in part to the damage done to his crops by straying cattle; whereas if it were employed in ranching, its owner would suffer the implicit loss of forgoing a $100 payment from the neighboring farmer (the owners of farmland bearing the cost of crop damage). Submarginal land by definition can be neither farmed nor ranched profitably.

Now let the rule of liability be changed so that ranchers become liable for crop damage. If there is to be a long-run effect, it must be true that the cost interrelationships change in a manner that causes either the conversion of ranchland to farmland or submarginal land to farmland. But neither conversion can be made profitable by the change in liability.

Acreage that was marginally profitable in ranching must remain ranchland because it had been earning net revenues in excess of the $100 damages done by cattle to surrounding farmland. If a producing ranch were to be switched from ranching to farming to avoid the new liability its owner would forgo revenues (in excess of $100) that exceeded the resulting reduction in liability ($100). The owner of what was marginal ranchland, therefore, will continue to employ this land in ranching under the new liability rule.

The land that previously was submarginal must remain submarginal. The changed liability rule will not attract this land into farming. Submarginal lands under the original rule of liability earned insufficient revenues in farming to cover the $100 cost of crop damage. Under the new rule of liability, neighboring ranchers will succeed in negotiating with the owners of this land to keep it out of farming. Operating ranches, under the old rule of liability, had been yielding net revenues in excess of $100; therefore it will be possible and profitable for ranchers, in order to avoid the $100 crop damage that otherwise would result, to offer an amount to the owners of submarginal land that is sufficient to keep the land out of farming.

There is a temptation at this point in the argument to believe that an error has been made. Suppose that the farmer suffers damages equal to $100 and the rancher enjoys a net return equal to $110. If the rancher is not liable he will choose to continue ranching and to refuse a payment from a neighboring farmer of $100 to stop ranching. But if the rule of liability is reversed, he will continue ranching only if his $110 net return is sufficient to cover the cost imposed on the farmer ($100) *plus* the payment required to keep submarginal land (which can be assumed to border on another boundary of the ranch) out of farming. There has been no error in the argument, but there is an error in introducing the second neighbor halfway through the analysis. With the rancher not liable, he would have elected to remain in ranching only if the net return to ranching exceeded the payments to leave ranching offered to him by *both* his neighbors. If the rancher finds it remunerative to remain in ranching in the face of both these offers, he must earn a sufficient net return from ranching, after the rule of liability is changed and he is held liable, to be able to pay damages to his neighboring farmer *and* to pay the owner of neighboring submarginal land to keep that land out of production.

The change in the rule of liability does not lead to a conversion of ranchland or submarginal land to farming. The use of land that maximized returns before the change in liability rule continues to maximize returns after the new rule is adopted, and the mix of output is unaffected by the choice of liability rule even when long-run considerations are analyzed. To understand the effect of altering the rule of liability it is important to recognize that the owner of a resource who finds it in his interest to employ that resource in a particular way when he bears the cost of an interaction will be paid to employ that resource *in the same way* when the rule of liability is reversed. What can happen, and in this case does happen, when the rule of liability is changed is that present owners of land having a comparative advantage in ranching suffer a *windfall* loss in the value of their land, while owners of farmland enjoy a *windfall* gain. But this redistribution of wealth cannot alter the uses of these lands.

III

The problem of "extortion" is part of the larger problem of wealth redistribution that may accompany a change in the rule of liability. Our concern here is with situations in which such a redistribution takes place. However, it should be noted that, when there is no restriction on contracting, a change in the rule of liability need not be accompanied by wealth redistribution. If owners of firms are made liable for industrial accidents, for example, then the equilibrium wage will move downward to reflect the shifting of this explicit cost from workers to employers. Employers no longer will need to cover the cost of industrial accidents in the wages they pay since this cost will be paid by them in the form of industrial accident insurance or self-insurance required by the new rule of liability. The general effect of shifting accident liability directly to firms will be merely to change the classification, not the amount, of remuneration. What under no employer liability were simply wages become under employer liability wages plus accident benefits. No redistribution of wealth accompanies the change in liability. Workers who, when they had to bear the cost of accidents directly, received \$*X* in wages will, under the new rule of liability, receive part of the \$*X* in the form of accident compensation and the remainder in wages, but there will be no change in their total income after taking account of expected accident costs under the two systems.

This holds strictly only if workers and employers are allowed to enter into voluntary contractual arrangements for reshifting the explicit cost back to workers, a matter that need not be discussed in detail here. If such agreements are disallowed by the law – i.e., if the costs of making such agreements is prohibitively high because of their illegality – then some wealth may be redistributed from those workers who would have found it advantageous to self-insure to workers who find it advantageous to buy insurance; such a law would force workers, in the wage reductions they must accept, to purchase insurance for industrial accidents from their employers.

The problem of "extortion" arises when a change in liability gives rise to a redistribution in wealth. In the farmer–rancher case, the relative values of nearby farm and ranchlands will be changed when the rule of liability is altered. Under one rule of liability, with farmers required to bear the cost of crop damage, farmers will need to pay ranchers to reduce herd size; under the other rule, ranchers will have to pay farmers for damages or for any alteration in the quantity of corn grown nearby. The change in the direction of payments must affect the rents that can be collected by owners of these lands and thus the market values of these lands.

In these cases the owner of the specialized resource, ranchland or farmland, that is not required to bear the cost of the interaction may threaten to increase the intensity of the interaction in an attempt to get his neighbor to pay him a larger sum than would ordinarily be required to obtain his cooperation in adjusting the intensity of the interaction downward. The owner of ranchland, if he is not liable for crop damage done by straying cattle, might, in the absence of a neighboring farmer, raise only 1,000 head of cattle. With proximity between farming and ranching, a neighboring owner of farmland might be willing to pay the rancher the sum required to finance a 200-head reduction in herd size. However, if the owner of ranchland *threatens* to raise 1,500 had, he may be able to secure more than this sum from the farmer because of the additional crop damage that would be caused by the larger herd size. With or without this ''extortion'' threat, the size of the herd will be reduced to 800 because that is the size, by assumption, that maximizes the total value of both activities. Given the interrelationship between the two activities, that is the herd size that will maximize the return to the farmer and, indirectly, the sum available for possible transfer to the rancher. What is at issue is the sharing of this maximum return.

To the extent that there exist alternative farm sites, the ability of the owner of ranchland to make such a threat credible is compromised. Competition among such owners will reduce the payment that farmers make to ranchers to that sum which is just sufficient to offset the revenue forgone by ranchers when herd size is reduced. No rancher could succeed in a threat to increase herd size above normal numbers because other ranchers would be willing to compete to zero the price that farmers are asked to pay to avoid abnormally large herd sizes. Abnormally large herd size, in itself, will generate losses to owners of ranchland, and for this reason competition among such owners will reduce the price that owners of farmland must pay to avoid such excessive herd sizes to zero.

But if a ranchland owner has a locational monopoly, in the sense that there are no alternative sites available to farmers, then the rancher may succeed in acquiring a larger sum from his neighboring farmer in order to avoid abnormally large herd sizes. The acquisition of a larger sum by the owner of ranchland generally will require him to incur some cost to make his threat credible, perhaps by actually beginning to increase herd size beyond normal levels. If the cost of making this threat credible is low relative to the sum available for transfer from the owner of farmland, the rancher will be in a good position to accomplish the transfer. The sum available for transfer will be the amount by which the value of the neighboring land when used as farmland exceeds its value in the next best use. If the rancher were to demand a larger payment from his neighbor, the neighboring land would be switched to some other use.

The temptation to label such threats extortion or blackmail must be resisted by economists, for these are legal and not economic distinctions. The rancher merely attempts to maximize profits. If his agreements with neighboring farmers are marketed in competition with other ranchers, profit maximization constrained by competition implies that an agreement to reduce herd size can be purchased for a smaller payment than if effective competition in such agreements is absent. The appropriate economic label for this problem is nothing more nor less than monopoly. It takes on the cast of such legal classifications as extortion only because the context seems to be one where the monopoly return is received by threatening to produce something that is not wanted – excessively large herds. The conventional monopoly problem involves a reduction or a threat to reduce the output of a desired good. In the unconventional monopoly problem presented here, there is a threat to increase herd size beyond desirable levels. But this difference is superficial. The conventional monopoly problem can be viewed as one in which the monopolist produces more scarcity than is desired, and the unconventional monopoly problem discussed here can be considered one in which the monopolist threatens to produce too small a reduction in crop damage. Any additional sum that the rancher succeeds in transferring to himself from the farmer is correctly identified as a monopoly return.

The temptation to resolve this monopoly problem merely by reversing the rule of liability must be resisted. Should the liability rule be reversed and the owner of ranchland now be held liable for damage done by his cattle to surrounding crops, the specific monopoly problem that we have been discussing would be resolved. But if the farmer enjoys a locational monopoly such that the rancher has nowhere else to locate, the shoe will now be on the other foot. The farmer can threaten to increase the number of bushels of corn planted, and hence the damage for which the rancher will be liable, unless the rancher pays the farmer a sum greater than would be required under competitive conditions. The potential for monopoly and the wealth redistribution implied by monopoly is present in principle whether or not the owner of ranchland is held liable for damages. Both the symmetry of the problem and its disappearance under competitive conditions refute the allegation that Coase's analysis implicitly endorses the use of resources in undesirable activities.

Should the law treat such classes of monopoly problem as "extortion" or "blackmail?" It may not be useful for the law to take this step, because the threat is made credible by increasing the output of an economic good – cattle if the rancher is not liable, corn if he is. Because it is difficult to sort desirable from undesirable increases in herd or crop size, there is a real danger of penalizing desirable increases in herd or crop size by mistake if such wealth transfers are treated as extortion. Activities to which anti-extortion laws normally apply typically involve the use of violence or the threat to take some action that falls within a general class of actions considered socially undesirable. The application of anti-extortion legal measures in such cases is less likely to penalize socially desirable actions by mistake. In other cases, it may be possible for the courts to limit the amount of payments to levels that are reasonable compensations for costs incurred (or profits forgone), although it is not clear how easily such determinations can be made by courts. Alternatively, it is possible to attempt to eliminate the source of the problem – monopoly – but the wisdom of relying on antitrust in this context is a matter on which the author is unprepared to speak.

IV

The costly interaction between farming and ranching is not properly attributed to the actions of either party individually, being "caused," instead, by resource scarcity, the scarcity of land and fencing materials. If transaction cost is negligible, it would seem that the choice of liability rule cannot depend on who "causes" the damage, since both jointly do, or on how resource allocation will be altered, since no such alteration will take place, but largely on judicial or legislative preferences with regard to wealth distribution.

Once significant transacting or negotiating cost is admitted into the analysis, the choice of liability rule will have effects on resource allocation, and it no longer follows that wealth distribution is the main or even an important consideration in choosing the liability rule. The assumption of negligible transacting cost can be only a beginning to understanding the economic consequences of the legal arrangements that underlie the operations of the economy, but little more can be done here than to illustrate the nature of the considerations.[10]

The most obvious effect of introducing significant transacting cost is that negotiations will not be consummated in those situations where the expected benefits from exchange are less than the expected cost of exchanging. Exchange opportunities will be exploited only up to the point where the marginal gain from trade equals the marginal cost of trade. Of course, there is nothing necessarily inefficient in halting exchange at this point. If this were all that could be said on the subject, there would be little more to do than call the reader's attention to the similar analytical roles of transport cost in international trade and transacting cost in exchange generally. But there *is* more to say.

Significant transacting cost implies that the rule of liability generally will have allocative effects (as Coase recognizes). Consider the problem of liability for automobile–pedestrian accidents. To the extent that "accident" has any economic meaning, it must mean that circumstances are such that voluntary negotiations between the driver and the pedestrian are prohibitively costly in many driving situations. The parties to an accident, either because of the speed with which the accident occurs or because of a failure to notice the presence of a competing claimant for the right of way, cannot conclude an agreement over the use of the right of way at costs that are low enough, *ex ante*, to make the effort worthwhile.

Partly as a consequence of the costliness of such negotiations, rules of the road are developed. Speed limits, traffic signals, and legal constraints on passing are substituted for the development of saleable private rights. In a specific case it may be possible to assign private rights to use the road in a way that makes the exchange of these rights feasible; but, in general, if these rules make economic sense it is precisely because the cost of transacting is expected to be too high in most cases to warrant the development of saleable private rights to the use of roads.

The practicality of such rules is not an argument for or against government action, but a rationale for the substitution of rules for negotiation. The use of rules to eliminate costly negotiations can be found in the management of privately owned parking lots and toll roads as well as in those that are publicly owned.

Such rules notwithstanding, accidents do take place. Assuming that the cost of transacting is too high to make negotiated agreements practical in such cases, we can compare the effect on resource allocation of the rule of liability that is chosen. If drivers are held liable in automobile–pedestrian accidents, the incentives for pedestrians to be careful about how and where they cross streets will be reduced. The incentives for drivers to be careful will be increased. Indeed, if each pedestrian could be guaranteed *full* compensation for all financial, physical, and psychological costs suffered in an accident, then pedestrians would become indifferent between being struck by an auto and not being struck. Drivers, however, would actively seek to avoid accidents since they would always be liable; whereas, if it were possible to have a system of complete and full pedestrian liability, it would be the drivers who became indifferent between accidents and no accidents and it would be the pedestrians who actively sought to avoid accidents.

In a regime in which transacting cost was zero, either system of liability would generate the same accident-avoiding behavior, as the Coase analysis suggests. With driver liability, drivers would themselves avoid accidents, or, if such avoidance could be purchased at lower cost from pedestrians, drivers would pay pedestrians to avoid accidents. Under a scheme of pedestrian liability, it would be the pedestrians who took direct action to avoid accidents or indirect action by paying drivers to avoid accidents. Under either rule of liability, those accidents are avoided for which the accident cost exceeds the least-cost method of avoiding accidents, where the least cost is the lesser of either the driver or pedestrian cost of avoiding accidents. Both rules of liability, assuming zero transacting cost, yield the same accident rate and the same accident-avoiding behavior. The effect of switching from one rule of liability to another is limited to wealth redistribution.

In a situation in which transacting cost is prohibitively high, driver liability leads to the avoidance only of those accidents for which the cost of avoidance to the *driver* is less than the expected accident cost, and pedestrian liability leads to the avoidance of only those accidents for which the cost of avoidance to the *pedestrian* is less than the expected accident cost. In general, the accident rate that results will differ under these two systems since the cost of avoiding accidents will not be the same for drivers and pedestrians. Both systems will lead to higher accident rates than would be true if transacting costs were zero. The effect of positive transacting cost is to raise the cost of avoiding accidents through the foreclosure of the use of possibly cheaper cost-avoidance techniques when these can be employed only by the other party to the accident. A similar conclusion can be reached for all liability problems when transacting cost is prohibitive and when the law cannot particularize the rule of liability to take account of who is the least-cost damage avoider in every instance.

One liability rule may be superior to another if transacting costs are more than negligible precisely because the difficulty of avoiding costly interactions is not generally the same for the interacting parties. It may be less costly for pedestrians to avoid accidents or for farmers to relocate their crops than it is for drivers to avoid accidents or ranchers to reduce the number of cattle they raise. If information about this were known, it would be possible for the legal system to improve the allocation of resources by placing liability on that party who in the usual situation could be expected to avoid the costly interaction most cheaply.

The use of words such as "blame," "responsible," and "fault" must be treated with care by the economist because they have no useful meanings in an economic analysis of these problems other than as synonyms for the party who could have most easily avoided the costly interaction. Whether the interaction problem involves crop damage, accidents, soot, or water pollution, the qualitative relationship between the interacting parties is symmetrical. It is the *joint* use of a resource, be it geographic location, air, or water, that leads to these interactions. It is the demand for scarce resources that leads to conflicting interests.

The legal system does produce rules for determining prima facie "fault," but in this context "fault" means only according to some acceptable and applicable legal precedent. In an accident involving a rear-end collision, the court generally will place the burden for proving the absence of negligence on the party driving the following car. If a car strikes a person running across a fenced expressway at night, the burden of proving the absence of negligence is likely to be placed on the pedestrian. In treating such cases differently, the law bases its decisions on acceptable and appropriate precedents, but the acceptability of these precedents should not be confused with the morality of the interacting parties. A deeper analysis of these precedents may reveal that they generally make sense from the economic viewpoint of placing the liability on that party who can, at least cost, reduce the probability of a costly interaction happening. Less care need be taken by the driver of the following car in the rear-end collison than would need to be taken by the lead driver to avoid the accident, and less care is needed by a pedestrian to refrain from running across an expressway than is needed by a driver to avoid striking the pedestrian. Nor need the acceptability of such precedents be based on restitution since, as these precedents become known, their long-run effect is to deter accidents at least cost. If courts are to ignore wealth, religion, or family in deciding such conflicts, if persons before the courts are to be treated with regard only to the cause of action and available proof, then, as a normative proposition, it is difficult to suggest any criterion for deciding liability other than placing it on the party able to avoid the costly interaction most easily.

NOTES

1 Coase (1960).

2 Coase (1960, pp. 2–8).

3 I ignore other possibilities such as building a fence. These are discussed by Coase (1960, p. 3). Consideration of them changes the exposition but not the results.

One further assumption is required for the mix of output to remain unchanged. Any redistribution of wealth resulting from a change in the rule of liability is assumed to have no consequences for the demands for the products produced. Owners of farmland and ranchland should be vegetarians in equal proportions, for otherwise a redistribution of wealth between these two groups would alter the market demands for corn and beef and thereby indirectly alter the mix of output produced. The wealth redistribution problem will be discussed later when we turn to the subject of extortion.

4 The reserve clause and other aspects of organized baseball are discussed in Rottenberg (1956, p. 242). The reasoning employed by Rottenberg is similar but not identical to the above argument. Rottenberg's argument is based partly on the premise, not used here, that it takes two fairly well matched teams to produce a good game.

5 Non-pecuniary aspects of his employment are discussed later, but it should be noted that the argument for retention of the reserve clause is not based on non-pecuniary job amenities.

6 Wellisz (1964, p. 345).

7 Calabresi (1965, p. 713).

8 Calabresi (1968, p. 67).

9 Nutter (1968, p. 503).

10 Other considerations that arise when the cost of transacting is positive are discussed in Demsetz (1966, p. 61).

REFERENCES

Calabresi, G. (1965). "The Decision for Accidents: An Approach to Nonfault Allocation of Costs." *Harvard Law Review*, 78.

—— (1968). "Transaction Costs, Resource Allocation, and Liability Rules: A Comment." *Journal of Law and Economics*, 11.

Coase, R. H. (1960). "The Problem of Social Cost." *Journal of Law and Economics*, 3.

Demsetz, H. (1966). "Some Aspects of Property Rights." *Journal of Law and Economics*, 9.

Nutter, G. W. (1968). "The Coase Theorem on Social Cost: A Footnote." *Journal of Law and Economics*, 11.

Rottenberg, S. (1956). "The Baseball Players' Labor Market." *Journal of Political Economy*, 64.

Wellisz, S. (1964). "On External Diseconomies and the Government Assisted Invisible Hand." *Economica*, 31.

5
The Cost of Transacting

The empirical work in this paper is a study of the cost of transacting on a very important market, the New York Stock Exchange; but the economics of transacting, of which this paper is a beginning, has an importance that extends beyond particular markets and argues against the general neglect accorded the subject by economists. This can be grasped by considering the operation of an economic system in which transaction cost is zero. The usual sources of inefficiency fail to exist in such an economic system.

Externalities? Persons subjected to harmful effects will, at zero negotiating and contracting cost, bring the value they attach to a reduction of these effects to the attention of whoever produces the harmful effects. The value placed on reducing these effects will be compared, again through costless negotiations, with the value attached by others to the benefits associated with the production of these effects. In response to such costless bidding by rivals, the output of harmful effects will be brought to efficient levels.

Monopolies? It will be profitable for agreements to be reached, again at zero transacting cost, between buyers and sellers that lead to efficient output rates in return for side payments. Efficient rates of output yield a bigger pie to be shared by all, so that, in a milieu of costless transactions, utility maximization will yield efficient allocations even in the presence of monopoly and monopsony.

Of course, the existence of positive transacting cost has no direct relevance to economic inefficiencies. As with any cost, the question that is relevant for efficiency is whether or not the cost is appropriately economized. In some cases it will be efficient to have markets in which negotiations are carried forth to bring costs and benefits to bear on economic decision units. The value of realigning resources as a result of such negotiations is expected to be worth the cost of transacting. In other cases it will be efficient not to negotiate; in a world of positive transacting cost some external and monopoly effects are

The author wishes to thank George J. Stigler for advice, encouragement, and particularly for his incessant prodding. Reprinted with permission from *Quarterly Journal of Economics*, 82, 1968.

consistent with efficiency. None of this makes unimportant the usual questions concerning the role of government in the resolution of externality and monopoly problems. For there are cases in which the cost of government action is less than the cost of transacting in markets. In such cases, we will employ government action that realigns resources more completely than can be achieved economically in the market place.[1]

In addition to these areas of application, the economics of transactions will be the core of an economic theory of money, for exchange will tend to be conducted in ways that economize on the cost of transacting.[2] An economic theory of money must inquire into what conditions favor the use of a specialized medium of exchange, for there seem to be circumstances in which barter appears more economical. "Portability, storability, and divisibility," words frequently marshaled to describe an economical money, become quantifiable characteristics when they are treated as methods for reducing the cost of transactions.[3]

The above subjects are beyond the scope of the present study, but the work presented below will shed some light on why the New York Stock Exchange (NYSE) has dominated for so long the organized trading of securities, and the empirical estimates to be given will enable us to re-evaluate intuitive notions about imperfections in the capital markets: how much of the difference in borrowing costs between large and small firms can be attributed to differences in the cost of transacting rather than to imperfections in the capital market?

But the more general question we seek to investigate is the extent to which transaction costs are affected by the scale of trading. This aspect of trading, always of interest to economists, has implications that extend beyond the NYSE. Do standardization and delegation of transacting authority result in marketing scale economies? The NYSE provides us with an important source of data by which the presence or absence of scale economies can be detected, and what will be studied below in detail for this important market is an application of Adam Smith's famous proposition:

> As it is the power of exchanging that gives occasion to the division of labour, so the extent of this division must always be limited by the extent of that power, or, in other words, by the extent of the market.

THE DEFINITION AND MEASUREMENT OF TRANSACTION COST ON THE NEW YORK STOCK EXCHANGE

Transaction cost may be defined as the cost of exchanging ownership titles. In the specific case of the NYSE, it is the cost of exchanging titles to money and to shares of stock. It is possible to increase or decrease this cost by a more or less inclusive definition of which activities are to be counted as transaction activities. From one viewpoint, the cost of producing assets is necessary to the exchange of assets, whereas from another viewpoint, only titles to assets need be produced for exchange to take place – the production of the assets themselves can be postponed indefinitely. And one could include in transaction cost the cost of being informed about the general nature of the market – the cost of making phone calls to one's broker or of reading the financial pages. Transaction cost is defined narrowly in this paper as the cost of using the NYSE to accomplish a quick exchange of stock for money. Broader interpretations lead to extremely difficult empirical and conceptual problems.

Given that titles to assets exist, given that decisions to exchange these titles have been made, and given that brokers or sales representatives have been informed of these decisions, what are the costs to buyers and sellers of using the NYSE to contract with each other? These remaining costs comprise transaction cost as the term is used in this paper. On the NYSE two elements comprise almost all of transaction cost: brokerage fees and ask–bid spreads. Transfer taxes could be included, but it is expedient to concentrate our attention on the two major components.

The inclusion of the ask–bid spread in transaction costs can be understood best by considering the neglected problem of "immediacy" in supply and demand analysis. Predictable immediacy is a rarity in human actions, and to approximate it requires that costs be borne by persons who specialize in standing ready and waiting to trade with the incoming orders of those who demand immediate servicing of their orders. The ask–bid spread is the markup that is paid for predictable immediacy of exchange in organized markets; in other markets, it is the inventory markup of retailer or wholesaler.

In figure 5.1, curves D_i and S_i illustrate the demand and supply flows per unit of time for security X_i on the part of those who desire that their buy or sell orders be serviced immediately. Intersection E_i shows the conventional view of equilibrium price. Suppose that E_i is, in fact, the average price for which X has been and will be exchanged. But a person wishing to sell shares of X_i at price E_i cannot automatically count on the presence of a buyer. An order to buy X_i at price E_i may come to the market only after a time delay of minutes, hours, or even days. And a person wishing to buy X_i at price E_i has no guarantee that a sell order will be available with which to match his buy order. Thus, D_i and S_i do not illustrate *always present* market orders; rather, they measure time rates of demand and supply for which, at any given time, no market orders need be present.

Now let some person or persons provide the service of standing ready to sell or buy at stated prices immediately upon receipt of a matching order. To cover the cost of standing ready, these persons will be willing to buy X_i at a price that is slightly below E_i and sell at a price that is slightly above E_i. The difference between these two prices is the ask–bid spread. Their geometric counterparts can be illustrated in Figure 5.1 as follows: S_i is the supply curve of those who wish to sell immediately. But persons willing to wait before selling, and who do so by keeping their selling offers active, must be compensated for the cost of waiting; to cover the cost of waiting, their supply curve will lie above S_i; S_i' shows the supply curve of asking prices for those who stand ready and waiting to sell to those who demand immediate servicing of their purchase orders. D_i is the demand curve for those who desire immediate purchases, so the intersection of D_i and S_i' yields the equilibrium ask price, A_i.

Similarly persons willing to supply securities according to schedule S_i require that these shares be sold as soon as they are offered. The service of immediately buying these shares is offered by persons willing to stand ready and waiting to buy as soon as sell orders reach the market. Waiting costs must be incurred by these persons, and, therefore, their demand prices will be somewhat lower than those who are not prepared to wait. A schedule of demand prices for those offering to wait for the arrival of selling orders is given by D_i'. The intersection of D_i' with S_i determines the equilibrium bid price, B_i, at which a sale can be executed immediately. The difference between A_i and B_i is the spread that is quoted on security X_i. There exist two equilibrium prices and not one – A_i for immediate sales and B_i for immediate purchases. E_i can be thought of as an arithmetic average of A_i and B_i. The spread measures the price of immediacy in both buying and selling securities and X_i (in the symmetrical presentation of figure 5.1) measures the volume of trading in each submarket. If buy orders and sell orders could be counted upon to arrive simultaneously, so that there would be no demand for the services of persons to stand ready and waiting,

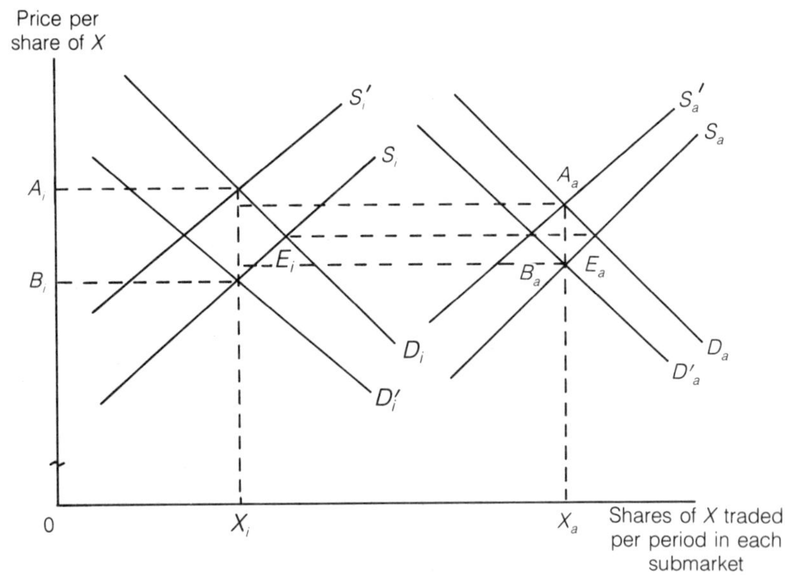

Figure 5.1

then E_i would determine the volume of trading. Without simultaneity, the volume of trading will be increased to the extent that those who stand ready and waiting specialize in reselling (rather than holding) what they have purchased. Thus, a specialist who buys at $98 and sells at $100 substitutes two transactions for what would be one transaction if the outside traders could count on their orders arriving simultaneously and at the same price, say $99. (The curves with subscript *a* will be referred to later.)

A person who plays an important role in these submarkets on the NYSE is the specialist. The specialist earns his income in two ways: by managing orders and by assuming risk. The former role is to manage orders left with him by traders who desire to move to other positions on the floor of the exchange. In this role, the specialist acts as a broker; he matches buy and sell orders. If he matches an order left to his care with an order that is subsequently presented to him by another floor trader, the specialist shares in the commission charged to the customer by the floor trader. This is the specialist's first source of income and in earning this income he serves as an information repository.

In his second role, the specialist may step in to match the order left with him by trading for his own account. If he does so, he acts as a trader and receives no part of the commission charged to the customer. Thus, if the first trader presents an order to sell (or buy) and the specialist buys (or sells) for his own account to match the trader's order, he does not earn any share of commissions on the exchange. However, such an operation can generate income for the specialist from other sources. He can engage in an opposite trading action at a preferential price differential later. If he buys for his own account, he can hope to resell later at a higher price than he paid; if he sells for his own account, he can expect to repurchase later at a lower price than he paid.

The specialist earns income through buying and selling for his own account by standing ready to step in during periods when ask–bid quotations submitted by outsiders are too far apart to keep trade active without wide jumps in price. The specialist can increase the rapidity of exchange with narrower price movements during such periods by offering a narrower ask–bid spread than outsiders are currently submitting. This role of the specialist involves judgment, investment, and risk-taking; it is a role that is difficult to computerize completely, although computer programs conceivably could aid the specialist in playing this role. The investment involved is common to that made by other inventory specialists such as retailers and wholesalers of commodities. It is the willingness to invest in inventory and to stand ready to exchange in order to offer quicker exchange at given cost to ultimate buyers and sellers. What makes the specialist important in this process is that he is obligated to fellow members of the exchange to make a market for the securities in which he specializes. If there exists no quotation from outsiders that is "reasonably" narrow, he must offer one of his own to facilitate trading. The specialist hopes, of course, to realize a profit on inventory turnover. Specialists in all types of markets perform essentially these same functions. All would like to acquire inventory at low prices and resell at high prices and to do so very rapidly; but competitive forces, to be discussed later, are at work in varying degrees in these markets, and the stronger are these forces the closer will these markups be to the cost of waiting and carrying inventory.

It is apparent from the discussion that under competitive conditions the ask–bid spread, or markup, will measure the cost of making transactions *without delay*. A person who has just purchased a security and who desires immediately to resell it will, on the average, be forced to suffer a markdown equal to the spread found in the market place. This markdown (plus brokerage commissions) measures the cost of an immediate round-trip exchange. Under less competitive conditions, this spread may somewhat exaggerate the underlying cost to those who stand ready and waiting of quick round-trip transactions, but, for any *given* degree of competition (since brokerage commissions do not vary with the time taken to complete a transaction), differences in spread will indicate differences in the cost of quick exchange. The typical spread for one security may be twice the percentage of price that it is for another; this can be taken to indicate that the cost of quick exchange per dollar invested in the first security is greater than it is for the second, and, perhaps, approximately twice as great. The spread, of course, can be thought of as measuring twice the cost of a one-way transaction; the last transaction price may be \$40 and the currently quoted spread may ask \$40½ and bid \$39½, so that a market order pays a half point penalty relative to the last transaction price.

If the cost of quick exchange is higher for one asset than it is for another, we may assume that the cost of exchanging with any given time delay will be higher also, although not necessarily proportionately higher. The forces at work in determining the cost of quick exchange, we shall see, are not such that they can be expected to work in opposite directions if we increase the time interval during which an exchange is concluded. Hence, the analysis that follows can be expected to determine the identity of variables and to measure the direction of their effect on the cost of making transactions in highly organized markets whatever the time allowed to conclude an exchange. The *magnitude* of the effects measured, however, can be associated with *quick* exchange only.

The ask–bid spread and the commission brokerage are determined by different procedures and institutional arrangements. Generally, commission brokerage depends only on the price of a share and is independent of whether or not the executed order is a market or limit order. The relationship of commissions to prices is established collectively by members of the NYSE. The spread is determined by persons acting individually, by specialists, by floor-traders, or by outsiders submitting market or limit orders. The spread component of transaction cost will vary according to several aspects of the market for a security. The *structural* requirements for competition are more clearly in evidence in determining the spread than they are in determining brokerage commissions.

Data to be discussed later reveal that the spread comprises about 40 per cent and the commission brokerage about 60 per cent of the total transaction cost. Total transaction cost is approximately 1.3 per cent of the value of one round lot of a $48 stock.

THE DETERMINATION OF THE ASK–BID SPREAD

Persons who stand ready and waiting to transact with incoming market orders submit limit orders quoting a minimum ask price or a maximum bid price. The prices stipulated by incoming limit orders arriving "simultaneously" do not cross except by accident, perhaps because market conditions change between the time that a limit order is submitted and the time at which it arrives on the floor of the exchange. A prospective purchaser either submits a market buy order, in which case he concludes an exchange at the lowest existing limit ask price, or, if he is prepared to stand ready and waiting, he submits a limit bid order stipulating an upper limit to the purchase price that he is willing to pay. This upper limit will be below the currently effective ask quotation. Likewise, a prospective seller will never ask a price below the currently effective bid price. Transactions generally occur between a market order and a limit order, although sometimes market orders will be crossed if the quoted spread is relatively large and if a buy and sell order arrive simultaneously. Only by accident will two limit orders, a bid and an ask, be crossed in the market place.

Those who stand ready to wait for incoming market orders pre-empt early positions in the trading queue by offering relatively high bid quotations and relatively low ask quotations (although occasionally disparities in the size of orders will alter this priority). The lower the ask and the higher the bid offered by a trader, *ceteris paribus*, the shorter the period he expects to wait before concluding an exchange with incoming market orders. Quotations distant from the last transaction price, if they are maintained, produce transactions after a longer wait than quotations maintained closer to the last transaction price; price cannot skip over these closer quotations; they must be acted upon before price can deviate further from the last transaction price.

Any given set of limit orders and associated ask–bid prices will be acted upon sooner the more rapidly market orders arrive, so that the expected waiting and inventory cost will be less for those who are at the front of the limit order queues. Of course, in response to lower waiting cost, the active securities may attract more limit orders, and this would tend to delay the execution of those limit orders not at the head of the queue; but, in equilibrium, the average spread brought about for active securities by competing limit orders will be smaller than for inactive securities. Whoever is at the head of the trading queue will trade more quickly if the security is active; hence, to get to the front of the queue, traders will be willing to lower their asking prices and raise their bidding prices. The fundamental force working to reduce the spread is the time rate of transactions. The greater the frequency of transacting, the lower will be the cost of waiting in a trading queue of specified length, and, therefore, the lower will be the spreads that traders are willing to submit to pre-empt positions in the trading queue.

Waiting costs are relatively important costs for trading in organized markets, and would seem to dominate the determination of spread. An inverse relationship between spread and time rate of transactions is to be expected unless there are rapidly rising marginal costs of communicating with respect to the number of orders transmitted to a single market place. The technology of communicating prices and transferring titles in the security markets is such that offsetting diseconomies are likely to arise only on those occasions when trading is so heavy that queues of *market* orders are formed. Since these occasions, in fact, are few, it would seem that the organized trading of a security is subject to a *form* of scale economies. *This need not be true of all markets, and more will be said later about this.* We assume here that *potential* waiting costs do, in fact, dominate security trading, and this leads us to the conclusion that trading is subject to scale economies on the NYSE, where scale refers to trading in a particular security and not necessarily to trading in a heterogeneous bundle of securities. Moreover, inventory and queuing theory leads us to believe that waiting costs will be reduced most rapidly when the transaction rate is small and increasing. The presence of economies in transacting is a major proposition to be tested in this paper.

The geometrical counterpart of our argument is illustrated in figure 5.1, where the spread generated by the curves with subscript *i* (for inactive security) is to be compared with the smaller spread generated by the curves labeled with the subscript *a* (for active security).

It is important to distinguish the relationship between waiting cost and *market* transaction rate in a particularly security, which is what is described above, and that between waiting cost and the *individual trader's* transaction rate. A person who submits only a single limit order will expect lower waiting costs for an actively traded security than for an inactively traded security, as will a person who submits many limit orders. Nonetheless, for both active and inactive securities, it is possible for the individual trader's marginal cost of transacting to increase as the rate at which he transacts increases. As the volume of trading in a particular security increases, waiting cost curves *shift* downward for all market participants, both frequent and infrequent traders. Whether or not the marginal cost curve for waiting is negatively sloped is a separate question about which the evidence is conflicting.

Over recent years on the NYSE there has been a rapid attrition in the number of specialists who keep book on any single security. At the present time there is one specialist only for each security, although many specialists handle more than one security. Specialists are a minority of the membership of the exchange, and the other members have an interest in the maintenance of small spreads, since small spreads will increase the volume of business that customers will do with them.

Since this increase in the specialization of specialists has been accepted and probably encouraged by the NYSE, it would seem that members act as though they believe that scale economies are present with regard to the activities of a single trader. But if such scale economies do exist, it is strange that the percentage of trading by volume in which the specialist participates in his own behalf seldom exceeds 50 percent, and, when it is in excess of 50 percent, it is usually for those securities that trade slowly. (See appendix 1 for supporting data.)

The question is of some interest to us because scale economies with respect to the transactions of a particular trader suggest natural monopoly and the possibility of a divergence between the observed spread and the underlying cost of transacting. The question is not crucial since our interest here is in the fee paid by outsiders for transacting quickly on the NYSE and not necessarily on the underlying cost. Moreover, our primary concern is with the behavior of spread as the transaction rate increases and not with the absolute level of spread; even in the presence of some degree of monopoly power, the behavior of spreads in relation to transaction rates should give some indication of the behavior of the monopolist's underlying cost. Nonetheless, the possibility of a divergence between spread and cost is important enough to warrant more attention.

Even though scale economies are present in the specialist's trading activities, there is little likelihood of his maintaining spread much above the cost of waiting. Competition of several types will keep the observed spread close to cost. The main types of competition emanate from (1) rivalry for the specialist's job, (2) competing markets, (3) outsiders who submit limit orders rather than market orders, (4) floor traders who may bypass the specialist by crossing buy and sell orders themselves, and (5) other specialists. Each of these competitive forces is considered briefly.

Competition affecting the spread will arise from rivalry for the job of specialist. It is in the interests of non-specialist members of the exchange, who are a majority, to have small spreads maintained, for this will increase the time rate of transactions and the time rate at which commissions are earned. Indeed, one of the stated NYSE guidelines for specialists is that of making an orderly market by keeping spreads narrow and close to the last transaction price. If the spread is maintained according to the *conventional* profit-maximizing solution of natural monopoly, and if this yields a large rent, it will be in the interest of non-specialist members of the exchange to compete for the job of specialist by offering to maintain narrower spreads. Effective rivalry for the job of specialist should keep spreads close to the cost of providing a ready market for outsiders. Thus, although scale economies with respect to each trader's activity imply that each security will be handled by one specialist, it is not true that this necessarily means that the spread will be maintained at the monopoly levels indicated by a conventional natural monopoly solution to the specialist's maximizing problem.[4]

Many securities are listed on more than one exchange and trading (unlisted) securities is permitted on many more exchanges. The maintenance of a large spread on the NYSE is an invitation to trade the security elsewhere. The effectiveness of this competition is, of course, limited by the scale economies offered by the high transaction rate of the NYSE.

Outsiders who submit limit orders to the NYSE offer effective competition to specialists and manage to participate in large percentages of the transactions made on the exchange. An objection might be raised that outsiders must pay commission brokerage and, therefore, compete at a disadvantage with the specialist. But outsiders pay this brokerage whether they submit limit orders or market orders. Their choice between the two types of orders, therefore, should be unaffected by brokerage commission. One can say that higher brokerage, as with any other price, reduces the volume of transactions on the NYSE, but it cannot be said that it affects the probability that an incoming order will be a market order rather than a limit order. Moreover, part of the brokerage paid by customers is transferred to the specialist when he completes a transaction for others, that is, when he acts as a broker; whereas, when he trades for his own account, he forgoes his share of a customer's commission. A relevant opportunity cost for the specialist when he trades for his own account is this forgone brokerage fee; if he is rational he will treat this as a cost of trading for his own account, just as an outsider should treat the brokerage he pays for trading on his account. Any financial barrier that must be overcome by outsiders in competing with specialists by submitting limit orders is probably slight.

Exchange members do not suffer from the limitations that might be assigned to outsiders. Members can compete with specialists by submitting limit orders of their own or by crossing orders for their customers, thus bypassing the specialist. If the spread quoted by the specialist is relatively large, exchange members can be expected to compete in this way.

Finally, specialists who handle different securities compete with each other. Offering a narrower spread than other specialists who handle different securities is one way a specialist can switch customers to his security and away from those handled by other specialists. Thus, a customer may ask his broker to secure quotations on several securities and allow differences in the spread (per dollar exchange) to affect his choice of which security to buy or sell. This is similar, for example, to the competition of furniture retailers who inventory highly similar furniture.

An enumeration of the forces of competition is not, by itself, convincing evidence of competition; the large share of trading in which the specialist does not participate is somewhat more convincing of the absence of "natural monopoly'' conditions. Unfortunately, unless the underlying cost of waiting is known, it is not possible to assess the competitiveness of the spread. It may be possible, however, to get some idea of the strength of the competitive forces operating internally on the NYSE: a negative relationship between spread and the number of competing markets on which a security is listed can be interpreted as indicating that spreads would have been higher on some securities had trading on other markets been prohibited. But, given the competition of other markets, the observed spreads cannot be taken as evidence of monopoly power since these other markets stand ready to compete and thus reduce the spread. The situation is complicated even further if we treat the listings on other markets as indications that the market in a particular security is more active than is indicated by the trading activity of the NYSE alone. There is some evidence that this is the case (to be discussed below), and, if it is, any negative relationship between spread and number of competing markets merely reflects the basic relationship between the spread and the transaction rate.

A security's price must also affect the spread quoted for quick exchange. Spread per share will tend to increase in proportion to an increase in the price per share so as to equalize the cost of transacting per dollar exchanged. Otherwise, those who submit limit orders will find it profitable to narrow spreads on those securities for which spread per dollar exchanged is larger. The tendency for these arbitrage activities to lead to spreads that are proportionate to prices will be strongest if the cost of transacting and of waiting is the same per dollar exchanged for high-priced and low-priced securities. Insofar as outsiders are concerned, the commission cost per dollar exchanged is lower for high-priced securities. To the extent that this disproportionality reflects underlying cost differences per dollar exchanged, then members of the exchange also will face declining cost per dollar exchanged as security price is raised, and this should attenuate somewhat the tendency toward strict proportionality. The strength of this attenuation depends on how important is the lack of proportionality in brokerage commission. If the non-proportional aspects of brokerage commissions are small in relation to total exchange and waiting cost, only a minor and difficult-to-detect effect on proportionality will be present. The brokerage paid by members in trading for their own accounts is considerably less than that paid by outsiders. The risk of adverse price changes and the cost of waiting are relatively more important than commissions insofar as exchange members are concerned. At best, we can assert a strong positive relationship between spread and price and inquire into the sign of the second derivative.

THE DETERMINATION OF THE TRANSACTION RATE

The basic relationship that has been specified is between the spread and the transaction rate. The transaction rate may be higher or lower for a day or two, perhaps because of a short-lived rumor, an accidental convergence of trading in the stock, or, more often, because the market for all stocks is temporarily active or inactive. It is not clear whether spreads will be related more closely to an average, normal, or long-run transaction rate or to the transaction rate of the moment. Two variables are used to measure the transaction rate: (1) number of transactions per day based on data for two (non-adjacent) days of trading, and (2) the number of shareholders. A few words about the use of number of shareholders is in order.

A plausible primary determinant of a long-run or "normal" transaction rate for assets belonging to a given asset class (shares of stock in different companies, automobiles of different makes, etc.) is the number of asset owners. A doubling of the number of participants will approximately double the transaction rate. Unless there is underway a sudden change in demand for the security, the number of persons presently owning shares will be positively related to the number of market participants interested in bidding on the asset. We expect, then, the number of shareholders will be strongly related to long-run transaction rates.

There is a minor statistical advantage to number of shareholders. The statistical work to follow is based on a random sample of 200 securities traded on the NYSE. Observations are recorded for two days (separated by about a month). Six securities were not traded both days and these cannot be used directly in regressions incorporating logarithmic or inverted forms of the transaction rate. No such problem is encountered with the number of shareholders.

STATISTICAL RESULTS

The following symbols identify the variables discussed above:

S = the ask–bid spread measured in dollars per share

T = the time rate of transactions defined as the number of separately recorded transactions per day on the board of the NYSE. A single transaction may be one in which any number of shares is traded, provided only that it is reported as a single transaction. A trade of 500 shares may represent an exchange between two persons, which it ordinarily will during the course of a day's trading, or between more than two persons, which it may represent when the market opens and is cleared of overnight orders.[5]

P = the price per share

N = the number of shareholders measured in hundreds

M = the number of markets on which the security is listed

The data used in the statistical analysis are a random selection of 200 securities listed on the NYSE. Incomplete data for 8 of these reduced the sample size to 192. Data on spread, price, and transaction frequency are calculated from the *Francis Emory Fitch Sheets*.[6] Observations on these variables are averaged for trading on two days, January 5 and February 28, 1965. The number of shareholders for each security is taken from *Moody's* and the number of markets from Standard & Poor's *Stock Guide*. Essentially, then, the data consist of cross-sectional measures of the variables.

Our interest is primarily in obtaining regression estimates for equations (IA) and (IB) and, secondarily, for equation (II):

$$S = f(T, P, M) \tag{IA}$$

$$S = g(N, P, M) \tag{IB}$$

$$T = h(N) \tag{II}$$

Indicating partial differentiation by subscripts, we expect to find the following constraints operative for equations (IA) and (IB):

$$S_T < 0 \tag{1}$$

$$S_{TT} > 0 \tag{2}$$

$$S_P > 0 \tag{3}$$

$$S_N < 0 \tag{4}$$

$$S_{NN} > 0 \tag{5}$$

There is ambiguity about the sign of T_{NN} and some reason to believe that (6) $S_{PP} \leq 0$ and (7) $S_M \leq 0$. Equation (II) will be discussed later.

Different transaction rates can be pictured geometrically as in figure 5.1. Smaller transaction rates are represented by the supply and demand curves located closer to the vertical axis and larger transaction rates by supply and demand curves farther to the right. The long-run transaction rate is determined primarily by exogenous forces, of which the dominating force seems to be *N*. (For example, *N* turns out to give a slightly better fit than number of shares outstanding.) The price of the security also is fundamentally determined by exogenous forces such as anticipated corporate earnings. The role of *M*, the number of markets in which the security is listed, is not obvious. It is inserted to gauge the degree to which listing on outside markets lowers the spread. But it must be remembered that *M* may also be related to trading activity, so that, for any given value of *N* or *T*, securities listed on more exchanges may tend to be more actively traded. Both views of the role of *M* suggest that, if increases in *M* play a role, it will be to reduce *S*.

It is important to note that it is not our purpose to estimate any of the curves shown in figure 5.1. We seek an explanation for any difference in spread between security *i* and security *a*. Our discussion suggests that prices and (short- or long-run) transaction rates will dominate as forces affecting the spread. The fee paid to others for standing ready and waiting to transact immediately is the dependent variable. If this fee is approximately competitive, it measures the cost per share of standing ready and waiting; this cost function is, we suppose, invariant with respect to the identity of the share traded, so that, in the competitive case, spreads are viewed as points on this stable cost function.

If the fee for trading quickly is not approximately competitive, difficulties arise in any attempt to estimate the underlying cost function; the margin above cost reflected by spreads in the absence of competition need not be the same for different securities. In the non-competitive case this margin will be affected by the shape of the underlying marginal cost curve for waiting and by differences in the elasticity of demand for quick exchange. Coping with these problems requires a model in which variables are included that are expected to be related to differences among securities in these respects. No attempt is made here to view the market as non-competitive.[7] But even though the spread be determined in non-competitive markets, a negative association between spread and transaction rate will indicate that waiting cost per share is negatively related to transaction rates (unless the demand for transacting quickly becomes less elastic as the transaction rate increases).

Least-square estimates of equations IA and IB have been calculated using both linear and logarithmic forms. The estimates for these are presented in appendix 2. The best-fitting regressions are linear in P and logarithmic in T and N. Linearity in P gives *slightly* better results than the use of ln P; however, the coefficient of ln P is highly significant and conforms to the condition $S_{PP}<0$. ln T and ln N, however, seem to give much better fits than T and N. The best-fitting regressions are presented below. The t-statistic is given in parentheses and the square of the correlation coefficient and the standard error of estimate are also indicated. For the sample size employed here, and assuming conditions of normality, t-values above 2 indicate significance levels above 0.95 probability for one-tailed tests of significance. Residuals from the equations are very well behaved.[8]

$$S = 0.38027 + 0.0080709\ P - 0.11527\ \ln\ T - 0.022906\ M \qquad \text{(IA)}$$
$$(5.80) \qquad (12.15) \qquad (6.46) \qquad (0.97)$$
$$r^2 = 0.57637 \qquad s_{y,x} = 0.28632$$

$$S = 0.48411 + 0.0088554\ P - 0.080911\ \ln\ N - 0.029691\ M \qquad \text{(IB)}$$
$$(5.65) \qquad (13.24) \qquad (5.10) \qquad (1.21)$$
$$r^2 = 0.5422 \qquad s_{y,x} = 0.29666$$

Both regressions give highly similar fits; although (IA) gives a slightly better fit, the use of number of shareholders does surprisingly well. All coefficients take on the expected algebraic signs and all except the M coefficient are highly significant. The coefficients of ln T and ln N yield the expected second derivatives. The coefficient of M cannot be judged to differ significantly from zero in the light of the evidence presented here. Readers will note that the significance of the M coefficient increases slightly when ln N is used in place of ln T. The reason for this is that M is associated slightly with differences in transaction rates that are not explained by differences in N. This can be seen below, where regression estimates of two versions of equation (II) are given:

$$T = 9.4897 + 0.02263\ N \qquad \text{(II)}$$
$$(6.72) \quad (14.49)$$
$$r^2 = 0.52489 \quad s_{y,x} = 18.69261$$

$$T = 10.837 + 0.03744\ P - 11.811\ S + 1.6527\ M + 0.02166\ N \qquad \text{(II}'\text{)}$$
$$(2.89) \quad (0.65) \quad (2.72) \quad (1.09) \quad (13.70)$$
$$r^2 = 0.55667 \quad s_{y,x} = 18.20096.$$

All coefficients take on signs that are consistent with the forces operating in the market. N dominates in both (II) and (II′), so that T is determined primarily by exogenous forces. Note that r^2 and $s_{y,x}$ do not improve significantly when P, S, and M are added. The signs of the coefficients of P and S are consistent with the roles played by these variables. Higher values of P, given S, imply lower transaction costs per dollar exchanged and, therefore, higher transaction rates. And higher values of S, given P, imply higher transaction cost per dollar exchanged and, therefore, lower transaction rates. The dominance of N undoubtedly reflects a strong tendency for S and P to be adjusted to their equilibrium values, so that the cost of transacting per dollar exchanged does not vary much from one security to another; N, however, does differ between securities and, given the equilibrium cost of transacting per dollar, accounts for most of the differences in observed transaction rates.

The (not significantly) positive coefficient of M in (II′) is consistent with the belief that, for given N, differences in M will be associated positively with differences in T. This is consistent with the (not significant) negative relationship between S and M indicated in equations (IA) and (IB). Finally, it should be noted that results not presented here reveal that the use of ln N significantly impairs the fit of regressions (II) and (II′).

SUMMARY AND COMMENTS

The statistical analysis strongly indicates that the cost of exchanging a security declines as trading activity in that security increases. It would seem that the centralization of trading activity on the NYSE can be explained by the lowering of transaction costs thereby achieved. These results probably hold for organized trading in commodities and currencies also. Adding additional securities or different commodities may increase transaction costs and eventually limit the number of securities or assets traded in a given market. Should this be the case, and this certainly has not been established here, we would have a plausible explanation for the dominance of the NYSE in trading the securities it does list and, at the same time, an explanation for the NYSE's self-imposed curb on the number of corporations listed.

The distinguishing characteristic of such trading on organized exchanges is the willingness of customers to forgo a personal examination of the goods bought and sold. This allows a high degree of standardization and enables communicating and title exchange costs to be kept low even for large transaction rates. When customers are willing to let others buy and sell for them, when they are willing to conclude an exchange without a personal prior examination of the goods, the concentration of trading on relatively few markets offers the prospect of lower transaction costs.

When customers are unwilling to forgo a personal examination of goods, markets must be able to cope with many more bodies, both human and automobile, per transaction. The associated crowding and the need for product display (as is required when shares of different corporation are traded) probably generates diseconomies. However, as long as it is possible to multiply the number of markets without significant increases in the rent earned by factor inputs, scale diseconomies for single markets need not and do not seem to produce scale diseconomies for the marketing industry as the number of competing markets grows.

In concluding this paper, it is interesting to examine the implications of the statistical evidence for measuring imperfections in capital markets. Differences in borrowing rates often are taken as indications of such imperfections, but differences in borrowing rates cannot be taken at face value since cost differences may exist that account for a part or all of the observed differences in rates. The cost of transacting is relevant to this problem since our evidence suggests that the markups required to market additional shares will be less for larger companies than for smaller companies if we accept what most certainly is true, that larger companies tend to have more shareholders.

Assume that two corporations desire to increase outstanding equity by the same percentage of existing equity. One corporation already has (or anticipates that it will have) 100,000 shareholders ($N = 1000$); the other has 1,000 shareholders ($N = 10$). Assume further that both shares will sell at *roughly* the same price so that commission brokerage per round lot is identical. The cost of inventorying the securities and of waiting will differ for the two issues according to the evidence presented above, so that we should expect the larger corporation to secure a price per share somewhat higher than the smaller corporation. The difference in price per share will reflect the difference in spread, or distribution markup, per share. This can be estimated from equation (IB). Holding price and number of markets constant, the difference in numbers of shareholders produces a difference in spread equal to about $0.37 per share. If the prices per share are assumed to be in the neighborhood of $40, then, for every $40 secured by the smaller company, $40.37 will be secured by the larger company, a difference equal to almost 1 percent in borrowing cost.

The results are only slightly less impressive if transaction cost per dollar exchanged is used directly as the dependent variable. Define: $X = S/P$. Using least squares to regress X on N and M yields

$$X = \underset{(11.58)}{0.019224} - \underset{(4.44)}{0.0015284} \ln N - \underset{(0.40)}{0.00021483}\, M. \qquad \text{(III)}$$

A difference in size of corporation of the magnitude indicated in the previous example generates a difference in borrowing cost equal to 0.7 percent. If the larger corporation has 1 million shareholders, the difference in borrowing cost becomes 1 percent. Of course, these calculations are based on the

Table 5.1 New York Stock Exchange Market volume *v.* specialist transaction participation rate (percentages of stock days[a] in each category of market volume falling into each range of specialist transaction participation rate)

	Specialist transaction participation rate[b]					
	0.01–16.00%	*16.01–26.00%*	*26.01–37.00%*	*37.01–50.00%*	*50.01%+*	*Total*
Market vol. (no. of shares)						
10,000 and over	42.5	18.9	18.9	8.0	1.7	100.0
5,701-10,000	28.8	26.7	24.8	15.0	4.7	100.0
3,901-5,700	25.9	23.1	25.7	15.6	9.7	100.0
2,801-3,900	25.8	19.9	23.8	18.9	11.6	100.0
2,101-2,800	24.7	19.1	23.7	18.1	14.4	100.0
1,501-2,100	22.5	19.4	20.7	18.5	18.9	100.0
1,101-1,500	17.7	19.1	22.4	18.8	22.0	100.0
701-1,100	14.4	18.7	19.3	21.5	26.1	100.0
401-700	4.1	26.2	13.7	25.1	30.9	100.0
10-400	0.4	7.9	15.2	25.1	51.4	100.0

[a]One stock day = a one day observation on one stock. Data are for three weeks ending January 27, March 24, and June 16, 1961.

[b]Number of specialist transactions as a percentage of the number of market transactions.

Source: Adapted from *Report of the Special Study of Security Markets*, 88th Congress, House Doc. no. 95, part 2, p. 459.

presumption that differences in transaction cost will be passed on to the borrower.

APPENDIX 1

Table 5.1 is adapted from the report of the *Special Study of Security Markets*. The tabulation contains the percentage of stock days (defined as one day's observation on one stock) falling into each cell. The cells relate the percentage of market transactions in which the specialist participated (the columns) to market volume. For example, the entry in row (1), column (1) indicates that, of those stocks trading 10,000 and more shares a day, 42.5 percent were observed to fall into the specialist participation rate category of 0.01–16.00 percent of market volume. Large cell entries are underlined twice and small cell entries are underlined once. It is clear that the more inactive the security, the greater the specialist participation rate tends to be.

APPENDIX 2

Linear forms:

(A) $S = 0.2101 + 0.008996\ P - 0.003589\ T - 0.04712\ M$
(3.45) (13.22) (4.42) (1.91)
$r^2 = 0.52689 \quad s_{y,x} = 0.30035$

(B) $S = 0.1787 + 0.009275\ P - 0.00008871\ N - 0.05477\ M$
(2.90) (13.30) (3.44) (2.17)
$r^2 = 0.50857 \quad s_{y,x} = 0.30611$

Log form:

$S = -0.2407 + 0.3522 \ln P - 0.1118 \ln N - 0.02808\ M$
(1.56) (10.37) (6.41) (1.05)
$r^2 = 0.4617 \quad s_{y,x} = 0.32036$

Best fitting forms (used in text):

(A) $S = 0.38027 + 0.0080709\ P - 0.11527 \ln T - 0.022906\ M$
(5.80) (12.15) (6.46) (0.97)
$r^2 = 0.57637 \quad s_{y,x} = 0.28632$

(B) $S = 0.48411 + 0.0088554\ P - 0.080911 \ln N - 0.029691\ M$
(5.63) (13.24) (5.10) (1.21)
$r^2 = 0.5422 \quad s_{y,x} = 0.29666$

NOTES

1 A more detailed discussion of the relationship between transaction cost and efficiency can be found in Coase (1960) and Demsetz (1964).
2 See Alchian and Allen (1967, pp. 49–50).
3 The cost of using a specialized medium of exchange is essentially the cost of holding an inventory of money. The greater is the number of goods whose prices are relatively independent, the lower will be the risks associated with fluctuations in the value of this inventory; and the greater is the time rate of exchange, the lower will be the expected cost per transaction of inventorying money.
4 The concept of rivalry introduced here and the difficulty it poses for the theory of natural monopoly are discussed more fully in Demsetz (1968).
5 The number of transactions and the volume traded per day are very highly correlated.
6 Francis Emory Fitch, Inc., 138 Pearl Street, New York.
7 Assuming that the spread is determined in markets best approximated by the competitive model is *not* the same as assuming that commission brokerage to outsiders is set competitively. Whatever is true about how the membership of the NYSE decides collectively (with the cooperation of the SEC) about brokerage commissions, it is not true that the spread is set collectively; nor is it true that the interest of most members of the NYSE is served by spreads that are larger than underlying costs.
8 Regression estimates in (IA) contain six fewer sample observations than in (IB) because $T = 0$ for six securities.

REFERENCES

Alchian, A. and Allen, W. (1967). *University Economics*. Belmont, Cal.: Wadsworth.
Coase, R. H. (1960). "The Problem of Social Cost." *Journal of Law and Economics*, 3.
Demsetz, H. (1964). "The Exchange and Enforcement of Property Rights." *Journal of Law and Economics*, 7.
—— (1968). "Why Regulate Utilities." *Journal of Law and Economics*, 11.

6
Minorities in the Market Place

The purposes of this essay are to argue that most legal constraints on the operation of the market penalize those in our society who are discriminated against, and that such groups can generally expect to fare worse in the polling place than in the free market place. This essay may serve a useful purpose in view of the support given by discriminated-against minorities to the transference of decisions from the market to the polling place. In the first section I define terms and make clear my assumptions. In the second section I consider the argument and offer some evidence. Some implications for political organization are presented in section III.

I

The words ''discrimination against'' or ''non-preference for'' persons will be used to express an aversion to association with these persons. A taste for discrimination I identify as a taste for segregation. The ''goodness'' or ''badness'' of particular tastes for association will not be a subject of this discourse, the purpose of which is to assess effects and not to make ethical judgments. However, lest the words to follow be interpreted as a general condemnation of discrimination, I shall pause for a paragraph to assert the useful role that can be played by discrimination and to reveal my broad use of the word.

Because they are discriminated against, women who are plain and overweight use the techniques of cosmetics, styling, diets, and exercise to beautify themselves, and uneducated persons desirous of associating with the educated find it advantageous to acquire more education. Only if we are not ready to admit that beauty and education are characteristics to which encouragement should be given can we claim that discrimination serves no useful purposes. Indeed, although mistakes are often made as to what are the ''appropriate'' or ''useful'' criteria upon which to discriminate, there can be no doubt that

This essay is reprinted from *North Carolina Law Review* 43(2), 1965.

discrimination is one of the strongest forces for change in a free society. Discrimination against the uneducated, the criminal, and the vulgar provides powerful incentives for persons to choose courses of action judged to be more desirable by those who are discriminating.[1] In cases where the characteristic being discriminated against allows for no choice alternative to a non-preferred person, as where color is discriminated against per se, discrimination cannot serve as an incentive for developing traits preferred by the discriminator. In such cases, the value of discrimination (but not of the right to discriminate) rests solely on the effect it has on the well-being of the discriminator and on that of the non-preferred. It cannot rest on the well-being that comes about through a change (in the color) in the non-preferred.

In assessing the effects of the market place and the polling place, I shall always adopt the viewpoint of the non-preferred. My evaluations will not necessarily be the same as those derivable from the opposite viewpoint, nor will they necessarily be different. Many of my conclusions about political processes will depend on the non-preferred being a political minority.

No men that are considered in this essay live only for association with preferred persons. My first assumption is that people are motivated by many desires. They prefer more of wealth, power, respect, leisure, goodwill, freedom, and association with preferred people. This list of desires is not complete, nor is it necessarily in order of importance. Our discussion will emphasize the desire for wealth and for association with preferred people.

The second assumption is that preferences are substitutable. Greater wealth can compensate one for less association with persons he prefers, and, likewise, greater association with preferred persons can compensate one for less wealth. Persons described in this essay can be induced to accept more association with non-preferred persons if, in return, they are offered more wealth.[2]

In evaluating the workings of the market and polling places, we shall, as I have said, judge according to the well-being of non-preferred persons. Which of two alternative situations enhances the well-being of a person is to be judged solely by which one he would choose. He may prefer a lower-paying job with non-pecuniary advantages to a higher-paying one without the same non-pecuniary advantages. In such cases, I judge the lower-paying job to be the one that enhances his well-being. This brings us to my third assumption. I assume that persons know what is best for themselves. This does not mean that I assume perfect knowledge; rather, I assume that, when making a decision as to whether or not to seek out someone more expert, persons act in their self-interest. It would be well for readers to pause and reflect on these assumptions, for much of what follows derives logically from them.

We shall be interested in how behavior can be modified so as to improve the lot of non-preferred persons. The following ways of altering behavior will set the limits of our discourse:

1 Individual compensation methods
  (a) Individual wealth compensation
  (b) Individual personal characteristic compensation[3]
2 The method of majoritarian democracy

This list excludes many methods of influencing behavior – violence, power, appeal to the hereafter – and concentrates our attention on the methods that will be of practical concern to us. The methods of individual compensation involve the use of rewards or penalties by individuals to influence the behavior of other individuals. The incentive provided by the offering or withdrawal of wealth compensation needs no elaboration. Personal characteristic compensation refers to the use by an individual of beauty, personality, race, religion, etc., to compensate another person for making a desired change in his behavior. A pleasant personality is more likely to produce a desired change in someone's behavior than is an unpleasant one, and the appeal of one's neighbor or relative is likely to be more effective than a stranger's. Either form of individual compensation is permissive of a wide variety of responses from individuals according to how each weights the offered reward.

The method of majoritarian democracy refers to the passage of laws by voting majorities, the intention of which is uniformly to prohibit or require a specified behavior. Such laws are assumed not to allow (legally) a variety of responses, nor can they be enacted by an individual. Both these descriptions are simplifications, but they catch the essence of the differences between the two methods. The simplification involved can best be brought out by way of example.

Suppose some of us desire that wheat be produced in larger quantities. A method of majoritarian democracy would be for the majority of voters to pass a law requiring all farmers to allocate more acreage to wheat. The method of individual (wealth) compensation involves the offering of higher prices to farmers through the effect of increases in the demands of individual consumers. The individual compensation method allows farmers to react in varying degrees to the incentive offered and allows some who are not aware of the higher prices being offered not to react at all. The laws we shall consider are of the type just described. Our stereotype for such laws will not, of course, fit all cases. For example, the majority, in the law they approve, may offer a subsidy for all wheat produced and allow the farmers to react as they please. This form of law moves closer to the compensation method, but it still is not an individual affair; everyone is taxed to pay the subsidy whether or not he personally desires more wheat at the tax price. If the law is changed still further, by declaring that taxpayers need contribute only the dollar amounts that they wish and that, in return, they will receive a pro rata share from the varying amounts of increased acreage planted, we shall have come full circle to the method of individual wealth compensation. If this happens, there is no purpose served by the law.

One final clarification is in order. When phrases such as "minority interests," "majority interests," etc., are used, they will mean in the interests of most persons, but not of everyone, in the group. "Public welfare," "social welfare," "public conscience," etc., are phrases that will be avoided. They are ambiguous to such a degree that they hamper exposition.[4]

II

Most legal modifications of the operation of the free market work through restrictions on prices, wages, profits, or who may participate in the market. In this category are minimum wage laws and price ceilings; licensing requirements for medical practice, union membership, banks, and other vendors; and regulation of profit rates in the electric, gas, telephone, and transportation (and the steel) industries. The modifications introduced by these laws seriously interfere with the use of (individual) wealth compensation for changing behavior. In the absence of appeal to further government action, these laws force the burden of influencing behavior to fall on personal characteristic compensation. The possibility of further political action and of political action along different lines will be considered later. For the present, we confine our attention to how the increased emphasis on personal characteristic compensation brought about by the above types of laws works to the disadvantage of non-preferred persons. The implications we shall derive from this examination are independent of whether or not the non-preferred are a minority.

It is one thing for a beautiful, young, white, Protestant woman, as an aid to buying a better cut of steak, to display her personal characteristics to a discriminating white, Protestant butcher. It is quite another for a plain, old, Jewish, Negro woman to try the same tactic with the same butcher. The personal characteristics by which some persons are identified as non-preferred are not useful for eliciting desirable behavior from those who discriminate. In this sense, contrary to the usual cliché, the market is not color-blind. The non-preferred can compensate in part for these characteristics by presenting other personal qualities thought to be desirable by discriminators. But the very need to overcompensate signifies a disadvantage in this form of compensation, and unless the non-preferred can discover some natural talent for overcompensation along other personal lines, this type of incentive system should be avoided by them.

The types of legislative modifications of the free market we are now considering, and certain current social attitudes, to the extent that they are effective, all work to concentrate compensation increasingly on personal characteristics. A minimum wage law prevents a non-preferred person from offering his services for a lower wage than is received by his preferred (but equally productive) fellow worker. A lower wage request by, or a lower market wage for, the non-preferred job applicant offers wealth compensation to discriminating employers that will reduce their consumption of discrimination.[5] The cost to employers of a continuance of the degree of discrimination they have been practicing is increased by allowing non-preferred workers to offer their services for lower wages. Prohibiting an employer from employing workers at wages lower than the legal minimum prohibits the offering of this wealth compensation to (or the imposition of this wealth cost on) discriminating employers. These employers will then choose from among competing applicants solely on the basis of personal characteristics. Non-preferred workers, turned away in larger numbers under these conditions, will be forced to accept less desirable employment elsewhere, possibly in occupations not covered by the minimum wage law, or will be forced into the ranks of the unemployed. Some non-preferred workers will be hired by discriminating employers if the productivities they can offer are high enough to warrant a wage sufficiently above the legal minimum to allow discriminating employers the wealth compensation they require. These workers, even though they are employed, do not directly benefit from minimum wage laws.

The problem is obvious. The law concentrates the criterion for employability on the personal characteristics of workers, a criterion under which the non-preferred will suffer. Legal minimum wage laws constitute a specific prohibition on the varied offers of and responses to wealth compensation. They fit neatly into our definition of the method of majoritarian democracy. Such laws, however, introduce only a legal uniform wage floor. Others introduce specific wage uniformity at wage levels above the minimum, and these work to the disadvantage of even the very productive non-preferred workers.

Two important types of laws that work toward the extension of wage uniformity are ''equal pay for equal work'' laws and laws that confer a high degree of monopoly power on unions. The method in which equal pay for equal work laws affect non-preferred persons is identical to that of minimum wage laws. Though workers have equal productivities, if some are preferred to others on grounds of personal characteristics, and if the same wage must be paid to both, the non-preferred either will not be hired or else will be hired in lesser jobs in which they are more productive than their preferred counterparts. Equal pay for equal work, as in the case of legal minimums, concentrates compensation on personal characteristics and thus works to the disadvantage of non-preferred persons.[6]

There are two respects in which the power of unions works to the disadvantage of non-preferred persons. First, in cases of craft unions, non-preferred persons may simply be kept out by various devices. This would not be important if craft unions were not often granted the effective monopolization of their trade by virtue of the coercive power they can wield over their employers. Majoritarian democracy again confronts us with a specific prohibition that works to the disadvantage of the non-preferred – employers are prohibited from employing non-union workers. The power for this prohibition stems from the specific exemption of unions from anti-trust laws and from majority tolerance of tactics such as coercive picketing.

Second, even in unions open to all, the insistence on equal pay for equal work for their members again reduces the employability of non-preferred workers by discriminating employers. Equal pay for equal work, whether emanating directly from equal pay laws or from the special legal treatment accorded unions, prohibits non-preferred persons from compensating discriminating employers by offering wealth compensation. Since no wage differential can be offered, since no cost can be imposed on employers who discriminate, fewer persons who are non-preferred will be hired for the jobs they seek. Forced to seek less desirable employment, non-preferred persons will suffer a reduction in their well-being. It should be emphasized that these non-preferred can be plain women or physically deformed persons as well as Jews or Negroes.[7]

The specific examples we have been discussing show the general principles at work. The existence of non-preference in combination with legal (or moral) prohibitions on the use of wealth incentives by non-preferred persons forces incentives to center on personal characteristics, a form of incentives that reduces the well-being of persons being discriminated against. Any existing degree of non-preference will reduce the well-being of non-preferred persons to a greater extent the more effective are the constraints placed on the use of wealth compensation. Legal measures taken by the government, which has a monopoly on law-giving and on police power, comprise some of the more effective constraints on the use of wealth. What is not so obvious is how indirectly such laws can work. Consider a union that enjoys an effective monopoly on employment in a certain trade or industry, the monopoly power stemming from the legal treatment we accord unions. Suppose further that neither employers nor employees are discriminators, but that union agents are. Let the union secure an attractive wage increase which enlarges the demand for union membership. Now, neither the government, employers, nor rank and file workers desire to discriminate, but all three groups frown on the sale of union membership by union agents to the highest bidders. The agents would be voted out of office if they resorted to the market in allocating memberships. This *moral* constraint, backed by the union's *monopoly power*, effectively prohibits non-preferred persons from using wealth incentives to overcome the discrimination of union agents. Union memberships will go primarily to preferred persons.[8] If applicants could avoid being channeled through the union hiring monopoly, if they could avoid the need for union membership and thus avoid the moral constraint on the sale of union membership, they would be hired by non-discriminating employers.

The relevance of monopoly, or the effectiveness of the constraint on the use of wealth, can be highlighted a little more. Suppose the government suppresses wage demands for reasons of national policy, and that union members, in fact, are discriminators. Prevented from exacting pecuniary monopoly profits in the form of wage increases, the union can instead use its power to secure more control over hiring procedures. In this way it can exact non-pecuniary gains in the form of more successful exclusion of non-preferred job applicants.

The essence of the problem is the coupling of non-preference with the ability to prevent the use of wealth incentives, an ability which, to be effective, must be backed by some significant market power. The most effective market power is that which can be enforced by the police power of the government.

The subject of our essay is discrimination, which we have defined only as an aversion to association. But it is worth mentioning that the kinds of laws and market power we have been discussing above also are disadvantageous to those workers who are relatively unproductive. These persons, if they are prevented from offering their services for wages lower than are received by more productive workers, will have difficulty securing employment. The existence of a strong positive correlation between persons who are discriminated against for reasons of personal characteristics and persons who are relatively unproductive will double the effect of wage and labor laws in reducing their well-being. Such persons will have difficulty securing employment from discriminating and non-discriminating employers. Non-discriminating employers will need to receive wealth compensation in the form of lower wage payments to offset low productivities. Discriminating employers require an additional wealth incentive to overcome their aversion to association.

Next, let us consider the attempt in this country to regulate the profit rates of several industries. To the extent that such regulation is effective, it reduces the well-being of non-preferred workers. The direct attempts to establish the rate of profit of railroads and public utilities at some normal level reduces the effectiveness of offers of wealth compensation in overcoming discriminatory behavior. Suppose the most profitable course available to firms in these industries is to employ non-preferred persons at lower wages than need be offered to preferred persons. If this hiring policy is expected to result in profit rates in excess of the allowed normal rate of return, firms will expect the regulatory process to prevent the capture of these returns. The offered wealth compensation for not discriminating is not realizable. In such cases, those who control the hiring policy will cater to their preferences for association to a greater degree than they would in the absence of a profit constraint. They would be more inclined toward desirable personalities, desirable religions, etc., and less inclined toward persons who are most productive per dollar of wage expenditure.[9]

However, there is a second way, which has no counterpart in wage laws, in which profit regulation works to the disadvantage of non-preferred persons. Not only are *rewards* reduced for hiring less costly, non-preferred labor because regulatory commissions attempt to keep profit rates to a normal level, but, in addition, *penalties* for hiring more costly preferred labor are reduced. Price increases may allow a normal profit rate to be obtained at higher cost levels.

Regulatory commissions, by virtue of their monopoly over prices, can allow prices to be raised to cover higher costs. One method of increasing cost levels is to cater to preferences even though pampering these preferences is costly. Employing workers who are preferred for reasons of association, but not productivity, will raise costs and may depress profit rates to below normal levels, but subsequently allowed price increases may go a long way toward offsetting the higher costs.

The effects of profit regulation of this type extend to the buying of supplies and materials as well as to the hiring of labor. Why trade with sellers who charge lower prices if you are not allowed to increase your profit rate and if you are protected from competition in the setting of higher prices which yield the normal rate? Instead, be willing to pay higher prices if you can deal with sellers with whom you prefer to associate. These effects, of course, depend on the general inability of regulatory commissions to specify appropriate cost levels. The whole production procedure is so complex, and varies so much among firms, that it is virtually impossible for a commission to be able to specify such cost levels.[10]

For our next case let us consider licensing. The attainment of professional and business positions by non-preferred persons, which would confer some hiring power to them, is itself often limited by requiring licenses or accreditation for practicing many professions and operating many businesses. Where law or morality effectively prohibits the sale for profit of these licenses, we can expect greater attention to be paid to personal characteristics compensation. The establishment of requirements and even the issue of licenses is often controlled by persons who are already members of the business or the profession. Craft unions and medical practice are examples. Such persons are generally prohibited from selling membership for profit. They will thus be more inclined to exercise their tastes for association. If a government official controls the licensing, he can be expected to give more attention to the personal characteristics he prefers *and* to the impact on votes particular applicants are expected to have. This is not the place to discuss other reasons for or against licensing procedures. My claim is the more modest one of pointing to the greater emphasis that will be given to personal characteristics compensation in the selection of applicants if membership cannot be sold for profit.[11]

As a final exercise in this part of the argument, let us consider the effects of legal price ceilings. Some discriminating sellers can be persuaded to allow some integration of their customers if non-preferred persons are allowed to bid for some of the services of such sellers by offering wealth compensation. A law that establishes an effective ceiling on the prices at which sellers can offer their wares prohibits the use of (direct) wealth inducements. It declares illegal the very force that can be used to divert emphasis away from personal characteristics and to direct some of the wares of discriminating sellers to non-preferred persons. When price ceilings are made effective by the power of the government, *and* when discriminating sellers are involved, we prevent the free market from improving the well-being of those actually discriminated against. It is important to note that I do not claim that all members of a group are made worse off by such laws. I claim that those actually discriminated against are hurt. It may be that other members of the group who are *not* discriminated against, and who have less purchasing power than other persons, are aided.

Up to this point, I have argued that most of the legal infringements on the operation of free markets can be expected to worsen the well-being of those being discriminated against. All conceivable anti-free-market laws need not produce these effects. It is a fact, however, that until very recently all major anti-free-market laws that have proved to be politically palatable have been of this type. The major exceptions have been some parts of Fair Employment Practice laws.[12] These attempt to directly reduce the degree of discrimination practiced in hiring practices. Whether we can expect this type of law to have a measurable impact on discrimination is a subject to which I shall return shortly. We shall then consider other possible anti-free market laws which could be expected, in and of themselves, to have effects more to the liking of non-preferred persons.[13] Before we consider these laws, it is necessary to embellish one aspect of the preceding arguments.

I have emphasized that this argument applies only to those who are actually discriminated against. The number of persons in a ''non-preferred group'' who are actually discriminated against is limited to those who are inclined to transact with trading partners who have discriminatory attitudes, and is further limited by the existence of any sizable costs for sorting out preferred from non-preferred persons. Although a seller of products (or a hirer of labor) may prefer non-association with certain groups of persons, if the costs of sorting non-preferred from preferred persons are too great in the type of market activity being carried on, he may choose not to indulge his taste for discrimination. Up to this point we have ignored these sorting costs, concentrating our attention instead on the cost that is imposed by the offer of wealth compensaton by non-preferred persons. In some cases sorting costs may be high relative to the benefits (to the discriminator) of discriminating.

The higher are the costs of sorting people, the fewer will be the number of discriminators who actually cater to their taste for association. Sorting costs are generally lower, for example, in the case of Negroes than they are for Jews. A picture on the job application or on the university admission application reveals the Negro but not the Jew. Should persons have an equal taste for discrimination against both groups, the higher cost of recognizing Jews will reduce the incidence of discrimination against them relative to that against Negroes.[14]

Sorting costs are prohibitively high when sales are made from vending machines, whereas in personal service stores clerks can merely ignore recognizable non-preferred persons. And the non-preferred person is likely to fare better at the self-service meat counter of a supermarket than at a cut-to-order meat store.

For our argument, however, the essential point is that, when the costs of sorting persons are high, it is necessary for us to hedge on some of the conclusions we have reached. Many of our conclusions still follow necessarily, but others follow only with a high degree of probability. As a strong example countering the logical necessity of one of our earlier conclusions, consider again the discriminating union agent who is restrained from selling union memberships to the highest bidders. If there is no cost to sorting persons, he will necessarily confer these memberships on only members of preferred groups; allowing him to sell these memberships will necessarily tend to reduce the degree of discrimination he practices. Alternatively, if the personal costs to him of interviewing and rejecting applicants is high relative to the personal advantage of preferred association, he may let some non-preferred persons acquire membership even though he cannot sell the memberships. Given the reduction in discrimination occasioned by these sorting costs, suppose he is now allowed to sell memberships. He may find preferred applicants willing and able to bid high enough to overcome some of the resistance to discrimination caused by the sorting costs. Consequently, sale of memberships may induce him to reduce the number of non-preferred persons in his union. For this event to occur, we require a very unlikely confluence of two circumstances: first, sorting costs must be high and they must be borne by the discriminator; second, preferred persons, in sufficient numbers, must be willing to outbid non-preferred persons.

Preferred persons may be willing to outbid non-preferred persons for monopoly wages, but would they be willing to pay more for commodities and services ordinarily purchased in the market? Probably not. Whites might generally be able to outbid Negroes for, say, union memberships, but would the cost of sorting out Negroes be high? Probably not. And, while the costs of sorting out Jews might be high, can we expect non-Jews to be able generally to out-bid Jews? I am told probably not. It cannot be denied that a simultaneous satisfaction of the three requirements might be found, but the frequency with which it is likely to be found seems sufficiently low for us to establish the credibility of the main conclusions of our earlier argument.

Let us now turn to anti-free market laws which are designed to beneficially affect non-preferred persons. These kinds of laws are not generally found in our legal framework and we shall require some imagination to conjure them onto these pages. This will not be as difficult as it might appear, but before exercising our imagination let us consider the one major case of existing statutory law designed specifically to aid non-preferred persons. Fair Employment Practices laws state that it is illegal to discriminate on the basis of color, religion, or nationality in the hiring of workers and in the terms on which they are hired. To the extent that such laws are effective, they can reduce the impact of discriminatory attitudes, in terms either of the degree to which segregation is practiced or of the degree to which non-preferred persons must offer wealth compensation to secure employment.

There are laws and then there are laws. All of them are not equally easy to enforce. The very nature of Fair Employment laws would lead us to believe that they are among the most difficult to make effective. For they do not require every firm to count among its employees 10 percent Negroes, 30 percent Catholics, and 1 percent Jews, standards that would be relatively easy to enforce. Instead, they require that firms must be reasonable and just in their hiring practices. Now, the greater the degree to which subjective evaluation, to which reasonableness and justice, enter into the criteria for legal behavior, the more difficult and expensive it becomes to enforce a law successfully. Reasonable men can disagree on the relative competence of workers and unreasonable men can find myriad ways in which to appear to be reasonable. This has two implications. First, to establish reasonableness, we will require *acceptable* enforcement of the law to undertake a case-by-case treatment, which will be very slow and very expensive; not many cases will be treated, and most who would be judged violators will escape examination. Second, since the criterion to be applied by the law is largely subjective, it will not be an acceptable enforcement practice to penalize violators severely. When persons can try to behave reasonably but cannot know the legal criterion for reasonable behavior, it is unlikely that the law will threaten them with weighty penalties. Those who desire to violate the law repeatedly will not be overly deterred from their practices. In most cases, these laws require a violator merely to rectify his behavior in a particular case.

Minimum wage laws and union equal pay demands are easier to enforce. It is one thing to say that below-minimum legal wages are being paid and that two union members in the same job classification are receiving different wages. It is quite another to say what is a just wage or a just job classification. The specificity of minimum wage laws and union wage rates eases the enforcement problem. This is not to say that such laws do not face considerable enforcement difficulty, but only that they face less difficulty than those involving more subjective evaluation of behavior. Likewise, it is not so difficult for regulatory commissions to control profit rates, given the cost base on which the control is based, as it is for the commissions to determine the appropriate or just cost base.[15]

The difficulty that can be encountered in enforcing even the more objective laws is highlighted by the following quotations on the effects of the $1 minimum wage law made effective on March 1, 1956:

> Minimum wage violations were found in 21% of investigations made for enforcement purposes between July and December, 1956. . . . Discovered underpayments of the minimum wage more than tripled between fiscal year 1956 and fiscal year 1957. . . . If, for every discovered violation of the minimum, three went undiscovered [this being the ratio of discovered to undiscovered underpayment estimated by the Department

of Labor for fiscal year 1958], then about 310,000 covered employees were paid less than the minimum in fiscal year 1957. . . . The Department estimated that total underpayments both discovered and undiscovered totalled $80 million.[16]

Nonetheless, the minimum wage law is sufficiently enforceable to leave traces of evidence. The effects of minimum wage laws can be revealed by examining the repercussions of changes in the level of legal minimum wage rates on the employment of household workers. Such an examination was recently published by Yale Brozen,[17] and I repeat here some of its findings:

The minimum wage clause of the Fair Labor Standards Act applies to most occupations. . . . Private household work is one of the few completely excluded occupations. Since it is an alternative opportunity for many workers affected by minimum wage rate provisions . . . the changes in this line of work can provide some clues as to the effect of the lifting of the wage floor in covered occupations. Trifling movements in employment opportunities in many other categories are concentrated on domestic service and should produce detectable effects. . . .

In each instance [since 1949], when the minimum wage rate rose, the number of persons employed as household workers rose. The rise was not the result of unemployed household workers finding jobs since there was also a rise in the percentage of household workers unemployed in each instance (except 1961–2, when the decline in unemployment percentage accounts for only 15 percent of the rise). Evidently, some persons lost jobs in the covered occupations (or persons who would normally have entered failed to find jobs) and sought jobs in non-covered household work. They found jobs, and household employment rose. Also, the competition of these additional workers made it somewhat more difficult for household workers who lost their positions to find new jobs.[18]

These findings are, of course, consistent with my conclusions. The use of the household workers category fits in well with our subject since most workers in this line are Negro. Even with this evidence, however, it is difficult for our purposes to sort out the effects of minimum wage laws on those who are discriminated against from the effects on those who have low productivities.

Alchian and Kessel present some evidence that bears directly on the degree to which profit constraints appear to influence hiring patterns.[19] They offered an analysis of data published by the American Jewish Congress, which surveyed the occupations of Jewish and non-Jewish Harvard Business School graduates. The data concerned 352 Harvard MBA graduates selected on the basis of a random sample. Of these, 224 were non-Jewish and 128 Jewish. The 352 Harvard graduates were classified by ten industry categories. Alchian and Kessel suggest that the proportion of Jews employed will be less in regulated industries and in highly concentrated industries, which, in fear of antitrust, can be expected not to maximize pecuniary profits.

The ten industries' categories are (1) agriculture, forestry and fisheries, (2) mining, (3) construction, (4) transportation, communication, and other public utilities, (5) manufacturing, (6) wholesale and retail trade, (7) finance, insurance, and real estate, (8) business services, (9) amusement, recreation, and related services, and (10) professional and related services.

Categories (4) and (7) must be regarded as relatively monopolized. Therefore, if the hypothesis presented here is correct, the relative frequency of Jews in these two fields is lower than it is for all fields combined. The relative frequency of Jews in all fields taken together, in the entire sample, is 36 percent. These data show that the frequency of Jews – 74 MBAs – in the two monopolized fields is less than 18 percent. If a sample of 352, of whom 36 percent are Jews, is assigned so that 74 are in monopolized and 278 in nonmonopolized fields, the probability that an assignment random with respect to religion will result in as few as 18 percent Jews in the monopolized fields (and over 41 percent in nonmonopolized fields) is less than 0.0005.[20]

Evidence of the above type that directly isolates the discrimination is difficult to find. There is much evidence, however, on the effectiveness of minimum wage laws that is consistent with the findings of Yale Brozen.[21]

Can evidence be produced on the impact of Fair Employment Practice laws? Some case studies of particular firms have been made, but evidence of general applicability is lacking. Some idea of the effectiveness of Fair Employment Practice laws can be had by comparing unemployment figures for those states with such laws and those without. Our task is somewhat simplified by the two-fold classification of states given by the United States Department of Labor and reported in the *Hearings on Equal Employment Opportunity*.[22] This classification lists states according to whether, in the judgment of the Department of Labor, they had effective Fair Employment Practice Commission laws in 1960. Fifteen states were listed as having effective laws.[23] The remainder (including Washington, DC) either had no laws or were thought to have ineffective laws. In each state we can get a partial index of how well non-whites fared in the labor market by dividing the unemployment rate among whites by the unemployment rate among non-whites. The lower the value of the resulting quotient, the greater the relative incidence of unemployment among non-whites. We can then average these quotients for each group of states and compare the average for states with effective laws with the average for states

Table 6.1 State averages of the unemployment rate among whites divided by the unemployment rate among non-whites

	1960	*1950*	*1940*
(a) States with effective laws in 1960	0.48	0.48	0.65
Other states:			
(b) Excluding the South	0.47	0.45	0.61
(c) The South*	0.59	0.59	1.10
(d) All other states	0.51	0.49	0.76

*The 11 states of the Confederacy.

Source: Calculated from U.S. Bureau of the Census, Dept. of Commerce, Census of Populations, (1960), Table 53.

with ineffective or no laws. The results are presented in table 6.1. They are tabulated for those states with laws deemed effective in 1960 and for other states.

The most relevant comparison is between the effective employment law states and other states excluding the South. The South can be expected to be atypical with respect to the index with which we are working for the following four reasons. (1) In the interval of years covered, the South experienced a considerable shift to industrialization and urbanization. (2) These states, nonetheless, remain more agriculturally oriented than most of the other states. (3) There has been a large emigration of Negroes from the South to the North. These emigrants may have been the more productive Negro residents of the South. (4) Social attitudes and institutions in the South about the races are alleged to differ fundamentally from those in the North and West. It is possible to speculate that the agricultural orientation of the South is fundamentally responsible for the better showing these states give with respect to the relative unemployment rates of the whites and non-whites in each of the years and, further, that rapid industrialization and urbanization, together with the emigration of more productive Negroes, account for most of the worsening of performance between 1940 and 1950.

Non-Southern states without effective employment laws are more closely matched to the effective-law states with regard to industrialization and urbanization, increases in Negro population, pace of economic change, and social attitudes and institutions toward the races. These states are, therefore, more relevant for testing the effectiveness of fair employment laws. Two things stand out if we compare row (a) with row (b). First, in 1960 there existed no statistically significant difference in our index. Non-whites fared about the same in terms of relative unemployment rates in both groups of states. Second, while increasing urbanization and industrialization probably account for most of the decline in the index from 1940 to 1960 in both groups of states, during this interval, *when most of the states with effective employment laws were acquiring the laws*, the index falls by 0.17 in effective-law states and by only 0.14 in non-effective-law states. Thus, the evidence reveals that there is generally no significant difference in unemployment rate ratios in 1960 for the two groups of states, and that there is probably no significant difference in the performance of these two groups of states while one group was acquiring effective laws and the other was not. These data are consistent with our assertions about the ineffectiveness of these laws.[24]

Thus far, I have argued that the logic of most legal infringements on the operation of the free market implies that they will work to the disadvantage of non-preferred persons. In the one major case where the logic does not carry this implication, I have argued that the law would be ineffective. Some evidence has been presented that is consistent with these arguments and more could have been marshalled from other sources. Is it an accident that the political processes have worked in this fashion? Or is there something about politics that makes this type of performance likely?

III

It is not impossible to devise laws that both infringe on the operation of the free market and effectively help non-preferred persons. It turns out that these would be almost the exact opposite of the laws we have been discussing (except for the Fair Employment Practices law). Instead of a legal minimum wage, we would require a carefully designed legal maximum wage. Rather than restricting profit rates, we should offer bonuses to firms able to earn high profit rates and impose penalties on those firms earning low profit rates. Moral aversion to the making of profits would need to be replaced with an attitude of respect and admiration. In short, if we changed our Constitution so that laws passed by Congress are carried out in reverse, and if we pass students on the basis of how well they fail most social welfare examinations, the world could be made better for the non-preferred at the same time that market controls were increased.

The payment of a government bonus every time a firm increases its profit rate will encourage the firm to accept the wealth compensations offered by non-preferred persons seeking employment. The firm will then weigh pecuniary returns more heavily and tastes for discrimination more lightly.

Wage ceilings designed to fall between the higher market wage received by preferred workers and the lower wage paid to non-preferred workers by discriminating employers will cause some preferred workers to leave the labor force and others to seek less demanding employment. The wage they could earn in covered employment would no longer be high enough to attract some of them. Employers would, to some extent, find it desirable to substitute non-preferred workers for those preferred refusing to offer their services at the legal ceiling wage rate.

But, of course, it is unlikely that we will ever see legislation of this type. Nor will we see Fair Employment Practices laws requiring the enforceable standard of 10 percent Negroes in every firm's labor force (except perhaps in the government's labor force). Most voters will feel such legislation inimical to their well-being and will not vote for it. Many firms are rather unsuccessful, and most are none too profitable. Why should they and their workers vote to penalize themselves and to subsidize the success of the few profitable firms? Why should most workers legally limit the maximum wages they can receive? And therein lies the difficulty faced by non-preferred minorities in turning to majoritarian democracy for anti-free-market laws which are more to their advantage. They are a voting minority. In a very real sense, we can substitute the phrase "vote compensation" for "majoritarian democracy" in our list of methods of altering behavior. Just as non-preferred persons will find it disadvantageous to compete in the arena of personal characteristics, so minorities will find it disadvantageous to compete in the arena of the polling place.

All political action to improve the position of minorities is not, of course, hopeless. But success requires the support of a widely based electorate. Such support can be had on issues that benefit non-preferred minorities *at the expense of preferred persons* only in exceptional circumstances.

Basically, there are two circumstances in which minorities can turn to national politics with some success on such issues. One is when the issue of concern to them is of secondary importance to others, so that, even though most people oppose the minority's desires, they will vote primarily on the basis of other issues. The groundwork is then set for the formation of a political coalition in which a faction of preferred persons agrees to back legislation favoring the non-preferred minority (even though the preferred find such legislation distasteful) in return for the support of the minority on more important issues which divide the majority of voters. For this method to have much success, it is necessary that the issue of interest to the minority be unimportant to the majority even though they oppose the minority desire. Success is unlikely on issues which the preferred believe would change significantly and to their disadvantage the relative economic positions of preferred and non-preferred. It is unlikely that measures such as setting maximum legal wages, subsidizing profits and penalizing losses, and 10 percent of non-preferred minorities in each firm's work force would be considered unimportant by most preferred persons.

The second case is one in which minorities find that large numbers of preferred persons actually favor the minority stand on an issue even though some preferred seriously oppose this stand. Recent civil rights legislation[25] (and Supreme Court action) is a good example. The essential parts of this legislation, such as the public accommodations section[26] and the section on voting rights,[27] have been a part of the Northerner's practice of life for many years and a part of his moral life for many more. And so has a single public school system for both white and non-white. On these issues the Northern white has sided with our Negro minority to provide the political strength and popular support needed for legislation and court decisions. Whatever effects these laws have will be felt in the Southern states and not in the Northern.

It is important to note that political success requires in the case of coalitions that the issue be unimportant. For important issues, the minority's view must already be accepted as part of the life of a substantial number of preferred persons. In the near future, we are unlikely to find much non-minority national popular support on issues such as open occupancy, forced neighborhood integration, or forced transportation of children to distant school districts. Nor will there be popular support for maximum legal wages, profit subsidization, etc. All these things are both important and are believed by the majority of voters to be contrary to their long-run interests. Recent appeals to the federal government by minorities were entirely rational because the support of Northerners could be counted on. Further appeals for actions that affect the way of life in both North and South may be irrational, and, in any case, will be much less successful.

Our negative conclusions about the prospects for new anti-free-market legislation which effectively helps non-preferred minorities does not, however, extend to pro-free-market legislation. Much more support can be picked up from members of the majority for restricting somewhat the monopoly power of unions, for keeping minimum legal wages below effective levels, for reductions in the number of legal licensing requirements, for removal of rent ceilings which still continue in some areas, and for changes in some of our regulatory practices. For many in the majority still identify their long-run interests with increased freedom of the individual. The restoration and protection of free markets is the practical political possibility of advantage to minorities because it is here that both minority and majority can find some long-run advantages.

The operation of the free market has implications for the structure of political power and institutions to which minorities should aspire. Four characteristics of the free market stand in contrast to the characteristics of the national polling place. (1) In the free market, the imposition of costs or the bestowal of benefits is largely an individual affair. It is unnecessary first to receive the approval of a majority of persons before individual wealth compensation can be brought to bear on a decision-maker. (2) The amount of wealth compensation that is brought to bear can vary considerably, depending on how much of his wealth a person is willing to commit to change behavior in the market place. A person can cut his wage request by very much or by very little, and he can likewise vary the price he is willing to pay. (3) In the free market, economic power is distributed thinly among decision-makers. (4) Finally, the market, through the forces of competition among many decision-makers, provides a mechanism for spreading the effects of wealth compensation to those on whom wealth incentives are not originally brought to bear.

In contrast, the national polling place allows no direct action on behavior unless a majority of voters support the disputed influence; action cannot be taken individually. In addition, each voter has only one vote to cast and cannot vary his vote compensation with the intensity of his feelings on a particular issue. Power in the current political structure is not spread thinly but is instead increasingly concentrated on two parties at the national level. Finally, a vote for a particular candidate fails to influence the behavior of the other party unless a very large number of votes accompanies it.

I have already dealt in some detail with the role of the first two free market characteristics in influencing behavior so that I need not dwell on them here. Moreover, it is unlikely that individuals will be given more than one vote to distribute or concentrate as they please, and even more unlikely that majority requirements will change. Examination of the political implications of these two characteristics of free markets, therefore, would be an injudicious use of words. We move on to consider characteristics (3) and (4).

Several persons who cooperate in casting their dollar votes or who independently cast them in the same way can, by virtue of the dispersal of market power among many decision-making centers, become very influential in changing the behavior of one such center. The Negroes of a Southern community who withhold patronage from discriminating bus lines or from other local vendors can force large costs on discriminators. Likewise, if many Negroes offer their services at low wages to a single firm, they effectively concentrate wealth incentives on a single decision-maker. This results from the relatively small size of most enterprises in this country and from the relatively large concentration of Negroes in certain geographic areas. Contrast this with the ineffectiveness of withholding purchases from all bus lines in the South *if* all Southern communities were populated according to the white and non-white national population averages. Or contrast the costs imposed on discriminating firms, given that 10 percent of their job applicants offer their services at lower wages as compared with 90 percent of their applicants. In the market, it is not only possible for an individual member of the minority to offer varying quantities of dollar votes in reward for non-discriminatory behavior; it is also possible for a minority group to saturate a local center of economic decision-making with dollar votes. This is not possible in national politics, where the maximum saturation with political votes that is possible depends only on the total number of minority votes compared with the total number of majority votes. In national politics, minorities are effectively prevented from concentrating political vote compensation.

With the ability to impose costs individually in the market place and to concentrate such costs on particular centers of economic decision-making, it is possible for minorities to influence behavior substantially in particular parts of the market place. The effect of this change in behavior will be extended by the market to other centers of decision-making. A firm hiring many non-preferred will be able to offer its product at lower prices than more discriminatory competitors. This will raise the cost of discriminating to these competitors, for in order to maintain their market, they will now be forced to lower price. If competitors lower price without increasing the number of non-preferred hired, they will need to suffer a personal wealth loss. This brings home the cost of discriminating to them and reduces the amount of discrimination they will practice. The spread of wealth compensation from its original point of application to other parts of the market can continue as long as non-preferred are willing and able to supply services to competitors.

It might be supposed that these competitive forces will work only if the ultimate buyers of products do not know or care what labor was used to produce products. Ultimate consumers often are indifferent, and in this respect, the market is color-blind. But consumers sometimes do care who produces a product or who consumes it with them. Even so, the market will still work to spread the effects of wealth compensation. A law requiring every can of produce to be marked to indicate whether it was produced with non-preferred or with preferred workers would allow consumers to discriminate in their purchases. Nonetheless, if the price of a can produced by non-preferred workers is lower, a wealth cost will be imposed on ultimate buyers who discriminate. Some or all such buyers will buy less of the product produced by preferred workers because of its higher relative cost. In similar fashion, the ability of non-preferred persons to bid appealing prices for homes, and thereby to acquire some homes, will force those who wish to discriminate to pay moving costs and otherwise to reduce their well-being. Prices for nearby homes will be forced down *if* their owners insist on selling only to preferred persons. Thus, the market will spread the costs of discriminating in these cases also. (It must be remembered that we are talking about a free market and not one in which preferred persons are allowed to collude to restrict the terms of sale of property.)

It is possible to modify the structure of political power so that majoritarian democracy will more closely resemble the operation of free markets. Democracy as we know it requires one vote per person and majority approval, so that it is not possible to imitate the first two important characteristics of the free market. Individuals do not have additional votes to concentrate, nor can they influence any political decision individually. However, a redistribution of political authority from the national and state levels to the level of local communities will allow non-preferred persons to control the majority of votes in those local communities where they reside in relatively large numbers.

States are too large to enable non-preferred groups easily to dominate political decisions. But, except for those cases where minority preferences have already been accepted by substantial numbers of preferred persons, cases that have already been largely exploited, a change in the distribution of political power upward to the central government is a move in the wrong direction for non-preferred minorities. At the national level their votes are necessarily outnumbered. The correct direction in which to shift power is to the community level. The resulting dispersal of political power parallels the dispersal of economic power in the market. And, in the same way that several members of the minority can concentrate their dollar votes on an economic decision center, they can effectively concentrate their political votes on a local center of political decision-making.

Control over political decisions at some local center will allow the (national) minority to adopt a political program that is ideal from its viewpoint. This does not mean a program that mercilessly penalizes the (nationally) preferred persons who reside in their community. If the local political platform is overzealous, preferred persons will leave the community, and in the short run (nationally) non-preferred persons may move in from other communities. (This shifting in residence is a competition among localities akin to the spread of wealth compensation in the market place.) The resulting segregation may be undesirable culturally and economically and not at all in the interest of the (national) minority. Instead, a more moderate program, possibly concentrating on equality of opportunity, might be optimal. Such a program could improve the position of non-preferred persons without producing undesirable amounts of segregation.

While minorities gain this advantage in some local communities, preferred persons will exercise the same powers in other communities. But preferred majorities will have this power over all communities if control is concentrated at the national level. To prevent the majority from using this power extravagantly in all communities, it is necessary to transfer power from the central government and states to local communities. And to prevent local communities which are controlled by preferred persons from adopting over-zealous programs of their own, it is necessary to abandon majoritarian democracy for some form of constitutional democracy. The long-run political interests of non-preferred minorities thus lie in the opposite direction from that which they usually pursue. The non-preferred minorities should now side with those who favor a freer market, stronger adherence to the Constitution, and greater dispersal of political power to local governments.

NOTES

1 This is true irrespective of the degree to which our present choices are determined by our past. If certain acts of discrimination are part of our past, we will behave differently than otherwise.

2 Many readers will recognize this as a form of the basic law of demand used in economics. The higher the cost of a preferred action, the less frequently will that action be taken.

3 For good treatments of personal characteristic compensation, see Becker (1957); Alchian and Kessel (1962).

4 These phrases sometimes seem to propose as criteria for action the welfare or conscience of a majority of persons, sometimes of a vocal minority, and sometimes of an intellectual minority. They are never used in a way which reasonably can be interpreted to mean the welfare or conscience of all, or there would be no need for a clarion call to action. It is always surprising to find that those who are inclined to use such phrases as criteria for action fail to realize that most of the measures taken in Nazi Germany met these criteria.

5 Discrimination on the part of an employer may merely reflect workers' discriminatory tastes.

6 We must be careful not to draw incorrect inferences about the profitability of discriminating. If we take the wages of preferred workers as being independent of the degree to which discrimination is practiced by a firm, it follows that an employer who discriminates pays for his discrimination by forgoing the profits he could earn by hiring non-preferred workers at wages below the value of their output. An employer can only increase his profitability by employing more non-preferred workers so long as their productivity exceeds the wage he must pay. It follows from this that an employer who does not discriminate according to personal characteristics will, *ceteris*

paribus, be the most profitable competitor in the market place. The offering of wealth compensation by non-preferred workers in the form of offering their services at lower wage rates will increase the relative profitability of those discriminating employers who, in response to this compensation, reduce the degree of discrimination they practice. Those who respond less to the offer of wealth compensation will operate their firms less profitably, whereas those who require little or no wealth compensation, i.e., those who do not discriminate, will run the most profitable firms. Of course, those who earn smaller nominal returns because they discriminate will earn non-monetary returns in their increased consumption of preferable association.

7 What about Jews hiring Jews and Negroes hiring Negroes, etc.? Although the direction of non-preference may change, my analysis remains applicable.

8 For a more detailed treatment of this example, see Alchian and Kessel (1962).

9 See Alchian and Kessel (1962).

10 The issue here is not whether presidents of utilities desire to discriminate or whether only particular utilities will so desire. The issue is the reduced emphasis on cost brought about by the regulatory process. Public utilities will treat costs more loosely and will not institute as careful policing action on internal operations. This looseness allows costs to be increased throughout the firm. The decreased emphasis on costs can result in the behavior described above by those doing the hiring and purchasing. One utility's cost may be raised because of discriminatory hiring, another's because of ineffective purchasing procedures.

11 The case against trade unions on this score is fairly well documented, and I give no specific references. The case against the American Medical Association can be found in Kessel (1958, p. 20). Further, we should note that many general licensing procedures for businesses, liquor stores for example, restrict owners to persons who have established credit and good reputation in the community. Such requirements are likely to work to the disadvantage of persons not preferred by the community.

12 E.g., NY Labor Law, section 220-e.

13 The phrase "in and of themselves" indicates that the long-run effect of these laws on such things as personal liberty is ignored. Also, I include anti-trust laws as pro-free-market even though they may curtail personal liberty.

14 A classic attempt to reduce the costs of sorting Jews from non-Jews was the Nazi requirement that Jews wear yellow arm bands. This attempt was frustrated for a short time in occupied Denmark by non-Jewish Danes who voluntarily placed yellow bands around their arms.

15 See Stigler and Friedland (1962, p. 1).

16 Macesich and Stewart (1960, pp. 288–9).

17 Brozen (1962, p. 103).

18 Brozen (1962, pp. 103–4).

19 Alchian and Kessel (1962).

20 Alchian and Kessel (1962, p. 171).

21 See Demsetz (1961, p. 80); Peterson (1957, p. 412).

22 *Hearings on S. 773, S. 1210, S. 1211, and S. 1937 Before the Subcommittee on Employment and Manpower of the Senate Committee on Labor and Public Welfare*, 88 Cong., 1st Sess. 109 (1962).

23 Alaska, California, Colorado, Connecticut, Massachusetts, Michigan, Minnesota,

New Jersey, New Mexico, New York, Ohio, Oregon, Pennsylvania, Rhode Island, and Wisconsin.

24 These findings are not conclusive, however. A more detailed study of the degree to which whites and non-whites are found in particular industries or job classifications in various states is needed for a more convincing demonstration.

25 Civil Rights Act of 1964, Pub. L. 88–352, 78 Stat. 241. Hereinafter, the act will be referred to only by section.

26 Sections 101–7.

27 Section 201.

REFERENCES

Alchian, A. and Kessel, R. (1962). ''Competition, Monopoly, and the Pursuit of Pecuniary Gain.'' *Aspects of Labor Economics*, 157.

Becker, G. (1957). *The Economics of Discrimination*. Chicago: University Press.

Brozen, Y. (1962). ''Minimum Wage Rates and Household Workers.'' *Journal of Law and Economics*, 5.

Demsetz, H. (1961). ''Structural Unemployment: A Reconsideration of the Evidence and the Theory.'' *Journal of Law and Economics*, 4.

Kessel, R. (1958). ''Price Discrimination in Medicine.'' *Journal of Law and Economics*, 1.

Macesich, G. and Stewart, C. (1960). ''Recent Department of Labor Studies of Minimum Wage Effects.'' *Southern Economic Journal*, 26.

Peterson, J. M. (1957). ''Employment Effects of Minimum Wages 1938–1950.'' *Journal of Political Economy*, 65.

Stigler, G. J. and Friedland, C. (1962). ''What Can Regulators Regulate? The Case of Electricity.'' *Journal of Law and Economics*, 5.

7
Toward a Theory of Property Rights

When a transaction is concluded in the market place, two bundles of property rights are exchanged. A bundle of rights often attaches to a physical commodity or service, but it is the value of the rights that determines the value of what is exchanged. Questions addressed to the emergence and mix of the components of the bundle of rights are prior to those commonly asked by economists. Economists usually take the bundle of property rights as a datum and ask for an explanation of the forces determining the price and the number of units of a good to which these rights attach.

In this paper, I seek to fashion some of the elements of an economic theory of property rights. The paper is organized into three sections. The first section discusses briefly the concept and role of property rights in social systems. The second section offers some guidance for investigating the emergence of property rights. The third section sets forth some principles relevant to the coalescing of property rights into particular bundles and to the determination of the ownership structure that will be associated with these bundles.

THE CONCEPT AND ROLE OF PROPERTY RIGHTS

In the world of Robinson Crusoe, property rights play no role. Property rights are an instrument of society and derive their significance from the fact that they help a man form those expectations that he can reasonably hold in his dealings with others. These expectations find expression in the laws, customs, and mores of a society. An owner of property rights possesses the consent of fellow men to allow him to act in particular ways. An owner expects the community to prevent others from interfering with his actions, provided that these actions are not prohibited in the specifications of his rights.

It is important to note that property rights convey the right to benefit or harm oneself or others. Harming a competitor by producing superior products may be permitted, while shooting him may not. A man may be permitted to

This paper is reprinted with permission from *AER*, May 1967.

benefit himself by shooting an intruder but be prohibited from selling below a price floor. It is clear, then, that property rights specify how persons may be benefitted and harmed, and, therefore, who must pay whom to modify the actions taken by persons. The recognition of this leads easily to the close relationship between property rights and externalities.

Externality is an ambiguous concept. For the purposes of this paper, the concept includes external costs, external benefits, and pecuniary as well as non-pecuniary externalities. No harmful or beneficial effect is external to the world. Some person or persons always suffer or enjoy these effects. What converts a harmful or beneficial effect into an externality is that the cost of bringing the effect to bear on the decisions of one or more of the interacting persons is too high to make it worthwhile, and this is what the term shall mean here. "Internalizing" such effects refers to a process, usually a change in property rights, that enables these effects to bear (in greater degree) on all interacting persons.

A primary function of property rights is that of guiding incentives to achieve a greater internalization of externalities. Every cost and benefit associated with social interdependencies is a potential externality. One condition is necessary to make costs and benefits externalities. The cost of a transaction in the rights between the parties (internalization) must exceed the gains from internalization. In general, transacting costs can be large relative to gains because of "natural" difficulties in trading or they can be large because of legal reasons. In a lawful society the prohibition of voluntary negotiations makes the cost of transacting infinite. Some costs and benefits are not taken into account by users of resources whenever externalities exist, but allowing transactions increases the degree to which internalization takes place. For example, it might be thought that a firm that uses slave labor will not recognize all the costs of its activities, since it can have its slave labor by paying subsistence wages only. This will not be true if negotiations are permitted, for the slaves can offer to the firm a payment for their freedom based on the expected return to them of being free men. The cost of slavery can thus be internalized in the calculations of the firm. The transition from serf to free man in feudal Europe is an example of this process.

Perhaps one of the most significant cases of externalities is the extensive use of the military draft. The taxpayer benefits by not paying the full cost of staffing the armed services. The costs that he escapes are the additional sums that would be needed to acquire men voluntarily for the services or those sums that would be offered as payment by draftees to taxpayers in order to be exempted. With either voluntary recruitment, the "buy-him-in" system, or a "let-him-buy-his-way-out" system, the full cost of recruitment would be brought to bear on taxpayers. It has always seemed incredible to me that so many economists can recognize an externality when they see smoke but not when they see the draft. The familiar smoke example is one in which negotiation costs may be too high (because of the large number of interacting parties) to make it worthwhile to internalize all the effects of smoke. The draft is an externality caused by forbidding negotiation.

The role of property rights in the internalization of externalities can be made clear within the context of the above examples. A law that establishes the right of a person to his freedom would necessitate a payment on the part of a firm or of the taxpayer sufficient to cover the cost of using that person's labor if his services are to be obtained. The costs of labor thus become internalized in the firm's or taxpayer's decisions. Alternatively, a law that gives the firm or the taxpayer clear title to slave labor would necessitate that the slaveowners take into account the sums that slaves are willing to pay for their freedom. These costs thus become internalized in decisions although wealth is distributed differently in the two cases. All that is needed for internalization in either case is ownership which includes the right of sale. It is the prohibition of a property right adjustment, the prohibition of the establishment of an ownership title that can thenceforth be exchanged, that precludes the internalization of external costs and benefits.

There are two striking implications of this process that are true in a world of zero transaction costs. The output mix that results when the exchange of property rights is allowed is efficient and the mix is independent of who is assigned ownership (except that different wealth distributions may result in different demands).[1] For example, the efficient mix of civilians and military will result from transferable ownership no matter whether taxpayers must hire military volunteers or whether draftees must pay taxpayers to be excused from service. For taxpayers will hire only those military (under the ''buy-him-in'' property right system) who would not pay to be exempted (under the ''let-him-buy-his-way-out'' system). The highest bidder under the ''let-him-buy-his-way-out'' property right system would be precisely the last to volunteer under a ''buy-him-in'' system.[2]

We will refer back to some of these points later. But for now, enough groundwork has been laid to facilitate the discussion of the next two sections of this paper.

THE EMERGENCE OF PROPERTY RIGHTS

If the main allocative function of property rights is the internalization of beneficial and harmful effects, then the emergence of property rights can be understood best by their association with the emergence of new or different beneficial and harmful effects.

Changes in knowledge result in changes in production functions, market values, and aspirations. New techniques, new ways of doing the same things, and doing new things – all invoke harmful and beneficial effects to which society has not been accustomed. It is my thesis in this section that the emergence of new property rights takes place in response to the desires of the interacting persons for adjustment to new benefit–cost possibilities.

The thesis can be restated in a slightly different fashion: property rights develop to internalize externalities when the gains of internalization become larger than the cost of internalization. Increased internalization, in the main, results from changes in economic values, changes which stem from the development of new technology and the opening of new markets, changes to which old property rights are poorly attuned. A proper interpretation of this assertion requires that account be taken of a community's preferences for private ownership. Some communities will have less well developed private ownership systems and more highly developed state ownership systems. But, given a community's tastes in this regard, the emergence of new private or state-owned property rights will be in response to changes in technology and relative prices.

I do not mean to assert or to deny that the adjustments in property rights which take place need be the result of a conscious endeavour to cope with new externality problems. These adjustments have arisen in Western societies largely as a result of gradual changes in social mores and in common law precedents. At each step of this adjustment process, it is unlikely that externalities per se were consciously related to the issue being resolved. These legal and moral experiments may be hit-and-miss procedures to some extent but in a society that weights the achievement of efficiency heavily, their viability in the long run will depend on how well they modify behavior to accommodate to the externalities associated with important changes in technology or market values.

A rigorous test of this assertion will require extensive and detailed empirical work. A broad range of examples can be cited that are consistent with it: the development of air rights, renters' rights, rules for liability in automobile accidents, etc. In this part of the discussion, I shall present one group of such examples in some detail. They deal with the development of private property rights in land among American Indians. These examples are broad ranging and come fairly close to what can be called convincing evidence in the field of anthropology.

The question of private ownership of land among aboriginals has held a fascination for anthropologists. It has been one of the intellectual battlegrounds in the attempt to assess the "true nature" of man unconstrained by the "artificialities" of civilization. In the process of carrying on this debate, information has been uncovered that bears directly on the thesis with which we are now concerned. What appears to be accepted as a classic treatment and a high point of this debate is Eleanor Leacock's memoir on "The Montagnes' 'Hunting Territory' and the Fur Trade."[3] Leacock's research followed that of Frank G. Speck, who had discovered that the Indians of the Labrador Peninsula had a long-established tradition of property in land.[4] This finding was at odds with what was known about the Indians of the American South-west and it prompted Leacock's study of the Montagnes who inhabited large regions around Quebec.

Leacock clearly established the fact that a close relationship existed, both historically and geographically, between the development of private rights in land and the development of the commercial fur trade. The factual basis of this correlation has gone unchallenged. However, to my knowledge, no theory relating privacy of land to the fur trade has yet been articulated. The factual material uncovered by Speck and Leacock fits the thesis of this paper well, and in doing so it reveals clearly the role played by property right adjustments in taking account of what economists have often cited as an example of an externality – the overhunting of game.

Because of the lack of control over hunting by others, it is in no person's interest to invest in increasing or maintaining the stock of game. Overly intensive hunting takes place. Thus a successful hunt is viewed as imposing external costs on subsequent hunters – costs that are not taken into account fully in the determination of the extent of hunting and of animal husbandry.

Before the fur trade became established, hunting was carried on primarily for purposes of food and the relatively few furs that were required for the hunter's family. The externality was clearly present. Hunting could be practiced freely and was carried on without assessing its impact on other hunters. But these external effects were of such small significance that it did not pay for anyone to take them into account. There did not exist anything resembling private ownership in land. And in the *Jesuit Relations*, particularly Le Jeune's record of the winter he spent with the Montagnes in 1633–4 and in the brief account given by Father Druilletes in 1647–8, Leacock finds no evidence of private land holdings. Both accounts indicate a socioeconomic organization in which private rights to land are not well developed.

We may safely surmise that the advent of the fur trade had two immediate consequences. First, the value of furs to the Indians was increased considerably. Second, and as a result, the scale of hunting activity rose sharply. Both consequences must have increased considerably the importance of the externalities associated with free hunting. The property right system began to change, and it changed specifically in the direction required to take account of the economic effects made important by the fur trade. The geographical or distributional evidence collected by Leacock indicates an unmistakable correlation between early centers of fur trade and the oldest and most complete development of the private hunting territory.

> By the beginning of the eighteenth century, we begin to have clear evidence that territorial hunting and trapping arrangements by individual families were developing in the area around Quebec. . . . The earliest references to such arrangements in this region indicate a purely temporary allotment of hunting territories. They [Algonkians and Iroquois] divide themselves into several bands in order to hunt more efficiently. It was their custom . . . to appropriate pieces of land about two leagues square for each group to

hunt exclusively. Ownership of beaver houses, however, had already become established, and when discovered, they were marked. A starving Indian could kill and eat another's beaver if he left the fur and the tail.[4]

The next step toward the hunting territory was probably a seasonal allotment system. An anonymous account written in 1723 states that the "principle of the Indians is to mark off the hunting ground selected by them by blazing the trees with their crests so that they may never encroach on each other. . . . By the middle of the century these allotted territories were relatively stabilized."[6]

The principle that associates property right changes with the emergence of new and re-evaluation of old harmful and beneficial effects suggests in this instance that the fur trade made it economic to encourage the husbanding of fur-bearing animals. Husbanding requires the ability to prevent poaching, and this, in turn, suggests that socioeconomic changes in property in hunting land will take place. The chain of reasoning is consistent with the evidence cited above. Is it inconsistent with the absence of similar rights in property among the South-western Indians?

Two factors suggest that the thesis is consistent with the absence of similar rights among the Indians of the south-western plains. The first of these is that there were no plains animals of commercial importance comparable to the fur-bearing animals of the forest, at least not until cattle arrived with Europeans. The second factor is that animals of the plains are primarily grazing species whose habit is to wander over wide tracts of land. The value of establishing boundaries to private hunting territories is thus reduced by the relatively high cost of preventing the animals from moving to adjacent parcels. Hence both the value and the cost of establishing private hunting lands in the South-west are such that we would expect little development along these lines. The externality was just not worth taking into account.

The lands of the Labrador Peninsula shelter forest animals whose habits are considerably different from those of the plains. Forest animals confine their territories to relatively small areas, so that the cost of internalizing the effects of husbanding these animals is considerably reduced. This reduced cost, together with the higher commercial value of fur-bearing forest animals, made it productive to establish private hunting lands. Frank G. Speck finds that family proprietorship among the Indians of the peninsula included retaliation against trespass. Animal resources were husbanded. Sometimes conservation practices were carried on extensively. Family hunting territories were divided into quarters. Each year the family hunted in a different quarter in rotation, leaving a tract in the center as a sort of bank, not to be hunted over unless forced to do so by a shortage in the regular tract.

To conclude our excursion into the phenomenon of private rights in land among the American Indians, we note one further piece of corroborating evidence. Among the Indians of the North-west, highly developed private family rights to hunting lands had also emerged – rights that went so far as to include inheritance. Here again we find that forest animals predominate and that the West Coast was frequently visited by sailing schooners whose primary purpose was trading in furs.[7]

THE COALESCENCE AND OWNERSHIP OF PROPERTY RIGHTS

I have argued that property rights arise when it becomes economic for those affected by externalities to internalize benefits and costs. But I have not yet examined the forces that will govern the particular form of right ownership. Several idealized forms of ownership must be distinguished at the outset. These are communal ownership, private ownership, and state ownership.

By communal ownership, I shall mean a right which can be exercised by all members of the community. Frequently the rights to till and to hunt the land have been communally owned. The right to walk a city sidewalk is communally owned. Communal ownership means that the community denies to the state or to individual citizens the right to interfere with any person's exercise of communally owned rights. Private ownership implies that the community recognizes the right of the owner to exclude others from exercising the owner's private rights. State ownership implies that the state may exclude anyone from the use of a right as long as the state follows accepted political procedures for determining who may not use state-owned property. I shall not examine in detail the alternative of state ownership. The object of the analysis that follows is to discern some broad principles governing the development of property rights in communities oriented to private property.

It will be best to begin by considering a particularly useful example that focuses our attention on the problem of land ownership. Suppose that land is communally owned. Every person has the right to hunt, till, or mine the land. This form of ownership fails to concentrate the cost associated with any person's exercise of his communal right on that person. If a person seeks to maximize the value of his communal rights, he will tend to overhunt and overwork the land because some of the costs of his doing so are borne by others. The stock of game and the richness of the soil will be diminished too quickly. It is conceivable that those who own these rights, namely, every member of the community, can agree to curtail the rate at which they work the lands if negotiating and policing costs are zero. Each can agree to abridge his rights. It is obvious that the costs of reaching such an agreement will not be zero. What is not obvious is just how large these costs may be.

Negotiating costs will be large because it is difficult for many persons to reach a mutually satisfactory agreement, especially when each hold-out has the right to work the land as fast as he pleases. But, even if an agreement among all can be reached, we must yet take account of the costs of policing the agreement, and these may be large, also. After such an agreement is reached, no one will privately own the right to work the land; all can work the land but at an agreed upon shorter work-week. Negotiating costs are increased even further because it is not possible under this system to bring the full expected benefits and expected costs of future generations to bear on current users.

If a single person owns land, he will attempt to maximize its present value by taking into account alternative future time streams of benefits and costs and selecting that one which he believes will maximize the present value of his privately owned land rights. We all know that this means that he will attempt to take into account the supply and demand conditions that he thinks will exist after his death. It is very difficult to see how the existing communal owners can reach an agreement that takes account of these costs.

In effect, an owner of a private right to use land acts as a broker whose wealth depends on how well he takes into account the competing claims of the present and the future. But with communal rights there is no broker, and the claims of the present generation will be given an uneconomically large weight in determining the intensity with which the land is worked. Future generations might desire to pay present generations enough to change the present intensity of land usage. But they have no living agent to place their claims on the market. Under a communal property system, should a living person pay others to reduce the rate at which they work the land, he would not gain anything of value for his efforts. Communal property means that future generations must speak for themselves. No one has yet estimated the costs of carrying on such a conversation.

The land ownership example confronts us immediately with a great disadvantage of communal property. The effects of a person's activities on his neighbors and on subsequent generations will not be taken into account fully. Communal property results in great externalities. The full costs of the activities of an owner of a communal property right are not borne directly by him, nor can they be called to his attention easily by the willingness of others to pay him an appropriate sum. Communal property rules out a "pay-to-use-the-property" system, and high negotiation and policing costs make ineffective a "pay-him-not-to-use-the-property" system.

The state, the courts, or the leaders of the community could attempt to internalize the external costs resulting from communal property by allowing private parcels owned by small groups of person with similar interests. The logical groups in terms of similar interests are, of course, the family and the individual. Continuing with our use of the land ownership example, let us initially distribute private titles to land randomly among existing individuals and, further, let the extent of land included in each title be randomly determined.

The resulting private ownership of land will internalize many of the external costs associated with communal ownership, for now an owner, by virtue of his power to exclude others, can generally count on realizing the rewards associated with husbanding the game and increasing the fertility of his land. This concentration of benefits and costs on owners creates incentives to utilize resources more efficiently.

But we have yet to contend the externalities. Under the communal property system, the maximization of the value of communal property rights will take place without regard to many costs, because the owner of a communal right cannot exclude others from enjoying the fruits of his efforts and because negotiation costs are too high for all to agree jointly on optimal behavior. The development of private rights permits the owner to economize on the use of those resources from which he has the right to exclude others. Much internalization is accomplished in this way. But the owner of private rights to one parcel does not himself own the rights to the parcel of another private sector. Since he cannot exclude others from their private rights to land, he has no direct incentive (in the absence of negotiations) to economize in the use of his land in a way that takes into account the effects he produces on the land rights of others. If he constructs a dam on his land, he has no direct incentive to take into account the lower water levels produced on his neighbor's land.

This is exactly the same kind of externality that we encountered with communal property rights, but it is present to a lesser degree. Whereas no one had an incentive to store water on any land under the communal system, private owners now can take into account directly those benefits and costs to their land that accompany water storage. But the effects on the land of others will not be taken into account directly.

The partial concentration of benefits and costs that accompany private ownership is only part of the advantage this system offers. The other part, and perhaps the most important, has escaped our notice. The cost of negotiating over the remaining externalities will be reduced greatly. Communal property rights allow anyone to use the land. Under this system it becomes necessary for all to reach an agreement on land use. But the externalities that accompany private ownership of property do not affect all owners, and, generally speaking, it will be necessary for only a few to reach an agreement that takes these effects into account. The cost of negotiating an internalization of these effects is thereby reduced considerably. The point is important enough to elucidate.

Suppose an owner of a communal land right, in the process of plowing a parcel of land, observes a second communal owner constructing a dam on adjacent land. The farmer prefers to have the stream as it is, and so he asks the engineer to stop his construction. The engineer says, "Pay me to stop." The farmer replies, "I will be happy to pay you, but what can you guarantee in return?" The engineer answers, "I can guarantee you that I will not continue constructing the dam, but I cannot guarantee that another engineer will not take up the task because this is communal property; I have no right to exclude him." What would be a simple negotiation between two persons under a private property arrangement turns out to be a rather complex negotiation between the farmer and everyone else. This is the basic explanation, I believe, for the preponderance of single rather than multiple owners of property. Indeed, an increase in the number of owners is an increase in the communality of property and leads, generally, to an increase in the cost of internalizing.

The reduction in negotiating cost that accompanies the private right to exclude others allows most externalities to be internalized at rather low cost. Those that are not are associated with activities that generate external effects impinging upon many people. The soot from smoke affects many homeowners, none of whom is willing to pay enough to the factory to get its owner to reduce smoke output. All homeowners together might be willing to pay enough, but the cost of their getting together may be enough to discourage effective market bargaining. The negotiating problem is compounded even more if the smoke comes not from a single smoke stack but from an industrial district. In such cases, it may be too costly to internalize effects through the market place.

Returning to our land ownership paradigm, we recall that land was distributed in randomly sized parcels to randomly selected owners. These owners now negotiate among themselves to internalize any remaining externalities. Two market options are open to the negotiators. The first is simply to try to reach a contractual agreement among owners that directly deals with the external effects at issue. The second option is for some owners to buy out others, thus changing the parcel size owned. Which option is selected will depend on which is cheaper. We have here a standard economic problem of optimal scale. If there exist constant returns to scale in the ownership of different sized parcels, it will be largely a matter of indifference between outright purchase and contractual agreement if only a single, easy-to-police, contractual agreement will internalize the externality. But, if there are several externalities, so that several such contracts will need to be negotiated, or if the contractual agreements should be difficult to police, then outright purchase will be the preferred course of action.

The greater are diseconomies of scale to land ownership, the more will contractual arrangement be used by the interacting neighbors to settle these differences. Negotiating and policing costs will be compared to costs that depend on the scale of ownership, and parcels of land will tend to be owned in sizes that minimize the sum of these costs.[8]

The interplay of scale economies, negotiating cost, externalities, and the modification of property rights can be seen in the most notable "exception" to the assertion that ownership tends to be an individual affair: the publicly held corporation. I assume that significant economies of scale in the operation of large corporations is a fact and, also, that large requirements for equity capital can be satisfied more cheaply by acquiring the capital from many purchasers of equity shares. While economies of scale in operating these enterprises exist, economies of scale in the provision of capital do not. Hence, it becomes desirable for many "owners" to form a joint-stock company.

But if all owners participate in each decision that needs to be made by such a company, the scale economies of operating the company will be overcome quickly by high negotiating cost. Hence a delegation of authority for most decisions takes place and, for most of these, a small management group becomes the *de facto* owners. Effective ownership, that is effective control of property, is thus legally concentrated in management's hands. This is the first legal modification, and it takes place in recognition of the high negotiating costs that would otherwise obtain.

The structure of ownership, however, creates some externality difficulties under the law of partnership. If the corporation should fail, partnership law commits each shareholder to meet the debts of the corporation up to the limits of his financial ability. Thus, managerial *de facto* ownership can have considerable external effects on shareholders. Should property rights remain unmodified, this externality would make it exceedingly difficult for entrepreneurs to acquire equity capital from wealthy individuals. (Although these individuals have recourse to reimbursements from other shareholders, litigation costs will be high.) A second legal modification, limited liability, has taken place to reduce the effect of this externality. *De facto* management ownership and limited liability combine to minimize the overall cost of operating large enterprises. Shareholders are essentially lenders of equity capital and not owners, although they do participate in such infrequent decisions as those involving mergers. What shareholders really own are their shares and not the corporation. Ownership in the sense of control again becomes a largely individual affair. The shareholders own their shares, and the president of the corporation and possibly a few other top executives control the corporation.

To further ease the impact of management decisions on shareholders, that is, to minimize the impact of externalities under this ownership form, a further legal modification of rights is required. Unlike partnership law, a shareholder may sell his interest without first obtaining the permission of fellow shareholders or without dissolving the corporation. It thus becomes easy for him to get out if his preferences and those of the management are no longer in harmony. This "escape hatch" is extremely important and has given rise to the organized trading of securities. The increase in harmony between managers and shareholders brought about by exchange and by competing managerial groups helps to minimize the external effects associated with the corporate ownership structure. Finally, limited liability considerably reduces the cost of exchanging shares by making it unnecessary for a purchaser of shares to examine in great detail the liabilities of the corporation and the assets of other shareholders; these liabilities can adversely affect a purchaser only up to the extent of the price per share.

The dual tendencies for ownership to rest with individuals and for the extent of an individual's ownership to accord with the minimization of all costs is clear in the land ownership paradigm. The applicability of this paradigm has been extended to the corporation. But it may not be clear yet how widely applicable this paradigm is. Consider the problems of copyright and patents. If a new idea is freely appropriable by all, if there exist communal rights to new ideas, incentives for developing such ideas will be lacking. The benefits derivable from these ideas will not be concentrated on their originators. If we extend some degree of private rights to the originators, these ideas will come forth at a more rapid pace. But the existence of the private rights does not mean that their effects on the property of others will be directly taken into account. A new idea makes an old one obsolete and another old one more valuable. These effects will not be directly taken into account, but they can be called to the attention of the originator of the new idea through market negotiations. All problems of externalities are closely analogous to those that arise in the land ownership example. The relevant variables are identical.

What I have suggested in this paper is an approach to problems in property rights. But it is more than that. It is also a different way of viewing traditional problems. An elaboration of this approach will, I hope, illuminate a great number of social-economic problems.

NOTES

1 These implications are derived by Coase (1960, pp. 1–44).
2 If the demand for civilian life is unaffected by wealth redistribution, the assertion made is correct as it stands. However, when a change is made from a "buy-him-in" system to a "let-him-buy-his-way-out" system, the resulting redistribution of wealth away from draftees may significantly affect their demand for civilian life; the validity of the assertion then requires a compensating wealth change. A compensating wealth change will not be required in the ordinary case of profit-maximizing firms. Consider the farmer–rancher example mentioned by Coase. Society may give the farmer the right to grow corn unmolested by cattle or it may give the rancher the right to allow his cattle to stray. Contrary to the Coase example, let us suppose that, if the farmer is given the right, he just breaks even; i.e., with the right to be compensated for corn damage, the farmer's land is marginal. If the right is transferred to the rancher, the farmer, not enjoying any economic rent, will not have the wherewithal to pay the rancher to reduce the number of head of cattle raised. In this case, however, it will be profitable for the rancher to buy the farm, thus merging cattle-raising with farming. His self-interest will then lead him to take account of the effect of cattle on corn.
3 Leacock (1954).
4 Cf. Speck (1926).
5 Leacock (1954, p. 15).
6 Leacock (1954, p. 15).
7 The thesis is consistent with the development of other types of private rights. Among wandering primitive peoples, the cost of policing property is relatively low for highly portable objects. The owning family can protect such objects while carrying on its daily activities. If these objects are also very useful, property rights should appear frequently, so as to internalize the benefits and costs of their use. It is generally true among most primitive communities that weapons and household utensils, such as

pottery, are regarded as private property. Both types of articles are portable and both require an investment of time to produce. Among agriculturally oriented peoples, because of the relative fixity of their location, portability has a smaller role to play in the determination of property. The distinction is most clearly seen by comparing property in land among the most primitive of these societies, where crop rotation and simple fertilization techniques are unknown, or where land fertility is extremely poor, with property in land among primitive peoples who are more knowledgeable in these matters or who possess very superior land. Once a crop is grown by the more primitive agricultural societies, it is necessary for them to abandon the land for several years to restore productivity. Property rights in land among such people would require policing cost for several years during which no sizable output is obtained, Since to provide for sustenance these people must move to new land, a property right, to be of value to them, must be associated with a portable object. Among these people it is common to find property rights to the crops, which, after harvest, are portable, but not to the land. The more advanced agriculturally based primitive societies are able to remain with particular land for longer periods, and here we generally observe property rights to the land as well as to the crops.

8 Compare this with the similar rationale given by R. H. Coase to explain the firm in "The Nature of the Firm," (Coase, pp. 386–405).

REFERENCES

Coase, R. H. (1937). "The Nature of the Firm." *Economica*, 4.

—— (1960). "The Problem of Social Cost." *Journal of Law and Economics*, 3.

Leacock, E. (1954). "The Montagnes 'Hunting Territory' and the Fur Trade." *American Anthropological Association*, 36, Memoir no. 78.

Speck, F. G. (1926). "Land Ownership among Hunting Peoples in Primitive America and the World's Marginal Areas." *Twenty-second International Congress of Americanists*, 2.

PART III
The Firm and the Problem of Control

8
Production, Information Costs, and Economic Organization

with Armen A. Alchian

The mark of a capitalistic society is that resources are owned and allocated by such non-governmental organizations as firms, households, and markets. Resource owners increase productivity through cooperative specialization, and this leads to the demand for economic organizations that facilitate cooperation. When a lumber mill employs a cabinetmaker, cooperation between specialists is achieved within a firm, and when a cabinetmaker purchases wood from a lumberman, the cooperation takes place across markets (or between firms). Two important problems face a theory of economic organization: to explain the conditions that determine whether the gains from specialization and cooperative production can better be obtained within an organization like the firm or across markets, and to explain the structure of the organization.

It is common to see the firm characterized by the power to settle issues by fiat, by authority, or by disciplinary action superior to that available in the conventional market. This is delusion. The firm does not own all its inputs. It has no power of fiat, no authority, no disciplinary action any different in the slightest degree from ordinary market contracting between any two people. I can "punish" you only by withholding future business or by seeking redress in the courts for any failure to honor our exchange agreement. That is exactly all that any employer can do. He can fire or sue, just as I can fire my grocer by stopping purchases from him or sue him for delivering faulty products. What then is the content of the presumed power to manage and assign workers to various tasks? Exactly the same as one little consumer's power to manage and assign his grocer to various tasks. The single consumer can assign his grocer to the task of obtaining whatever the customer can induce the grocer to provide at a price acceptable to both parties. That is precisely all that an employer can do to an employee. To speak of managing, directing, or assigning workers to various tasks is a deceptive way of noting that the employer continually is

Acknowledgment is made for financial aid from the E. Lilly Endowment, Inc. grant to UCLA for research in the behavioral effects of property rights. Reprinted with permission from *AER*, 62(5), 1972.

involved in renegotiation of contracts on terms that must be acceptable to both parties. Telling an employee to type this letter rather than to file that document is like my telling a grocer to sell me this brand of tuna rather than that brand of bread. I have no contract to continue to purchase from the grocer and neither the employer nor the employee is bound by any contractual obligations to continue their relationship. Long-term contracts between employer and employee are not the essence of the organization we call a firm. My grocer can count on my returning day after day and purchasing his services and goods even with the prices not always marked on the goods – because I know what they are – and he adapts his activity to conform to my directions to him as to what I want each day; he is not my employee.

Wherein, then, is the relationship between a grocer and his employee different from that between a grocer and his customers? It is in a *team* use of inputs and a centralized position of some party in the contractual arrangements of *all* other inputs. It is the *centralized contractual agent in a team productive process* – not some superior authoritarian directive or disciplinary power. Exactly what is a team process, and why does it induce the contractual form, called the firm? These problems motivate the inquiry of this paper.

THE METERING PROBLEM

The economic organization through which input owners cooperate will make better use of their comparative advantages to the extent that it facilitates the payment of rewards in accord with productivity. If rewards were random, and without regard to productive effort, no incentive to productive effort would be provided by the organization; and if rewards were negatively correlated with productivity, the organization would be subject to sabotage. Two key demands are placed on an economic organization: metering input productivity and metering rewards.[1]

Metering problems sometimes can be resolved well through the exchange of products across competitive markets, because in many situations markets yield a high correlation between rewards and productivity. If a farmer increases his output of wheat by 10 percent at the prevailing market price, his receipts also increase by 10 percent. This method of organizing economic activity meters the *output directly*, reveals the marginal product, and apportions the *rewards* to resource owners in accord with that direct measurement of their outputs. The success of this decentralized, market exchange in promoting productive specialization requires that changes in market rewards fall on those responsible for changes in *output*.[2]

The classic relationship in economics that runs from marginal productivity to the distribution of income implicitly *assumes* the existence of an organization, be it the market or the firm, that allocates rewards to resources in accord with their productivity. The problem of economic organization, the economical means of metering productivity and rewards, is not confronted directly in the classical analysis of production and distribution. Instead, that analysis tends to assume sufficiently economic – or zero-cost – means, as if productivity automatically created its reward. We conjecture the direction of causation is the reverse – the specific system of rewarding that is relied upon stimulates a particular productivity response. If the economic organization meters poorly, with rewards and productivity only loosely correlated, then productivity will be smaller; but if the economic organization meters well, productivity will be greater. What makes metering difficult and hence induces means of economizing on metering costs?

TEAM PRODUCTION

Two men jointly lift heavy cargo into trucks. Solely by observing the total weight loaded per day, it is impossible to determine each person's marginal productivity. With team production it is difficult, solely by observing total output, to either define or determine *each* individual's contribution to this output of the cooperating inputs. The output is yielded by a team, by definition, and it is not a *sum* of separable outputs of each of its members. Team production of Z involves at least two inputs, X_i and X_j, with $\partial^2 Z/\partial X_i \partial X_j \neq 0$.[3] The production function is *not* separable into two functions, each involving only inputs X_i or only inputs X_j. Consequently there is no *sum* of Z of two separable functions to treat as the Z of the team production function. (An example of a *separable* case is $Z = aX_i^2 + bX_j^2$ which is separable into $Z_i = aX_i^2$ and $Z_j = bX_j^2$, and $Z = Z_i + Z_j$. This is not team production.) There exist production techniques in which the Z obtained is greater than if X_i and X_j had produced separable Z. Team production will be used if it yields an output enough larger than the sum of separable production of Z to cover the costs of organizing and disciplining team members – the topics of this paper.[4]

Usual explanations of the gains from cooperative behavior rely on exchange and production in accord with the comparative advantage specialization principle with separable additive production. However, as suggested above, there is a source of gain from cooperative activity involving working as a *team*, wherein individual cooperating inputs do not yield identifiable, separate products which can be *summed* to measure the total output. For this cooperative productive activity, here called "team" production, measuring *marginal* productivity and making payments in accord therewith is more expensive by an order of magnitude than for separable production functions.

Team production, to repeat, is production in which (1) several types of resources are used and (2) the product is not a sum of separable outputs of each cooperating resource. An additional factor creates a team organization problem: (3) not all resources used in team production belong to one person.

We do not inquire into why all the jointly used resources are not owned by one person, but inquire instead into the types of organization, contracts, and informational and payment procedures used among owners of teamed inputs. With respect to the one-owner case, perhaps it is sufficient merely to note that (a) slavery is prohibited, (b) one might assume risk aversion as a reason for one person's not borrowing enough to purchase all the assets or sources of services rather than renting them, and (c) the purchase–resale spread may be so large that costs of short-term ownership exceed rental costs. Our problem is viewed basically as one of organization among different people, not of the physical goods or services, however much there must be selection and choice of combination of the latter.

How can the members of a team be rewarded and induced to work efficiently? In team production, marginal products of cooperative team members are not so directly and separably (i.e., cheaply) observable. What a team offers to the market can be taken as the marginal product of the team but not of the team members. The costs of metering or ascertaining the marginal products of the team's members is what calls forth new organizations and procedures. Clues to each input's productivity can be secured by observing the *behavior* of individual inputs. When lifting cargo into the truck, how rapidly does a man move to the next piece to be loaded, how many cigarette breaks does he take, does the item being lifted tilt downward toward his side?

If detecting such behavior were costless, neither party would have an incentive to shirk, because neither could impose the cost of his shirking on the other (if their cooperation was agreed to voluntarily). But since costs must be incurred to monitor each other, each input owner will have more incentive to shirk when he works as part of a team than if his performance could be monitored easily or if he did not work as a team. If there is a net increase in productivity available by team production, net of the metering cost associated with disciplining the team, then team production will be relied upon rather than a multitude of bilateral exchanges of separable individual outputs.

Both leisure and higher income enter a person's utility function.[5] Hence, each person should adjust his work and realized reward so as to equate the marginal rate of substitution between leisure and production of real output to his marginal rate of substitution in consumption. That is, he would adjust his rate of work to bring his demand prices of leisure and output to equality with their true costs. However, with detection, policing, monitoring, measuring, or metering costs, each person will be induced to take more leisure, because the effect of relaxing on *his realized* (reward) rate of substitution between output and leisure will be less than the effect on the *true* rate of substitution. His realized cost of leisure will fall more than the true cost of leisure, so he "buys" more leisure (i.e., more non-pecuniary reward).

If his relaxation cannot be detected perfectly at zero cost, part of its effects will be borne by others in the team, thus making *his* realized cost of relaxation less than the true total cost to the team. The difficulty of detecting such actions permits the private costs of his actions to be less than their full costs. Since each person responds to his private realizable rate of substitution (in production) rather than the true total (i.e., social) rate, and so long as there are costs for other people to detect his shift toward relaxation, it will not pay (them) to force him to readjust completely by making him realize the true cost. Only enough efforts will be made to equate the marginal gains of detection activity with the marginal costs of detection; and that implies a lower rate of productive effort and more shirking than in a costless monitoring, or measuring, world.

In a university, the faculty use office telephones, paper, and mail for personal uses beyond strict university productivity. The university administrators could stop such practices by identifying *the* responsible person in each case, but they can do so only at higher costs than administrators are willing to incur. The extra costs of identifying each party (rather than merely identifying the presence of such activity) would exceed the savings from diminished faculty "turpitudinal peccadilloes." So the faculty is allowed some degree of "privileges, perquisites, or fringe benefits." And the total of the pecuniary wages paid is lower because of this irreducible (at acceptable costs) degree of amenity-seizing activity. Pay is lower in pecuniary terms and higher in leisure, conveniences, and ease of work. But still every person would prefer to see detection made more effective (if it were somehow possible to monitor costlessly) so that he, as part of the now more effectively producing team, could thereby realize a higher pecuniary pay and less leisure. If everyone could, at zero cost, have his reward-realized rate brought to the true production possibility real rate, all could achieve a more preferred position. But detection of the responsible parties is costly; that cost acts like a tax on work rewards.[6] Viable shirking is the result.

What forms of organizing team production will lower the cost of detecting "performance" (i.e., marginal productivity) and bring personally realized rates of substitution closer to true rates of substitution? Market competition, in principle, could monitor some team production. (It already *organizes* teams.) Input owners who are not team members can offer, in return for a smaller share of the team's rewards, to replace excessively (i.e., overpaid) shirking members. Market competition among potential team members would determine team membership and individual rewards. There would be no team leader, manager, organizer, owner, or employer. For such decentralized organizational control to work, outsiders, possibly after observing each team's total output, can speculate about their capabilities as team members, and, by a market competitive process, revised teams with greater productive ability will be formed and sustained. Incumbent members will be constrained by threats of replacement by outsiders offering services for lower reward shares or offering greater rewards to the other members of the team. Any team member who shirked in the expectation that the reduced output effect would not be attributed to him will be displaced if his activity is detected. Teams of productive inputs, like business units, would evolve in apparent spontaneity in the market – without any central organizing agent, team manager, or boss.

But completely effective control cannot be expected from individualized market competition, for two reasons. First, for this competition to be completely effective, new challengers for team membership must know where, and to what extent, shirking is a serious problem, i.e., know they can increase net output as compared with the inputs they replace. To the extent that this is true, it is probably possible for existing fellow team members to recognize the shirking. But, by definition, the detection of shirking by observing team output is costly for team production. Second, assume the presence of detection costs, and assume that in order to secure a place on the team a new input owner must accept a smaller share of rewards (or a promise to produce more). Then his incentive to shirk would still be at least as great as the incentives of the inputs replaced, because he still bears less than the entire reduction in team output for which he is responsible.

THE CLASSICAL FIRM

One method of reducing shirking is for someone to specialize as a monitor to check the input performance of team members.[7] But who will monitor the monitor? One constraint on the monitor is the aforesaid market competition offered by other monitors, but for reasons already given, that is not perfectly effective. Another constraint can be imposed on the monitor: give him title to the net earnings of the team, net of payments to other inputs. If owners of cooperating inputs agree with the monitor that he is to receive any residual product above prescribed amounts (hopefully, the marginal value products of the other inputs), the monitor will have an added incentive not to shirk as a monitor. Specialization in monitoring plus reliance on a residual claimant status will reduce shirking; but additional links are needed to forge the firm of classical economic theory. How will the residual claimant monitor the other inputs?

We use the term "monitor" to connote several activities in addition to its disciplinary connotation. It connotes measuring output performance, apportioning rewards, observing the input behavior of inputs as means of detecting or estimating their marginal productivity, and giving assignments or instructions in what to do and how to do it. (It also includes, as we shall show later, authority to terminate or revise contracts.) Perhaps the contrast between a football coach and team captain is helpful. The coach selects strategies and tactics and sends in instructions about what plays to utilize. The captain is essentially an observer and reporter of the performance at close hand of the members. The latter is an inspector/steward and the former a supervisor manager. For the present, all these activities are included in the rubric "monitoring." All these tasks are, in principle, negotiable across markets, but we are presuming that such market measurement of marginal productivities and job reassignments are not so cheaply performed for team production. And in particular, our analysis suggests that it is not so much the costs of spontaneously negotiating contracts in the markets among groups for team production as it is the detection of the performance of individual members of the team that calls for the organization noted here.

The specialist *who receives the residual rewards* will be the monitor of the members of the team (i.e., will manage the use of cooperative inputs). The monitor earns his residual through the reduction in shirking that he brings about, not only by the prices that he agrees to pay the owners of the inputs, but also by observing and directing the actions or uses of these inputs. *Managing or examining the ways to which inputs are used in team production is a method of metering the marginal productivity of individual inputs to the team's output.*

To discipline team members and reduce shirking, the residual claimant must have power to revise the contract terms and incentives of *individual* members without having to terminate or alter every other input's contract. Hence, team members who seek to increase their productivity will assign to the monitor not only the residual claimant right but also the right to alter individual membership and performance on the team. Each team member, of course, can terminate his own membership (i.e., quit the team), but only the monitor may unilaterally terminate the membership of any of the other members without necessarily terminating the team itself or his association with the team; and he alone can expand or reduce membership, alter the mix of membership, or sell the right to be the residual claimant–monitor of the team. It is this entire bundle of rights, (1) to be a residual claimant; (2) to observe input behavior; (3) to be the central party common to all contracts with inputs; (4) to alter the membership of the team; and (5) to sell these rights, that defines the *ownership* (or the employer) of the *classical* (capitalist, free-enterprise) firm. The coalescing of these rights has arisen, our analysis asserts, because it resolves the shirking-information problem of team production better than does the non-centralized contractual arrangement.

The relationship of each team member to the *owner* of the firm (i.e., the party common to all input contracts *and* the residual claimant) is simply a "quid pro quo" contract. Each makes a purchase and sale. The employee "orders" the owner of the team to pay him money in the same sense that the employer directs the team member to perform certain acts. The employee can terminate the contract as readily as can the employer, and long-term contracts, therefore, are not an essential attribute of the firm. Nor are "authoritarian," "dictational," or "fiat" attributes relevant to the conception of the firm or its efficiency.

In summary, two necessary conditions exist for the emergence of the firm on the prior assumption that more than pecuniary wealth enters utility functions. (1) It is possible to increase productivity through team-oriented production, a production technique for which it is costly to directly measure the marginal outputs of the cooperating inputs. This makes it more difficult to restrict shirking through simple market exchange between cooperating inputs. (2) It is economical to estimate marginal productivity by observing or specifying input behavior. The simultaneous occurrence of both these preconditions leads to the contractual organization of inputs, known as the *classical capitalist firms* with (a) joint input production, (b) several input owners, (c) one party who is common to all the contracts of the joint inputs, (d) who has rights to renegotiate any input's contract independently of contracts with other input owners, (e) who holds the residual claim, and (f) who has the right to sell his central contractual residual status.[8]

OTHER THEORIES OF THE FIRM

At this juncture, as an aside, we briefly place this theory of the firm in the contexts of those offered by Ronald Coase and Frank Knight.[9] Our view of the firm is not necessarily inconsistent with Coase's; we attempt to go further and identify refutable implications. Coase's penetrating insight is to make more of the fact that markets do not operate costlessly, and he relies on the cost of using markets to *form* contracts as his basic explanation for the existence of firms. We do not disagree with the proposition that, *ceteris paribus*, the higher is the cost of transacting across markets, the greater will be the comparative advantage of organizing resources within the firm; it is a difficult proposition to disagree with or to refute. We could with equal ease subscribe to a theory of the firm based on the cost of managing, for surely it is true that, *ceteris paribus*, the lower is the cost of managing, the greater will be the comparative advantage of organizing resources within the firm. To move the theory forward, it is necessary to know what is meant by a firm and to explain the circumstances under which the cost of "managing" resources is low relative to the cost of allocating resources through market transaction. The conception of and rationale for the classical firm that we propose takes a step down the path pointed out by Coase toward that goal. Consideration of team production, team organization, difficulty in metering outputs, and the problem of shirking are important to our explanation but, so far as we can ascertain, not to Coase's. Coase's analysis, insofar as it had heretofore been developed, would suggest open-ended contracts but does not appear to imply anything more – neither the residual claimant status nor the distinction between employee and subcontractor status (nor any of the implications indicated below). And it is not true that employees are generally employed on the basis of long-term contractual arrangements any more than on a series of short-term or indefinite length contracts.

The importance of our proposed additional elements is revealed, for example, by the explanation of why the person to whom the control monitor is responsible receives the residual, and also by our later discussion of the implications about the corporation, partnerships, and profit sharing. These alternative forms for organization of the firm are difficult to resolve on the basis of market transaction costs only. Our exposition also suggests a definition of the classical firm – something crucial that was heretofore absent.

In addition, sometimes a technological development will lower the cost of market transactions while, at the same time, it expands the role of the firm. When the "putting out" system was used for weaving, inputs were organized largely through market negotiations. With the development of efficient central sources of power, it became economical to perform weaving in proximity to the power source and to engage in team production. The bringing in of weavers surely must have resulted in a reduction in the cost of negotiating (forming) contracts. Yet, what we observe is the beginning of the factory system in which inputs are organized within a firm. Why? The weavers did not simply move to a common source of power which they could tap like an electric line, purchasing power while they used their own equipment. Now team production in the joint use of equipment became more important. The measurement of marginal productivity, which now involved interactions between workers, especially through their joint use of machines, became more difficult though contract negotiating cost was reduced, while managing the *behavior* of inputs became easier because of the increased centralization of activity. The firm as an organization expanded even though the cost of transactions was reduced by the advent of centralized power. The same could be said for modern assembly lines. Hence the emergence of central power sources expanded the scope of productive activity in which the firm enjoyed a comparative advantage as an organizational form.

Some economists, following Knight, have identified the bearing of risks of wealth changes with the director or central employer without explaining why that is a viable arrangement. Presumably, the more risk-averse inputs become employees rather than owners of the classical firm. Risk averseness and uncertainty *with regard to the firm's fortunes* have little, if anything, to do with our explanation, although they help to explain why all resources in a team are not owned by one person. That is, the role of risk, taken in the sense of absorbing the windfalls that buffet the firm because of unforeseen competition, technological change, or fluctuations in demand, is not central to our theory, although it is true that imperfect knowledge, and therefore risk, in *this* sense of risk, underlies the problem of monitoring team behavior. We deduce the system of paying the manager with a residual claim (the equity) from the desire to have efficient means to reduce shirking so as to make team production economical, and not from the smaller aversion to the risks of enterprise in a dynamic economy. We conjecture that "distribution-of-risk" is not a valid rationale for the *existence* and organization of the *classical* firm.

Although we have emphasized team production as creating a costly metering task and have treated team production as an essential (necessary?) condition for the firm, would not other obstacles to cheap metering also call forth the same kind of contractual arrangement here denoted as a firm? For example, suppose a farmer produces wheat in an easily ascertained quantity but with subtle and difficult-to-detect quality variations determined by how the farmer grew the wheat. A vertical integration could allow a purchaser to control the farmer's behavior in order to more economically estimate productivity. But this is not a case of joint or team production, unless "information" can be considered part of the product. (While a good case could be made for that broader conception of production, we shall ignore it here.) Instead of forming a firm, a buyer can contract to have his inspector on the site of production, just as home builders contract with architects to supervise building contracts; that arrangement is not a firm. Still, a firm might be organized in the production of many products wherein no team production or jointness of use of separately owned resources is involved.

This possibility rather clearly indicates a broader, or complementary, approach to that which we have chosen. (1) As we do in this paper, it can be argued that the firm is the particular policing device utilized when joint team production is present. If other sources of high policing costs arise, as in the wheat case just indicated, some other form of contractual arrangement will be used. Thus, to each source of informational cost there may be a different type of policing and contractual arrangement. (2) On the other hand, one can say that where policing is difficult across markets, various forms of contractual arrangements are devised, but there is no reason for that known as the firm to be uniquely related or even highly correlated with team production, as defined here. It might be used equally probably and viably for other sources of high policing cost. We have not intensively analyzed other sources, and we can only note that our current and readily revisable conjecture is that (1) is valid, and has motivated us in our current endeavor. In any event, the test of the theory advanced here is to see whether the conditions we have identified are necessary for firms to have long-run viability rather than merely births with high infant mortality. Conglomerate firms or collections of separate production agencies into one owning organization can be interpreted as an investment trust or investment diversification device – probably along the lines that motivated Knight's interpretation. A holding company can be called a firm, because of the common association of the word "firm" with any ownership unit that owns income sources. The term "firm" as commonly used is so turgid of meaning that we can not hope to explain every entity to which the name is attached in common or even technical literature. Instead, we seek to identify and explain a particular contractual arrangement induced by the cost of information factors analyzed in this paper.

TYPES OF FIRMS

Profit-sharing firms

Explicit in our explanation of the capitalist firm is the assumption that the cost of *managing* the team's inputs by a central monitor, who disciplines himself because he is a residual claimant, is low relative to the cost of metering the marginal outputs of team members.

If we look within a firm to see who monitors – hires, fires, changes, promotes, and renegotiates – we should find him being a residual claimant or, at least, one whose pay or reward is more than any others correlated with fluctuations in the residual value of the firm. He more likely will have options or rights or bonuses than will inputs with other tasks.

An implicit "auxiliary" assumption of our explanation of the firm is that the cost of team production is increased if the residual claim is not held entirely by the central monitor. That is, we assume that, if profit-sharing had to be relied upon for *all* team members, losses from the resulting increase in central monitor shirking would exceed the output gains from the increased incentives of other team members not to shirk. If the optimal team size is only two owners of inputs, then an equal division of profits and losses between them will leave each with stronger incentives to reduce shirking than if the optimal team size is large, for in the latter case only a smaller percentage of the losses occasioned by the shirker will be borne by him. Incentives to shirk are positively related to the optimal size of the team under an equal profit-sharing scheme.[10]

The preceding does not imply that profit-sharing is never viable. Profit-sharing to encourage self-policing is more appropriate for small teams. And, indeed, where input owners are free to make whatever contractual arrangements suit them, as generally is true in capitalist economies, profit-sharing seems largely limited to partnerships with a relatively small number of *active*[11] partners. Another advantage of such arrangements for smaller teams is that it permits more effective reciprocal monitoring among inputs. Monitoring need not be entirely specialized.

Profit-sharing is more viable if small team size is associated with situations where the cost of specialized management of inputs is large relative to the increased productivity potential in team effort. We conjecture that the cost of managing team inputs increases if the productivity of a team member is difficult to correlate with his behavior. In "artistic" or "professional" work, watching a man's activities is not a good clue to what he is actually thinking or doing with his mind. While it is relatively easy to manage or direct the loading of trucks by a team of dock workers where input activity is so highly related in an obvious way to output, it is more difficult to manage and direct a lawyer in the preparation and presentation of a case. Dock workers can be directed in detail without the monitor himself loading the truck, and assembly line workers can be monitored by varying the speed of the assembly line, but detailed direction in the preparation of a law case would require in much greater degree that the monitor prepare the case himself. As a result, artistic or professional inputs, such as lawyers, advertising specialists, and doctors, will be given relatively freer reign with regard to individual behavior. If the management of inputs is relatively costly, or ineffective, as it would seem to be in these cases, but if team effort is nonetheless more productive than separable production with exchange across markets, then there will develop a tendency to use profit-sharing schemes to provide incentives to avoid shirking.[12]

Socialist firms

We have analyzed the classical proprietorship and the profit-sharing firms in the context of free association and choice of economic organization. Such organizations need not be the most viable when political constraints limit the forms of organization that can be chosen. It is one thing to have profit-sharing when professional or artistic talents are used by small teams. But if political or tax or subsidy considerations induce profit-sharing techniques when these are not otherwise economically justified, then additional management techniques will be developed to help reduce the degree of shirking.

For example, most, if not all, firms in Yugoslavia are owned by the employees in the restricted sense that all share in the residual. This is true for large firms and for firms that employ non-artistic, or non-professional, workers as well. With a decay of political constraints, most of these firms could be expected to rely on paid wages rather than shares in the residual. This rests on our auxiliary assumption that general sharing in the residual results in losses from enhanced shirking by the monitor that exceed the gains from reduced shirking by residual-sharing employees. If this were not so, profit-sharing with employees should have occurred more frequently in Western societies where such organizations are neither banned nor preferred politically. Where residual sharing by employees is politically imposed, as in Yugoslavia, we are led to expect that some management technique will arise to reduce the shirking by the central monitor, a technique that will not be found frequently in Western societies since the monitor retains all (or much) of the residual in the West and profit-sharing is largely confined to small, professional–artistic team production situations. We do find in the larger-scale residual-sharing firms in Yugoslavia that there are employee committees that can recommend (to the state) the termination of a manager's contract (veto his continuance) with the enterprise. We conjecture that the workers' committee is given the right to recommend the termination of the manager's contract precisely because the general sharing of the residual increases "excessively" the manager's incentive to shirk.[13]

The corporation

All firms must initially acquire command over some resources. The corporation does so primarily by selling promises of future returns to those who (as creditors or owners) provide financial capital. In some situations resources can be acquired in advance from consumers by promises of future delivery (for example, advance sale of a proposed book). Or, where the firm is a few artistic or professional persons, each can "chip in" with time and talent until the sale of services brings in revenues. For the most part, capital can be acquired more cheaply if many (risk-averse) investors contribute small portions to a large investment. The economies of raising large sums of equity capital in this way suggest that modifications in the relationship among corporate inputs are required to cope with the shirking problem that arises with profit-sharing among large numbers of corporate stockholders. One modification is limited liability, especially for firms that are large relative to a stockholder's wealth. It serves to protect stockholders from large losses no matter how they are caused.

If every stockowner participated in each decision in a corporation, not only would large bureaucratic costs be incurred, but many would shirk the task of becoming well informed on the issue to be decided, since the losses associated with unexpectedly bad decisions would be borne in large part by the many other corporate shareholders. More effective control of corporate activity is achieved for most purposes by transferring decision authority to a smaller group, whose main function is to negotiate with and manage (renegotiate with) the other inputs of the team. The corporate stockholders retain the authority to revise the membership of the management group and the authority over major decisions that affect the structure of the corporation or its dissolution.

As a result, a new modification of partnerships is induced – the right to sale of corporate shares without approval of any other stockholders. Any shareholder can remove his wealth from control by those with whom he has differences of opinion. Rather than try to control the decisions of the management, which is harder to do with many stockholders than with only a few, unrestricted salability provides a more acceptable escape to each stockholder from continued policies with which he disagrees.

Indeed, the policing of managerial shirking relies on across-market competition from new groups of would-be managers as well as competition from members within the firm who seek to displace existing management. In addition to competition from outside and inside managers, control is facilitated by the temporary congealing of share votes into voting blocs owned by one or a few contenders. Proxy battles or stock-purchases concentrate the votes required to displace the existing management or modify managerial policies. But it is more than a change in policy that is sought by the newly formed financial interests, whether of new stockholders or not. It is the capitalization of expected future benefits into stock prices that concentrates on the innovators the wealth gains of their actions if they own large numbers of shares. Without capitalization of future benefits, there would be less incentive to incur the costs required to exert informed decisive influence on the corporation's policies and managing personnel. Temporarily, the structure of ownership is reformed, moving away from diffused ownership into decisive power blocs, and this is a transient resurgence of the classical firm with power again concentrated in those who have title to the residual.

In assessing the significance of stockholders' power, it is not the usual diffusion of voting power that is significant but instead the frequency with which voting congeals into decisive changes. Even a one-man-owned company may have a long term with just one manager – continuously being approved by the owner. Similarly, a dispersed voting power corporation may be also characterized by a long-lived management. The question is the probability of replacement of the management if it behaves in ways not acceptable to a majority of the stockholders. The unrestricted salability of stock and the transfer of proxies enhances the probability of decisive action in the event current stockholders or any outsider believes that management is not doing a good job with the corporation. We are not comparing the corporate responsiveness to that of a single proprietorship; instead, we are indicating features of the corporate structure that are induced by the problem of delegated authority to manager–monitors.[14]

Mutual and nonprofit firms

The benefits obtained by the new management are greater if the stock can be purchased and sold, because this enables *capitalization* of anticipated future improvements into present *wealth* of new managers who bought stock and created a larger capital by their management changes. But in nonprofit corporations, colleges, churches, country clubs, mutual savings banks, mutual insurance companies, and "coops," the future consequences of improved management are not capitalized into present wealth of stockholders. (As if to make more difficult that competition by new would-be monitors, multiple shares of ownership in those enterprises cannot be bought by one person.) One should, therefore, find greater shirking in nonprofit, mutually owned enterprises. (This suggests that nonprofit enterprises are especially appropriate in realms of endeavor where more shirking is desired and where redirected uses of the enterprise in response to market-revealed values is less desired.)

Partnerships

Team production in artistic or professional intellectual skills will more likely be by partnerships than other types of team production. This amounts to market-organized team activity and to a non-employer status. Self-monitoring partnerships, therefore, will be used rather than employer–employee contracts, and these organizations will be small to prevent an excessive dilution of efforts through shirking. Also, partnerships are more likely to occur among relatives or long-standing acquaintances, not necessarily because they share a common utility function, but also because each knows better the other's work characteristics and tendencies to shirk.

Employee unions

Employee unions, whatever else they do, perform as monitors for employees. Employers monitor employees and similarly employees monitor an employer's performance. Are correct wages paid on time and in good currency? Usually, this is extremely easy to check. But some forms of employer performance are less easy to meter and are more subject to employer shirking. Fringe benefits often are in non-pecuniary, contingent form; medical, hospital, and accident insurance and retirement pensions are contingent payments or performances partly in *kind* by employers to employees. Each employee cannot judge the character of such payments as easily as money wages. Insurance is a contingent payment – what the employee will get upon the contingent event may come as a disappointment. If he could easily determine what other employees had gotten upon such contingent events he could judge more accurately the performance by the employer. He could "trust" the employer not to shirk in such fringe contingent payments, but he would prefer an effective and economic monitor of those payments. We see a specialist monitor – the union employees' agent – hired by them and monitoring those aspects of employer payment most difficult for the employees to monitor. Employees should be willing to employ a specialist monitor to administer such hard-to-detect employer performance, even though their monitor has incentives to use pension and retirement funds not entirely for the benefit of employees.

TEAM SPIRIT AND LOYALTY

Every team member would prefer a team in which no one, not even himself, shirked. Then the true marginal costs and values could be equated to achieve more preferred positions. If one could enhance a common interest in non-shirking in the guise of a team loyalty or team spirit, the team would be more efficient. In those sports where team activity is most clearly exemplified, the sense of loyalty and team spirit is most strongly urged. Obviously the team is better, with team spirit and loyalty, because of the reduced shirking – not because of some other feature inherent in loyalty or spirit as such.[15]

Corporations and business firms try to instill a spirit of loyalty. This should not be viewed simply as a device to increase profits by *over*working or misleading the employees, nor as an adolescent urge for belonging. It promotes a closer approximation to the employees' potentially available true rates of substitution between production and leisure and enables each team member to achieve a more preferred situation. The difficulty, of course, is to create economically that team spirit and loyalty. It can be preached with an aura of moral code of conduct – a morality with literally the same basis as the Ten Commandments – to restrict our conduct toward what we would choose if we bore our full costs.

KINDS OF INPUTS OWNED BY THE FIRM

To this point the discussion has examined why firms, as we have defined them, exist. That is, why is there an owner–employer who is the common party to contracts with other owners of inputs in team activity? The answer to that question should also indicate the kind of the jointly used resources likely to be owned by the central owner–monitor and the kind likely to be hired from people who are not team-owners. Can we identify characteristics or features of various inputs that lead to their being hired or to their being owned by the firm?

How can the residual claimant, the central employer–owner, demonstrate his ability to pay the other hired inputs the promised amount in the event of a loss? He can pay in advance, or he can commit wealth sufficient to cover negative residuals. The latter will take the form of machines, land, buildings, or raw materials committed to the firm. Commitments of labor wealth (i.e., human wealth), given the property rights in people, are less feasible. These considerations suggest that residual claimants – owners of the firm – will be investors of resalable capital equipment in the firm. The goods or inputs more likely to be invested than rented by the owners of the enterprise will have higher resale values relative to the initial cost and will have longer expected use in a firm relative to the economic life of the good.

But beyond these factors are those developed above to explain the existence of the institution known as the firm – the costs of detecting output performance. When a durable resource is used it will have a marginal product and a depreciation. Its use requires payment to cover at least use-induced depreciation; unless that user cost is specifically detectable, payment for it will be demanded in accord with *expected* depreciation. And we can ascertain circumstances for each. An indestructible hammer with a readily detectable marginal product has zero user cost. But suppose that the hammer were destructible, and that careless (which is easier than careful) use is more abusive and causes greater depreciation of the hammer. Suppose in addition that the abuse is easier to detect by observing the way it is used than by observing only the hammer after its use, or by measuring the output scored from a hammer by a laborer. If the hammer were rented and used in the absence of the owner, the depreciation would be greater than if the use were observed by the owner and the user charged in accord with the imposed depreciation. (Careless use is more likely than careful use – if one does not pay for the greater depreciation.) An absentee owner would therefore ask for a higher rental price because of the higher *expected* user cost than if the item were used by the owner. The expectation is higher because of the greater difficulty of observing specific user cost, by inspection of the hammer after use. Renting is therefore in this case more costly than owner use. This is the valid content of the misleading expressions about ownership being more economical than renting – ignoring all other factors that may work in the opposite direction, like tax provision, short-term occupancy, and capital risk avoidance.

Better examples are tools of the trade. Watch repairers, engineers, and carpenters tend to own their own tools, especially if they are portable. Trucks are more likely to be employee-owned than are other equally expensive team inputs because it is relatively cheap for the driver to police the care taken in using a truck. Policing the use of trucks by a nondriver owner is more likely to occur for trucks that are not specialized to one driver, like public transit buses.

The factor with which we are concerned here is one related to the costs of monitoring not only the gross product performance of an input but also the abuse or depreciation inflicted on the input in the course of its use. If depreciation or user cost is more cheaply detected when the owner can see its use than by only seeing the input before and after, there is a force toward owner use rather than renting. Resources whose user cost is harder to detect when used by someone else tend on this count to be owner-used. Absentee ownership, in the lay language, will be less likely. Assume momentarily that labor service cannot be performed in the absence of its owner. The labor owner can more cheaply monitor any abuse of himself than if somehow labor-services could be provided without the labor owner observing its mode of use or knowing what was happening. Also, his incentive to abuse himself is increased if he does not own himself.[16]

The similarity between the preceding analysis and the question of absentee landlordism and of sharecropping arrangements is no accident. The same factors that explain the contractual arrangements known as a firm help to explain the incidence of tenancy, labor hiring, or sharecropping.[17]

FIRMS AS A SPECIALIZED MARKET INSTITUTION FOR COLLECTING, COLLATING, AND SELLING INPUT INFORMATION

The firm serves as a highly specialized surrogate market. Any person contemplating a joint-input activity must search and detect the qualities of available joint inputs. He could contact an employment agency, but that agency in a small town would have little advantage over a large firm with many inputs. The employer, by virtue of monitoring many inputs, acquires special superior information about their productive talents. This aids his *directive* (i.e., market hiring) efficiency. He "sells" his information to employee-inputs as he aids them in ascertaining good input combinations for team activity. Those who work as employees or who rent services to him are using him to discern superior combinations of inputs. Not only does the director–employer "decide" what each input will produce, he also estimates which heterogeneous inputs will work together jointly more efficiently, and he does this in the context of a privately owned market for forming teams. The department store is a firm and is a superior private market. People who shop and work in one town can as well shop and work in a privately owned firm.

This marketing function is obscured in the theoretical literature by the assumption of homogeneous factors. Or it is tacitly left for individuals themselves to do via personal market search, much as if a person had to search without benefit of specialist retailers. Whether or not the firm arose because of this efficient information service, it gives the director–employer more knowledge about the productive talents of the team's inputs, and a basis for superior decisions about efficient or profitable combinations of those heterogeneous resources.

In other words, opportunities for profitable team production by inputs already within the firm may be ascertained more economically and accurately than for resources outside the firm. Superior combinations of inputs can be more economically identified and formed from resources already used in the organization than by obtaining new resources (and knowledge of them) from the outside. Promotion and revision of employee assignments (contracts) will be preferred by a firm to the hiring of new inputs. To the extent that this occurs, there is reason to expect the firm to be able to operate as a conglomerate rather than persist in producing a single product. Efficient production with heterogeneous resources is a result not of having *better* resources but in *knowing more accurately* the relative productive performances of those resources. Poorer resources can be paid less in accord with their inferiority; greater accuracy of knowledge of the potential and actual productive actions of inputs, rather than having high productivity resources, makes a firm (or an assignment of inputs) profitable.[18]

SUMMARY

While ordinary contracts facilitate efficient specialization according to comparative advantage, a special class of contracts among a group of joint inputs to a team production process is commonly used for team production. Instead of multilateral contracts among all the joint inputs' owners, a central common party to a set of bilateral contracts facilitates efficient organization of the joint inputs in team production. The terms of the contracts form the basis of the entity called the firm – especially appropriate for organizing team production processes.

Team productive activity is that in which a union, or a joint use, of inputs yields a larger output than the sum of the products of the separately used inputs. This team production requires – like all other production processes – an assessment of marginal productivities if efficient production is to be achieved. Non-separability of the products of several differently owned joint inputs raises the cost of assessing the marginal productivities of those resources or services of each input owner. Monitoring or metering the productivities to match marginal productivities to costs of inputs and thereby to reduce shirking can be achieved more economically (than by across market bilateral negotiations among inputs) in a firm.

The essence of the classical firm is identified here as a contractual structure with: (1) joint input production; (2) several input owners; (3) one party who is common to all the contracts of the joint inputs; (4) who has rights to renegotiate any input's contract independently of contracts with other input owners; (5) who holds the residual claim; and (6) who has the right to sell this central contractual residual status. The central agent is called the firm's owner and the employer. No authoritarian control is involved; the arrangement is simply a contractual structure subject to continuous renegotiation with the central agent. The contractual structure arises as a means of enhancing the efficient organization of team production. In particular, the ability to detect shirking among owners of jointly used inputs in team production is enhanced (detection costs are reduced) by this arrangement, and the discipline (by revision of contracts) of input owners is made more economic.

Testable implications are suggested by the analysis of different types of organizations – nonprofit, proprietary for profit, unions, cooperatives, partnerships, and by the kinds of inputs that tend to be owned by the firm in contrast to those employed by the firm.

We conclude with a highly conjectural but possibly significant interpretation. As a consequence of the flow of information to the central party (employer), the firm takes on the characteristic of an efficient market in that information about the productive characteristics of a large set of specific inputs is now more cheaply available. Better recombinations or new uses of resources can be more efficiently ascertained than by the conventional search through the general market. In this sense inputs compete with each other within and via a firm rather than solely across markets as conventionally conceived. Emphasis on interfirm competition obscures intrafirm competition among inputs. Conceiving competition as the *revelation and exchange* of knowledge or information about qualities, potential uses of different inputs in different potential applications, indicates that the firm is a device for enchancing competition among sets of input resources as well as a device for more efficiently rewarding the inputs. In contrast to markets and cities which can be viewed as publicly or nonowned market places, the firm can be considered a privately owned market; if so, we could consider the firm and the ordinary market as competing types of markets, competition between private proprietary markets and public or communal markets. Could it be that the market suffers from the defects of communal property rights in organizing and influencing uses of valuable resources?

NOTES

1 To meter means to measure and also to apportion. One can meter (measure) output, and one can also meter (control) the output. We use the word to denote both; the context should indicate which.

2 A producer's wealth would be reduced by the present capitalized value of the future income lost by loss of reputation. Reputation, i.e., credibility, is an asset, which is another way of saying that reliable information about expected performance is both a costly and a valuable good. For acts of God that interfere with contract performance, both parties have incentives to reach a settlement akin to that which would have been reached if such events had been covered by specific contingency clauses. The reason, again, is that a reputation for "honest" dealings – i.e., for actions similar to those that would probably have been reached had the contract provided this contingency – is wealth.

Almost every contract is open-ended in that many contingencies are uncovered. For example, if a fire delays production of a promised product by *A* to *B*, and if *B* contends that *A* has not fulfilled the contract, how is the dispute settled and what recompense, if any, does *A* grant to *B*? A person uninitiated in such questions may be surprised by the extent to which contracts permit either party to escape performance or to nullify the contract. In fact, it is hard to imagine any contract which, when taken solely in terms of its stipulations, could not be evaded by one of the parties. Yet that is the ruling, viable type of contract. Why? Undoubtedly, the best discussion that we have seen on this question is by Stewart Macaulay (1968).

There are means not only of detecting or preventing cheating, but also for deciding how to allocate the losses or gains of unpredictable events or quality of items exchanged. Sales contracts contain warranties, guarantees, collateral, return privileges and penalty clauses for specific non-performance. These are means of assignment of *risks* of losses of cheating. A lower price without warranty – an "as is" purchase – places more of the risk on the buyer while the seller buys insurance against losses of his "cheating." On the other hand, a warranty or return privilege or service contract places more risk on the seller with insurance being bought by the buyer.

3 The function is separable into additive functions if the cross-partial derivative is zero, i.e., if $\partial^2 Z/\partial X_i \partial X_j = 0$.

4 With sufficient generality of notation and conception, this team production function could be formulated as a case of the generalized production function interpretation given by our colleague, E. A. Thompson (1970).

5 More precisely: "if anything other than pecuniary income enters his utility function." Leisure stands for all non-pecuniary income for simplicity of exposition.

6 Do not assume that the sole result of the cost of detecting shirking is one form of payment (more leisure and less take-home money). With several members of the team, each has an incentive to cheat against each other by engaging in more than the average amount of such leisure if the employer can not tell at zero cost which employee is taking more than average. As a result, the total productivity of the team is lowered. Shirking detection costs thus change the form of payment and also result in lower total rewards. Because the cross-partial derivatives are positive, shirking reduces other people's marginal products.

7 What is meant by performance? Input energy, initiative, work attitude, perspiration, rate of exhaustion? Or output? It is the latter that is sought – the *effect* or output. But performance is nicely ambiguous because it suggests both input and output. It is *nicely* ambiguous because, as we shall see, sometimes by inspecting a team member's input activity we can better judge his output effect, perhaps not with complete accuracy but better than by watching the output of the *team*. It is not always the case that watching input activity is the only or best means of detecting, measuring, or monitoring output effects of each team member, but in some cases it is a useful way. For the moment, the word "performance" glosses over these aspects and facilitates concentration on other issues.

8 Removal of (b) converts a capitalist proprietary firm to a socialist firm.

9 Recognition must also be made to the seminal inquiries by Morris Silver and Richard Auster (1969), and by H. B. Malmgren (1961).

10 While the degree to which residual claims are centralized will affect the size of the team, this will be only one of many factors that determine team size, so as an approximation, we can treat team size as exogenously determined. Under certain assumptions about the shape of the "typical" utility function, the incentive to avoid shirking with unequal profit-sharing can be measured by the Herfindahl index.

11 The use of the word "active" will be clarified in our discussion of the corporation, which follows below.

12 Some sharing contracts, like crop sharing, or rental payments based on gross sales in retail stores, come close to profit-sharing. However, it is gross output sharing rather than profit-sharing. We are unable to specify the implications of the difference. We refer the reader to S. N. Cheung (1969).

13 Incidentally, investment activity will be changed. The inability to capitalize the investment value as "take-home" private property *wealth* of the members of the firm means that the benefits of the investment must be taken as annual income by those who are employed at the time of the income. Investment will be confined more to those with shorter life and with higher rates or pay-offs if the alternative of investing is paying out the firm's income to its employees to take home and use as private property. For a development of this proposition, see the papers by Eirik Furobotn and Svetozar Pejovich (1970), and by Pejovich (1969).

14 Instead of thinking of shareholders as joint *owners*, we can think of them as investors, like bondholders, except that the stockholders are more optimistic than bondholders about the enterprise prospects. Instead of buying bonds in the corporation, thus enjoying smaller risks, shareholders prefer to invest funds with a greater realizable return if the firm prospers as expected, but with smaller (possibly negative) returns if the firm performs in a manner closer to that expected by the more pessimistic investor. The pessimistic investors, in turn, regard only the bonds as likely to pay off.

If the entrepreneur–organizer is to raise capital on the best terms to him, it is to his advantage, as well as that of prospective investors, to recognize these differences in expectations. The residual claim on earnings enjoyed by shareholders does not serve the function of enhancing their efficiency as monitors in the general situation. The stockholders are "merely" the less risk-averse or the more optimistic member of the group that finances the firm. Being more optimistic than the average and seeing a higher mean value future return, they are willing to pay more for a certificate that allows them to realize gain on their expectations. One method of doing so is to buy claims to the distribution of returns that "they see," while bondholders, who are more pessimistic, purchase a claim to the distribution that they see as more likely to emerge. Stockholders are then comparable to warrant holders. They care not about the voting rights (usually not attached to warrants); they are in the same position in so far as voting rights are concerned as are bondholders. The only difference is in the probability distribution of rewards and the terms on which they can place their bets.

If we treat bondholders, preferred and convertible preferred stockholders, and common stockholders and warrant holders as simply different classes of investors – differing not only in their risk averseness but also in their beliefs about the probability distribution of the firm's future earnings, why should stockholders be regarded as "owners" in any sense distinct from the other financial investors? The entrepreneur–organizer, who let us assume is the chief operating officer and sole repository of control of the corporation, does not find his authority residing in common stockholders (except in the case of a take-over). Does this type of control make any difference in the way the firm is conducted? Would it make any difference in the kinds of behavior that would be tolerated by competing managers and investors (and we here deliberately refrain from thinking of them as owner–stockholders in the traditional sense)?

Investment old timers recall a significant incidence of nonvoting common stock, now prohibited in corporations whose stock is traded on listed exchanges. (Why prohibited?) The entrepreneur in those days could hold voting shares, while investors held nonvoting shares which in every other respect were identical. Nonvoting shareholders were simply investors devoid of ownership connotations. The control and behavior of inside owners in such corporations has never, so far as we have ascertained, been carefully studied. For example, at the simplest level of interest, does the evidence indicate that nonvoting shareholders fared any worse because of not having voting rights? Did owners permit the nonvoting holders the normal return available to voting shareholders? Though evidence is prohibitively expensive to obtain, it is remarkable that voting and nonvoting shares sold for essentially identical prices, even during some proxy battles. However, our casual evidence deserves no more than interest-initiating weight.

One more point. The facade is deceptive. Instead of nonvoting shares, today we have warrants, convertible preferred stocks, all of which are solely or partly "equity" claims without voting rights, though they could be converted into voting shares.

In sum, is it the case that the stockholder–investor relationship is one emanating from the *division* of *ownership* among several people, or is it that the collection of investment funds from people of varying anticipations is the underlying factor? If the latter, why should any of them be thought of as the owners in whom voting rights, whatever they may signify or however exercisable, should reside in order to enhance efficiency? Why voting rights in any of the outside, participating investors?

Our initial perception of this possibly significant difference in interpretation was precipitated by Henry Manne. A reading of his paper makes it clear that it is hard to understand why an investor who wishes to back and ''share'' in the consequences of some new business should necessarily have to acquire voting power (i.e., power to change the manager–operator) in order to invest in the venture. In fact, we invest in some ventures in the hope that no other stockholders will be so ''foolish'' as to try to toss out the incumbent management. We want him to have the power to stay in office, and for the prospect of sharing in his fortunes we buy nonvoting common stock. Our willingness to invest is enhanced by the knowledge that we can act legally via fraud, embezzlement and other laws to help assure that we outside investors will not be ''milked'' beyond our initial discounted anticipations.

15 *Sports leagues*: Professional sports contests among teams is typically conducted by a *league* of teams. We assume that sports consumers are interested not only in absolute sporting skill but also in skills *relative* to other teams. Being slightly better than opposing teams enables one to claim a major portion of the receipts; the inferior team does not release resources and reduce costs, since they were expected in the play of contest. Hence, absolute skill is developed beyond the equality of marginal investment in sporting skill with its true social marginal value product. It follows there will be a tendency to overinvest in training athletes and developing teams. (''Reverse shirking'' arises, as budding players are induced to overpractice hyperactively relative to the social marginal value of their enhanced skills. To prevent overinvestment, the teams seek an agreement with each other to restrict practice, size of teams, and even pay of the team members (which reduces incentives of young people to overinvest in developing skills). Ideally, if all the contestant teams were owned by one owner, overinvestment in sports would be avoided, much as ownership of common fisheries or underground oil or water reserve would prevent overinvestment. This hyperactivity (to suggest the opposite of shirking) is controlled by the league of teams, wherein the league adopts a common set of constraints on each team's behavior. In effect, the teams are no longer really owned by the team owners but are supervised by them, much as the franchisers of some product. They are not full-fledged owners of their business, including the brand name, and can not ''do what they wish'' as franchises. Comparable to the franchiser is the league commissioner or conference president, who seeks to restrain hyperactivity, as individual team supervisors compete with each other and cause external diseconomies. Such restraints are usually regarded as anti-competitive, anti-social, collusive-cartel devices to restrain free open competition, and reduce players' salaries. However, the interpretation presented here is premised on an attempt to avoid hyperinvestment in team sports production. Of course, the team operators have an incentive, once the league is formed and restraints are placed on hyperinvestment activity, to go further and obtain the private benefits of monopoly restriction. To what extent overinvestment is replaced by monopoly restriction is not yet determinable; nor have we seen an empirical test of these two competing, but mutually consistent, interpretations. (This interpretation of league sports activity was proposed by Earl Thompson and formulated by Michael Canes.) Again, athletic teams clearly exemplify the specialization of monitoring with captains and coaches; a captain detects shirkers while the coach

trains and selects strategies and tactics. Both functions may be centralized in one person.

16 Professional athletes in baseball, football, and basketball, where athletes, having sold their source of service to the team owners then enter into sports activity, are owned by team owners. Here the team owners must monitor the athletes' physical condition and behavior to protect the team owners' wealth. The athlete has *less* (not, *no*) incentive to protect or enhance his athletic prowess since capital value changes have less impact on his own wealth and more on the team owners'. Thus, some athletes sign up for big initial bonuses (representing present capital value of future services). Future salaries are lower by the annuity value of the prepaid "bonus" and hence the athlete has *less* to lose by subsequent abuse of his athletic prowess. Any decline in his subsequent service value would in part be borne by the team owner who owns the players' future service. This does not say these losses of future salaries have no effect on preservation of athletic talent (we are not making a "sunk cost" error). Instead, we assert that the preservation is reduced, not eliminated, because the amount of loss of wealth suffered is smaller. The athlete will spend less to maintain or enhance his prowess thereafter. The effect of this revised incentive system is evidenced in comparisons of the kinds of attention and care imposed on the athletes at the "expense of the team owner" in the case where athletes' future services are owned by the team owner with that where future labor service values are owned by the athlete himself. Why athletes' future athletic services are owned by the team owners rather than being hired is a question we should be able to answer. One presumption is cartelization and monopsony gains to team owners. Another is exactly the theory being expounded in this paper – costs of monitoring production of athletes; we know not on which to rely.

17 The analysis used by Cheung (1969) in explaining the prevalence of share-cropping and land tenancy arrangements is built squarely on the same factors – the costs of detecting output performance of jointly used inputs in team production and the costs of detecting user costs imposed on the various inputs if owner-used or if rented.

18 According to our interpretation, the firm is a specialized surrogate for a market for team use of inputs; it provides superior (i.e., cheaper) collection and collation of knowledge about heterogeneous resources. The greater the set of inputs about which knowledge of performance is being collated within a firm, the greater are the present costs of the collation activity. Then, the larger the firm (market), the greater the attenuation of monitor control. To counter this force, the firm will be divisionalized in ways that economize on those costs – just as will the market be specialized. So far as we can ascertain, other theories of the reasons for firms have no such implications.

In Japan, employees by custom work nearly their entire lives with one firm, and the firm agrees to that expectation. Firms will tend to be large and conglomerate to enable a broader scope of input revision. Each firm is, in effect, a small economy engaging in "intranational and international" trade. Analogously, Americans expect to spend their whole lives in the United States; and the bigger the country, in terms of variety of resources, the easier it is to adjust to changing tastes and circumstances. Japan, with its lifetime employees, should be characterized more by large, conglomerate firms. Presumably, at some size of the firm, specialized knowledge about inputs becomes as expensive to transmit across divisions of the firms as it does across markets to other firms.

REFERENCES

Canes, M. (1970). "A Model of a Sports League." Unpublished doctoral dissertation, UCLA.

Cheung, S. N. (1969). *The Theory of Share Tenancy*. Chicago.

Coase, R. H. (1937). "The Nature of the Firm." *Economica*, 4; reprinted in G. J. Stigler and K. Boulding (eds.), *Readings in Price Theory*. Homewood, Ill., 1952.

Furobotn, E. and Pejovich, S. (1970). "Property Rights and the Behavior of the Firm in a Socialist State." *Zeitschrift für Nationalökonomie*, 30.

Knight, F. H. (1965). *Risk, Uncertainty and Profit*. New York.

Macaulay, S. (1968). "Non-contractual Relations in Business: A Preliminary Study." *American Sociological Review*, 28.

Malmgren, H. B. (1961). "Information, Expectations and the Theory of the Firm." Quarterly Journal of Economics, 75.

Manne, H. (1967). "Our Two Corporation Systems: Law and Economics." *Virginia Law Review*, 53.

Pejovich, S. (1969). "The Firm, Monetary Policy, and Property Rights in a Planned Economy." *Western Economic Journal*, 7.

Silver, M. and Auster, R. (1969). "Entrepreneurship, Profit, and the Limits on Firm Size." *Journal of Business, University of Chicago*, 42.

Thompson, E. A. (1970). "Nonpecuniary Rewards and the Aggregate Production Function." *Review of Economics and Statistics*, 52.

9
The Theory of the Firm Revisited

From the birth of modern economics in 1776 to 1970, a span of almost 200 years, only two works seem to have been written about the theory of the firm that have altered the perspectives of the profession: Knight's *Risk, Uncertainty, and Profit* (1921) and Coase's "The Nature of the Firm" (1937). This neglect is attributable fundamentally to the preoccupation of economists with the price system; the study of the price system, characterized as it is by Marshall's representative firm and Walras's auctioneer, undermines serious consideration of the firm as a problem-solving institution.

Coase's contribution is seminal for several reasons, but certainly for calling attention to the absence of a theory of the existence of the firm and to the importance (to this theory) of the fact that markets do not operate costlessly. Nonetheless, the theory of the firm is still incomplete and unclear in ways that are discussed in the middle part of this paper. A more complete theory of the firm must give greater weight to information cost than is given either in Coase's theory or in theories based on shirking and opportunism. This is discussed in the final part of the paper. Information cost figures importantly in transaction cost theory because information cost is an important component of transaction cost. It also figures importantly in Knight's risk-sharing and in agency theories of the firm. Its importance, however, is more fundamental than even these theories contemplate. It is useful therefore to begin this paper with a discussion of why the costless information that is assumed in the perfect competition model renders the model ineffective for studying the firm.

This paper was presented at a conference at Yale University honoring R. H. Coase on the fiftieth anniversary of the publication of his classic paper, "The Nature of the Firm." Coase himself gave three lectures at the conference; these are referred to in passing in the text. The author wishes to thank Rebecca Demsetz, Kevin James, Ben Klein, George Stigler, Mike Waldman, and Rupert Windisch for useful comments and questions.

PERFECT DECENTRALIZATION

What parades as perfect competition is a model that has much to say about the price system, but little to say about competition or the organization of firms. This probably is due to its intellectual origins in the eighteenth-century debate between mercantilists and free traders. The debate was not about competition per se, and it certainly was not about the organization of the firm. It was about the proper scope of government in the economic affairs of England and Europe. Is central economic planning necessary to avoid chaotic economic conditions? Smith's answer, though preserving a limited role for the state, was persuasively in the negative. The subsequent conflict between ''Smithian'' and dissenting views led to a closer examination of the conditions necessary for the price system to function in a manner that substantiates Smith's arguments. Almost two hundred years later, these conditions became formalized in the perfect competition model.

The intellectual achievement of this model is its complete abstraction from centralized control of the economy (Demsetz, 1982). What is modeled is not competition but extreme decentralization, and one can assess through its use whether extreme decentralization leads to chaotic resource allocation. The actors in this model maximize utility or wealth, and they do so in complete disregard of the decisions of others or, indeed, even the existence of others. The same decisions follow from the same prices (and technology) whether or not anyone else is ''out there'' reacting to these parameters. If such impersonal maximizing behavior is competition, it is a very restricted variety. As Knight points out, doing better than others is not involved. No small amount of mischief has resulted from identifying this model with competition. Its appropriate name is perfect *decentralization*.

Perfect decentralization is realized theoretically through assumptions guaranteeing that authority, or command, plays no role in coordinating resources. The only parameters guiding choice are those that are given – tastes and technologies – and those that are determined impersonally on markets – prices. All parameters are beyond the control of any of the model's actors or institutions, so these assumptions effectively deprive authority of any role in allocation. They are fully justified by the theory's remarkable yield – a compact, coherent, subtle yet simple model for deducing the equilibrium consequences of extreme decentralization of resource ownership. The model is a powerful tool not only for understanding how prices guide decisions in a decentralized economy, but also for assessing the impact of exogenous changes in the parameters that are taken as given by the model. The impact of changes in tax rates or tariffs, or the consequences of price supports, can be deduced with comparative ease.

The model contributes little to our understanding of the workings of a command economy or of political processes that might be structured around authority. Its use in public finance, for example, is to understand how the price system "digests" taxes, not to understand the behavior of political parties. The model also casts little light on legal institutions. Exchange is viewed as taking place without regard to problems of theft or fraud. The property right system, so important to the functioning of the price system, is implicitly assumed to operate costlessly in matters of exchange. These abstractions are defensible because the real objective of the model is to study allocation in the absence of authority.

More to the point of this paper, the model sets the maximizing tasks of the firm in a context in which decisions are made with full and free knowledge of production possibilities and prices. The worldly roles of management – to explore uncertain possibilities and to control resources consciously, where owners of such resources have a penchant for pursuing their own interests – are not easily analyzed in a model in which knowledge is full and free. "Firm" in the theory of price is simply a rhetorical device adopted to facilitate discussion of the price system. Tasks normally to be expected of management are given only the most superficial, formal discussion; they are performed without error and costlessly, as if by a free and perfect computer. The real tasks of management – to devise or discover markets, products, and production techniques, and actively to manage the actions of employees – have no place in the perfect decentralization model because it assumes that all products, markets, production techniques, and prices are fully known at zero cost.

The only management task that seems to remain, and which is the focus of attention in the firm of traditional price theory, is the selection of profit-maximizing quantities of outputs and inputs. But, since the required information for doing this is also freely in hand, and the required calculations are costless to make, the model strips management of any meaningful productivity in the performance of even these tasks. The *cost of maximizing* is ignored or implicitly assumed to be zero. De facto, the resources that might be required to make maximizing decisions are treated as if they are not scarce.[1]

The sole (seeming) exception to this generalization is the rationale sometimes adopted to justify U-shaped average cost curves – diminishing returns to "entrepreneurial capacity." Entrepreneurial decision capacity is assumed to be limited, and therefore costly. Because this capacity cannot be increased in proportion to increases in other inputs, cost curves ultimately turn up. However, this rationale is inconsistent with the model's assumptions, and it must be thought of as ad hoc and exogenous. The model assumes free and full information about technical relationships and prices, thus making it difficult to rationalize why size of the firm should affect the owner/entrepreneur's decision-making capacities.[2]

The absence of substantive managed coordination is the *sine qua non* of the perfect decentralization model. This is its intellectual achievement and its source of strength in providing an understanding of the price system in a situation of extreme decentralization. It is its source of weakness in analyzing managed coordination. Clearly, our understanding of firms can be improved by recognizing that management is a scarce resource employed in a world in which knowledge is incomplete and costly to obtain. This is explicitly recognized by Knight and Coase, and it is an important component of theories based on monitoring cost. Knight's analysis of the firm as an institution for efficient risk-sharing is based on risk aversion and costly knowledge; Coase's theory, known as the transaction cost theory of the firm, has as its central theme the relevance of costly managing and exchanging, which certainly contains important components of information cost.

THE TRANSACTION COST THEORY OF THE FIRM: SOME PROBLEMS

Before turning to a discussion of transaction cost theory, it is desirable to clarify terminology. Throughout this paper, I use "transaction cost" and "management cost" to refer to the costs of organizing resources, respectively, across markets and within firms. This accords with Coase's terminology. Recent writings on the theory of the firm sometimes use "transaction cost" to refer indiscriminately to organizational costs whether these arise from within the firm or across the market. This rather inept language forces textual discussion to make distinctions that would be better left to single word labels. For example, Williamson frequently is forced to use phrases such as "the governance costs of internal organization exceed those of market organization." If readers feel more comfortable with the newer terminology, although I cannot see why they should, they may translate my use of management and transaction costs for the governance costs, respectively, of organization achieved through firms and organization achieved across markets.

The early development of the transaction cost paradigm deals with the question of the existence of firms. Why do firms emerge as viable institutions when the perfect decentralization model amply demonstrates the allocative proficiency of the prices that emerge from impersonal markets? The question is asked and answered by Coase. Profit maximization (or efficiency) requires the substitution of firms for markets if the cost of using markets becomes large relative to the cost of managing. With compelling skill, Coase plays transaction cost against management cost to arrive at the formal condition that defines the extent of the firm. Equality between the marginal values of these costs, with respect to extending the tasks undertaken by the firm, defines a boundary on one side of which resources are managed within the firm and on the other side of which they are price-directed across markets. This comparison of transaction and management costs has become the focusing conceptualization of the transaction cost theory in all applications to the theory of the firm of which I am aware. Difficulties with it have gone unrecognized. Some of these are discussed next.

It is not so easy to distinguish purchase across a market from in-house production because in-house production involves the use of inputs that are *purchased*. Purchasing inputs (across markets) is substituted for purchasing goods that are more nearly complete (across markets). Hence, in-house production does not constitute a clear elimination of transaction cost. Similarly, purchasing goods from another firm, rather than producing these in-house, involves an implicit purchase of the management services undertaken by the other firm, so management cost is not eliminated by purchasing more nearly complete goods across markets. The correct question to ask, if we remain within the Coasian framework, is not whether management cost is more or less than transaction cost, but whether the sum of management and transaction cost incurred through in-house production is more or less than the sum of management and transaction cost incurred through purchase across markets, since either option entails expenditures on both cost categories.

This problem can be considered from a slightly different angle. If transaction cost is zero yet management cost is positive, the transaction cost theory predicts the demise of the firm. But what can this mean? It can mean only that each individual acts as a firm, selling the output of his efforts to other individuals acting in similar fashion. But it is a mistaken belief of the transaction cost theory that this organization of production eliminates management cost. Management is not eliminated, except, perhaps, by definition. It is functioning in more diffuse fashion across very many firms, since management cost is incurred by each such individual as he plans and executes his production activities unless the meaning of management is restricted to dealing with others.

Moreover, the inference drawn, that all production is individualized if transaction cost is zero, is wrong. Whether individuals act independently, as just described, or cooperate through a multi-person firm depends on the extent of scale economies to management. Multi-person firms are fully consistent with zero transaction cost if management is subject to scale economies. Zero transaction cost informs us only that these cooperating efforts will be organized with greater reliance on explicit negotiations than would be true if transaction cost were positive. Greater reliance on explicit negotiations may be of importance in some contexts but not others. The difference between these organizing techniques does not carry substantive consequences if the cooperating individuals would perform essentially the same actions, with the same continuity of association over time, when they rely on a series of explicit transitory negotiations as when they rely on an "employment contract." In either case, the substance of the firm is reflected in the style of cooperative behavior that obtains. This may be the same with both organizing techniques.

Another informative way to view the problem is to recognize that the output of another firm can be purchased, or, in substitution for this, that the other firm can be purchased. Purchasing the other firm is in-house production because it amounts to the purchase of the inputs required to produce the good. If transaction cost is assumed to be zero while management cost is assumed to be positive, the answer given by transaction cost theory is to purchase the good, for it will cost something to manage in-house production. But there is a cost to managing the other firm when it stands independently, and this cost must factor into the price of the good that is to be purchased. This implicit management cost must be paid whether the firm or its output is purchased. Hence, the decision rests on a traditional consideration – is management subject to economies of scale? And, in the more realistic context in which management, transaction, and production costs are all assumed to be positive, the correct decision is reached by assessing whether merger or independent production yields the lowest unit cost, taking all these costs into account, over the relevant range of output. Transaction cost is relevant to this judgment, but so are the other costs.

The degree to which coordination is vertically decentralized is no longer simply a matter of transaction cost, or even of transaction cost relative to management cost. Firms purchase inputs when they can secure them more cheaply than by producing them. The cost of transacting is one element of the cost of purchasing from others, but only one. There are a variety of others, including what we ordinarily call production costs. A firm purchases an input if the price asked for the input, which reflects the production cost of prospective sellers, when added to the costs of transacting and transporting, comes to less than the cost of making the input in-house. Thus, to say that firms produce their own inputs when it is cheaper to do so is *not* equivalent to saying that firms will purchase from others if the cost of transacting is less than the cost of managing. The decision also hinges on the internal costs of production that burden the potential purchaser and supplier. Quite simply, it depends on a comparison of *all* the gains and losses that attach to external procurement relative to in-house production. Indeed, an increase in the cost of transacting leads not to a substitution of managed coordination for market coordination, as users of the transaction cost theory assert, but to a substitution of managed coordination within fewer, larger, firms for managed coordination in more numerous, smaller, firms. *Managed* transfer of inputs between the departments of a (now larger) firm is substituted for *managed* buying and selling. One type of management substitutes for another.

It is with respect to the above points that new terminology is especially confusing. By using governance or transaction costs to refer to all costs, whether they be within the firm or across markets, it is easy to assert that the newer writings utilizing transaction cost theory refer to the necessity for taking account of all costs (at least of all costs of organizing). If so, have we come to the point of saying that firms are used when they are cheaper, all costs considered, but not when markets are cheaper? I am quite prepared to accept this position for what it is worth, but my point is that it deprives transaction cost theory of any predictive content. Moreover, the broader considerations that occupy some of the newer writings about the firm puts them at some distance from the transaction cost theory being discussed here. For example, Williamson (1985) uses the first part of his book about the institutions of capitalism to claim that its foundation lies in transaction cost considerations, but he fails to make substantive use of transaction cost throughout the remainder of the book. The only link to predictive content that remains is to be found in asset specificity, which he interprets to imply higher cost of using market governance of activities. But, as I argue later, and as Coase himself argues, the linkage is weak.

The emphasis that has been given to transaction cost (or that has been claimed to be given) dims our view of the full picture by implicitly assuming that all firms can produce goods or services equally well. ''Implicitly,'' because the ''other'' firm is represented by the ''market,'' and the market is treated as a perfect substitute in production for a firm. The only comparison sought is between the cost of transacting across this market and the cost of in-house managing. Since firms may not be perfect substitutes in the production of goods and services, and since they generally will not be if information cost is positive, it might be in the interest of a firm to produce its own inputs even if transaction costs were zero and management costs were positive. The production cost of other firms might simply be so high as to make in-house production superior to relying on these other firms. Or, if the production cost incurred by other firms is sufficiently low, it might serve the firm to purchase its inputs even though the cost of managing in-house production is zero.[3]

The confusion that exists in the literature derives from a hidden presumption that we are still guided by the perfect decentralization model, and that, in some respects, information remains full and free. Although information is treated as being costly for transaction or management control purposes, it is implicitly presumed to be free for production purposes. What one firm can produce, another can produce equally well, so the make-or-buy decision is not allowed to turn on differences in production cost. The only choice criterion that remains is that which compares transaction and in-house management costs, or, more correctly, the sum of these costs in each alternative offered by the make-or-buy choice. In this manner, the transaction cost theory of the firm ignores differences between firms when these lie outside the control function and discourages a search for such differences. Merged firms may be unable to duplicate the sum of what independently standing firms can accomplish for a variety of reasons, and many of these may be resistant to an analysis that is guided by the management and transaction cost categories. Productivity may be affected by considerations that are not plausibly included in these cost categories. Each firm is a bundle of commitments to technology, personnel, and methods, all contained and constrained by an insulating layer of information that is specific to the firm, and this bundle cannot be altered or imitated easily or quickly. The components of this bundle that are emphasized by transaction cost theory are important, but not exclusively so.

In a brief general critique of transaction cost theory, such as this, there is bound to be some oversimplification and some neglect of more subtle uses of the theory. Justice cannot be done to everyone who has used the theory in a broader sense than the interpretation given to it here. Nonetheless, the main emphasis and usage of transaction cost theory surely is to compare transaction and management costs so that conclusions may be drawn about organization. This emphasis has led to the neglect of other determinants of economic organization (one of which is discussed below), even though some of these are mentioned in passing, as it were, by those who make (or claim to make) transaction cost theory their paradigm of institutional organization. It is the paradigmatic use of transaction cost theory that is at issue here.[4]

Beyond considerations of production functions and the total cost of organization, the power of transaction cost theory turns on our ability to make it operational and to bring it to bear on substantive issues. This is not so easily done. It is difficult to discuss the relevance of transaction, management, and production costs without a clear distinction between these, and none is provided. One person phones another and directs him to purchase specific assets by a certain time if they can be acquired for less than a stipulated price. Is this activity transacting or managing? Knowing the answer would allow us to determine if an increase in the cost of this activity is expected to lead to the substitution of one firm for two or two for one. Since the call might be from an owner/manager of a firm to his employee in the purchasing department or from a customer/investor to the brokerage house whose services he purchases, it is hard to know whether we are dealing with a transaction or management cost until we *already know* whether we are discussing a firm or a market. This is true for the general case even though it might be possible in a specific instance, such as in the case of a tax on transactions, to be certain that we are dealing with only one of these costs. This makes it difficult to use the magnitude of "transaction" cost relative to "management" cost to predict how changed circumstances affect economic organization. The inherent difficulty is that the same organizing activities often characterize exchange *and* management.

Assuming that the problem of disentangling these costs is somehow resolved, there is still the problem of being able to stipulate the conditions that tend to make the relative magnitude of these costs high or low. This is necessary if we are to apply the theory of transacting positively to explain the structure of economic organization. Does an increase in the size of the market decrease transaction cost relative to management cost? Does dealing in services rather than products? Does dealing across national boundaries? Questions such as these must have answers about which we are confident if the transaction cost theory of the firm is to be applicable to the study of firms. As of now, we know very little about the forces that might influence the relative magnitude of these costs.

Klein, Crawford, and Alchian (1978), Riordan and Williamson (1985), and Williamson (1985) adopt the view that asset specificity is one such force. Asset specificity raises the prospect for opportunism. This heightened prospect is presumed to raise the cost of transacting. I am not sure that it costs (much) more to detail the terms of a contract when asset specificity is involved than when it is not. Even if it does, the change in the cost of contracting is unlikely to be very great. Asset specificity problems may be almost as easy to resolve through contract as through vertical integration, the latter being the option preferred by these authors. Truth is, it is not a predictably significant variation in transaction cost that motivates the vertical integration solution offered by these authors: it is the presumption that losses are greater if an agreement fails when asset specificity is involved than when it is not. This can be the case (although I am not sure that it is) even if transaction cost is unaffected by the presence or absence of asset specificity. It is simpler and less misleading to state that asset specificity increases the loss attendant on failure of agreement than that it increases the cost of transacting.

If we suppose that activities that increase transaction cost are distinguishable from those that increase management cost, there remains a problem of understanding just which issues are illuminated by using transaction cost theory. Consider the long-term contract that Coase identifies with the employment relationship. From Coase's perspective, costly transactions lead to greater reliance on longer-term contracts. The firm hires an employee for a duration rather than for each day or for each instant. There is much truth to this, but (in principle at least), since employees can quit at any instant, or be fired, we have a long-term arrangement only because it is in the interest of both parties to continue in association. The avoidance of costly transacting is part of the motivation for this interest, but our focus on this has led us to ignore other, possibly more important, reasons for continued association. If these other reasons exist, and some are discussed below, then a durable association replicating that achievable through a long-term contract would be sought even if transaction cost were zero. A series of costless transitory market negotiations would bring the same employers and employees together, so that, de facto, the firm that is characterized in terms of employment contracts would be achieved through repeated market negotiations. The same behavioral interrelationship might arise when transaction cost is zero as when it is positive. If we conceive of "the" firm as a set of particular behavioral interactions guided by agreements of one sort or another, transaction cost would then determine only how the firm is achieved, not whether it exists. How the firm is achieved is of interest in some contexts, but the behavior that characterizes the firm, which may be achieved through a variety of contractual arrangements, would seem to be a substantive issue determined by considerations that go beyond those highlighted by the transaction cost theory of the firm.

MORAL HAZARD, SHIRKING, AND OPPORTUNISM

Writings about the theory of the firm began to diverge from the simple transaction cost format during the 1970s. Increasing attention was given to the problem of achieving incentive alignment. Attention began turning toward the issue raised by Berle and Means (1932) in *The Modern Corporation and Private Property* – the alleged separation between ownership and control – with the important difference that, unlike for Berle and Means, the task became one of understanding how firms organize to resolve the problem. The recent investigation of the ownership structure of the firm undertaken by Ken Lehn and myself (Demsetz and Lehn, 1985) is a continuation of this line of development.

This issue does not permit one to ignore the task of understanding the inner organization of the firm, whereas the transaction cost approach encourages one to dwell on questions like, Why do firms exist? or Why is there vertical integration? Moral hazard analysis, shirking, and opportunism – the problems of incentive compatibility – yield explanations of the internal organization of the firm that are difficult to derive from transaction cost considerations alone. It is true that transaction cost is involved in the existence of these problems, at least for a (too) broad definition of transaction cost.[5] They presuppose a positive cost of negotiating them completely out of existence. However, the role of transaction cost in explaining the manner in which organization responds to these problems is like the role of gravity in explaining chemical reactions; gravity influences chemical reactions, but seldom is it the key variable whose behavior importantly explains variations in the reactions observed.

Thus, Alchian and Demsetz (1972) rely on differences in shirking opportunities to understand the organization of the firm, rather than differences in transaction cost. Their focus is on how the organization of the firm can be accounted for by the differences in the monitoring needs that result.[6] Similarly, as discussed above, the literature on opportunism really relies on a presumed correlation between asset specificity and the loss to be expected from contract failure, and not on variations in transaction cost. The organizations selected and the incentive systems brought into play to moderate incentive incompatibilities are analyzed through variations in the nature of the monitoring problem that is faced, not through variations in the cost of transacting. It is because of this that incentive incompatibilities offer an alternative to transaction cost analysis in the developing theory of the firm, even though transaction cost is embedded in the organization problem. However, the shirking–opportunism alternative has shortcomings of its own. These are now outlined briefly.

Alchian and Demsetz view shirking as an activity to which firm-like organization (to be discussed more fully below) is particularly susceptible. This is because the revenues of the firm must be shared by the various owners of inputs used by the firm without the full guidance or protection normally offered by intervening competitive markets. These markets would exist if the firm purchased goods from other firms rather than producing them in-house. The centralization of production in firm-like (team) organization therefore is more productive under particular conditions if it survives in the face of the greater shirking costs it must bear. The reason for firm-like production is to be found in the special productivity it offers in some circumstances. Alas, although Alchian and Demsetz make this clear, they fail to discuss the sources of this special productivity. Abating the cost of shirking helps explain the firm's inner organization but provides no rationale for the firm's existence. The extension of this analysis to general agency problems (Jensen and Meckling, 1976) fails to remedy this defect.

The literature on post-contractual opportunistic behavior extends the notion of shirking to contractual exchange, but it takes a position that is different from, and possibly contrary to, Alchian and Demsetz. Thus, Klein, Crawford, and Alchian (and Riordan and Williamson also) lean toward a position in which firm-like production, through vertical integration, reduces the severity of opportunism in the presence of asset specificity. This position implicitly views market contracting as bearing the special costs of opportunism (shirking across markets), but then an explanation is needed as to why markets exist if firm-like organization reduces the cost of opportunism more than does the market. The existence of markets is rationalized by the belief that they offer "high-powered" incentives not provided by the firm, but Alchian and Demsetz view the keener incentives offered by the market as a reason why firms are subject to more shirking than are markets! This brings us to the awkward position of stating that firm-like organization is preferred when the advantages of managing opportunism internally outweigh the advantages of managing them through markets; that is, firm organization is preferred when it is superior.

This awkwardness is alleviated somewhat by the fact that Alchian and Demsetz stress team production without special reference to vertical relationships; their emphasis is on the problem of free-riding when production is joint, even when this "jointedness" occurs within a single "horizontal" activity level. The literature on opportunism stresses vertical relationships, and the emphasis is on reneging or guile. It may well be that firm-like organization raises the cost of dealing with free-riding while lowering the cost of dealing with guile. Awkwardness might also be alleviated by asset specificity considerations, for asset specificity can be used to index those situations in which firm-like organization has more of an advantage (but, as Coase points out in his lectures, possibly not enough of an advantage). As of now, this is a frail reed upon which to build a theory of the firm. It is silent in regard to the survivability of firm-like organization in the absence of asset specificity, and it is directed primarily at explaining the vertical depth of firms rather than the existence of firms or other aspects of their internal organization. Moreover (as Coase also points out in his lectures), the opportunism that is associated with asset specificity may be easier to resolve through contract stipulation.

Perhaps more important, asset specificity may reduce the non-opportunistic costs of maintaining vertically separated organizations. There is less need to manage (through vertical integration) the coordination of assets when they are "dedicated" to specific uses, as they are likely to be under conditions of asset specificity. In such a case, if the legal system is a sufficiently good enforcer of contracts, asset specificity may give rise to vertical disintegration.

The major use to which asset specificity has been put is to make the predictive statement that vertical integration is more likely when assets are specific, vertical integration being presumed to circumvent the opportunistic problems caused by asset specificity. Riordan and Williamson (1985) adopt this position in their commendable attempt to make predictive statements about vertical integration. Their claim is that, when conditions are such as to require asset specificity to achieve low-cost production, vertical integration is more likely.

But there is more to asset specificity than what is contemplated in their paper (and in the important paper by Klein, Crawford, and Alchian, 1978). Owners and management make commitments to each other in order to solicit many years of devoted service; human capital specificity arises as a result of long tenure (and this specificity may be exacerbated by the use of physical assets that are highly specific). Conditions change, requiring these commitments to be broken if the firm is to survive. Unlike the claim made by the literature on opportunism, owners or top management do not rush out to break these commitments. They seek to keep them, both for reasons of personal honor and for reasons of continuing to solicit devoted duty from other employees. This is one reason why mergers or takeovers occur. A new broom sweeps clean, and these commitments give way to the exigencies of economic conditions.[7] Such is the claim of much of the writings about takeovers. Here we find mergers (initially) taking place to facilitate opportunism toward those who have invested in human capital. Behavior that is opportunistic toward employees is facilitated through mergers, possibly vertical ones, by bringing in new owners and management who are personally free of these past commitments.

There is much more to the problem of economic organization than is plausibly subsumed under transaction and monitoring cost. Perhaps the transaction and monitoring approaches to the theory of the firm have confined our search too much. Firms would exist in a world in which transaction and monitoring costs are zero, although their organization might be considerably different. In the space that remains, I consider an alternative approach, one based on aspects of information cost considerations that are different from those captured by transaction and monitoring costs. No well developed model is offered. My intent is only to illustrate one way in which we have ignored considerations that seem important to a theory of the firm. It is desirable first to give some notion of what it is that we wish to explain with a theory of the firm.

FIRM-LIKE ORGANIZATION

The firm properly viewed is a "nexus" of contracts. Our interest might center on explaining (1) the persistence of certain types of contracts that are found in this nexus, (2) the variation observed in other types of contracts that are "more or less" included in this nexus, and (3) the (horizontal and vertical) scope of activities covered by these contracts. No doubt this list can be extended greatly. For example, we might want to understand the relationship between the existence of firm-like contracts and problems of unemployment and politics. Past and current interest in the existence, the internal organization, and the vertical and horizontal scope of "the firm" fit comfortably into the three areas of inquiry listed above, and it is in these that I wish to show that information cost has relevance that extends beyond its significance in transaction cost and moral hazard problems.

The defining content of the nexus of contracts referred to above remains rather vague in literature on the theory of the firm.[8] We may as well recognize that we have no clear notion of firm-like contractual arrangements, especially since we now recognize the difficulty of distinguishing between coordination achieved "across markets" and coordination achieved "within firms." It might be useful to adopt legal notions of what a firm is and what it is not, for there do arise cases in which this determination has been called forth because of the important impact it has on which body of law determines the liabilities of the parties involved. I prefer instead to identify three aspects of the nexus of contracts that plausibly influence firm-like coordination. (At least two of them receive mention in case law.) These aspects of firm-like contractual arrangements brush aside the question of absolutes – When is a nexus of contracts *a firm*? – and substitute instead a question of relatives – When is a nexus of contracts *more firm-like*?

A common feature of corporate charters is a statement about the business of the firm. While this may change over time, one aspect that persists is that the firm produces goods that are to be sold. This implies an agreement to *specialize*, by which I mean to produce mainly for persons who are not members of the firm's team. The complement to this is self-sufficiency or production by and *for* the same persons, which, in the limit, is one person doing for himself without the cooperation of others. Specialization, which can differ in degree between firm-like institutions, is adopted as a characteristic of firm-like contracts in order to maintain compatibility with the theory of price. The firm in the theory of price does not consume what it produces: it sells to others.[9]

The second aspect of the nexus of contracts is the expected length of time of association between the same input owners. Do the contractual agreements entered into contemplate mainly transitory, short-term association, which in the extreme would be characterized by spot market exchanges, or do these agreements contemplate a high probability of continuing association between the same parties? The firm viewed as team production exhibits significant reassociation of the same input owners. The third facet is the degree of conscious direction that is used to guide the uses to which resources are to be put; this is minimal in spot market transactions, but more important in a context in which continuity of association is relied upon. The direction of some by others catches the spirit of managed coordination.

Our interest centers mainly on the cooperative efforts of more than one person, but the one-person firm is not ruled out by these characteristics. The financial advisor, working alone, offers specialized services. Continuity of association and directability of behavior would seem more difficult to imagine in the case of a one-person firm. Still, a person must deal with himself in a relationship that is continuous over a lifetime, and conflicts do arise between the capabilities and tastes of a person today, or in one set of circumstances, and those of the "same" person tomorrow, or in a different set of circumstances. Because of these conflicts, a person somtimes finds it desirable to restrict his activities by entering into binding precommitments that control his future behavior (Thaler and Shefrin, 1981). Deadlines are often accepted as a self-enforcing device, and costs are imposed on future errant (from today's perspective) behavior (as when Christmas savings clubs are joined). The agency problem resides within each of us as well as in interactions between us.

Specialization, continuity of association, and reliance on direction are characteristics of firm-like coordination. They substitute for self-sufficiency and spot markets. These are frequently found characteristics of firm-like organization because they are productive in many circumstances. This productivity derives in part from transaction and monitoring cost considerations, but it also depends on other conditions. Particularly important are the conditions that underlie the acquisition and use of knowledge.

KNOWLEDGE AND THE ORGANIZATION OF SPECIALIZATION

Adam Smith has enshrined forever the idea that specialization is productive, but Smith's focus is on the changes wrought in the individual worker. The problem of how the activities of cooperating specialists are organized so as to mesh better is largely ignored. He ascribes the productivity gains achieved through specialization to three aspects of the division of labor: improvement in dexterity realized by each workman, time saved by avoiding switching from one task to another, and ease with which workmen conceive of innovating improvements when they are steadily occupied in a single task. He writes as if the examples of specialization that he discusses take place within different departments of a firm, but they could also take place across different firms. Indeed, this is the interpretation adopted by Stigler (1951) in his discussion of the impact of market size on vertical integration. It is safe to ignore the organization problem only if the gains achievable through specialization are independent of the way in which specialization is achieved. This seems implausible, and surely would be thought so by Smith, who saw in natural liberty an organizing principle vastly superior to central planning. Even if the details of this organization are best left to the invisible hand of natural liberty, its broad outline is important to the theory of the firm.

Information is also a subject upon which much has been written, at least since Stigler's "The Economics of Information" (1961). It is a subject that has obvious connections to moral hazards and transactions, but here I want to emphasize other, neglected, connections to the theory of the firm. Economic organization, including the firm, must reflect the fact that knowledge is costly to produce, maintain, and use. In all these respects, there are economies to be achieved through specialization. Although the true conglomerate firm is a puzzle, we generally identify industries, and firms in these industries, as repositories of specialized knowledge and of the specialized inputs required to put this knowledge to work. Steel firms specialize in different stocks of knowledge and equipment from those of firms in investment banking or industrial chemicals, and even firms in the same industry differ somewhat in the knowledge and equipment upon which they rely.

Knowledge does not directly convert to utility or living standards. If each of us specialized in a single branch of knowledge, but attempted to use this knowledge without relying on others, the standard of living achievable would be less than if everyone had become a jack-of-all-trades. Although knowledge can be learned more effectively in specialized fashion, its use to achieve high living standards requires that a specialist somehow use the knowledge of other specialists. This cannot be done only by *learning* what others know, for that would undermine gains from specialized learning. It cannot be done only by *purchasing* information in the form of facts, for in many cases the theory that links facts must be mastered if facts are to be put to work.

This difference between the economics of acquiring and using knowledge has profound implications for social organization. "Common knowledge," particularly of language and arithmetic, is useful because its possession allows *greater* specialization. There must be a low-cost method of communicating between specialists and the large number of persons who either are non-specialists or are specialists in other fields. Since this communication cannot consist of extensive education in this knowledge without losing the gains from specialized learning, and since the bare facts contained in this knowledge are often uninterpretable, much communication must consist in the giving of *directions*. These directions may pertain to product use or to work activity. The large cost born to educate masses of persons in language and calculating skills is worth bearing because it facilitates the giving and taking of directions.

Firms and industries must form a pattern of economic organization that takes account of the need for acquiring knowledge in a more specialized fashion than the manner in which it will be used. Those who are to produce on the basis of this knowledge, but are not to be possessed of it themselves, must have their activities *directed* by those who possess (more of) the knowledge. Direction substitutes for education (that is, for the transfer of the knowledge itself). Direction may be purchased through short- or long-run commitments, depending partly on the cost of transacting. In either case, direction is involved, and direction is an important dimension of managed coordination. A second way to put information to work without sacrificing specialization in knowledge is to produce and sell goods that require less information to use than is required to produce them; *direction*, in the form of instructions, is involved, but, unlike the direction of employees, who are expected to respond in details of timing and execution of their assigned tasks, the users of purchased goods have greater discretion about the timing and application of the instructions that accompany purchased goods. The larger the number of different bodies of knowledge that are required to produce a good, or the more specialized the knowledge that is required, the greater the reliance that must be placed on the direction of some by others. The division of this direction between the direction of employees and the direction of buyers of the good is relevant to the issue of vertical integration. The vertical depth of the firm may be considered from the perspective of the need for conserving on information costs. Other costs matter also, but I wish to focus attention on the consequences of costly knowledge, and I wish to do so without reference to the information costs inherent in transaction and moral hazard problems.

Because it is uneconomical to educate persons in one industry in the detailed knowledge used in another, recourse is had to developing or encapsulating this knowledge into products or services that can be transferred between firms cheaply because the instructions needed to use them do not require in-depth knowledge about how they are produced (and because of transport considerations). The economical use of industrial chemicals by steel firms does not generally require knowledge of how these chemicals are produced; similarly, the use of steel by industrial chemical firms does not require transfer of knowledge of how the steel is produced. A production process reaches the stage of yielding a salable product when downstream users can work with, or consume, the "product" without themselves being knowledgeable about its production. Short of this point, it would be necessary to educate downstream users more fully, and this would sacrifice the gains from specialized learning.

However, "products" could continue to be processed into downstream derivatives that are even easier to use. Steel could be set into its structural places by producers rather than by construction companies; this would reduce the need for construction companies to learn the properties of steel that are relevant to riveting and integrating the structure. Steel could be driven for its buyers when they use it in the form of an automobile. The process of further product refinement is halted when the next version of the product will be put to many multiple uses downstream that rely on different bodies of knowledge. A single firm if it were vertically integrated would have difficulty acquiring and maintaining the stocks of knowledge necessary to control cost and quality and to make good managerial decisions when downstream uses are multiple in this sense.

The many uses that are made of steel generally require knowledge that is substantially different from that which is required to produce steel. It is therefore costly to house production of steel in the same firm that is to produce many of these downstream products. Instead, steel is sold. Title passes to others who are masters of the knowledge required to use steel to produce derivative products and services.

Roughly speaking (since other things also matter), the vertical boundaries of a firm are determined by the economics of conservation of expenditures on knowledge. A single firm works a product into new, simpler-to-use (on the basis of directions) products until the diversity of uses further downstream is so great as to require this firm, if it is to continue developing product lines, to bear greater costs of information acquisition and maintenance than are avoided by potential users when there is additional simplication of each product line. Title to "the" product is likely to change hands when this point in the development of product lines is reached; but even if title does not change, further work on derivative products is likely to become the task of other firms. The boundary defining degree of vertical integration will have been established.

It will normally be the case that the boundary suitable for changing title is not coterminous with the point at which one person can economically possess the knowledge required to bring the process to this boundary. Still, the firm that is owned, managed, and operated by a single person is more common than might be supposed. It exists when a person's capacity to absorb knowledge, and to become expert in its use, is great enough for him to learn and use those skills required to bring a product to the boundary at which title is likely to change. The town baker may find it expedient to master knowledge of kitchen chemistry, recipes, and cash accounting himself, and to purchase only ingredients from others. In the more important case, however, the capacity of an individual to acquire and use knowledge is too limited to allow this boundary to be reached without requiring the services of several people each of whom is occupied in a different vertical stage of production.

Economies of scale with respect to number of persons optimally linked to the use of other inputs at any given horizontal level of economic activity may also call for many more than just one person at each stage of production.

Information cost may play a role here also. The giving of directions (in substitution for educating) to others may be subject to scale economies of a limited sort. The utilization of the services of a "direction giver" may demand the presence of several "direction receivers" if these services are to be used efficiently.

This brings us to the question of how these services are secured, and to the issue of continuity of association. In many cases it is not practical to purchase the knowledge itself unless someone is to become expert in it; hence, in one way or another a growing reliance on additional knowledge requires securing the services of additional persons. Such services can be secured through short-term transitory purchases or through long-term, less frequently repeated, purchases. Transaction cost will influence this decision, but it is not the only important consideration. The decision also turns on the productivity *benefits* derivable from different arrangements. Two firms facing the same labor transaction costs may choose different employment arrangements because the benefits they derive from these arrangements differ. Particularly important in determining these benefits are knowledge-based considerations. Continuing association of the same persons makes it easier for firm-specific and person-specific information to be accumulated. (See the large literature on specificity of human capital.) Knowledge about the objectives and organization of the firm is learned "cheaply" through continuing association, and so is knowledge about the capabilities and limitations of the persons involved in this association. Continuing association, however, implies commitment, and commitment has the disadvantage of inflexibility. The benefits to be derived from continuing association must be set against the cost of inflexibility in determining the best manner in which to acquire the talents and services of many persons.

Short-term arrangements become more favorable when firms are more likely to change what they are doing in the important respects of objectives, locations, tasks, and style. Long-term arrangements are more suitable when the conditions under which a firm operates are stable. The considerable changes in quantities and types of labor services required by firms who have been forced to shift from a relatively stable regulated environment to a more volatile unregulated environment reflects these considerations, and my guess is that deregulated firms choose an average continuity of association with the typical employee that is shorter than they chose in a regulated environment.

The complete absence of variability in the tasks that are likely to be required by a firm is an incentive to substitute machinery for personnel. Machinery, being very durable, can be thought of as usable on a continuing basis by the firm. As task variability increases, the inflexibility of machines exacts a toll. Labor services increase in relative productivity. Great variability in the likely uses to which an employee is to be put creates an even stronger need for flexibility, and long-term employment tends to give way to short-term. Thus, while long-term employment relies on the direction of employees in a changing pattern of tasks, great variability in such tasks makes any one employee less suitable than a series of employees each better suited to the immediate requirements of the job. The resulting variation in continuity of association is affected by transaction cost, but it is also affected (more importantly, I believe) by how the relative productivities of tenure change when the stability of the knowledge requirements of an employee changes.

Theories of transaction cost and agency have greatly enriched our understanding of the nature of firm-like organization. Coase's insight into the importance of the cost of using markets helped to stimulate much of the work that has been done on this topic during the last two decades. My concern is that our thinking may be too constrained by our past successes. Some important problems are amenable to solution by application of the logic of both transaction cost theory and agency theory, but other problems, equally important, are not. Coase's work is best honored by using it as the foundation upon which to build a still richer set of tools. One step in this construction has already been added – the theory of agency relationships. In the present effort to encourage the taking of additional steps, I have found it necessary to outline some of the weaknesses in what has already been accomplished, while suggesting a new direction of inquiry. This would not be needed except for the fact that the work that Coase has done, and that which he has prompted others to do, remains so compelling.

NOTES

1 Free information about production and prices may be contrasted with information about consumption. Knowledge about production and prices is assumed to be *universally* knowable at zero cost. With no one privy to this information, there is no role for a specialized input called management. Knowledge about personal tastes is freely knowable only to the person whose tastes they are; hence, individuals as consumers must manage their own affairs, including the hiring of experts, but this requirement for personalized decisions is also satisfied costlessly.

It is this asymmetric, theoretical treatment of knowledge – universally knowable in the case of production, only personally knowable in the case of consumption – that makes socialism appear appealing. The state is viewed by intellectuals as capable when it comes to production, where it is presumed to possess knowledge as good as anyone else's, but incapable when it comes to psychological trade-offs between consumption goods and between work and leisure. The policy that flows quite naturally from such assumed asymmetry in knowledge is nationalization of industry combined with privatization of consumption and work.

2 If free and full information about technical relationships and prices make it difficult to cap the size of firms in the model of perfect decentralization, they also make it difficult to develop a theory of market concentration. Short of making information costly, the only way out of these dilemmas is to conjure other sources of diseconomies of scale. Conjuring is necessary, because economic theory makes no pretention at knowing these sources or when they will be more and less operative.

3 This analysis of the make-or-buy decision is infra-marginal in nature. If the problem of make-or-buy is viewed in the context of completely divisible adjustments, it must be that on the margin all firms are indifferent between making inputs or buying them. The fact that some firms make considerable quantities of their inputs, even while they purchase the same inputs from others, simply reveals that infra-marginal comparisons show that over some range of output the sum of these costs is lower if inputs are produced in-house.

4 Williamson may be cited again. In *The Economic Institutions of Capitalism* (1985), he discusses in three pages (pp. 92–4) the role of scale economies in raising the cost of enlarging the scope of activities included within a single firm; and he discusses different ways of organizing work later in the book. It would be wrong to claim that he has completely ignored production cost. Yet, his discussion of these does not emphasize the *differences* that may exist between firms within the same industry. His discussion of scale economies is confined to the problem of where on a given production function, available to all firms, the firm functions (similarly with regard to choice of method of organizing work). That the history of a firm may impose constraints on its knowledge about and its ability to alter the way it functions plays no key role in his discussions. Indeed, preceding his discussion of scale economies, in another short section (pp. 86–90), he rejects the importance of technological conditions to economic organization. With respect to asset specificity (which he fails to recognize as at least partly technical), it is not with technology that he is concerned but with the (asserted) fact that asset specificity raises the cost of governance through market arrangements. Even "bounded rationality" is not used to emphasize the *differences in the content of the information* that may be possessed by the personnel and traditions of different firms. It is used to limit the span of control that may be exercised by one person over others, and, thereby, to create a monitoring problem.

5 The question of how transaction cost is to be defined is raised in my paper, "The Exchange and Enforcement of Property Rights." (Demsetz, 1964). The questions raised are of two sorts: (1) Should the cost of enforcing agreements be a transaction cost? (2) Should the cost of avoiding the "under-revelation" of demand (as when collective goods are purchased) be a transaction cost? My preference is for a more restricted definition, dealing with the cost of negotiating. Otherwise, we come seriously close to a definition of transaction cost that amounts to "the cost of solving a problem."

6 Recognition of the relevance of moral hazard for the theory of the firm both precedes and follows Coase's seminal work on transaction cost. Many writers using the moral hazard theme take the discussion of shirking in Alchian and Demsetz (1972) as a starting reference, but Knight, in his classic Risk, Uncertainty, and Profit (1921), anticipates much of what they say. Knight clearly understands the shirking problem, which he calls moral hazard; he also recognizes its relationship to the organization of the firm. The failure to appreciate his contribution fully is mainly due to Knight himself, and this for two reasons. First, his interest really is not in the firm, but in the enterprise *system*, so he does not bring his ideas about the inner workings of the firm to center-stage or to full maturity. Second, his theoretical perspective is overwhelmed by his belief in the importance of allocating risk (of compensation loss) efficiently, and this leads him to make the existence of risk his dominant and pervasive explanation for the existence and organization of firms. He views the separation of claims on the firm's revenues into a stable component – the wage that is received

by employees – and a less stable component – the profit that is received by owner/entrepreneurs – as reflecting different degrees of aversion to and competence in handling risk. It is this theme that attracts the criticism of Alchian and Demsetz, Coase, and other writers too, and that diverts them from Knight's discussion of the relationship between economic organization and moral hazard. Just as there can be little doubt that transaction cost is relevant to the existence of the firm, and to the existence of moral hazard problems, so there cannot be much doubt that moral hazard problems influence the internal organization of the firm.

7 This role of mergers was brought to my attention by an unpublished econometric exercise of my research assistant, John Simpson.

8 Alchian and Demsetz (1972) define the firm implicit in classical economics by the bundle of rights that determines the permissable action of the owner–monitor. He has the right (1) to be a residual claimant; (2) to observe input behavior; (3) to be the central party common to all contracts with input owners; (4) to alter the membership of the team; and (5) to sell these rights.

9 The large number of activities carried on in specialized fashion is too broad to meet the needs of an inquiry seeking to explain firms as these are commonly identified. Every person who acts as a specialist, and every combination of such persons who act as a team of specialists, can be considered a firm, and in many respects they are different firms. The calculus of choice that motivates a person who provides engineering service to GM is not much different if he functions as an "independent" consultant or as an "employee." Nonetheless, a particular combination of the above dimensions may define a firm that is of special interest and importance. This combination is likely to be a *multi-person* team involving a *central contracting agent* operated mainly for *profit*, whose members associate together on a *continuing* basis and have their actions coordinated in large part by *direction*.

REFERENCES

Alchian, Armen A. and Demsetz, H. (1972). "Production, Information Costs, and Economic Organization." *American Economic Review*, 62.

Berle, A. A. and Means, G. C. (1932). *The Modern Corporation and Private Property*. London: Macmillan.

Coase, R. H. (1937). "The Nature of the Firm." *Economica*, 4.

Demsetz, H. (1964). "The Exchange and Enforcement of Property Rights." *Journal of Law and Economics*, 7.

—— (1982). *Economic, Legal and Political Dimensions of Competition*. Amsterdam: North-Holland.

—— and Lehn, K. (1985). "The Structure of Corporate Ownership: Causes and Consequences." *Journal of Political Economy*, 93.

Jensen, M. C. and Meckling, W. H. (1976). "Theory of the Firm: Management Behavior, Agency Costs, and Ownership Structure." *Journal of Financial Economics*, 3.

Klein, B., Crawford, R. G. and Alchian, A. A. (1978). "Vertical Integration, Appropriable Rents, and the Competitive Contracting Process." *Journal of Law and Economics*, 21.

Knight, F. H. (1921). *Risk, Uncertainty, and Profit*. New York: Hart, Schaffner and Marx (republished by Harper and Row, 1965).

Riordan, M. H. and Williamson, O. E. (1985). ''Asset Specificity and Economic Organization.'' *International Journal of Industrial Organization*, 3.

Stigler, G. J. (1951). ''The Division of Labor is Limited by the Extent of the Market.'' *Journal of Political Economy*, 59.

—— (1961). ''The Economics of Information.'' *Journal of Political Economy*, 69.

Thaler, R. H. and Shefrin, H. M. (1981). ''An Economic Theory of Self-control.'' *Journal of Political Economy*, 89.

Williamson, Oliver E. (1985). *The Economic Institutions of Capitalism*. New York: Free Press; London: Macmillan.

10
Vertical Integration: Theories and Evidence

Vertical integration is discussed in many contexts. Antitrust, barriers to entry, successive monopoly, and the theory of the firm all play a part in these discussions. The first part of this chapter critically reconsiders some of the theories currently deployed to rationalize vertical integration. Special attention is given to market size, asset specificity, and risk explanations. In the second part, some evidence bearing on the explanatory power of four of these explanations – market size, asset specificity, monopoly, and risk – is presented. Although each of these explanations may serve a useful explanatory function in a specific, restricted context, the evidence to be presented creates doubt about the ability of any of these (excepting possibly market size) to offer an explanation of vertical integration that has generalizable explanatory power.

THE SIZE OF THE MARKET

Stigler (1951) sets forth an explanation of vertical integration that is based on Adam Smith's proposition that specialization is limited by the extent of the market. An increase in specialization is interpreted by Stigler to imply an increase in the number of stages in the vertical chain of production, each stage being occupied by firms specialized to it. The "completely" vertically integrated firm undertaking all necessary activities in-house is burdened by inefficiencies that arise from the (plausible) fact that these activities do not achieve minimum average cost levels at the same implied rate of final output. As the market grows in size, it becomes easier to avoid these inefficiencies by separating the vertical stages of production into separate industries populated with specialized firms whose numbers and sizes are determined by the scale economies that prevail in the stage of production they serve.

This interpretation of Smith takes too narrow a view of how specialization may be achieved. Specialization can take place within a firm, as well as between firms, by reorganizing it into more numerous specialized departments. To realize all potential economies, such departments would be sized differently. Some of the output from larger departments would be used internally and the remainder sold to other firms. Even for very small markets, in which none of the various vertically related activities can be scaled to exhaust scale economies, it is impossible to determine if a single firm will undertake all vertically related activities or if distinctly specialized firms will occupy each stage of production. Which organization of production is used to realize the potentiality of specialization cannot be ascertained simply by considerations of differences in the degree to which scale economies characterize these vertically related activities. The issue turns on the benefits and costs of managing vertically related activities in-house *v.* coordinating them across markets.

Stigler's theory, although in need of a broader perspective on how specialization may be achieved, nonetheless remains valid in substance. Whether increased specialization is achieved within a firm or across firms, the typical firm must become more specialized as its market grows. Activities subject to greater scale economies are increased relative to other activities in some firms, either in firms wholly specialized to these activities or in departments of firms not so specialized. The typical firm becomes more specialized in either case as market size grows, but less so if rationalization of production takes place in a firm that remains integrated (but in a more unbalanced fashion). There is more specialization and less vertical integration in both cases, but the degree of vertical integration that is characteristic of the typical firm differs.

In one of these two ways, a continued increase in market size leads to more specialization, but only to a point. This point obtains when market size has become large enough to allow firms (whether partly or completely specialized) to exhaust economies of scale in all vertically related activities. Further increases in market size need not be accompanied by further increases in specialization. A doubling of market size beyond this point may result only in the replication of existing firms. The empirical detection of Stigler's prediction would seem to depend on the existence of a sufficient number of situations in which market size falls short of this point.

The size of the market may also influence the comparative advantages of trading goods and trading labor services. To the extent that there are greater scale economies in the exchange of goods than in the exchange of labor services, the separation of vertical stages of production will continue as the market grows. Growth in market size also may impact the prices of factor inputs. Prices for inputs used to exchange goods may be affected differently from prices of inputs used to exchange labor services. Our ignorance of relevant facts and theories about such matters blocks any easy conclusion.[1]

These considerations frustrate the deduction of logically valid and verifiable predictions about the relationship between vertical integration and market size. Because the inverse correlation between market size and degree of vertical integration deducible from Stiglerian considerations rests on unexploited scale economies, it is necessary first to have some confidence about whether markets have grown large enough to exhaust all important sources of scale economies in the various levels of vertically related activities. Second, it is necessary to be able to make plausible claims about how the cost of exchanging goods relative to the cost of exchanging labor services is altered by market size. An empirical investigation of vertical integration cannot presume knowledge about these matters; indeed, it is more likely to provide such knowledge than to test Stigler's view of the importance of market size.

MORAL HAZARD AND ASSET SPECIFICITY

Moral hazard problems appear in two guises in the evolving theory of the firm – as shirking and as post-contractual opportunistic behavior – and in these guises they seem to call sometimes for vertical integration and sometimes for vertical separation. In Alchian and Demsetz (1972), shirking, which may be thought of as behaving opportunistically toward an employment agreement, is an obstacle to the use of team production.[2] The firm, being an important form of team production, is limited in its scope by the more difficult shirking problems caused by larger size. This applies to both the horizontal and the vertical size of the firm, although a case can be made that horizontal size is more likely to bring an increase in the cost of shirking than is vertical size. A necessary condition for a firm, and for a particular size of a firm, to be a viable form of organization is that the increase in productivity that it brings about must outweigh the increase in shirking cost that it also brings about. Situations likely to imbue team production with severe shirking problems increase the probability that production will be organized across markets instead of within firms. In the context of vertical integration, such situations give rise to the separation of vertically related activities. The opposite view is taken in the literature on opportunism. Opportunism tends to be viewed as a cost of using market agreements, and situations more likely to be burdened with opportunism are those in which vertical integration is viewed as more likely. (See Klein, Crawford, and Alchian, 1982.) The substitution of employment within the firm for transactions across markets is seen as the solution to opportunism.

The current state of literature concerning the relationship between moral-hazard-type problems and the organization of production, at least from my own perspective, is ambiguous. We may think of moral hazard as arising from a variety of sources. Some sources suggest the proper solution lies in vertical integration, others that it lies in vertical separation. Asset specificity may offer a cutting edge by which to separate some of these sources. Recent writings on vertical integration rely on this characteristic of assets to identify situations in which vertical integration is likely. Riordan and Williamson (1985) use asset specificity in this way. In their view, vertical integration becomes more preferred the more important asset specificity is to the achievement of low-cost production. Such assets, once committed to a particular cooperative effort, bear large losses in value if switched to other uses. To avoid opportunism when specific assets are required to achieve low costs, the organization of production bypasses potential intervening markets in favor of vertical integration. This proposition is plausible enough, but, as we shall see, closer examination suggests there is need for caution.

Our tendency is to think of asset specificity *only* in the context of moral hazard problems, but asset specificity may affect other costs of economic organization also. The manner in which these other costs are affected can lead to vertical separation.

We may distinguish at least two types of coordination costs: those associated with opportunistic behavior, and (opportunism aside) those associated with integrating knowledge effectively.[3] Asset specificity increases the first type of cost, but it plausibly lowers the second type of cost. The more the second type of cost is reduced, the less is the need for relying on vertical integration to smooth the interface between stages of production. Asset specificity is likely to be associated with uniqueness of function. Large oil pipelines, once built, are not much good for anything but transporting liquid between terminal points. Coordinating the use of pipelines with crude oil production and with refineries, considered from the perspective of timing, pacing, and sequencing of operations (all of which involve integrating knowledge), is not likely to be very costly to achieve *even* if the pipeline is independently owned. (Indeed, it is this "necessary" linkage that underlies the moral hazard potential of committing assets in this fashion.) Thus, although asset specificity raises an issue in regard to price, it also lowers the cost of coordinating physical linkages across markets. It is not clear, therefore, whether greater asset specificity generally implies greater vertical integration.

If people do not generally succumb to the temptation of opportunism, or if tight contractual agreements can be monitored effectively by the legal system, so that opportunism in regard to price becomes a minor problem, then the relationship between asset specificity and vertical integration may be reversed by considerations of using knowledge effectively to control vertically related activities. Vertical separation of ownership becomes more practical the more dedicated in use are the assets used in vertically related activities.

Even in the absence of social incentives to behave honorably, asset specificity may be linked inversely to vertical integration. One important but unconventional situation may be used to illustrate this. A firm that has sunk none of its assets into plant, equipment, and site is in a position to deploy its still liquid resources in a large variety of ways. Such a firm holds no assets laden with specificity. Because of this, it cannot easily tap outside public markets for capital; its lack of commitment to a particular activity creates moral hazard problems for a diffuse set of public shareholders or bondholders who have reason to fear opportunism by insiders. Once asset-specific commitments are made, insiders have far fewer opportunities to use the firm's assets in ways unexpected by public investors. Hence the public is more willing to invest, and capital is provided in much greater degree by outsiders who have little hope of being able to control insider decisions. A market between providers of capital and users of capital (vertical separation) can exist and be tapped more readily because of asset specificity. Absent asset specificity, the provision of capital and the control of the firm must be more integrated.

Setting aside the above considerations, let us now reconsider asset specificity in its currently popular role of putting quasi-rent at risk. Presumably, vertical integration is a device for holding down the costs of coping with opportunism in the face of behavior that is expected to arise after negotiations are completed.[4] How vertical integration accomplishes this is not quite clear. Vertically integrating assets that already exist and are separately owned allows no escape from the distributional consequences of opportunism because the price at which such assets are merged surely reflects how the owners' assets are locked in. In this case, integration would be motivated more by the desire to avoid risk than by the possibility of avoiding the expected distributional consequences of opportunism.[5]

This suggests that a desire to avoid the distributional consequences of opportunism leads to the use of "original" vertical integration - vertical integration set in place by a sole owner of the assets rather than through merger. Even this does not avoid the problem of opportunism unless such an owner produces for himself those assets laden with specificity. A simple purchase of such assets from independent suppliers would allow the buyer to behave opportunistically toward suppliers since the degree of specificity of their products increases as these products near completion. Until title to these assets actually changes hands, these suppliers are exposed to opportunism. The firm must use its own employees to produce such assets.

This method of avoiding the cost of opportunism is viable only under certain conditions. It must be the case that shirking (opportunism within the firm) is not so exacerbated by asset specificity that the increase in cost attributable to shirking outweighs any saving attributable to the resulting reduction in opportunism. Asset specificity is more likely to increase the probability of vertical integration when this condition is met and to decrease the probability when it is not. That one of these outcomes is more likely than the other depends partly on the underlying system of legal rights. The employee in charge of the pipeline division of an integrated petroleum company does not have the same incentives as the employee in charge of the refinery. The pipeline division may "demonstrate" an incapability of delivering as much crude oil as expected, claiming that it needs more corporate resources to do the job right. This claim is harder to ignore the more specific to the pipeline is the refinery investment. Opportunism may flourish in the bureaucratic structure of firms.

The CEO arbitrates such disputes, but, then, the "court" that might be used to arbitrate contractual disputes between independent agents simply has been replaced by, or moved to, the firm's central office. Alternatively, the CEO may attempt to devise an incentive system that reduces the propensity to behave opportunistically. This, too, may be costly. Such an incentive system undoubtedly would need to limit freedom of action and stifle initiative.

Internal adjudication may be more effective than independent courts in such matters because the head of the pipeline division can be *fired* or *demoted* without thereby depriving the refinery of access to the pipeline. The ability of the firm to retain access to specialized assets while severing the employment relationship depends on the underlying system of enforceable rights. Differences in the control over assets by owners and employees are a key to establishing the greater attractiveness of vertical integration in situations where assets exhibit greater specificity. If striking employees are allowed to deprive the firm of the use of assets, the superiority of the vertical integration solution is undermined, and it is undermined to a greater degree the more dependent the firm is on these assets. Such dependency is undoubtedly greater the more these assets exhibit specificity. The transfer of ownership rights to employees in this fashion compromises the ability of "vertical integration" to solve moral hazard problems arising from asset specificity; for if employees retain the right to strike and lock out management, full integration of *ownership* has not been achieved. It may be that the "hold-up" exercisable by striking employees is more threatening than that exercisable by an independent firm. To the extent that independent firms are effectively owned, and unions are not, firms will have more concern for reputation in their dealings with others.

The possibility of relying on outside contractors (vertical separation) to circumvent the ability of unions to tie up assets in the event of labor disputes has not escaped the attention of private and state owners of firms. It even merits its own name – "out-sourcing." The apparent attractiveness of this option belies the ease with which one can draw conclusions about vertical integration from the fact of asset specificity.

If limits are placed on the ability of employees to deny the use of assets to the firm, a reverse problem of opportunism arises. Employees, including those who might have been independent owner–managers of the separate parts of a vertically separated alternative to an integrated firm, are exposed to a greater risk of opportunistic behavior by the firm's management (or owners). This risk is heightened to the extent that employee human capital is characterized by specificity. To some extent this risk is ameliorated through independent ownership of vertically related assets. If the human capital created by management and employees is highly specific to the enterprise in which they work, the ownership and operation of a separate firm conveys an ability to deprive other parts of the vertical chain of production of the use of these assets. This provides management and employees with some protection against an appropriation of their human capital quasi-rents. The existence of a risk of such appropriations therefore raises the cost of relying on a vertically integrated ownership structure. The desirability of integrating vertically turns on the trade-offs implicit in two types of asset specificity: that which is linked to the human capital of employees and that which is linked to non-human capital.

For both of the reasons discussed above (the one deriving from considerations of operational efficiency absent guile and the other from the opportunism, shirking trade-offs just discussed), the relationship between vertical integration and moral hazard problems remain ambiguous even when asset specificity is present. We may be certain that asset specificity has led to vertical integration in specific cases, yet be uncertain about *general* tendencies. Vertical integration may be uncorrelated with the degree to which asset specificity characterizes the desirable production process.

The few case studies that have been undertaken on this issue do provide some verification that asset specificity leads to closer vertical *ties*. Paul Joskow (1985), in an examination of the relationship between coal mining and coal-burning electric utilities, demonstrates a positive correlation between site specificity and vertical integration *or* length of contract. Even here caution is in order; long-term contracts may mark an ability to cope with aspect specificity without resorting to full vertical integration. Other case studies tend to rely on interpretation of material contained in court cases, as in the dispute between General Motors and Fisher Body. The weaknesses of these lie primarily in selectivity problems: selectivity in regard to the cases chosen for interpretation, and selectivity in regard to the type of opportunistic behavior that is likely to ripen into a court case. A selection of examples from contract disputes may give a biased perspective of the causes of vertical organizations. Situations in which vertical reorganization stems from efficiency considerations *absent guile* are likely to be under-represented.

OTHER SOURCES OF VERTICAL INTEGRATION: THE SUSPECTS MULTIPLY

Empirical testing of theories of vertical integration is complicated by the existence of still more theories of vertical integration. In addition to size of market and asset specificity theories, and the theory of operational efficiency absent guile discussed above, there are theories based on risk reduction, price regulation, monopolization, and successive monopoly.

Risk refers here to wide fluctuations in sales or profits. This explanation is based on the expectation that variations in sales or profit in one segment of the vertical chain of production will tend to be canceled out by opposite variations upstream or downstream. Thus, if the supply of crude oil should unexpectedly become greater, its price will fall and so will the profitability of producing it. The fall in the price of crude, however, has a positive impact on refinery profits and sales. A merger between these two activities should yield more stable profit and sales. If the supply of crude should become smaller unexpectedly, a similar canceling of effects, this time in the opposite direction, takes place.[6]

Of course, such smoothing of outcomes can be achieved by investors through appropriate portfolio diversification. But costly information may frustrate this way of avoiding risk. Investors may desire to rely on the managements of firms to find better "fitting" vertical arrangements; or, insulated from the discipline of owner interests by agency cost, managements may seek such fits for reasons of their own risk averseness.

Price regulation refers to vertical integration to avoid inefficiencies inherent in price controls. Effective price ceilings and floors create disparities between the demands for and supply of goods, including inputs. The longer price controls persist, the greater the extent to which vertically related stages of production will be merged to avoid these disparities. Vertical integration becomes a more compelling solution in the presence of asset specificity because asset specificity makes it more difficult for those who are queuing in response to price controls to shift resources out of industries severely affected by price control. This motive for vertically integrating, although linked to asset specificity, is not dependent on opportunistic behavior.

The monopolization explanations view vertical integration as a technique for raising barriers to entry in order to obtain higher profit. Different rationalizations of this belief exist in the literature. These frequently seem poorly thought out, very speculative in nature, or presumptuous in the conditions required. Often, the allegation is that vertical integration forces potential entrants to face more severe capital requirements by compelling them to enter at several stages of production in order to compete with existing vertically integrated firms. Sometimes it is asserted that tactical superiority is gained by producing at several stages of production.

Other treatments of the problem of deterring entry rely on investments in specific assets, such investments being used to convince potential entrants of the commitment made by existing firms to retain market share in the face of entry. This tactic involves vertical integration only to the extent that specificity of assets is best obtained through vertically integrated operations. Here we have another explanation of vertical integration predicting a positive correlation between asset specificity and vertical integration on grounds other than opportunistic behavior, although there is an unusual and perverse sense in which opportunism may be said to be involved. The situation may be viewed as one in which existing firms seek to establish an understanding or an *implicit* agreement with potential entrants that they will be met with punishing competition should they actually attempt entry. However, if entry really is tried, the existing firms may find it in their interest to tolerate the entrants, choosing to share the market rather than to engage in costly competition. The deviation between the actual and "pretended" behavior of existing firms may be interpreted as opportunism. An investment in specific assets, by reducing the probability that such opportunism takes place, may be viewed as *reducing* the probability that the implicit agreement with potential entrants will be violated.

Another association between vertical integration and monopoly is the well known use of vertical integration to solve the successive monopoly problem. Inefficiencies created by dealings between successive monopolists can be reduced or eliminated through vertical integration. Vertical integration is not viewed as a source of monopoly, in distinction to the position taken by those seeking to link vertical integration to barriers to entry; the successive monopoly problem views vertical integration as a way to reduce the cost that would otherwise derive from monopoly that already exists. Such monopoly may derive from pre-existing legal restrictions on competition (patents), copyrights, and trademarks.

The variety and complexity of these alternative explanations make it impossible at the present time to conduct an empirical investigation capable of assessing in convincing fashion the relative importance of all of them. Nonetheless, it is possible to acquire a sense of the *general* importance of some of them. General tendencies, of course, do not bar contrary findings in special cases.

QUANTIFYING ASSET SPECIFICITY AND VERTICAL INTEGRATION

Asset specificity

Perhaps the major hurdle to any study purporting to gather evidence about the general importance of opportunism as a source of vertical integration is that of devising a broadly applicable index of asset specificity. What data does the theory tell us to collect? In some cases, such as that investigated by Joskow, high transport cost may place vertically related operations in such close and isolated locations that they may be viewed as bound together by specificity once locational commitments are made. In a more general sense, however, it is difficult to detect the presence of asset specificity. Asset specificity defined by the losses that would be suffered by the reassignment of assets to other uses hardly gives a clue about the information that should be sought to detect its presence. It is necessary to improvise. The improvisation adopted here is far from satisfactory, and it is necessary to warn the reader that the empirical work bearing on asset specificity may be carrying a heavy load of "garbage."

An important component of the indexes of asset specificity adopted here is investment in durable assets. Most discussions of asset specificity associate durability of assets with costly reassignment of their use. The placing of a *durable* pipeline, *durable* refinery, *durable* seam of coal, and *durable* electric power generating station are but a few examples of the importance of asset durability that can be found in the literature of opportunistic behavior. The exposure to opportunism that is associated with the post-contractual situation depends in large part on the fact that fungible assets are converted into durable varieties in order to fulfill the terms of the contract. While durability of assets exacerbates fears of opportunism, the rapid physical depreciation of assets mutes them.

It is true that not all durable assets exhibit a high degree of specificity. Coins and currency are highly durable but are hardly specific to a particular use. Much equipment is durable but is redeployable in alternative uses at little sacrifice in value. But it is plausibly true as a statistical proposition that firms which rely in larger degree on durable assets are more likely to experience the consequences of asset specificity. Moreover, if not all durable assets are highly specific, most assets that are specific are likely to be durable. Hence, if asset specificity is a powerful source of vertical integration, we can plausibly expect to find a positive relationship between vertical integration and the importance in the production process of durable relative to non-durable assets. The degree to which durable assets are relied upon in the production process is calculated here by one of three ratios: the ratio of investment in plant to current assets, the ratio of investment in plant to number of employees, and the ratio of the gross value of durable assets to number of employees.

The values of plant and current assets are pure balance sheet calculations, and their ratio purports to measure the relative importance of non-fungible to fungible assets. Whether it is a good measure depends on the degree of freedom one associates with the use of current assets. To the extent that current assets are inextricably tied to servicing the volume of sales, their fungibility is lessened. Investment in plant per employee purports to index the importance of asset specificity in the mix of inputs used to produce a product. The number of workers employed might also be interpreted as an index of the importance of human capital; if so interpreted, this second index can be taken to measure physical asset specificity relative to human capital specificity.

The firm's plant is composed largely of buildings that are site-specific. It may be the case, however, that the use of buildings may be altered without great loss. It is difficult to know whether, or to what extent, this is the case, but investment in plant may be too rough a measure of asset specificity to yield statistically observable results. A broader measure of asset specificity is offered by durable asset intensity, as measured by the value of durable assets per employee. This measure surely includes investments in durable assets that possess moderate and great specificity. Compared with the use of a broad spectrum of labor and materials, the other main inputs in the production process, investment in durable assets should correlate with greater specificity in the inputs used.

Vertical integration

The substantive measure of degree of vertical integration relied on here is the ratio of value added to sales. This measure is also not without problems. When measuring vertical integration at the level of an industry, the index's denominator is the size of the market; this creates errors in variable problems when market size is one of the explanatory variables we seek to examine. Similar problems appear in the numerator of the index because of the wage and depreciation charges contained therein; the asset specificity explanatory variable is measured by the importance of investment in plant, sometimes relative to the number of employees, so potential errors in variable problems emerge here also.

On a different level of difficulties, it has been suggested by Adelman (1955) that this index is more biased against a showing of vertical integration the closer is a firm's product to the final good in the chain of production. As an example, consider three firms located at different positions in the same vertical production chain: raw materials, manufacturing, and retailing. Each firm, we shall suppose, adds equal value (one-third of final product value) to the final product. Suppose the raw material producer purchases no inputs, but produces everything he needs in-house. He sells his output to a manufacturer, who adds one-third to the value of his purchases from the raw material producer and then sells his output to a retailer. The retailer adds the final one-third to the value of the product before it is sold to consumers. Even though each firm adds an equal increment to the value of the product, the ratio of value added to sales would be 1 for the raw material producer (on the assumption that it purchases no inputs), 1/2 for the manufacturer, and 1/3 for the retailer. The decline in the value of the ratio that is associated with production farther downstream is, of course, attributable to the accompanying increase in the sales base. Yet, some base such as sales is needed because value added taken by itself can be large not just because of vertical integration but also because of large horizontal size. Dividing by some measure of horizontal size tends to negate the latter source of value added, thus creating an index that is more reflective of value added secured through vertical integration.

It is not clear how strong is the bias pointed to by Adelman; its strength in the illustrative example depends in part upon a very unlikely condition: that the upstream firm purchases no inputs from others. The study reported here attempts to reduce bias from this source by relying only on firms and industries classified as primarily in manufacturing activity. Retailers, wholesalers, utilities, finance, insurance, transporter, mining, construction, and agriculture are among the several activities excluded. This focuses the study on an intermediate layer of economic activity. Alternatively, dummy variables could be assigned to different types of economic activity. This has not been done here because market concentration measures, which are also used, have not been tailored carefully for many industries outside the manufacturing sector.

QUANTIFYING OTHER VARIABLES

Market concentration and profit rate are used to index the degree to which monopoly might be present. These variables should be positively related to vertical integration if the monopoly explanations of vertical integration are important. The well-known difficulties with such variables as indexes of monopoly need not be repeated here, but these indexes are so often relied upon in industrial organization research that it is of interest to examine their impact on vertical integration. There are special ambiguities in their use for this purpose, because their role is not likely to lie exclusively in tracking the importance of monopoly for vertical integration. Market concentration may also reflect difficulty in finding substitute firms with which to deal, and so it may be associated with vertical integration through the problem of opportunism as well as through the presence of monopoly. Moreover, both market concentration and profit rate may reflect the presence of scale economies rather than (just) monopoly, and thus they may relate to the market size explanation of vertical integration.

The impact of market size on vertical integration is determined by relating vertical integration to industry sales. A negative relationship between degree of vertical integration and industry sales is supportive of such an explanation. The critical evaluation of this theory undertaken above suggests caution here. If firms are small relative to the market, we may have a sign that scale economies in the various activities undertaken by these firms have been largely dissipated; this suggests that we should not observe any relationship between vertical integration and market size for markets that are very large relative to firms. Unlike the measure of asset specificity adopted here, we may have more confidence that industry and firm sales are reasonable measures of size in the context of Stigler's theory. Nonetheless, there are measurement problems that should be brought to the attention of readers unfamiliar with such data. Firms sometimes have considerable sales in industries other than those into which they are placed by official data sources. This makes industry size and firm size less commensurate with each other than might be thought.

One remaining issue of interpreting Stigler's theory of vertical integration bears on its testing. The theory certainly proposes a negative relationship between vertical integration and the size of a *particular* market as it grows (or as it exists in different locations). As the market matures, vertical integration is displaced by increasing specialization; if the size of the industry begins to diminish, a reverse process of vertical integration sets in. The impact of industry growth on vertical integration is one of the subjects to be explored below, but is Stigler's theory silent about comparisons between industries? If one industry is bigger than another, should we expect relatively more specialization and less vertical integration in it? Clearly, conditions of production differ across industries, and what is a large market relative to available scale economies in one industry may be small in another.

This suggests that not much can be inferred from a cross-section analysis of industries. Yet, this simply means that factors other than market size also influence the degree of vertical integration, and that these are not included in the theory. If these other factors can be taken to be distributed randomly across industries, a cross-section analysis may still shed light on the validity of the relationship between vertical integration and market size. Still more to the point, these other factors are likely to be closely related to the presence or absence of significant scale economies. The greater the degree to which scale economies are available to a set of vertically related activities, the larger must the market be to elicit a given degree of vertical disintegration. This suggests the validity of cross-section analyses of industries if firm size is added to market size as an explanatory variable. The theory as described by Stigler may be interpreted to say that when markets are large relative to the firms that comprise them, firms tend to be less vertically integrated.

The risk explanation of vertical integration is tested by determining which firms experience greater variability in both firm sales and firm profit rates. The greater are these variabilities, the greater the degree of vertical integration that should be observed. Since vertical integration, according to this explanation, should attenuate the variability in sales and profit rate, this is at best a rough test of the risk explanation. A more sophisticated treatment would endogenize variability. I assume that any attenuation of risk that arises as a result of vertical integration leaves firm sales and profit rates less stable than those of firms that choose not to vertically integrate. On this supposition, if the risk explanation is correct, variability and vertical integration should be positively correlated.

It seems clear to me that the market size theory of vertical integration is more certainly tested here than either the risk or monopolization theories. The test of the risk theory depends on an assumption that vertical integration does not largely eliminate the instability to which it is asserted to be a response. The monopolization theory relies on a theoretically blemished measure of degree of monopoly achieved. The strength of the test of asset specificity depends on the confidence that can be placed in the values of plant and durable assets as indexes of asset specificity.

DATA SOURCES

This study of vertical integration is based on annual COMPUSTAT data obtained for the twenty-year period 1962–81 and on US Census data for 1963–77. A broad range of industries is investigated. Preciseness in detecting specificity of assets, as is achieved in Joskow's case study, is sacrificed here in favor of enlarging sample size considerably and using variables that allow some comparison to alternative theories.

Two classes of variables are used: those measured at the level of the firm, and those measured at the level of the four-digit SIC industries. Market concentration and industry sales derive from census industry data. Firm sales and firm profit rate derive from COMPUSTAT data. Variables purporting to measure degree of vertical integration and asset specificity are alternatively measured on the basis of firm and industry data. Lower-case letters are used to indicate data measured at the level of the firm, upper-case letters to indicate census industry data.

Vertical integration measured at the level of the firm is calculated from COMPUSTAT data by summing annual expenditures in those accounts most likely to contain expenditures on the firm's internally provided inputs. Primarily, these are labor, advertising, research and development, rental expenses, and depreciation and amortization charges. Profit is thus excluded from this measure of value added. Alternative estimates were made including and excluding interest charges. This measure of value added is divided by annual firm sales to obtain an index of vertical integration for firms that we may designate as *vi*. Unlike COMPUSTAT, the US Census provides a direct summary measure of value added at the level of the industry (which, however, includes industry profit in its definition). Dividing this summary measure by industry sales yields a second index of vertical integration, designated here as VI.

The following section more carefully defines the variables used in this study. Some of these variables are borrowed from three earlier studies undertaken by the author to examine problems unrelated to vertical integration. The study of firm data is limited to manufacturing firms contained in the intersection of these three studies. In combination with problems arising because some firms failed to report some data to COMPUSTAT, this limits the sample size to 146 firms. The study of industries (not specific firms), although much more limited in number of variables, is based on 219 four-digit census manufacturing industries.

DEFINITIONS

vi = index of vertical integration measured at the level of the firm from COMPUSTAT data

VI = index of vertical integration measured at the level of the industry from US Census data

np = net values of plant per manufacturing firm

c = current assets per firm

e = number of employees per manufacturing firm (thousands)

DA = gross value of durable assets per manufacturing industry
E = employment per manufacturing industry
*R*4 = four-firm concentration ratio defined to vary between 0 and 100 percent per four-digit SIC industry
S = value of sales per four-digit SIC industry ($ m)
f = values of sales per manufacturing firm ($ m)
z = profit/assets per manufacturing firm
Var *f* = variance (over time) of firm sales
Var *z* = variance (over time) of firm profit rate

EVIDENCE OF A SORT

Tables 10.1, 10.2, and 10.3 report results when vertical integration is measured at the level of the firm from COMPUSTAT data. Table 10.4 reports results when

Table 10.1 OLS estimates of vertical integration (*vi*) regressed on input mix, market concentration, profit rate, market size, and risk (Annual observations, 1962-1981; *t*-values in parentheses)

	1962-81		*1962-71*	*1972-81*
Intercept	0.329	0.327	0.398	0.312
	(6.08)	(6.07)	(7.33)	(5.31)
np/c	−0.134	—	−0.0451	−0.129
	(−2.14)		(−0.69)	(−1.99)
$(np/c)^2$	0.0255	—	−0.00278	0.0224
	(1.11)		(−0.12)	(0.87)
*R*4	−0.00865	−0.000680	−0.00198	−0.000619
	(−1.11)	(−0.89)	(−2.29)	(−0.76)
S	0.000038	0.000036	0.000060	0.000034
	(2.83)	(2.69)	(2.45)	(3.2)
S^2	−4.206E-09	−4.037E-09	−1.048E-08	−2.558E-09
	(−3.74)	(−3.63)	(−3.25)	(−4.00)
f	0.000204	0.000191	0.000168	0.00145
	(4.80)	(4.57)	(1.95)	(4.88)
f^2	−3.075E-08	−3.082E-08	−4.115E-08	−1.971E-08
	(−2.00)	(−2.02)	(−1.04)	(−2.46)
Var *f*	−3.545E-08	−2.624E-08	8.374-08	−1.757E-08
	(−1.03)	(−0.77)	(0.66)	(−0.39)
z	−0.452	−0.470	−0.808	−0.595
	(−1.27)	(−1.33)	(−2.55)	(−1.61)
Var *z*	2.352	1.928	−6.137	3.746
	(0.40)	(0.33)	(−1.24)	(0.53)
np/e	—	−0.0060	—	—
		(−1.77)		
$(np/e)^2$	—	0.000045	—	—
		(0.69)		
Adj. R^2	0.21	0.23	0.14	0.21
N	146	146	146	146

Table 10.2 OLS estimates of vertical integration (*vi*) regressed on input mix, market concentration, profit rate, market size, and risk (Annual observations, 1962-1981; *t*-values in parentheses)

	1962-81		*1962-71*	*1972-81*
Intercept	0.269	0.271	0.370	0.256
	(5.03)	(5.25)	(7.14)	(4.46)
np	−0.231E-03	−0.172	−0.558E-03	−0.115E-03
	(−1.66)	(−1.26)	(−1.95)	(−1.10)
c	0.304E-03	—	0.150E-03	0.251E-03
	(2.31)		(0.62)	(2.62)
e	—	0.0076	—	—
		(3.53)		
R4	−0.697E-03	−0.529E-03	−0.0018	−0.629E-03
	(−0.88)	(−0.68)	(−2.13)	(−0.77)
S	0.316E-04	0.354E-04	0.502E-04	0.311E-04
	(2.39)	(2.73)	(2.09)	(2.99)
S^2	−3.526E-09	−3.959E-09	−9.175E-09	−2.327E-09
	(−3.25)	(−3.69)	(−2.95)	(−3.75)
f	0.993E-04	−0.356E-04	0.254E-04	0.403E-04
	(1.29)	(−0.39)	(1.84)	(0.66)
f^2	−2.904E-08	−3.819E-08	−4.179E-08	−1.414E-08
	(1.29)	(−0.39)	(1.84)	(0.66)
Var *f*	−7.323E-09	7.190E-08	1.348E-08	−4.890E-09
	(−0.20)	(1.65)	(0.10)	(−0.10)
z	−0.440	−0.404	−0.779	−0.549
	(−1.22)	(−1.15)	(−2.44)	(−1.49)
Var *z*	4.744	3.953	−4.99	5.387
	(0.80)	(0.69)	(−0.10)	(0.76)
Adj. R^2	0.20	0.24	0.13	0.21
N	146	146	146	146

vertical integration is measured at the level of the industry from Census data. Additional statistical results, not presented in tabular form, are discussed in the text. Tables 10.1–10.3 are discussed first.

Tables 10.1, 10.2, and 10.3 differ in the way the same essential variables are calculated. Table 10.1 uses *np/c* and *np/e*, the ratios of book value of net plant to current assets and to number of employees, to index degree of asset specificity. Table 10.2 uses these variables in linear form. (The substitution of gross plant for net plant yields no changes of interest and is not reported here.) Table 10.3 uses *S/f* to measure industry size relative to firm size, whereas tables 10.1 and 10.2 use these variables in linear form. In each of these tables, the first, third, and fourth columns use the same explanatory variables but measure them over different time periods, whereas the second column substitutes dollars of depreciated plant per employee for dollars of depreciated plant per dollar of current assets as the measure of asset specificity.

The conclusion that emerges in tables 10.1, 10.2, and 10.3, taken as a whole and noting the reformulation of form and partitioning of time periods they offer, is that

Table 10.3 OLS estimates of vertical integration (*vi*) regressed on input mix, market concentration, profit rate, market size, and risk (Annual observations, 1962-1981; *t*-values in parentheses)

	1962-81		*1962-71*	*1972-81*
Intercept	0.340	0.345	0.391	0.356
	(6.14)	(6.14)	(7.34)	(5.82)
np/c	−0.054	—	0.0127	−0.0322
	(0.28)		(0.190)	(−0.45)
(*np/c*)	0.00715	—	−0.162	0.000128
	(0.80)		(−0.65)	(0.01)
*R*4	0.000108	0.000239	−0.00106	0.000219
	(0.13)	(0.29)	(−1.21)	(0.24)
S/f	−0.000210	−0.000206	−0.000409	−0.000123
	(−2.03)	(−2.02)	(−2.16)	(−1.70)
$(S/f)^2$	5.310E-08	5.232E-08	2.203E-07	1.570E-08
	(1.31)	(1.31)	(1.57)	(1.26)
Var *f*	2.104E-08	2.067E-08	1.809E-07	2.503E-08
	(1.67)	(1.65)	(1.75)	(1.23)
z	−0.176	−0.213	−0.485	−0.486
	(−0.46)	(−0.55)	(−1.52)	(−1.17)
Var *z*	3.117	2.408	−3.579	−0.949
	(0.46)	(0.36)	(−0.67)	(−0.12)
np/e	—	−0.00165	—	—
		(−0.46)		
$(np/e)^2$	—	−0.206E-04	—	—
Adj. R^2	0.03	0.05	0.05	0.00
N	146	146	146	146

only firm and market size bear a convincing relationship to vertical integration measured at the firm level. Market concentration, profit rate, and measure of riskiness fail to exhibit a strong relationship in any of the tables reported in this study. No empirical support is provided that the risk and monopoly explanations describe generally important sources of vertical integration. The relationship between vertical integration and asset specificity, although exhibiting some strength in table 10.1, does not in tables 10.2 and 10.3; more important, the relationship tends to be perverse in direction to what is called for by the asset specificity theory, whether asset specificity is measured by *np/c* or *np/e*.

The statistical evidence supporting Stigler's interpretation of Adam Smith in tables 10.1 and 10.2 is somewhat complex. Once the quadratic forms of the relationships between vertical integration and firm size, and between vertical integration and market size, are analyzed, a negative relationship emerges for values of these variables in excess of their mean values. (If the quadratic form of *S* is replaced by a simple linear form, a negative relationship dominates the connection between *vi* and *S*.) For large firms and for large markets, increases in either firm or market size yield a reduction in vertical integration. Table 10.3

Table 10.4 Vertical integration (*Vi*) regressed on durable assets per employee, product value and growth in product value
219 four-digit SIC manufacturing industries, annual data (1963 and 1977)

Intercept	0.601	0.547	0.623	0.556
	(26.56)	(28.08)	(28.50)	(28.47)
AV(*DA*/*E*)	−0.731E-05	−0.217E-05		
	(−5.33)	(−4.22)		
AV (*DA*/*E*)^2	6.146E-11			
	(4.02)			
AV(*S*)	−0.127E-04	−0.739E-05		
	(−2.07)	(−2.52)		
AV(*S*)^2	3.352E-10			
	(1.24)			
Gro*S*	0.00393	0.000809	0.000297	−0.00310
	(0.58)	(0.12)	(−0.04)	(−0.44)
77 (*DA*/*E*)			−0.653E-05	−0.180E-05
			(−7.06)	(−5.32)
77 (*DA*/*E*)^2			3.084E-11	
			(5.45)	
77 (*S*)			−0.703E-05	−0.549E-05
			(−1.73)	(−2.71)
77 (*S*)^2			1.189E-10	
			(0.94)	
Adj. R^2	0.16	0.10	0.25	0.15

Notes: AV = average of 1963 and 1977, including dependent variable
Gro*S* = {*S* (1977) − *S*(1963)}/*S*(1963)
77 ( ) = 1977 only, including dependent variable *VI*.

examines the relationship between *S*/*f* and vertical integration, and an analysis of the quadratic form used in this table reveals a predominantly negative relationship throughout the range of sample data. However, the substitution of *S*/*f* for the non-ratioed forms in which these variables appear in tables 10.1 and 10.2 results in a considerable reduction in the adjusted R^2, so significant a reduction that only a trivial percentage of variation in vertical integration is now explained.

Obviously, *S* and *F* in non-ratioed form contribute heavily to the explanatory power of the regression equations reported in tables 10.1 and 10.2. The squared forms of these variables take signs strongly opposite to those that attach to the linear forms. For the period 1962–81, the mean values of *S* and *f* are approximately the values that maximize degree of vertical integration in the first regression equation of table 10.1, so there is a considerable range of observations over which the relationship between vertical integration and either firm size or market size is negative. The relationships between vertical integration and market size, and between vertical integration and firm size, are predominantly negative when both variables are large. This is consistent with an interpretation of Stigler's proposition which recognizes that specialization can take place within firms as well as across firms. When firms and markets are large, increases in these variables are associated with increases in specialization. By ratioing these variables, as is done in table 10.3 with *S/f*, these effects are muted to the extent that *S* and *f* are correlated, which they tend to be. Hence, although *S/f* performs as Stigler's proposition would suggest, its explanatory power is reduced considerably.

However, when values of *S* and *f* are less than their mean values, the negative relationship between these variables and vertical integration no longer holds. It is replaced by a predominantly positive relationship for which no theoretical explanation is available. Indeed, one would expect the negative relationship to prevail more strongly in situations in which firm and market size are not yet large, because it is in such situations that potential scale economies are more likely to remain to be exploited. Yet, the fact that firm size and market size are small, by a reversal of causation, may itself indicate situations in which potential scale economies are trivial; this interpretation would be more congenial to the Stiglerian view.

Table 10.4 examines the statistical evidence about the relationship between *VI* and asset specificity and size of market using four-digit US Census industry data. Asset specificity is measured by the gross value of durable assets; the relationship between net value of durable assets and *VI* is weaker but still exhibits strength in the negative direction. No variables in this table are measured at the level of the firm. All are measured at the level of Census four-digit industries. The top half of the table uses an average of 1963 and 1977 data, indicated by *AV*( ). The bottom half uses 1977 data only, indicated by 77( ). Market size is inversely related to vertical integration, as in tables 10.1 and 10.2. Durable assets per employee is negatively related to *VI*, but more strongly than net plant per employee (in tables 10.1–10.3). Although this negative relationship is perverse to what is suggested by the asset specificity theory, its strength calls for explanation.

Table 10.4 reveals no relationship between vertical integration and the growth in market size, *GroS*, between 1963 and 1977. A negative relationship is suggested by Stigler's interpretation of Adam Smith. The search for this relationship was repeated for firm-level data of the kind used in tables 10.1 and 10.2. Change in vertical integration, both absolute and percentage, was made a function of change in market size, change in firm size, and change in *np/c*, and these relationships were considered with and without using the initial level of vertical integration as an explanatory variable. Throughout this search for an explanation of changes in *vi*, the only relationship to reveal itself was a negative one between vertical integration and the initial level of vertical integration. None of the theoretically important explanatory variables showed any recognizable relationships to vertical integration.

The empirical part of this study lends some support to the notion that firm and market size are related to vertical integration. Although the linear relationship between vertical integration and market size is negative, estimates of the quadratic form of this relationship reveal that it is not monotonic, a finding that is inconsistent with the theory as presently formulated. Moreover, the negative relationship between vertical integration and market size called for by the theory does not reveal itself in studies of the change in vertical integration over time. There is also some indication of a negative relationship between vertical integration and capital intensity, whether this is measured by plant or by durable assets; but we have no explanation for such a relationship.

The overall results must be counted as undermining the notion that we really know the dominant causes of vertical integration. To me, this suggests that more attention should be paid to problems of timing, sequencing, and quality control in a context in which opportunism plays no important role. The focus should be on information and transaction costs in a guileless society, and on how different technologies yield different matrices of these costs. None of the above theories considers vertical integration from this perspective.

NOTES

1 The cost of transacting on *organized* exchanges reveals persistent scale economies (Demsetz, 1968; Tinic, 1972); in itself, this argues for a continued decrease in degree of vertical integration as the market continues to grow.

2 Alchian and Demsetz (1972) are often cited as the originators of this theme, but Knight also notes the importance of moral hazard to the theory of the firm. He clearly understands not only the shirking problem, which he calls "moral hazard," but also its relevance to the organization of managed coordination. Unfortunately, his ideas on these matters are not brought to maturation. Partly this is because his interest really is not in the firm, but in the enterprise *system*, and partly because, when he does deal with the firm, his thoughts about moral hazard are overwhelmed by his belief that the firm's viability as an institution is attributable to the role it plays in allocating risk efficiently. The result is that his views on moral hazard have tended to be neglected. Alchian and Demsetz, for example, and Coase also, critically comment on Knight's dominant theme of efficient risk allocation, overlooking his discussion of the relationship between economic organization and moral hazard.

3 See chapter 9 above entitled "The Theory of the Firm Revisited" for a discussion of both the importance of knowledge to the organization of the firm and the ambiguity in the logic connecting asset specificity to vertical integration.

4 Other methods are available for ameliorating the problem without resorting to vertical integration, for example, an "up front" payment from the party most likely to behave opportunistically to the other party. The pay or take contract is another; the party supplying the specific assets is explicitly entitled to payment whether or not the other party takes delivery, thus reducing the probability of later "hold-up" behavior.

5 The absence of an explanation for how problems of opportunism are resolved simply by altering the status of one of the interacting parties from that of independent owner to that of employee is noted by Grossman and Hart (1986).

6 Asset specificity may be involved in this explantion. Greater swings in profit or sales may be expected from any given variation in underlying conditions when assets cannot be moved into or out of the business easily. By exacerbating the risk of wide swings, asset specificity may encourage vertical integration for risk-abating reasons that have little to do with opportunistic behavior.

REFERENCES

Adelman, M. A. (1955). "Concept and Statistical Measurement of Vertical Integration." In G. J. Stigler (ed.), *Business Concentration and Price Policy*. Princeton, NJ: National Bureau of Economic Research.

Alchian, A. A. and Demsetz, H. (1972). "Production, Information Costs, and Economic Organization." *American Economic Review*, 62.

Demsetz, H. (1968). "The Cost of Transacting." *Quarterly Journal of Economics*, 82. Reproduced as chapter 5 above.

—— (1988). "The Theory of the Firm Revisited." *Journal of Law, Economics, and Organization*, 4. Reproduced as chapter 9 above.

Grossman, S. J. and Hart, O. D. (1986). "The Costs and Benefits of Ownership: a Theory of Vertical and Lateral Integration." *Journal of Political Economy*, 94.

Klein, B. (1980). "Transaction Cost Determinants of "Unfair Contractual Agreements." *American Economic Review*, 70.

—— Crawford, R. G. and Alchian, A. A. (1978). "Vertical Integration, Appropriable Rents and the Competitive Contracting Process." *Journal of Law and Economics*, 21.

—— and Kenny, R. (1987). "Contractual Flexibility." Unpublished paper.

Joskow, P. L. (1985). "Vertical Integration and Long-term Contracts: The Case of Coal-burning Electric Generating Plants." *Journal of Law, Economics and Organization*, 1.

Riordan, M. H. and Williamson, O. E. (1985). "Asset Specificity and Economic Organization." *International Journal of Industrial Organization*, 3.

Stilger, G. J. (1951). "The Division of Labor is Limited by the Extent of the Market." *Journal of Political Economy*, 59.

Tinic, S. (1972). "The Economics of Liquidity Services." *Quarterly Journal of Economics*, 86.

Williamson. O. E. (1983). "Credible Commitments: Using Hostages to Support Exchange." *American Economic Review*, 83.

11
The Structure of Ownership and the Theory of the Firm

The separation of ownership and control in the modern corporation, an issue brought to the fore so effectively by Berle and Means fifty years ago, retains a central position in recent writings about the economic theory of the firm. The problem is stated succinctly by Berle and Means:

> The separation of ownership from control produces a condition where the interests of owner and of ultimate manager may, and often do, diverge, and where many of the checks which formerly operated to limit the use of power disappear. . . .
>
> In creating these new relationships, the quasi-public corporation may fairly be said to work a revolution. It . . . has divided ownership into nominal ownership and the power formerly joined to it. Thereby the corporation has changed the nature of profit-seeking enterprise.[1]

The holder of corporate stock experiences a loss of control over his resources because ownership is so broadly dispersed across large numbers of shareholders that the typical shareholder cannot exercise real power to oversee managerial performance in modern corporations. Management exercises more freedom in the use of the firm's resources than would exist if the firm were managed by its owner(s), or at least, if ownership interests were more concentrated. Because management and ownership interests do not naturally coincide when not housed in the same person, Berle and Means perceive a conflict of interest, which, with ownership dispersed, is resolved in management's favor.

To Berle and Means, this signifies a serious impairment of the social function of private property. Profit maximization constrained and guided by competition is the link between private ownership and efficient resource utilization, a link presumably broken by a structure of ownership that reduces the incentives of corporate managers to maximize profit. Corporate wealth is used to further ends other than profit maximization. The logical consequences of decentralization through private ownership of the means of production, then, are

This study benefitted from suggestions made by Professors Ken Lehn and Barry Weingast, and a Sloan Foundation grant to UCLA. Reprinted with permission from *Journal of Law & Economics*, XXVI 1983.

no longer those deduced with the aid of a theory of price based on owner-managed firms. The argument is as appealing to socialists as it is credible to non-interventionists. Indeed, businessmen themselves implicitly support the central thesis of separation. They are among the first to deny the dominance of the profit motive in business decisions, frequently appealing to the evidence that exists in the record of corporate financial support of various charitable and educational endeavors.

Other social critics have welcomed the modern corporation because it seems to provide a vehicle by which efficiency can be restored. Thorstein Veblen, for example, saw the alleged separation of ownership and control as a transfer of control from capitalists to engineers.[2] He believed capitalists were mainly interested in creating scarcity through monopolization, while engineers were mainly interested in technical efficiency and output growth. For Veblen, the separation of ownership and control turned control over to efficiency-seeking management. Growth was unwelcome to one of Veblen's more famous students, J. K. Galbraith, who gave to the technostructure the desire and power to produce an undesirably large growth of the private sector.

For all these commentators on the modern corporation, the cutting edge is the separation between ownership and control. A closer look at the problem of ownership structure is warranted, if for no other reason than that these commentators fail to examine either the theoretical problem or the empirical premise carefully. In the discussion that follows, I will be recovering some subject matter that has emerged in recent writings by economists on organization theory,[3] but the views taken in this paper offer some difference in emphasis and mild disagreement.

I view the ownership structure of the firm as an endogenous outcome of a maximizing process in which more is at stake than just accommodating to the shirking problem. A broader perspective on the problem of the optimum ownership structure makes the fears of Berle and Means meaningless. I conclude with a discussion of evidence bearing on the empirical premise assumed by the alleged separation between ownership and control.

THE FIRM IN ECONOMIC THEORY

Two concepts of the firm motivate Berle and Means to level the charge of social inefficiency at the modern corporation: their conception of the firm in economic theory, and their contrasting conception of the real modern corporation. The first of these associates the profit-maximizing firm of economic theory with the pre-corporation firms that populated the business world during most of the nineteenth century. The theoretical firm is viewed as a good approximation of pre-corporate real firms, and the theory pictures these as lean, no-nonsense institutions devoid of managerial amenities. The second conception is a firm largely controlled by a management possessing an insignificant interest in the profitability of the firm's activities. À la Baumol,[4] the firm may seek to keep shareholders contented with a minimum acceptable positive return, but beyond that, profit is traded off to increase the *utility* of management. Utility-maximizing managerial behavior requires the use of the firm's resources to provide on-the-job amenities. These might include not only the usual amenities but also abnormally high managerial wages and excessively large firms. If the organization pictured by the firm of economic theory promotes efficiency, then, for Berle and Means, the organization they perceive as the real corporation surely does not. These two conceptions of the firm draw a contrast that remains popular and guides much of the clamor for radically reorganizing corporate law, if not the private sector.[5]

It is a mistake to confuse the firm of economic theory with its real-world namesake. The chief mission of neoclassical economics is to understand how the price system coordinates the use of resources, not to understand the inner workings of real firms.[6] There are two broad divisions of use to which resources may be put: consumption and production. One of the important tasks of the theory of price is to explain how prices influence each of these uses. To this end, the theory *defines* the household, not to approximate the activities of a family of four, but as the theoretical institution in which rational decisions about consumption take place. Correspondingly, the firm is *defined*, not to approximate the activities of a real firm, pre- or post-corporate organization, but as the theoretical institution in which production (for others) takes place. This distorts some characteristics of real families and real firms. Some family activity is devoted to production and, as such, is guided primarily by profit considerations (the family rents rooms in its house to boarders), and no doubt the persons who manage real firms consume while on the job; but this is unimportant to the theory's objective, for the theory does not seek to understand the actual loci of consumption and production. Its concern is with how these activities are affected by exogenous changes (such as a tax change) and with how the price system determines the quantities and mixtures of goods consumed and produced.

The study of these problems is simplified considerably by defining households and firms to be specialized, respectively, to consumption activity and production activity. Consumption, by definition, creates utility, so the household's decisions in theory are utility-maximizing decisions. Production is devoid of direct utility-creating activities (which are defined as consumption), so the firm's decisions are guided only by profit considerations. However, the maximization of the firm's profit delivers to its owners a maximum capability for (indirect) utility-creating consumption in their households. The entire process really is concerned with utility maximization, but some activities, identified as production (for use by others), deliver utility indirectly to factor owners through the easing of their household budget constraints.

Real firms, whether or not they are owner-managed, are not so specialized in their activities. This does not undermine the relevance of the theoretical firm for explaining the guidance given to economic activity by prices. To see why the conclusions of economic theory remain valid in this task even when consumption, as well as production, takes place in real firms, let us consider an owner-managed firm that houses both activities. For the present discussion, let us be concerned only about *known* on-the-job consumption.

The compensation received by the owner–manager of such a firm potentially contains three components: pecuniary wages of management, known amenities of office, and profit of owner. The behavior of such an owner–manager surely is guided by utility maximization, not simply the pursuit of profit. One owner may prefer spotlessly clean surroundings for the large part of the day he spends at the office. Another values managing a larger or faster-growing firm. A third values associating with laborers who practice a particular religion or who have a particular skin color. Nothing in the theory of the price system bars the owner from indulging these desires. The theory of competitive markets, which is based on full knowledge of such consumption, requires only that he pay for these indulgences, just as if he were purchasing them as a consumer. (This is common knowledge among students of labor markets, and it has frequently been documented quantitatively by them.)

Because a good part of a real owner–manager's life is on the job, he very well may decide in favor of on-the-job consumption. This more realistically depicted firm, because of the resources used to provide on-the-job consumption, appears to add needlessly to its cost of producing goods. This seems to be at odds with the firm of economic theory, which minimizes the cost of producing goods that its customers will consume. The appearance is a delusion. Because those who consume on the job pay for their amenities, such consumption will take place only when it *reduces* the cost of producing goods for others. Competitive markets for the firm's goods prevent its owner–manager from financing his amenities through customers' contributions to his revenue. Customers always can purchase from firms whose owners prefer to confine their consumption in greater degree to their households. Competitive markets for labor similarly block an owner–manager from taxing his workers to pay for his amenities; and, finally, investors always can put their funds elsewhere if they cannot receive a competitive return (corrected for risk) from a firm whose owner–manager consumes on the job.

Because the owner–manager pays for his amenities by accepting a reduction in his implicit managerial compensation, he will not consume while on the job unless the cost of doing so, per unit of utility received, is *less* than if he consumed at home. The same must be true of all workers, including hired managers. If the owner–manager or his employees desire to consume on the job, paying for what they consume, then their services can be acquired more cheaply by allowing such consumption than by barring it, for in such a case the cost of on-the-job amenities is smaller than would be the increase in take-home pay required to maintain identical utility levels for these employees. On-the-job consumption, when known, occurs only if there is a utility advantage to consuming at the firm, because the equivalent value in larger take-home pay is more fungible than is on-the-job consumption. If consumption at home is more efficient, then it will not take place on the job; the increase in pecuniary compensation required to compensate persons for not consuming on the job will be less than the cost of providing such consumption if workers' or managers' utility level is to be unchanged.

The assumption that firms minimize the cost of producing goods for others, derived so easily from the profit-maximizing assumption, remains valid even when the firm is permitted to provide on-the-job amenities. The producing activity of the firm is carried on at least cost because such consumption possibilities are available. The neoclassical theory of the firm merely simplifies the study of the price system by implicitly assuming, or defining, consumption activity to be more efficient in households.

It follows that the claim, and presumed empirical observation, that consumption takes place on the job cannot refute either profit maximization or efficiency in the production of goods by real firms. The deployment of resources in firms may differ because of different degrees of on-the-job consumption, but firms that supply more such amenities are producing them more cheaply for their employee–consumers (or perhaps, more accurately, are producing more utility per dollar expended) than if these employee–consumers were forced to consume substitute "amenities" at home. Hence, goods that are produced for employee consumption on the job and goods produced for outside consumers (which the firm of economic theory is designed to explain) are both produced at as low an opportunity cost as is possible. The firm of economic theory may be only a sketch of real firms, but it nonetheless yields useful insights about resource utilization in a decentralized economy.

SHIRKING

To this point, I have discussed only known consumption on the job by individual employees. In a model of the firm in which monitoring cost is zero, this would be the only possible on-the-job consumption; each quality of worker, including managers, receives his market-determined wage, but the way in which that wage is received depends on whether the worker prefers to consume on the job or at home. Once we turn to a model of the firm in which monitoring cost is positive, the inverse correlation between take-home wages and on-the-job consumption is weakened, at least in the case of the individual worker. If positive monitoring cost means anything, it certainly means the weakening of this inverse correlation.

Take-home wages for an identifiable quality grouping of workers will be inversely correlated with their *collective* on-the-job consumption even when monitoring cost is positive, but some workers in the group will consume more on the job than others, and the amount of collective consumption by the group will be higher (than with zero monitoring cost) by virtue of the fact that this inverse relationship cannot be preserved so strongly when compensating each individual. Correspondingly, the group's take-home pay will be lower. We may interpret the amount by which on-the-job consumption, given positive monitoring cost, exceeds the amount of consumption that would take place when modeled with zero monitoring cost as *shirking*. Shirking is a non-activity in the zero monitoring cost model. Unlike the mutually advantageous on-the-job consumption that takes place when monitoring cost is zero, shirking can be reduced and both employer and employees made better off if the monitoring cost required to reduce shirking is less than the value of the resources consumed in shirking. Presumably, shirking is reduced to its optimal level by various pressures from within and outside the firm, but shirking nonetheless will exist.

The average quality of employees contained in an identifiable quality group determines the compensation that is paid, per employee, to this group. This compensation contains a larger fraction of on-the-job consumption than it would in a zero monitoring cost model. In firms that have more difficulty (higher costs) in monitoring, this fraction will be greater. The fraction that is take-home pay will be lower than for the same quality group of employees employed in a low monitoring cost firm.

AGGREGATE ON-THE-JOB CONSUMPTION

There are thus two sources of on-the-job consumption: known individual consumption (possibly the owner–manager's), which reflects personal taste, and unknown individual consumption – shirking – which reflects the existence of positive monitoring cost. Once this is recognized, it is no longer clear that diffuse ownership gives rise to more on-the-job consumption. Where is it written that the owner–manager of a closely held firm prefers to consume only at home?

Consider an owner–manager who delights in associating with people of his own religion or skin color. Because he spends most of his waking hours on the job, this is where he will choose to indulge his preferences. If, to indulge his taste for on-the-job consumption, he must employ workers who are less productive in supplying the goods that he sells to others, then consuming in the firm will force him to accept lower pecuniary returns. For him, this may be superior to higher income and less preferred on-the-job associations.

Imagine now that this same person becomes specialized to the task of owning, not managing, the firm. Let us suppose that the professional managers that he employs to replace him in the firm's management share his tastes in fellow workers. In his new role as specialized owner, however, he derives no utility from the composition of the labor force, for he no longer puts in time at the office. He prefers instead the higher pecuniary returns that can be had with a less homogeneous mixture of laborers. His desire for profit now leads him to search for a management that is less prone to discriminate by religion and color. Alternatively, he may insist on reducing the pecuniary compensation of his hired managers until his net return rises to what could be secured from a new and different management.

The reduction in the compensation of existing management may nonetheless be insufficient to keep this management in the managing game. The owner, when he was manager, was prepared to accept some reduction in pecuniary income because *he* consumed on-the-job amenities, and he preferred this to higher take-home compensation because his utility from such consumption is time- and place-specific. Because he sacrifices this specificity when he consumes at home, he will insist on a greater reduction in the compensation of hired management than he was prepared to accept when he managed the firm; now it is hired management, not he, that enjoys these time- and place-specific amenities. He will ask a greater financial sacrifice from such a management than he would have asked of himself, were he managing, if he is to be just as well off consuming at home. The net result of his becoming a specialized owner, therefore, may very well be a reduction in on-the-job consumption.

This important aspect of specialization in ownership has largely gone unnoticed. The specialized owner derives little or no direct utility from on-the-job consumption by his management. He may be unaffected by such consumption if his management is prepared to stay on the job while absorbing *enough* of a wage cut to compensate the specialized owner for the resulting increase in other costs. But because of the time and place specificity of on-the-job consumption, the required wage cut will be larger than would have been required by the owner were he managing his own firm. In general, we can expect that specialized ownership, in and of itself, creates pressure for less on-the-job consumption so long as monitoring cost is not a barrier to guaranteeing that what is promised by management is what is delivered.

We thus have two opposing forces at work. The "pure" effect of specialized ownership is to reduce on-the-job consumption below levels that would obtain if owners were also managers. The opposing force is the increase in monitoring cost associated with organizational structures most likely to create specialized ownership interests. The shareholder of a large publicly held corporation derives no direct utility from on-the-job consumption of management, so his interests are fixed on the bottom line of the profit and loss statement. The more broadly based is the ownership of the firm, however, the greater is the cost of monitoring management.

It is clearly an error to suppose that a firm managed by its only owner comes closest to the profit-maximizing firm postulated in the model firm of economic theory. The owner–manager of such a firm may or may not be motivated only by the search for profit. He may habitually consume on the job. This consumption can take many forms. It need not be the proclivity for association with homogeneous fellow workers described above. The senior Ford, who built the Ford Motor Company into a position of dominance in the automobile industry, is said to have had such a proclivity. But also, in his later years, he proved to be stubborn, singleminded, and without managerial flexibility. He ''consumed'' dominance over his fellow workers at the sacrifice of profit to himself. His lieutenants were disgruntled but helpless as they witnessed the decline of the company. Ford survived as the managerial leader of his company only because it was *his* company. Had the Ford Motor Company been a publicly held corporation, it is unlikely that he would have been allowed to indulge his taste for dominance for so long. Those who criticize the publicly held corporation for favoring on-the-job consumption may be aiming at the wrong target.

Whether on-the-job consumption finds its source in the personal tastes of owners and employees of the firm or in the cost of monitoring is irrelevant to either profit maximization or efficiency. Specialization of business activity into one set of rights that we identify as share ownership and which we may, if we insist, call ownership of the corporation, and a second set that we call managerial control, surely raises the utility level achievable by those with funds to invest and those with managerial skills to sell. This division of property rights allows persons the option of combining ''ownership'' and control in any mixture that they wish, given the budget constraints they face. Investment funds *and* control, therefore, become available at *lower* costs to society than would be possible were fractional ownership barred. The advent of the modern corporation, organized exchanges, and corporation law have reduced the cost of specializing one's interest as between the different tasks of owning and managing.

THE EQUILIBRIUM BUSINESS ORGANIZATION

If greater monitoring cost is associated with one type of business organization (perhaps the large publicly held corporation) than with another (perhaps the small closely held corporation), then we may expect differences in the uses to which resources are put because of differences in *shirking*. The high-monitoring-cost business will use a larger fraction of its resources to deliver compensation to management in the form of on-the-job consumption, where this may include larger firm size and faster growth as well as the usual amenities. The pecuniary component of managerial compensation, over time and on average, will adjust downward appropriately, so that the sum of amenities and take-home pay for a group of like-quality managers is the same as they could obtain from the second firm, but the first firm's deployment of resources will nonetheless differ from the second firm's.

The existence of alternative business organizations (meaning different capabilities for monitoring employee behavior) implies a predictable self-selection process, in which managerial talent (of a given quality) with a taste for on-the-job consumption will tend to manage firms that have chosen a high-monitoring-cost organization. Such firms cannot easily prevent on-the-job consumption, so it is to their advantage to accept larger amounts of it in return for lower take-home compensation. Managerial talent with a preference for take-home pay will find its comparative advantage in low-monitoring-cost firms, because these firms, by virtue of their ability to monitor on-the-job consumption, are willing to offer a larger fraction of compensation in the form of take-home wages.

The different deployments of the resources of firms called forth by differences in monitoring cost are consistent with the requirements of efficiency. They represent ways of accommodating to the different tastes of investors and managers. The preferences of some investors for diversification of their capital and for absence of monitoring responsibility, and of some managers for on-the-job consumption, are catered to efficiently by a different deployment of the firm's resources, and a different ownership structure, than would be the case for investors and managers who have other preferences. Underlying technical and market conditions will set boundaries to the type of business organization through which investors and managers may combine financial and human resources to achieve their goals in a mutually advantageous manner, and within these limits cooperation will be achieved efficiently by different resource deployment.

It is important to treat monitoring cost as we would treat any other cost of production if we are to develop a useful perspective for assessing the consequences of a diffuse ownership structure. The structure of ownership that emerges is an endogenous outcome of competitive selection in which various cost advantages and disadvantages are balanced to arrive at an equilibrium organization of the firm. One cannot simply assert that diffuse ownership fails to yield maximum profit or maximum value of the firm, or that it fails to yield efficient resource allocation. On-the-job consumption, and even control by owners, cannot be judged independently of other aspects of the equilibrium organization.

The monitoring cost that must be incurred to reduce shirking to its optimal level is a function of the way the firm has been organized and of the technological conditions that underlie the production of its goods. The cost is borne by the firm, not its employees. Because a given quality group of employees must receive the same total compensation (although its mix may differ) whether the group works for a firm with a high or a low monitoring cost, the cost of monitoring cannot be passed on to the employees. In making its choice of business organization, the firm (or its owners) therefore must pay attention to how this choice affects the cost of monitoring and whether a higher-monitoring-cost organization will also bring with it reductions in other costs that make the higher monitoring cost worth bearing.

Consider the model of the owner–managed, hierarchically organized business firm. Lines of control branch out from the president's office, occupied, naturally, by the only owner of the firm. He supervises middle management. In turn, middle management supervises shop foremen, and the foremen monitor the rest of the firm's labor force (which receives agreed-upon fixed wages). Middle management may be paid by fixed salary and/or a share in the profit of the firm. The owner–president's income is derived wholly from the revenue left after paying these agreed-upon wages and other costs, including monitoring cost, of operating the firm.

This type of firm will maximize the value of the owner's assets only under a limited set of conditions, even though there is *no* separation between ownership and control of the kind associated with a diffuse ownership structure. For such an organization to be effective in holding down cost, the tasks performed by those working under the middle management's direction, or, perhaps, under the foremen's direction, must be relatively easy to direct and monitor. When laborers receive fixed wages, not at all influenced (in the short run) by the profitability of the firm, they have a powerful incentive to shirk. If the tasks performed by these workers are physical, repetitive ones, perhaps turning out intermediate parts for the assembly of a final product, this shirking can be held within tolerable limits when fixed wages have been agreed upon. The owner–president's task is to direct and monitor middle management, reducing the degree to which it shirks. Because the president's income is the revenue that remains after paying other factors of production, he has no incentive to *shirk* (which is *not* to say he never consumes on the job). Shirking by middle management may be reduced if they are allowed to share in profits, because their tasks are unlikely to be so easy to monitor. Sharing in profit gives some incentive to curtail *voluntarily* the degree of shirking.

The viability of such a business organization depends on how well three conditions are satisfied. (1) The tasks of fixed-wage workers must be easy to monitor. (2) The funds that the owner–president is able and willing to commit to the equity of the firm must be sufficient to maintain an effective scale of operations. (3) The owner's taste for managing and his ability to lead the firm must be appropriate to the situation in which the firm finds itself. These three conditions will not be satisfied by every situation in which a firm may exist, and when they are not, competitive pressures will call for a different organization. A firm whose scale requirement is relatively small but in which the tasks that need to be performed are less easy to monitor may rely to a greater extent on profit-sharing, or partnership. When scale requirements are large, especially when the survival of the firm requires a rapid attainment of large scale, then there will be economic pressure to satisfy the consequent need for sizable equity capital by turning to a diffuse ownership structure so as to reduce the wealth that must be committed to this single enterprise by a typical investor. The greater monitoring cost that might arise from such an ownership structure may be more than offset by the reduction in risk-associated capital cost, so that maximization of the value of the assets of the firm actually requires a diffuse ownership structure.

The ownership structure likely to maximize the value of the firm's assets depends on the technology of the tasks required of the firm's labor force, on the desired scale of operation, and on the managerial ability of potential owners of the firm. No single ownership structure is suitable for all situations if the value of the firm's assets is to be maximized. In particular, from the viewpoint of the owner(s), the optimal distribution of profits is 100 percent to a single owner–manager only in special circumstances.

As the number of shareholders increases, the wealth of each will depend less on the success of the firm, and it will be more difficult to organize very diffuse ownership interests into an effective instrument for monitoring management. But this carries no implication of a resulting reduction in the value of the firm. As the prospective typical purchaser of ownership shares recognizes the minimal effect that small shareholders have on the control of the firm, there must be a compensating reduction in risk and in the annoyance of monitoring management if he is to provide equity capital. The terms on which he purchases his shares must be competitive with what he requires to concentrate his funds in a single enterprise that he would monitor. It is unreasonable to suppose that diffuse ownership has destroyed profit maximization as a guide to resource allocation. Indeed, profit maximization may require a diffuse ownership structure. But it is equally unreasonable to suppose that potentially valuable assets will not be controlled effectively by some groups of owners. In general, self-interest, functioning within the framework of private ownership of shares, surely propels effective control by owners into existing vacuums in control.

THE ALLEGED VACUUM IN CONTROL BY OWNERS

The issue of the alleged separation between ownership and control is based on an empirical presumption that ownership of the modern corporation is so diluted among the multitude of shareholders that their interests are essentially unrepresented when corporate management makes its decision. Sensible rejoinders to this charge have been made. Essentially, these claim that, when the need arises, dispersed ownership will become sufficiently concentrated to give proper guidance to, perhaps to ''boot'' out, an ineffective management. This congealing of ownership may take the form of a takeover, a rebellion by a group of cooperating shareholders, or the acquisition of large shareholdings by one or a few shareholders. These events, because they are possible and, indeed, actually do take place, put a constraint on management even when they are not currently operative. In addition, of course, management does worry about the prices of the firm's stocks and bonds because these give the terms on which capital will be supplied to the corporation. Even shirking managers desire cheaper financing of amenities. Managerial personnel are also quite concerned about the value of their services to other firms that may seek to employ them. The many years of investment in human capital and reputation are not lightly put at risk in the pursuit of the advantages offered by shirking. Nonetheless, temptations arise, the cost of concentrating ownership is not negligible, and such concentration *after* a poor showing is at best a partial remedy. For these reasons there would seem to be a demand for an ongoing supervision of management or for a linking of the interests of management to those of shareholders. This is supplied partly from the board of directors, but the members of the board may themselves have little actual ownership interest in the firm. It is also supplied by correlating managerial wages and corporation performance.

The allegation of effective separation between ownership and control, if true, would pose a genuine puzzle. The alleged vacuum of control surely should not exist, for the self-interest of owners calls for avoiding the surrender of the control of valuable assets except to others who have similar interests. Not every owner of shares can or wishes to control management, but those who purchase shares do presume that in the typical case there will be some owners with enough at stake to oversee management.

There have been a few studies of the degree to which corporate share ownership is structured so as to assure a significant representation of ownership interests. Various standards are used to determine whether such representation is present. The fraction of shares owned by the largest single ownership unit, by the five largest ownership units, the ten largest, and the twenty largest are among the standards used to define minority ownership interests, while

Table 11.1 Ownership interest of corporate directors and management

	Unweighted ave., 1973-82	
	% of shares (1)	*Value of shares (2) ($'000)*
Manufacturing firms:		
Ten largest on 1975 Fortune 500	2.1	151,621
Middle ten on 1975 Fortune 500	19.3	124,560
Last ten on 1975 Fortune 500	20.4	27,134
Ten too small for 1975 Fortune 500 (randomly selected)	32.5	66,486
Ten public utility firms (randomly selected)	13.5	14,271
Average over all fifty firms	17.5	76,623

Note: Out of the total of 500 data points, 4 were secured by extrapolation from neighboring data. Extrapolations of data for 1973 and 1974 were also required in some instances.
Source: Percentage of shares owned by management secured from Value Line Survey of Corporations.

5, 10, and 20 percent of outstanding shares are among the standards used to identify the ownership significance of these minorities. These alternatives tend to identify numerous firms as "owner-controlled," although, of course, the number so identified varies inversely with the toughness of the criterion adopted. Nonetheless, roughly speaking, about 50 percent of large corporations fall into the owner-controlled category.

These studies underestimate the degree of ownership representation because they generally ignore the fact that corporate executives, while not often among the largest shareholders, receive incomes that are highly correlated with stock performance. This correlation derives not only from bonuses but also, to a surprising degree, from managers' ownership of stock. Ownership and control are not so separate as is often supposed.

Column (1) of table 11.1 reveals that a substantial fraction of outstanding shares are owned by directors and management of corporations in all but the very largest firms. In the ten largest firms in the Fortune 500 (ranked in 1975), the average share of stock owned by management over a ten-year period was only slightly over 2 percent. But an average of twenty firms, ten in the middle and ten at the bottom of the 500 list, reveals that corporate managers owned about 20 percent of outstanding shares, and for ten firms too small to make the Fortune list, this share rises to 32 percent. If we suppose that regulation reduces the productivity of linking management interests to owner interests, the smaller fraction of shares owned by the managements of utilities makes sense.

Column (2) shows a much smaller variation in the value of the shareholdings of corporate management. The fraction of shares owned by management in the ten largest corporations is roughly one-tenth the fraction owned in smaller corporations, but because of the difference in number and price of the shares the value of managers' holdings in the largest corporations is roughly twice the average of the thirty smaller manufacturing firms.

Assorted ambiguities are embedded in these data. For example, the variations in the table may reflect differences in shares owned per corporate executive or differences in the relative size of the managerial components of these firms, but such interpretation problems cannot undercut the conclusion that managers' shareholdings create a substantial linkage between the financial interests of management and those of outside shareholders.

A Senate report[7] contains data for 1976 on stockholdings of 122 major corporations. A variety of industry sectors are covered, including manufacturing, finance, transportation, retail, and utilities. The average share of stock held by the twenty largest holdings is slightly more than 20 percent. From these data, it is possible to supplement the management shareholdings with outsider shareholdings for the ten largest firms shown in the table, for which management owned an average of slightly over 2 percent of outstanding shares. The twenty largest share-owners owned an average of 18 percent of the shares of these firms, so that, when outsider ownership of shares is taken into account, all groups of firms in the table, including the largest firms, exhibit substantial sources of profit-motivated control.

How important to managers' income is the stock-based compensation received by management through its holdings of shares? Wilbur G. Lewellen[8] calculated the value of managers' remuneration received in the form of stock, dividend income, and capital gains for fifty of the nation's largest manufacturing firms for every year between 1940 and 1963. He also estimated the after-tax income that management derived from its nonstock wages. Lewellen found that stock-based compensation for the top executive, averaged over all firms in his sample, exceeded four times the after-tax wages, and for the top five executives, averaged over all firms, stock-based compensation was almost five times as great as wages.

The picture painted by management shareholdings, the importance of stock-based managerial income, and the size of minority shareholdings is that of a strong linkage between management and owner interests. While it cannot be argued on the basis of these data that there is a perfect correlation between these interests, it is clear that there is an ongoing considerable interest in profit-maximizing behavior. It is also clear that the problems of congealing diffuse outsider shareholdings, to discipline the management of the largest corporations when the need arises, is not so formidable, because these shareholdings are not so diffusely owned as is often supposed. How could it be otherwise? In a world in which self-interest plays a significant role in economic behavior, it is foolish to believe that owners of valuable resources systematically relinquish control to managers who are not guided to serve their interests.

NOTES

1 Berle and Means (1933, pp. 6–7).
2 Veblen (1924).
3 See Williamson (1964); Alchian and Demsetz (1972, p. 777); Jensen and Meckling (1976, p. 305); Fama (1980, p. 288). My mild disagreement with this literature revolves around the following issues: I do not believe that resorting to agency relationships reduces the value of the firm to its owners. On the contrary, it increases this value. I do not believe that on-the-job consumption is necessarily, or even probably, greater with professional management than with management by owners. The cost of agency, I believe, is borne by the firm, not by the agents. I am not prepared to presume the fact of diffuseness in the ownership of the modern corporation.
4 Baumol (1967).
5 See Nader, Green, and Seligman (1976); and Galbraith (1967).
6 See Demsetz (1982), for an extended discussion of the task of neoclassical economic theory.
7 US Senate (1978).
8 Lewellen (1969, p. 299).

REFERENCES

Alchian, A. and Demsetz, H. (1972). "Production Information Costs and Economic Organization." *American Economic Review*, 62.

Baumol, W. I. (1967). *Business Behavior, Value, and Growth*. New York: Harcourt, Brace and World.

Berle, A. A. and Means, G. C. (1933). *The Modern Corporation and Private Property*. New York: Macmillan.

Demsetz, H. (1982). *Economic, Legal, and Political Dimensions of Competition*. Amsterdam: North-Holland.

Fama, E. (1980). "Agency Problems and the Theory of the Firm." *Journal of Political Economy*, 88.

Galbraith, J. K. (1967). *The New Industrial State*. Boston: Houghton Mifflin.

Jensen, M. C. and Meckling, W. H. (1976). "Theory of the Firm: Managerial Behavior, Agency Costs, and Ownership Structure." *Journal of Financial Economics*, 3.

Lewellen, W. G. (1969). "Management and Ownership in the Large Firms." *Journal of Finance*, 24.

US Senate (1978). *Voting Rights in Major Corporations*. Staff study. Washington, DC: US Senate Subcommittee on Reports, Accounting, and Management of the Committee on Governmental Affairs.

Veblen, T. (1924). *The Engineers and the Price System*. New York: Viking Press.

Williamson, O. E. (1964). *The Economics of Discretionary Behavior: Managerial Objectives in a Theory of the Firm*. Englewood Cliffs, NJ: Prentice-Hall.

12
The Structure of Corporate Ownership: Causes and Consequences

with Kenneth Lehn

Large publicly traded corporations are frequently characterized as having highly diffuse ownership structures that effectively separate ownership of residual claims from control of corporate decisions. This alleged separation of ownership and control figures prominently both in the economic theory of organization and in the ongoing debate concerning the social significance of the modern corporation, a debate that we join later in this paper.[1] Our primary concern, however, is to explore some of the broad forces that influence the structure of corporate ownership. Our conjectures about the determinants of ownership structure are examined empirically.

Inspection of ownership data reveals that the concentration of equity ownership in US corporations varies widely. For a sample of 511 large US corporations, table 12.1 lists the distribution of three measures of ownership concentration: the percentage of a firm's outstanding common equity owned by the five largest shareholders ($A5$), the percentage of shares owned by the 20 largest shareholders ($A20$), and an approximation of a Herfindahl measure of ownership concentration (AH). This sample and these data will be described more fully later in the paper. We simply note here the variation in ownership concentration. The value of $A5$ ranges from 1.27 to 87.14 around a mean value of 24.81. Similar variation is found in the values of $A20$ and AH: $A20$ ranges from 1.27 to 91.54 and AH ranges from 0.69 to 4,952.38. The corresponding average values of these two variables are 37.66 and 402.75, respectively.

We approach the task of explaining the variation in these data by considering the advantages and disadvantages to the firm's shareholders of greater diffuseness in ownership structure. The most obvious disadvantage is the

This paper reprinted with permission from *Journal of Political Economy* 93(6) 1985.

greater incentive for shirking by *owners* that results. The benefit derived by a shirking owner is his ability to use his time and energies on other tasks and indulgences; this benefit accrues entirely to him. The cost of his shirking, presumably the poorer performance of the firm, is shared by all owners in proportion to the number of shares of stock they own. The more concentrated is ownership, the greater the degree to which benefits and costs are borne by the same owner. In a firm owned entirely by one individual, all benefits and costs of owner shirking are borne by the sole owner. In this case, no "externalities" confound his decision about attending to the tasks of ownership. In a very diffusely owned firm, the divergence between benefit and costs would be much larger for the typical owner, and he can be expected to respond by neglecting some tasks of ownership.

The inefficiency implied by such externalities, of itself, dictates against diffuse ownership structures, and we would observe no diffuse ownership structures in a "rational" world unless counterbalancing advantages exist. Since these advantages do exist, a decision to alter a firm's ownership structure in favor of greater diffuseness presumably is guided by the goal of value maximization. A theory of ownership structure is based largely on an understanding of what makes these advantages vary in strength from firm to firm.

DETERMINANTS OF OWNERSHIP STRUCTURE

Of the possible general forces affecting ownership structure, three seem important enough to merit investigation. One of these, the *value-maximizing size* of the firm, is not surprising. The second, more subtle and difficult to measure, is the profit potential from exercising more effective control, to which we ascribe the name *control potential*. The third is *systematic regulation*, the general purpose of which is to impose, in one form or another, constraints on the scope and impact of shareholder decisions. In addition to these, we consider the *amenity potential* of firms, about which more will be said below.

Value-maximizing size

The size of firms that compete successfully in product and input markets varies within and among industries. The larger is the competitively viable size, *ceteris paribus*, the larger is the firm's capital resources and, generally, the greater is the market value of a given fraction of ownership. The higher price of a given fraction of the firm should, in itself, reduce the degree to which ownership is concentrated. Moreover, a given degree of control generally requires a smaller share of the firm the larger is the firm. Both these effects of size imply greater diffuseness of ownership the larger is a firm. This may be termed the risk-neutral effect of size on ownership.

Table 12.1 (a) Frequency distribution of *A5*, *A20*, and *AH* for 511 firms in sample

	A5		*A20*			AH	
Range	*Frequency*	*Cumulative percentage*	*Frequency*	*Cumulative percentage*	*Range*	*Frequency*	*Cumulative percentage*
0-4.99	16	3.13	11	2.15	0-19.99	28	5.48
5-9.99	50	12.92	13	4.70	20-39.99	46	14.48
10-14.99	86	29.75	13	7.24	40-59.99	70	22.70
15-19.99	98	48.92	32	13.50	60-79.99	44	31.31
20-24.99	72	63.01	41	21.53	80-99.99	42	39.53
25-29.99	45	71.82	67	34.64	100-119.99	38	46.97
30-34.99	37	79.06	59	46.18	120-139.99	28	52.45
35-39.99	27	84.34	66	59.10	140-159.99	22	56.75
40-44.99	19	88.06	57	70.25	160-179.99	16	59.88
45-49.99	18	91.59	39	77.89	180-199.99	11	62.04
50-54.99	9	93.35	34	84.54	200-219.99	14	64.78
55-59.99	10	95.30	22	88.85	220-239.99	9	66.54
60-64.99	10	97.26	21	92.96	240-289.99	17	69.86
65-69.99	7	98.63	19	96.67	290-369.99	21	73.97
70-74.99	4	99.41	9	98.43	370-479.99	24	78.67
75-79.99	1	99.61	2	98.83	480-539.99	22	82.98
80-84.99	0	99.61	3	99.41	540-779.99	21	87.08
85-89.99	2	100.00	1	99.61	780-1,219.99	25	91.98
90-94.99	0	100.00	2	100.00	1,220-2,279.99	20	95.89
95-100.00	0	100.00	0	100.00	2,280-4,959.99	21	100.00

(b) Summary statistics of *A5*, *A20*, and *AH* for 511 firms in sample

Variable	N	*Mean*	*Standard deviation*	*Min.*	*Max.*
A5	511	24.81	15.77	1.27	87.14
A20	511	37.66	16.73	1.27	91.54
AH	511	402.75	722.99	0.69	4,952.38

Risk aversion should reinforce the risk-neutral effect. An attempt to preserve effective and concentrated ownership in the face of larger capital needs requires a small group of owners to commit more wealth to a single enterprise. Normal risk aversion implies that they will purchase additional shares only at lower, risk-compensating, prices. This increased cost of capital discourages owners of larger firms from attempting to maintain highly concentrated ownership.

As the value-maximizing size of the firm grows, both the risk-neutral and the risk-aversion effects of larger size ultimately should weigh more heavily than the shirking cost that may be expected to accompany a more diffuse ownership structure, so that an inverse relationship between firm size and concentration of ownership is to be expected. Larger firms realize a lower *overall* cost with a more diffuse ownership structure than do small firms. The choice by owners of a diffuse ownership structure, therefore, is consistent with stockholder wealth (or utility)-maximizing behavior.

Control potential

Control potential is the wealth gain achievable through more effective monitoring of managerial performance by a firm's owners. If the market for corporate control and the managerial labor market perfectly aligned the interests of managers and shareholders, then control potential would play no role in explaining corporate ownership structure (although it might then explain the degree to which ownership by professional management is concentrated). We assume, however, that neither of these markets operates costlessly. In addition to the transaction and information costs associated with the acquisition and maintenance of corporate control, Jarrell and Bradley (1980) have shown that there are significant regulatory costs associated with control transactions. These nontrivial costs act effectively as a tax on corporate control transactions. Although we are unaware of similar empirical studies of transaction costs associated with the managerial labor market, we assume that this market also imperfectly disciplines corporate managers who work contrary to the wishes of shareholders. Our view is that these transaction costs impose a specific identity and control potential on firms. Alterations in the structure of corporate ownership, in part, can be understood as a response to these costs.

We seek to uncover elements of a firm's environment that are pervasive and persistent in their effect on control potential. Firm-specific uncertainty is one such factor. Firms that transact in markets characterized by stable prices, stable technology, stable market shares, and so forth are firms in which managerial performance can be monitored at relatively low cost. In less predictable environments, however, managerial behavior simultaneously figures more prominently in a firm's fortunes and becomes more difficult to monitor. Frequent changes in relative prices, technology, and market shares require timely managerial decisions concerning redeployment of corporate assets and personnel. Disentangling the effects of managerial behavior on firm performance from the corresponding effects of these other, largely exogenous, factors is costly, however.[2] Accordingly, we believe that a firm's control potential is directly associated with the noisiness of the environment in which it operates. The noisier a firm's environment, the greater the payoff to owners in maintaining tighter control. Hence, noisier environments should give rise to more concentrated ownership structures.[3]

Clearly, we take the view that owners *believe* they can influence the success of their firms and that all outcomes are neither completely random nor completely foreseeable. This belief constitutes an assertion of the existence of risks, opportunities, and managerial shirking that are in some degree controllable by owners for the profit of owners. The profit potential from exercising a given degree of owner control is, we believe, correlated with instability in the firm's environment.

This instability may be measured in many ways – by fluctuations in product and input prices of relevance to a firm, for example, or by variations in a firm's market share. We rely on instability of a firm's profit rate, measured by variation in both stock returns and accounting returns. Profit data are readily available, and profit variability offers a global measure of the impact of the various subcomponents of instability in its environment; profit also is the "bottom line" that so interests stockholders.

The three measures of instability examined here are (1) firm-specific risk (*SE*), as measured by the standard error of estimate calculated from fitting the "market model," (2) the standard deviation of monthly stock market rates of return (STD_s), and (3) the standard deviation of annual accounting profit rates (STD_a). Our intuition favors firm-specific risk as the factor most strongly associated with the type of instability for which control is most useful. The exercise of control should be particularly important to those operations of a firm that can be influenced and responded to most easily. These would seem to include the inner functioning of the firm and its operations in the markets in which it purchases and sells, both of which are proximate and specific to the firm. In contrast to these sources of instability, economy-wide events such as the rate of growth of money supply or fluctuations in government tax expenditure flows are beyond a firm's control and, at best, can be reacted to intelligently. Because of these reactive possibilities, even this more distant and less firm-specific instability is likely to call forth more concentrated ownership, but greater control potential is offered by instability that is more specific to the firm.

We include instability in accounting rates of return among our measures, though we recognize many defects of accounting data. One of these defects is purely statistical: whereas we have collected monthly stock return data, our accounting data are annual data. For any time period, then, there are 12 times as many observations with which to calculate a stock return variance as there are for calculating an accounting return variance. Accounting profits, however, may reflect year-to-year fluctuations in underlying business conditions better than stock market rates of return, since stock market rates of return reflect expected future developments that may cloak contemporary fluctuations in business conditions. We say "may" because today's accounting rate of return is influenced by past investment expenditures (and other carryover accounting entries), and this also attenuates the impact of "today's" instabilities. It is not clear on *a priori* grounds which measure is better suited to measure day-to-day or year-to-year variability in the firm's environment.

Regulation

Systematic regulation restricts the options available to owners, thus reducing control potential in ways that may not be reflected fully in profit instability. Regulation also provides some subsidized monitoring and disciplining of the management of regulated firms. A bank whose balance sheet looks too risky to regulators will find itself under considerable pressure to replace its management. These "primary" effects of regulation should reduce ownership concentration to a greater degree than would be predicted simply on the basis of profit instability.

We expect the net impact of regulation to be dominated by these primary effects, which call for greater diffuseness of ownership in regulated industries. There are also well-known problems of amenity consumption by management in a regulated setting. These should be more important than in non-regulated firms because cost-plus price-setting regulation reduces the incentive to hold down cost while it dulls competition. Greater control of management by owners would seem to be called for and, hence, greater concentration of ownership. However, owner incentives to reduce managerial amenity consumption are also dulled by the tendency of commissions to adjust prices toward levels that leave the profit rate unchanged, and this counteracts the desire for greater control of management.

Amenity potential of a firm's output

Those who own large fractions of the outstanding shares of a firm either manage the firm themselves or are positioned to see to it that management serves their interests. Maximizing the value of the firm generally serves these interests well, for this provides the largest possible budget for a shareholder to spend as a "household". The advantage of maximizing profit through the firm and then consuming in the household is based on the implicit assumption that specialization in consumption is productive of maximum utility. However, when owners can obtain their consumption goals better through the firm's business than through household expenditures, they will strive to control that firm more closely to obtain these goals. Just as the potential for higher profit creates a demand for closer monitoring of management by owners, so does the potential for firm-specific amenity consumption.

We refer here to the utility consequences of being able to influence the type of goods produced by the firm, not to the utility derived from providing general leadership to the firm. We believe that there is non-pecuniary income associated with the provision of general leadership and with the ability to deploy resources to suit one's personal preferences, but we are not now prepared to assert how this varies across firms or different ownership structures.[4] However, we do believe that two industries are likely to call forth tight control in order to indulge such personal preferences. These are professional sports clubs and mass media firms. Winning the World Series or believing that one is systematically influencing public opinion plausibly provides utility to some owners even if profit is reduced from levels otherwise achievable. These consumption goals arise from the particular tastes of owners, so their achievement requires owners to be in a position to influence managerial decisions. Hence, ownership should be more concentrated in firms for which this type of amenity potential is greater. Unfortunately, other than a shared perception that the sports and media industries are especially laden with amenity potential for owners, we have no systematic way of tracking amenity potential. On balance, we consider amenity potential a more speculative explanation of ownership concentration in these special industries than are size, control potential, and regulation.

DATA AND MEASUREMENTS

This study uses ownership data obtained from three directories published by Corporate Data Exchange (CDE): *CDE Stock Ownership Directory: Energy* (1980), *Banking and Finance* (1980), and *Fortune 500* (1981). The sample consists of 511 firms from major sectors of the US economy, including regulated utilities and financial institutions. These firms represent all firms for which we were able to obtain ownership data, accounting data (from the COMPUSTAT tape), and security price data (from the Center for Research on Security Prices, CRSP, tape). We also examine a manufacturing and mining subsample composed of 406 firms.

The ownership data consist of a ranking of all publicly identifiable stockholders who exercised investment power over 0.2 percent or more of the company's common equity. The CDE used the same definition of investment power as that used by the Securities and Exchange Commission (SEC) in application of 13(f) regulations. Specifically, this definition includes all shares over which the stockholder has the power to buy or sell.

The CDE used various SEC forms to secure data, including forms 3, 4, 13f, 14d-1, and 144; and, in addition, it examined corporate proxy statements, secondary offering and merger prospectuses, public pension plan portfolios, employee stock ownership plan reports, and foundation and educational endowment portfolios. Where institutional investors held shares in a management capacity (e.g., investment advistory agreements or trust agreements), the party for whom they managed the shares is identified as the holder with investment power. Similarly, when nominees held stock, the party for whom they held the stock is identified as the holder with investment power. Holdings by diversified financial holding companies, investment banks, brokerage firms, and investment company managers are listed in the ''street name'' of the firms when the firms are not holding the shares in a management capacity.

Our statistical work relies heavily on the percentage of shares owned by the most important shareholders, *A*5 and *A*20, and the approximation of the Herfindahl index, *AH*. Different notation is introduced when we discuss institutional and non-institutional shareholders.

In our regression equations we measure the percentage of shares owned by the top 5 and top 20 shareholders by applying a logistic transformation to these percentages, using the formula

$$\log \frac{\text{percentage concentration}}{100 - \text{percentage concentration}}.$$

The transformation is made to convert an otherwise bounded dependent variable into an unbounded one. A logarithmic transformation is applied to the Herfindahl measure of ownership concentration.[5] We designate the transformed variable by prefixing *L*, as in *LA*5, *LA*20, and *LAH*.

A glance at a simple correlation matrix of *A*5, *A*20, and *AH* indicates that we can expect similar empirical results from using these alternative measures. The correlation between *A*20 and *AH* is weakest, but it is still 0.71. For purposes of constructing an index of ownership concentration, the 20 largest ownership interests establish a workable outer limit. Beyond 20, it is difficult to interpret the measure as a meaningful index of ownership concentration (see table 12.2).

Our measure of firm size (*EQUITY*) is the average annual market value of the firm's common equity during the period 1976–80, with units in thousands of dollars. We have experimented with other size measures (e.g., book value of assets), but the general nature of the statistical result is unaffected by this choice. Since our ownership data pertain to the ownership of common equity, we prefer to proxy size with a measure of the value of common equity. Our

Table 12.2 Correlation of ownership measures for 511 regulated and non-regulated firms

	A5	*A20*
A20	0.92	—
AH	0.86	0.71

measures of instability of a firm's environment (SE and STD_s) are based on stock market rates of return as determined by 60 monthly stock market returns during the five-year period 1976–80.[6] Instability measured by the standard deviation in accounting profit rates (STD_a) is based on five annual profit rates over the period 1976–80. Dummy variables take a value of one if the firm is a regulated utility (*UTIL*), regulated financial institution (*FIN*), or media firm (*MEDIA*), and zero otherwise.

The second part of our empirical work tests the Berle–Means thesis, which implies that diffuse ownership structures adversely affect corporate performance. We test this by assessing the impact of ownership structure on accounting profit rate ($RETURN_a$). In doing so, it is necessary to control for other factors that may affect accounting profit rate. These other factors include the size of the firm as measured by the book value of assets averaged over 1976–80 (*ASSET*) and a set of variables that seek to standardize for accounting artifacts. These variables are ratios to sales of capital expenditures (*CAP*), advertising (*ADV*), and R & D expenses (*RD*), all measured as averages from the 1976–80 time period.

Summary definitions of all variables used in this paper appear below. Summary statistics for these variables for the 511 firms in our sample are shown in table 12.3.

Description of variables

A5	Percentage of shares controlled by top five shareholders. *Sources: CDE Stock Ownership Directories: Banking and Finance* (1980), *Energy* (1980), and *Fortune 500* (1981)
A20	Percentage of shares controlled by top 20 shareholders. *Sources:* same as *A5*
AH	Herfindahl index of ownership concentration. Calculated by summing the squared percentage of shares controlled by each shareholder. *Sources:* same as *A5*
F5	Percentage of shares controlled by top five families and individuals. *Sources:* same as *A5*
I5	Percentage of shares controlled by top five institutional investors. *Sources:* same as *A5*
UTIL	One if firm is electric utility, natural gas pipeline, or natural gas distributor; zero otherwise. *Source:* COMPUSTAT
FIN	One if firm is bank, saving and loan institution, insurance company, or securities firm; zero otherwise. *Source:* COMPUSTAT
MEDIA	One if firm is newspaper publisher, book publisher, magazine publisher, or broadcaster; zero otherwise. *Source:* COMPUSTAT
EQUITY	Market value of common equity ($'000; annual average, 1976–80). *Source:* CRSP
$RETURN_s$	Stock market rate of return (average monthly return, 1976–80). *Source:* CRSP

$RETURN_a$	Accounting rate of return (annual average of net income to book value of shareholders' equity, 1976–80). *Source:* COMPUSTAT
SE	Standard error of estimate from market model in which firm's average monthly return (1976-80) is regressed on the average monthly return on value-weighted market portfolio (1976–80). *Source:* CRSP
STD_s	Standard deviation of monthly stock market rates of return, 1976–80. *Source:* CRSP
STD_a	Standard deviation of annual accounting rates of return, 1976–80. *Source:* COMPUSTAT
CAP	Ratio of capital expenditures (annual average, 1976–80) to total sales. *Source:* COMPUSTAT
ADV	Ratio of advertising expenditures (annual average, 1976–80) to total sales. *Source:* COMPUSTAT
RD	Ratio of research and development expenditures (annual average, 1976–80) to total sales. *Source:* COMPUSTAT
$ASSET$	Value of total assets ($ m; annual average, 1976–80). *Source:* COMPUSTAT

STATISTICAL ANALYSIS OF OWNERSHIP CONCENTRATION

Ordinary least squares (OLS) regression estimates of $LA5$ on three alternative measures of profit instability and four other variables are shown in table 12.4.

Table 12.3 Summary statistics of variables for 511 firms in sample

Variable	*Mean*	*Standard deviation*	*Min.*	*Max.*
A5	24.81	15.77	1.27	87.14
A20	37.66	16.73	1.27	91.54
AH	402.75	722.99	0.69	4,952.38
F5	9.08	13.03	0	69.39
I5	18.39	11.52	0.75	87.14
UTIL	0.10	0.30	0	1
FIN	0.11	0.31	0	1
MEDIA	0.03	0.16	0	1
EQUITY	$1,221,754	$2,698,140	$22,341	$40,587,203
$RETURN_s$	0.017	0.012	−0.013	0.074
$RETURN_a$	0.238	0.105	−0.077	0.824
SE	0.067	0.025	0.031	0.398
STD_s	0.084	0.029	0.034	0.412
STD_a	0.055	0.050	0.002	0.320
CAP	0.089	0.103	0	0.841
ADV	0.011	0.023	0	0.200
RD	0.012	0.020	0	0.200
ASSET	$3,505	$8,114	$48	$94,162

Table 12.4 OLS estimates of *LA*5

Intercept	−1.53	−2.10	−1.53	−2.02	−1.20	−1.29
	(13.6)	(11.9)	(12.3)	(10.1)	(20.3)	(15.8)
UTIL	−1.31	−1.20	−1.27	−1.15	−1.36	−1.33
	(11.1)	(10.0)	(10.4)	(9.0)	(11.6)	(11.3)
FIN	−0.47	−0.47	−0.45	−0.44	−0.45	−0.45
	(4.2)	(4.3)	(4.1)	(3.9)	(4.0)	(4.0)
MEDIA	0.67	0.70	0.67	0.68	0.63	0.62
	(3.2)	(3.4)	(3.2)	(3.3)	(3.0)	(3.0)
*EQUITY**	−4.50	−3.51	−4.64	−3.99	−5.94	−5.70
	(3.5)	(2.7)	(3.6)	(3.1)	(4.6)	(4.5)
SE	6.86	17.94	—	—	—	—
	(4.8)	(5.9)				
SE^2	—	−39.38	—	—	—	—
		(4.1)				
STD_s	—	—	5.44	13.77	—	—
			(4.2)	(4.7)		
STD_s^2	—	—	—	−28.59	—	—
				(3.1)		
STD_a	—	—	—	—	2.84	5.49
					(4.1)	(2.9)
STD_a^2	—	—	—	—	—	−11.78
						(1.5)
N	511	511	511	511	511	511
R^2	0.31	0.33	0.30	0.32	0.30	0.30
F	45.0	41.5	43.6	38.6	43.3	36.5

Note: t-statistics are in parentheses.
*All coefficient estimates on *EQUITY* should be multiplied by 10^{-8}.

All three measures of instability are significantly and positively related to ownership concentration. In addition to linearly estimating ownership concentration as a function of instability, we also estimated this relationship in nonlinear form by including the squared value of the instability measure. The squared values of these variables are negatively related to ownership concentration, indicating that at higher values of these variables the increase in concentration of ownership associated with a given increase in instability diminishes. Of the three instability measures, the standard error of estimate from the market model enters most significantly, and the standard deviation in accounting profit rates enters least significantly.[7]

All other variables take the expected signs, and all of the estimated coefficients are statistically significant at the 0.05 level. Size of firm, as measured by the market value of equity, is negatively related to ownership concentration.[8] The dummy for systematic regulation indicates that the average concentration of ownership for the regulated firms is significantly less than for other firms. The ownership structure of utility firms is affected more by regulation than is that of financial firms. Media firms exhibit significantly more ownership

Table 12.5 OLS estimates of ownership concentration

Measurement of ownership concentration	*Full sample (N = 511)* LA5	LA20	LAH	*Non-regulated sample (N = 406)* LA5	LA20	LAH
Intercept	−2.10	−1.01	3.83	−1.92	−0.68	4.21
	(11.9)	(6.0)	(13.5)	(9.7)	(4.0)	(13.8)
UTIL	−1.20	−1.44	−2.07	—	—	—
	(10.0)	(12.6)	(10.8)	—	—	—
FIN	−0.47	−0.49	−0.78	—	—	—
	(4.3)	(4.7)	(4.4)	—	—	—
MEDIA	0.70	0.75	0.94	0.68	0.72	0.91
	(3.4)	(3.8)	(2.8)	(3.3)	(4.0)	(2.8)
*EQUITY**	−3.51	−2.98	−4.25	−3.90	−3.82	−5.09
	(2.7)	(2.4)	(2.0)	(2.9)	(3.3)	(2.5)
SE	17.94	11.14	26.46	14.83	5.60	20.11
	(5.9)	(3.9)	(5.4)	(4.4)	(1.9)	(3.9)
SE^2	−39.38	−25.26	−59.70	−31.98	−12.14	−44.49
	(4.1)	(2.8)	(3.9)	(3.2)	(1.4)	(2.9)
N	511	511	511	406	406	406
R^2	0.33	0.36	0.33	0.12	0.09	0.09
F	41.5	46.5	41.2	13.4	9.3	10.0

Note: *t*-statistics are in parentheses.
*All coefficient estimates on *EQUITY* should be multiplied by 10^{-8}.

concentration, on average, than other firms, a finding that is consistent with the notion that tighter control is required to achieve the amenity potential offered by the unique output of these firms.

The variation in *LA*5 explained by these equations is at least 30 percent. When firm-specific risk is the instability measure, 33 percent of the variation is explained. The coefficients of all other variables and their significance are largely unaffected by the measure of instability chosen. Most altered is the coefficient on the market value of equity, which varies from − 3.51(E-08) for the nonlinear firm-specific risk equation to − 5.94(E-08) for the linear equation that includes the standard deviation of accounting profit rate.

Different measures of ownership concentration are regressed on identical sets of explanatory variables for two samples of firms in table 12.5. The left side of the table continues our investigation of the full sample of regulated and non-regulated firms. The right side of the table uses a smaller sample which systematically excludes regulated firms. Logistically transformed values of the percentage of shares owned by the five and by the 20 largest stockholding interests and the Herfindahl index are used as alternative measures of ownership concentration. We note the large impact of regulation on R^2.

In table 12.6 we measure ownership concentration separately for all investors (*A*5), family and individual investors (*F*5), and institutional investors (*I*5). The percentage of shares owned by the five largest shareholding interests (not

Table 12.6 Ownership concentration by type of owner

	Dependent variable A5	*Dependent variable* F5	*Dependent variable* I5
Intercept	9.98	1.74	10.66
	(3.0)	(0.6)	(4.3)
UTIL	−14.21	−6.86	−9.64
	(6.4)	(3.5)	(5.7)
FIN	−7.32	−3.26	−5.48
	(3.6)	(1.8)	(3.5)
MEDIA	13.30	13.30	1.40
	(3.5)	(3.9)	(0.5)
*EQUITY**	−5.00	−3.64	−2.88
	(2.1)	(1.7)	(0.16)
SE	306.47	154.63	165.85
	(5.4)	(3.1)	(3.9)
SE^2	−607.14	−388.16	−315.53
	(3.8)	(2.5)	(2.3)
N	511	511	511
R^2	0.23	0.10	0.16
F	24.7	9.7	15.5

Note: *t*-statistics are in parentheses.
*All coefficient estimates on *EQUITY* should be multiplied by 10^{-7}.

logistically transformed) of each shareholder class is the dependent variable in these regressions.[9] We examined these classifications of owners to discover whether the significance of the coefficient on the media variable is attributable to the behavior of family and individual owners or to institutional owners. Since the assumption of amenity potential is strongly governed by personal tastes, we do not expect ownership concentration to be significantly higher for institutional owners if the firm is a media firm.

Table 12.6 reveals that the greater ownership concentration in media firms is attributed almost exclusively to greater family and individual holdings. The coefficient estimate on *MEDIA* is the identical value, 13.30, and it is statistically significant in the equations in which *A*5 and *F*5 are the dependent variables. When *I*5 is the dependent variable, the coefficient estimate on *MEDIA* drops to 1.40, and is not statistically significant. These results are consistent with the interpretation we have given to the amenity potential associated with control of media firms.[10]

Additional evidence that suggests the amenity potential explanation of ownership structure is found by examining ownership data for professional sports clubs. Although we lack systematic ownership, profit, and size data for individual clubs, we show in table 12.7 aggregate ownership data for 121 clubs in five major sports. These clubs are much more tightly controlled than the 511 firms in our sample. Among the 121 sports clubs, there are 238 owners, an

Table 12.7 Ownership data on 121 sports firms and 511 non-sports firms

Sample	*No. of firms*	*No. of shareholders owning 10% or more of the firm's shares*	*No. of shareholders owning 10% or more of the firm's shares per firm*
Sports clubs:			
Major league baseball	26	54	2.1
North American Soccer League	24	54	2.3
National Basketball Association	22	52	2.4
National Football League	28	38	1.4
National Hockey League	21	40	1.9
All sports clubs	121	238	1.97
Demsetz-Lehn sample	511	218	0.43

Source: For sports data, North American Soccer League (NASL) *v.* NFL, no. 78, Civ. 4560-CSH US District Court, SD, New York, February 21, 1979.

average of 1.97 per club, who either are general partners or control at least 10 percent of the club's stock. Among the 511 firms in our sample, the corresponding numbers are 218 owners and an average of 0.43 owners per firm. Admittedly, sports clubs are smaller than the 511 firms in our sample, which in part explains the increased ownership concentration in the sports industry, and they may operate in less stable environments, although we do not know this to be a fact. Nonetheless, these data are consistent with the amenity explanation of ownership structure.

The impact of regulation on ownership concentration is examined from another perspective in table 12.8. Salomon Brothers rates the regulatory climates in which electric utility firms operate, assigning letter grades based on such factors as the allowed rate of return, the rate base test period used, the cost items allowed in the rate base, and the time taken by commissions to decide rate appeals. The 1979 rating we use is an average of regulatory jurisdictions, calculated by using revenue weighting for utilities operating in more than one jurisdiction. We divide the electric utilities in our sample into two groups: those that operate in regulatory climates that are less "stringent" than the median (i.e., "more favorable" for investment purposes) and all other electric utilities. The dummy variable, *REGULATORY CLIMATE*, takes the value of one if the utility is in the former group and zero otherwise.

We expect that this index of regulatory climate is positively related to ownership concentration, less stringent regulation offering owners more control potential through fewer restrictions and less commission monitoring of

Table 12.8 OLS estimates of LA5 for 37 electric utilities

Intercept	−3.94	−8.28	−3.79	10.45	1.18	0.29
	(7.4)	(5.4)	(5.3)	(5.2)	(1.9)	(0.3)
EQUITY	6.03*	1.10†	6.59*	2.07†	1.72†	2.33†
	(0.3)	(0.7)	(0.3)	(1.0)	(0.5)	(0.6)
REGULATORY CLIMATE	0.44	0.13	0.68	0.27	0.92	0.81
	(2.1)	(0.6)	(2.5)	(1.0)	(2.2)	(1.9)
SE	22.78	178.21	—	—	—	—
	(2.3)	(3.4)				
SE^2	—	−1,202.00	—	—	—	—
		(3.0)				
STD_s	—	—	28.63	244.71	—	—
			(2.3)	(3.9)		
STD_s^2	—	—	—	−1,594.26	—	—
				(3.5)		
STD_a	—	—	—	—	54.85	156.69
					(2.5)	(2.1)
STD_a^2	—	—	—	—	—	−2,374.75
						(1.4)
N	37	37	37	37	37	37
R^2	0.27	0.43	0.30	0.49	0.28	0.32
F	4.0	6.0	4.8	7.8	4.3	3.8

Note: t-statistics are in parentheses.
*Coefficient estimates are multiplied by 10^{-8}.
†Coefficient estimates are multiplied by 10^{-7}.

management. In all three equations where the instability measure enters linearly and in the equation where STD_a enters nonlinearly, *REGULATORY CLIMATE* enters with a significant and positive estimated coefficient. When *SE* and STD_s enter in nonlinear form, the estimated coefficient on *REGULATORY CLIMATE* remains positive but is not significant. The firm size variable, contrary to expectations, is not significantly related to ownership concentration. All three of the instability measures are significantly related to ownership concentration in the anticipated direction.

THE SEPARATION ISSUE

The discussion to this point has focused on the *determinants* of ownership structure. We now empirically examine the alleged *consequence* of diffuse ownership structures for the separation of ownership and control. Berle and Means brought the issue to center-stage in 1933 with the publication of *The Modern Corporation and Private Property*. Their interpretation of the issue has remained the focus of debate for more than half a century. Diffuseness in ownership structure, by modifying the link between ownership and control, is seen by them as undermining the role of profit maximization as a guide to resource allocation. Diffuseness of ownership is said to render owners of shares powerless to constrain professional management. Since the interests of management need not, and in general do not, naturally coincide perfectly with those of owners, this would seem to imply that corporate resources are not used entirely in the pursuit of shareholder profit. Although Berle and Means make no great effort to describe how corporate resources are allocated, later discussions of the corporation dwell on management's consumption of amenities at the expense of owner profits.

Berle and Means's work was anticipated by Thorstein Veblen's (1924) volume, *The Engineers and the Price System*. Veblen believed that he was witnessing the transfer of control from capitalistic owners to engineer–managers, and that the consequences of this transfer were to become more pronounced as diffusely owned corporations grew in economic importance. In the wake of this transfer of power, Veblen saw the end of the type of profit-seeking he associated with capitalists, for he believed that capitalistic owners sought neither efficiency nor increased output so much as monopolistic restrictions to raise prices. The engineers, trained and acculturated to seek technological efficiency, would see to it that the production from the firms they now controlled would rise to higher and socially more desirable levels. The profits of monopoly would be sacrificed on the altar of efficiency.

One of Veblen's famous disciples, John Kenneth Galbraith, shared his teacher's assessment of the change in control but evaluated the outcome differently. In *The New Industrial State* (1967) he argued that the technocrats who had gained control of the diffusely owned modern corporation would sacrifice owner profit to increase output beyond levels that served the real interests of consumers. Enticed to purchase these large output rates by powerful advertising campaigns, consumers would cause the private sector to grow too rapidly and at the expense of the public sector.[11]

Although the three views discussed above concerning the consequences of diffuse ownership structures offer somewhat different evaluations, they unanimously imply a positive correlation between ownership concentration and profit rate. If diffuseness in control allows managers to serve their needs rather than tend to the profits of owners, then more concentrated ownership, by establishing a stronger link between managerial behavior and owner interests, ought to yield higher profit rates.

We expect no such relationship. A decision by shareholders to alter the ownership structure of their firm from concentrated to diffuse should be a decision made in awareness of its consequences for loosening control over professional management. The higher cost and reduced profit that would be associated with this loosening in owner control should be offset by lower capital acquisition cost or other profit-enhancing aspects of diffuse ownership if shareholders choose to broaden ownership. Standardizing on other determinants of profit, Demsetz (1983) has argued that ownership concentration and profit rate should be unrelated.

Table 12.9 Recursive estimates of mean accounting profit rate

Intercept	0.24	0.27	0.35
	(6.2)	(11.7)	(4.2)
UTIL	−0.13	−0.10	−0.13
	(3.4)	(2.4)	(3.1)
FIN	−0.07	−0.06	−0.07
	(3.6)	(3.3)	(3.5)
CAP	0.04	0.05	0.04
	(0.7)	(0.8)	(0.7)
ADV	0.42	0.47	0.42
	(1.9)	(2.3)	(1.9)
RD	−0.11	−0.07	−0.11
	(0.4)	(0.3)	(0.4)
*ASSET**	5.70	8.14	5.97
	(0.8)	(1.2)	(0.9)
SE	−0.29	−0.43	−0.29
	(1.1)	(2.0)	(1.1)
LA5	−0.02	—	—
	(0.9)		
LA20	—	−0.004	—
		(0.2)	
LAH	—	—	−0.02
			(0.9)
N	511	511	511
R^2	0.10	0.10	0.10
F	7.2	7.2	7.1

Note: t-statistics are in parentheses.
*Coefficient estimates on *ASSET* are multiplied by 10^{-7}.

Table 12.9 reports recursive estimates for coefficients of a profit rate equation in which the key independent variables are alternative predicted measures of ownership concentration: *LA5*, *LA20*, and *LAH*.[12] The dependent variable is the mean value of annual accounting profit after taxes, as a percentage of the book value of equity. The mean is calculated for the five-year period 1976–80. Stock market rates of return presumably adjust for any divergences between the interests of professional management and owners, so we rely on accounting rates of return to reveal such divergences.

In addition to ownership concentration, we include several other independent variables in this equation. The utilities and financial dummies isolate the impact of systematic regulation. The coefficient on the financial dummy may be explained by accounting procedures, which for these firms include outstanding loans in the asset base. The potential upward bias in asset measurement that results is likely to depress the measured accounting profit rate. Capital, advertising, and R & D expenditures, all as a percentage of sales, standardize for accounting artifacts associated with the decision to expense some of these investments but to depreciate others. The size of the firm is measured by the book value of assets.

The general explanatory power of the profit rate equation is quite low, but regulation does seem to have a negative impact on accounting profit rate. Table 12.9 shows no significant relationship between ownership concentration and accounting profit rate, and especially no significant positive relationship.[13] The data simply lend no support to the Berle–Means thesis.[14]

We have suggested above that certain industries may be characterized as offering greater amenity potential and that this would lead to more concentrated ownership. This does not assert that the more concentrated is ownership, the greater is the tendency to cater to amenity potential. If we were to make such an assertion, it would imply a negative correlation between profit rate and ownership concentration, and this would tend to hide the opposite correlation suggested by Berle and Means. But, then, this would constitute no evidence more favorable to the Berle–Means hypothesis. Catering to amenity potential *is* maximizing owner *utility* if not owner profit. Such maximization hardly constitutes evidence of a separation between ownership and control.

CONCLUDING COMMENTS

We have argued, both conceptually and empirically, that the structure of corporate ownership varies systematically in ways that are consistent with value maximization. Understanding some of the forces that determine corporate ownership structure is valuable in its own right, but we also think that our results are germane to a more general theory of property rights. For example, can the land enclosure movement in England be explained in part by the enhanced control potential of landownership during periods of population growth and rising prices of farm and ranch products? Similarly, does greater predictability of an industry's environment make industry regulation politically more tolerable because collectivization of control is likely to be less damaging in such cases? Our analysis suggests a framework for new studies that may shed some light on these broader questions.

NOTES

1 Recent literature that has examined the separation of ownership and control includes Jensen and Meckling (1976) and Fama and Jensen (1983a, 1983b). The debate concerning the social implications of diffuse ownership of corporate equity had its genesis in Berle and Means (1933).

2 The effect of imperfect information on monitoring costs is developed formally in Holmström (1979, 1982).

3 An interesting variant of the hypothesis that corporate ownership structure is, in part, dependent on the stability of a firm's environment is found in Smith (1937, pp. 713–14): "The only trades which it seems posible for a joint stock company to carry on successfully, without an exclusive privilege, are those, of which all the operations are capable of being reduced to what is called a routine, or to such a uniformity of method as admits of little or no variation."

4 Ad hoc examples of the power of dominant owner–managers can be given. The share prices of Disney, Gulf and Western, and Chock Full O'Nuts all rose dramatically on the deaths of their dominant owners. Allegedly, the prices of these stocks had been depressed by the policies of Walt Disney to keep a considerable library of Disney films from television, of Charles Bluhdorn to use Gulf and Western to hold a large portfolio of stocks in other companies, and of Charles Black to use Chock Full O'Nuts to maintain large real estate investments. All three policies are associated by the financial community with the personal preferences of the then dominant owner–managers of these companies. Shortly after the deaths of Disney, Bluhdorn, and Black, share prices rose, respectively, 25, 42, and 22 percent. We have no systematic procedure for determining when dominant owners are more likely to exercise their personal preferences in "non-profit-maximizing ways" except for our belief in the amenity potential of mass media and sports industries.

5 Our empirical results remain significant when the equations are estimated using non-transformed ownership variables.

6 We calculated *SE* by regressing the firm's monthly returns on the returns to a value-weighted market portfolio.

7 Two additional specifications of the ownership equation deserve comment. As an alternative proxy for control potential, we included the intra-industry variability (using four-digit SIC codes) in average accounting profit rates (1976–80) as an independent variable. Plausibly, greater differences in profit rates among firms in the same industry provide an index of the difference in performance that can be wrought by superior control decisions. However, no significant relationship exists between this new index of control potential and ownership concentration. When it is entered as the sole control potential variable, the intra-industry variability of profit rate enters with a positive but statistically insignificant coefficient, and it does not significantly affect the other regression coefficients. When this variable is added to the regression equations in which SE proxies for control potential, it enters with a positive and statistically insignificant coefficient, and it again leaves all other coefficient estimates essentially unaffected. The simple correlation of the intra-industry variability of profit rate with *SE*, STD_s, and STD_a never exceeds 0.10. High values of the intra-industry variability of profit rate may correlate with poor census definitions of industries, or they may reflect accounting artifacts that increase the divergence between profit rates within industries, but there is no positive evidence of a linkage to control potential. This absence receives confirmation from a statistical study that regresses ownership concentration on equity, *SE*, SE^2, and 41 dummy variables, one for each two-digit industry containing our sample firms. The coefficients of only four industries exhibited statistical significance, and these were either mass media or regulated industries. Industry characteristics other than these bear no relationship to ownershp concentration. This absence of significance is puzzling to us, but its implication may be important to industrial organization studies. What the data seem to be saying is that firms are

significantly different, even within traditional industry classifications, and that many individual firms may constitute quasi-industries in and of themselves in regard to ownership concentration.

8 We also estimated a regression equation in which we entered the logarithm of *EQUITY* as an independent variable. This variable entered with a negative and statistically significant coefficient, and its inclusion did not significantly affect the other coefficients. Similarly, we included the squared value of *EQUITY* in addition to *EQUITY* and the other independent variables. *EQUITY* continued to enter with a significant, negative coefficient, and its squared value entered with a positive but insignificant coefficient. The other coefficient estimates remained unaffected in this equation.

9 The variables *F*5 and *I*5 occasionally take a value of zero, at which point the logistic transformation is undefined. For purposes of estimating these equations, we do not transform the ownership variables.

10 "Softer" evidence reinforces the amenity explanation of ownership concentration in the media industry. In 1984, Dow Jones & Company, 56 percent owned by the Bancroft family, attempted to issue a stock dividend in the form of a new class of stock that would have 10 votes per share compared with the one vote per share of the firm's original common equity. The Dow Jones chairman described the rationale behind this decision: "The purpose . . . is to try to assure the long-term future operation of *The Wall Street Journal* and Dow Jones' other publications and services under the same quasi-public trust philosophy that Clarence Barron and his descendants have followed during the company's history. The Bancroft family always has zealously guarded the integrity and independence of the Journal and Dow Jones' other publications. This has been crucial to their growth and financial success. The family . . . also has encouraged management always to take a long-term view, investing heavily for the purpose of building future strength and investment values. The family and the board, acting unanimously and with management's enthusiastic support, are seeking to protect and build Dow Jones' publications in the same manner in the years ahead through continued family control" ("Dow Jones Votes," 1984, p. 5). Similarly, DeAngelo and DeAngelo (1983), in a study of 45 firms that have dual classes of common stock, found that both the *New York Times* and the *Washington Post* have dual classes of common stock that trade with different voting rights.

11 The entire discussion of the separation thesis presumes that diffuseness of ownership is a pervasive phenomenon. Our data cast doubt on this presumption. Our sample is heavily weighted by Fortune 500 firms, precisely the firms that are supposed to suffer from diffuse ownership structures. Yet the mean values of *A*5 and *A*20, respectively, are 24.8 and 37.7 percent.

12 The predicted measures of *LA*5, *LA*20, and *LAH* were estimated from an OLS equation that included the following independent variables: *UTIL*, *FIN*, *MEDIA*, *EQUITY*, *SE*, and SE^2. The results reported in table 12.9 do not change significantly when the ownership equations are estimated using alternative specifications that were previously reported.

13 Not reported here is a replication of table 12.9 in which the profit rate equation is estimated using the actual, not predicted, value of the ownership variable. No changes in conclusions are called for by this replication. We also replicated table 12.9 on a set of firms for which we were able to obtain the industry four-firm

concentration ratio. The concentration ratio enters the profit rate equation with a negative and statistically significant sign, but the coefficient estimates on all three ownership variables remain not significant. Earlier studies of the profit-concentration relationship show a weakening of the usual positive correlation during periods of rising price levels. The negative relationship revealed in our work may, however, reflect the inflationary tenor of the late 1970s. The estimated ownership equation for this subset of firms performs weaker than it does when estimated for the entire sample.

14 Our results are consistent with those of Stigler and Friedland (1983). They reject the separation thesis by demonstrating that management salaries are no higher in ''management-controlled'' than in ''owner-controlled'' industries.

REFERENCES

Berle, A. A., and Means, G. C. (1933). *The Modern Corporation and Private Property*. New York: Macmillan.

DeAngelo, H., and DeAngelo, L. (1983). ''The Allocation of Voting Rights in Firms with Dual Classes of Common Stock.'' Mimeographed paper, University of Rochester.

Demsetz, H. (1983). ''The Structure of Ownership and the Theory of the Firm.'' *Journal of Law and Economics*, 26. Reprinted as chapter 11 above.

''Dow Jones Votes New Class of Common as Stock Dividend, Raises Payout 20%.'' *Wall Street Journal*, January 19, 1984.

Fama, E. F., and Jensen, M. C. (1983a). ''Agency Problems and Residual Claims.'' *Journal of Law and Economics*, 26.

—— (1983b). ''Separation of Ownership and Control.'' *Journal of Law and Economics*, 26.

Galbraith, J. K. (1967). *The New Industrial State*. Boston: Houghton Mifflin.

Holmström, B. (1979). ''Moral Hazard and Observability.'' *Bell Journal of Economics*, 10.

—— ''Moral Hazard in Teams.'' *Bell Journal of Economics*, 13.

Jarrell, G. A., and Bradley, M. (1980). ''The Economic Effects of Federal and State Regulation of Cash Tender Offers.'' *Journal of Law and Economics*, 23.

Jensen, M. C., and Meckling, W. H. (1976). ''Theory of the Firm: Managerial Behavior, Agency Costs and Ownership Structure.'' *Journal of Financial Economics*, 3.

Smith, Adam (1937). *An Inquiry into the Nature and Causes of the Wealth of Nations*. New York: Modern Library.

Stigler, G. J., and Friedland, C. (1983). ''The Literature of Economics: The Case of Berle and Means.'' *Journal of Law and Economics*, 26.

Veblen, Thorstein (1924). *The Engineers and the Price System*. New York: Viking Press.

13
Corporate Control, Insider Trading, and Rates of Return

The attention focused on the role of corporate takeovers in disciplining management has led to the neglect of a more important method for joining management and owner interests – an ownership structure appropriately concentrated under normal circumstances to deliver an efficient level of monitoring. A study of ownership concentration in over 500 very large corporations by myself and Kenneth Lehn (1985), referred to hereafter as the D–L study, discovered that the five largest ownership interests controlled over 25 percent of shares in 1980, and that differences in concentration across firms in the sample respond to the benefits and costs of monitoring management. This reflects the existence of a monitoring mechanism more basic to and more continuously operating than the corporate takeover.

It was also observed from this sample that, when individual and family ownership interests owned large fractions of a firm, these same interests failed to own significant amounts of shares in other firms. Important institutional owners did not specialize their portfolios in this fashion, nor did they own such large fractions of a firm's shares. Both differences may reflect the legal and fiduciary constraints facing institutional investors. It is doubtful if there would exist much incentive to monitor management in the absence of investment specialization of the sort exhibited by dominant individual and family owners. For this reason, I shall identify individual and family owners who own relatively large blocks of shares in any one firm as *controlling* shareholders of that firm.

This 511-firm sample tells us nothing about other investments that might be made by controlling shareholders, but I ask the reader to assume that the specialization of investments revealed in this sample correctly identifies a tendency by them to concentrate the uses to which they put their wealth. The tendency to specialize investment in a single firm burdens them with a cost

Ken Lehn and the SEC cooperated in data provision and analysis. Carol Simon made useful comments, and Susan Woodward's insights about the impact of insider trading on stock rates of return motivated the last part of this study. Reprinted with permission from *AEA Papers and Proceedings* 76(2) 1986.

not borne by minority shareholders – firm-specific risk. Another finding of the D–L study indicates that controlling shareholders bear even more firm-specific risk; ownership is more concentrated in firms exhibiting higher firm-specific risk. What benefits motivate investors to become controlling owners in the face of greater firm-specific risk?

Undoubtedly, many persons own a large fraction of shares in a firm because they have, or feel they have, a comparative advantage in exercising control, and that this advantage is worth utilizing to realize pecuniary and non-pecuniary returns. This must be the primary explanation for ownership concentration of the stable variety that is of concern here. Controlling owners also may be descendants of the firm's founding family, locked by capital gains tax avoidance into retaining a controlling position, but this incentive disappears when an estate is transferred at time of death. The central questions of this paper are whether insider trading offers a secondary compensation to controlling shareholders, and, if so, what its characteristics and consequences are.

The greater the percentage of shares owned, the greater is the power to obtain representation on the board of directors and to exercise influence over the management team. This power, and the continuing contact with the firm's affairs that it implies, provides access to insider information. Given the requisite large holding of the firm's shares, controlling shareholders are much more interested in having "their" firm experience good news rather than bad, so insider trading augments comparative advantage in encouraging the establishment of effective and beneficial control of management. Competition of substitute controlling shareholders determines the price of acquiring control. Combined with the inability of controlling shareholders to alter their substantial stock holdings quickly without dramatically affecting share prices, this serves to limit the return they can obtain.

Studies have shown, and we have every reason to believe, that trading profits are greater for traders possessed of insider information. For example, Joseph Finnerty (1976) shows that, after insiders sell a stock heavily, its price falls by an abnormal amount, and, after they buy heavily, its price rises by an abnormal amount. These studies, however, shed little light on the ability of controlling shareholders to tap insider information. It is so plausible that they have superior access that a demonstration seems unnecessary, but indirect evidence can be given. I base this on the expectation that greater access to more profitable inside information should lead to more active trading.

The SEC data on insiders for 1980 have been used to calculate insider trading volume as a percentage of insider stock holdings for two sets of firms drawn from the D–L study. The first subset contains the 28 firms exhibiting the highest degree of ownership concentration.[1] The second contains the 28 firms exhibiting such low concentration of ownership that no one shareholder owned more than 0.02 percent of the shares. If accessibility to more profitable insider information is greater for shareholders owning relatively more shares, the first subsample should show greater involvement in trading by those classified as insiders by the SEC. In fact, there is seven times more involvement in insider trading. Shares actually traded by persons classified as insiders, as a percentage of shares owned, is 0.64 percent for the first subset. This is to be compared to 0.09 percent for the second subset. Access to insider information does seem to be related to importance of shareholdings. Actual insider trading volume undoubtedly exceeds these reported values, but probably has no significant effect on their relative sizes.

A direct test of the importance of insider trading profit as an incentive for maintaining controlling ownership positions would examine the relationship between *profitability* of insider trading and ownership concentration. This would avoid the problem of under-reporting of insider trading *volume* to the SEC. Unfortunately, comprehensive data by firm on profitability of insider trading are not now available.

Firm-specific risk is itself a plausible measure of the profit potential of insider trading. Higher systematic risk firms are those whose fortunes in greater degree are tied to factors that also influence the fortunes of other firms. High firm-specific risk firms are those whose fortunes tend to be tied to factors that do not influence many other firms. Information about common factors, such as growing tightness in capital markets, will be known in advance to many persons in many firms that stay in contact with capital markets. Profiting from this information is difficult because intensive competition to do so is faced from all who are well positioned to have the same information. In contrast to this, advanced knowledge about a successful closing in a new large contract is more likely to be restricted to persons in firms doing the contracting. Trading on the basis of such firm-specific information is likely to be less competitive and more profitable. It is information that impacts the fortunes of a specific firm that provides the best opportunity to profit. Such information is most frequently encountered in those firms exhibiting high firm-specific risk. In fact, calculations on a 159 firm subset of the D–L sample shows a high correlation between the ratio of insider trading to total trading (measured for 1980) and firm-specific risk (measured over the period 1975–80). The correlation is 0.45 (with a t of 6.4).[2]

For this reason, the statistically significant positive relationship between ownership concentration and firm-specific risk found in the D–L study indirectly supports the proposition that the supply of controlling owners is positively related to the potential profitability of insider trading. The positive relationship between ownership concentration and firm-specific risk is interpreted in the D–L study as reflecting a greater demand for monitoring in firms subject to greater instability in the immediate environments in which they compete. Firm-specific risk is taken as an index of this instability. On this view, greater firm-specific risk implies a larger demand for controlling shareholders. This demand cannot bring forth more controlling shareholders without compensating them for bearing greater firm-specific risk. The larger part of this compensation presumably comes from the production of more valuable firms through the exercise of controlling ownership, a compensation that would be greater in those firms facing the most unstable conditions. But it will also be true that insider trading profits should be greater in these same firms. This constitutes a secondary source of compensation.

That insider information allows insiders to obtain a higher than average rate of return in the market for shares has been documented in other studies, but the interpretation given to such findings is misleading. Insiders bear special costs insofar as they are controlling shareholders. The cost of firm-specific risk is not recorded as an expense of the firm. It is borne personally by controlling shareholders. The higher rate of return *recorded* by insider trading in the market for shares, therefore, cannot be interpreted to mean that controlling shareholders receive a higher *personal* return than is enjoyed by outsiders.

Of course, controlling shareholders are not the only persons who come into possession of advance information. Others with access to such information would include key employees, bankers, and others who do business with the firm. Are they profiting from insider trading without improving the firm's operations? Some of them undoubtedly are in any given episode of new information. But economists should be suspicious of free lunches. The appearance of one often reflects our inability to observe the price easily. In this case, it probably reflects our ignorance of what is required of persons seeking regular access to insider information. Key employees bear the risk of specializing their human capital to the needs of the firm. Bankers and others who do important business with a firm not only receive information from the firm, but they also bring information to the firm. Insider information is a way of paying for services such as these, which, in their very nature, are difficult to reward through explicit contracts.

Trading with insider information, of course, creates opportunistics to profit at the expense of other traders. These wealth transfers, to the extent they impact minority shareholders, may be viewed as part of the cost borne by minority shareholders to encourage more effective monitoring of the firm. Since this cost falls in greater degree on minority shareholders who trade more frequently, minority shareholders should hold stock for longer periods than they would in the absence of insider trading. Buy-and-hold strategies will not give perfect protection against insider trading because they impose illiquidity costs on investors. Insider trading profits thus give rise to problems of equity, not only between insiders and "outsiders," but also between minority shareholders facing different liquidity costs. Equity problems such as these are a primary source of opposition to insider trading. But legislation seeking to reduce insider trading profit makes it more difficult to maintain controlling ownership interests so useful for monitoring purposes.

The wealth transfers associated with insider trading may be smaller than is thought if outsiders can anticipate which stocks confront them with higher probabilities of informationally disadvantaged trading. It is not clear that such anticipations can be formed confidently. Forecasts of insider trading must be made for periods long enough to make buy-and-hold strategies meaningful. Controlling stockholders, key employees, and persons with important business relationships all have access to insider information, so it is not clear that a relationship exists between insider trading and concentration of ownership. Although the general tendency of a stock to be traded intensely by insiders gives a plausible guide to future insider trading, the expected financial impact of insider trading on outsiders may be too small per trade to warrant careful investigation. All in all, it may be better simply to accept the average amount of insider trading that characterizes a diversified portfolio. To the extent that outsiders can and do make such forecasts, they can limit their losses to insiders by reducing their demand for stocks most likely to confront them with informationally disadvantaged trades. Investors would discount these stocks, or they would require higher dividends from them, so as to equalize rates of return *realized* after losses to insiders. This implication of efficient markets requires *recorded* rates of return, measured before losses to insiders, to be higher for stocks more likely to present outsiders with informationally disadvantaged trades. Difference in recorded rates of return will not be arbitraged away by outsiders because they are necessary to equalize realized rates of return.

Based on a 159-firm subset of the D–L data, there is a significant correlation between the recorded market rates of return, R, measured over the period 1975–80, and the ratio of insider trading, v, to total trading, V, measured for 1980 (t-statistics are shown in parentheses):

$$\underset{(15.8)}{R = 0.016} + \underset{(3.8)}{0.0005 v/V}; \qquad R^2 = 0.08;\ F = 14$$

This result supports the notion that investors discount stocks traded in intensely by insiders, but it may also reflect the happenstance that a disproportionate share of insider trading was done in anticipation of good news. On the other hand, for these same stocks, no significant correlation exists between this measure of the importance of insider trading and intercepts of the market model (estimated for 1975–80 in the D–L study). This suggests that further analysis is required to isolate the effects of insider trading from riskiness of investment, a task likely to be difficult if both reflect the rate at which new information impacts stock price.

NOTES

1 I arbitrarily chose 60 firms to measure differences in intensity of involvement in insider trading and 160 firms to measure the correlation between insider trading and

firm-specific risk. Missing data forced me to delete firms, and the publishing deadline of the *Proceedings* barred the replacement of these firms with others. Hence, I use 28 firms exhibiting high-ownershp concentration and 28 exhibiting low-ownership concentration to measure differences in the ratio of insider trading to shares owned by insiders, and I use 159 firms to correlate firm-specific risk and insider trading as a fraction of total trading.

2 See note 1.

REFERENCES

Demsetz, H. and Lehn, K. (1985). "The Structure of Corporate Ownership: Causes and Consequences." *Journal of Political Economy*, 93; reprinted as chapter 12 above.

Finnerty, J. E. (1976). "Insiders and Market Efficiency." *Journal of Finance*, 31.

14
The Control Function of Private Wealth

THE SEEKING OF WEALTH

Probably no large topic in economics is so likely to spark heated debate as wealth and its distribution. The debate centers on the social desirability of materialistic behavior and, with unnoticed inconsistency, on the degree to which wide disparities in income are defensible. Economists show less hostility than other social scientists to "materialism" and to inequality in the distribution of wealth. Only partly does this derive from the higher earnings of economists. It also stems from the belief they generally share that wealth-seeking ultimately promotes the common good by guiding resources into more productive uses, and, through competition between wealth-maximizers, by broadly distributing the gains that result.

There is dissent from this belief. One critical allegation is that wealth often is acquired in ways that are socially unproductive. Fortunes are made through theft, fraud, and drug trafficking. Monopoly and externalities of one sort or another also may reduce the correlation between wealth-maximizing behavior and social productivity. This truth suggests the need for greater discrimination on the part of those who assert that wealth-maximizing activity is always socially productive, and also the need for restrictions on the manner in which wealth may be acquired.

Another allegation is that differences in wealth largely reflect accidents of timing, place, and parentage rather than the arrangement of superior resource allocations. A related dissent asserts that wealth is not really important to the happiness of a people. This opinion can be found even in the writings of Adam Smith, who not only created the invisible hand, the movement of which surely is prompted by wealth-maximizing behavior, but who also analyzes this movement in a book boldly titled *The Wealth of Nations*. In *The Theory of Moral Sentiments*, Smith puts forward the view that "all men, sooner or later, accommodate themselves to whatever becomes their permanent situation . . . ; that, between one permanent situation and another, there was, with regard to real happiness, no essential difference . . .''[1] For the overwhelming plurality of persons, the allegation simply is believed to be false; were it voiced in households and taverns across the world, the din from the ridicule and scorn of those who work *for a living* would be deafening. Moreover, both of these allegations, which hold that the distribution of income is unrelated to productivity, may be judged false on the basis of evidence. Differences in wealth are demonstrably explained by differences in investment in human capital, intelligence, hours worked, risk of employment, and so on. Not only do persons invest in ways that are explainable as attempts to maximize wealth, but also, demands and supplies for all goods and services behave as if people are motivated strongly by wealth considerations.

THE HAVING OF WEALTH

But, whatever the validity or falseness of such allegations, it is clear that the important defenses of differences in individual wealth are found in the seeking of wealth rather than in the having of it. They emphasize expected socially desirable consequences of seeking wealth. Clearly, these defenses must also assume, or must imply, that the *having* of wealth is also desirable. Why worry about improving the allocation of resources, the main consequence of which is to increase wealth, if the having of wealth is not itself desirable?[2] The defense of wealth-seeking depends not only on the typical person's strong preference for having wealth, but also, generally speaking, on the belief that wealthy lives are a desirable social goal, that such lives are more satisfying (happy?) than those constrained by poverty.[3]

The defenses of wealth acquisition, we have seen, are of two sorts: a defense of the seeking of wealth, based on wealth-increasing *productivity* consequences, and a defense of the having of wealth, based largely on *consumption* (better life) consequences. The question to be asked here is whether the *having* of wealth (and the inequality with which wealth is distributed) has desirable productivity consequences that have been overlooked by focusing on wealth-*seeking* in matters of production. For example, it has been alleged that relatively wealthy people are needed to experiment in the consumption of new products and services, thus providing a testing ground for these before they are produced for and consumed by large numbers of not-so-wealthy persons. To the extent that this allegation is correct, this testing service is essentially a productivity consequence of the having, not the seeking, of wealth. The productive aspect of the having of wealth, which is discussed below, is I believe considerably more important and less speculative than this example. I wish to call attention to an important but neglected productivity-enhancing role of the having of *private* wealth, and of the inequality of its distribution.

THE CONTROL PROBLEM

This role is based on the problem of maintaining beneficial control over resources in the presence of economies of size. I do not refer here to the wealth required to pay for inputs on a scale demanded by large firms, but, rather, to the wealth required to reduce the degree to which ownership is separated from the control of these resources. The maintenance of such control requires large amounts of *individual, private* wealth in settings where large-scale enterprise would be efficient except for resolving the problem of control. The large-scale enterprise requires an ownership interest sufficiently large to encourage the owner(s) to undertake the task of overseeing management and other inputs, and of setting a proper course for the enterprise.

A diffuse ownership structure discourages this undertaking because of well-known free rider problems. No owner of a trivial fraction of equity has enough interest or power to take the problem of control seriously; leaving this task to someone else makes more sense. However, this someone, if he or she is to exist, must own a large personal stake in the firm. An undivided large equity stake requires considerable personal wealth when the efficient size of the firm is large.

Collectively owned assets, whether owned by the state through socialism or through diffuse corporate shareholdings, do not offer a practical substitute for a large private and personal equity stake. The collective characteristic of such alternatives frustrates the resolution of the free rider problem. Neither nationalization nor diffuse private shareholdings can be expected to establish the beneficial control that is characteristic of a large, private, individual equity stake. Hence, if large enterprises are to be maintained efficiently, it is important that many individuals hold enough private wealth to finance large equity stakes in these firms. Resolution of the control problem is a productive function of the having of wealth.

WEALTH INEQUALITY

This function is unlikely to be served well, even in wealthy societies, if wealth is equally distributed. Demsetz and Lehn (1985) measure the degree to which ownership is concentrated in over 500 large publicly held US corporations.[4] The five largest ownership interests, institutional and individual, in each corporation, controlled on average 25 percent of shares issued. The five largest individual and family ownership interests controlled, on average, 9 percent of shares issued. This probably understates the personal stake of individual and family owners because some ownership will be hidden. In any case, let us assume that five ownership interests are few enough to overcome serious free rider problems.

The mean market value of equity for these corporations was about $1.20 billion averaged over 1975–80, so that 9 percent of shares issued represents over $100 million invested, or over $20 million for each of the five largest individual and family ownership interests in the typical case. For the largest corporations in this sample, and for those owned in more concentrated fashion, individual stakes tend to be much higher. If a 9 percent ownership stake, summed over no more than five individual ownership interests, is required to deliver effective working control of large corporations, then the private net worth of the US population (in 1976), *if divided equally* among all households, would be inadequate to establish effective working control in any large corporation because the wealth of too many individuals would need to be combined to do so. An equal distribution of wealth would assure each household a private net worth between $7,000 and $8,000. Five such households could muster $40,000 at most, whereas $100 million would be required.

If wealth were distributed equally, we would need to either forsake effective control of efficient sized firms or forsake large-scale production where size is important to efficiency. The lower is per capita wealth relative to the financial size of efficient productive units, the greater is the degree of inequality in its distribution that is required to maintain effective control. For a given state of technology, the size structure of enterprise and the distribution of wealth are not independent, although wealthier (per capita) societies can maintain practical control of enterprise with a greater measure of egalitarianism.

INCENTIVES TO CONTROL

This interrelationship between wealth and the organization of industry differs from that which is part of standard price theory. The focus of existing theory is on the *capacity* of owner–entrepreneurs to cope with the flow of information; this capacity is determined by the physical and mental limitations of calculating and deciding, not by attenuation of the owner–entrepreneur's *incentive* to exercise control. The theory presumes a single owner forced to create and rely on an increasingly bureaucratic structure to make decisions as the size of the firm increases. Utilization of this structure at small firm sizes exploits indivisibilities, but at larger firm sizes it strains the capacity of the bureaucracy to handle information, giving rise to the standard U-shaped average cost curve.

Assume instead constant returns to scale with respect to information-handling capacity, so that the decision-making bureaucracy works equally well at small and large output rates as judged by its information-handling ability. There nonetheless remains a problem in *incentives*, a problem in the willingness to bear the risk and cost of making and monitoring decisions. This problem is resolvable (only) by bringing the costs and benefits of decisions to bear in a way that reduces the free rider problem. Private, concentrated, ownership is required, where "private" is taken to mean that persons exercising control over the firm's resources bear a considerable part of the costs and benefits visited upon the firm from the uses they make of these resources. Concentrated ownership need not be presumed by theory; it is an imperative of the need for control incentives. The required concentration of ownership, however, is securable to a society on a broad scale only if the society is privately wealthy and tolerant of a skewed distribution of wealth. Thus, effective control imparts to private wealth the ability to perform a productive function for which it is difficult to find a substitute in the presence of important indivisibilities in other factor inputs.

SPECULATIONS

We may speculate a bit, beginning with more general considerations and proceeding to narrower ones, about the consequences of this relationship between private wealth and the incentive to control business organization.

Societies poor in private wealth cannot control resources effectively if they attempt to take advantage of the (presumed) existence of frequently encountered economies of large size; and if they attempt to improve control by relying on smaller firms, for which less personal wealth is required to maintain control, they forgo realization of the advantages of large scale offered by indivisibilities in other inputs. Assuming that scale economies are more prevalent in industrial undertakings, this suggests that patient accumulation of private wealth, and toleration for skewness in its distribution, are a part of the preconditions for accelerated industrial development. Considerable protection of private wealth is required, thus reflecting the need for accepting a social system containing a large enclave of private property rights;[5] but, in addition, there is need for a period of time and a set of activities in which private wealth is actually accumulated.

Can the timing of the "take-off" into sustained economic growth, which we associate with the industrial revolution, and which did not take place simultaneously across Western nations, be explained by differences in the degree to which private wealth had been accumulated? Private wealth could have been accumulated over many years in activities not susceptible to the control problem discussed above. These would be activities in which scale economies are not especially pronounced, and which, therefore, could be controlled adequately without a prior accumulation of concentrated private wealth holdings. Agriculture and trading activities are obvious candidates. This suggests that a period of prosperity in agriculture and trading, long enough for concentrations of private wealth to emerge, would be likely precursors to the development of industry, which, because of differences in technology, exhibited greater scale economies than either agriculture or trade.

It will also be true that business organizations will be devised whose objective is to attenuate the incentive limitations on control imposed by private wealth constraints. The limited partnership and the corporation are examples. However, the greater the fraction of the firm's equity that derives from more numerous small investments, the more serious becomes the separation between ownership and control.

Wealth may also be borrowed. This allows the owners of a firm to acquire more resources than their private wealth can purchase, presumably allowing them to retain a dominant ownership position without possessing great private wealth. However, extensive borrowing cannot be relied upon to avoid problems of control incentives. Agency theory tells us that suppliers of borrowed funds should become increasingly reluctant about lending additional funds (at given interest rates) as their fear grows that this will entice owners of equity to invest in increasingly risky ventures.[6] Hence, for a given level of private wealth security offered by owners to back their borrowings, and for a given level of borrower expectations about the firm's success, the larger the firm's debt–equity ratio, the higher is the interest rate that lenders require. The higher interest rate offsets the greater risk to lenders of the firm going bankrupt because high debt–equity ratios encourage owners of equity to undertake riskier investments.

Beyond these methods of acquiring wealth are those that rely on ''pyramiding.'' A relatively small financial stake buys control of a holding company which in turn buys control of other investments; and so on. By retaining enough of an ownership interest at each stage of the pyramid, the onset of incentive problems is postponed, but at ever increasing costs of bureaucracy and information processing. Such organizations can at best merely delay the constraints on firm size that are imposed by private wealth and its distribution. Ultimately, these are brought into play by the traditional conception of limitations on firm size – the inability of bureaucracies to digest increasing amounts of information with undiminished efficiency.

NOTES

1 Smith (1982, p. 149).

2 A similar point may be made in reference to another defense of wealth-maximizing behavior. This sees the building of strength of character in the struggle to acquire wealth. Stigler imputes this defense to the classical economists (Stigler 1949, pp. 1–11). The struggle to acquire wealth can be an important source of character-building only if the having of wealth is important to people: else, why not rely on struggles over other ''prizes'' to build character?

3 That which is called ''materialism'' is unfairly labeled a lack of appreciation for finer things. Wealth not only helps to sustain life, it also brings an important release from the onerous tedium of a life forever devoted to sustaining life. Materialism, no less than spiritualism, seeks real improvement in the quality of life for common men.

The great variety of goods possessed by people in an affluent society – television, theatre, fashion, travel, sporting facilities – reveal not decadence, although decadence there is, but lives that are more interesting and varied than can be secured on Walden Pond. Those seeking to migrate from poorer to wealthier nations, because they desire wealth, should not be judged to love freedom less; the greater control over life that flows from wealth is difficult to distinguish from greater freedom.

4 Demsetz and Lehn (1985).

5 The requirement of a substantial private property enclave is, of course, consistent with the requisites for economic growth set forth in North and Thomas (1973). Their emphasis and argument, however, does not focus on the problem of establishing effective control over sizable agglomerations of productive assets, or on the role of private wealth in overcoming the control problem.

6 Jensen and Meckling (1976, pp. 305–60).

REFERENCES

Demsetz, H. and Lehn, K. (1985). "The Structure of Corporate Ownership: Causes and Consequences." *Journal of Political Economy*, 93; reproduced as chapter 12 above.

Jensen, M. C. and Meckling, W. H. (1976). "Theory of The Firm: Managerial Behavior, Agency Costs, and Ownership Structure." *Journal of Financial Economics*, 3.

North, D. C. and Thomas, R. P. (1973). *The Rise of the Western World*. Cambridge: University Press.

Smith, Adam (1982). *The Theory of Moral Sentiments*, ed. D. D. Raphael and A. L. Macfie. Indianapolis: Liberty Classics.

Stigler, G. J. (1949). *Five Lectures on Economic Problems*. London: Macmillan.

15
Profit as a Functional Return: Reconsidering Knight's Views

Perhaps the best and most influential of Knight's work is his 1921 classic *Risk, Uncertainty, and Profits*. The scope of the book extends well beyond the limits of its title, delving into the nature of science, knowledge, and social choice. The present paper ignores these broader topics and confines its discussion to the book's primary topics. These are the subjects listed in the book's title. Some attention is given to the theory of the firm, but Knight's interest is mainly in how risk and uncertainty impinge on the economic *system*.

Knight's main objectives are (1) to draw out the basic assumptions of the perfect competition model; (2) to show that the existence of profit requires the violation of these assumptions; and (3) to argue that a violation of the assumption of complete knowledge, particularly through the presence of uncertainty, is needed to explain the phenomenon of profit. Judged by the absence of viable alternative views on these matters over a period of 65 years, Knight's arguments must be judged a success. Indeed, modern developments in the theories of finance and rational expectations rest upon theoretical propositions that seem to differ little in substance from what Knight had to say about how competition would wring the profit out of behavior that seeks to take advantage of forecastable future developments.

Knight begins the substance of his argument by pointing out that the assumption of complete knowledge in a competitive environment implies that the resources devoted to satisfying any market demand will be just sufficient to the task. Product prices in all markets must equal unit costs at least on the margin. Any excess of total revenues over total costs can only be rents, attributable to rising supply conditions, and cannot be profits. Under this condition, competition allocates resources so as to deprive any market of profit or loss. This point, associated with the notion of static equilibrium under perfectly competitive conditions, seems unassailable, and early recognition of it was not confined to Knight.

Knight becomes more creative when attacking one prevailing view of the source of profit. This view asserts that real economies are never in static equilibrium, that change is always taking place, and that it is change that gives rise to profit. Knight is critical of this approach because change itself may be predictable. If it is, it cannot give rise to profit. Profit, Knight argues, must therefore be associated with lack of perfect foresight.

Most of the literature dealing with imperfect foresight during Knight's time associated lack of perfect foresight with riskiness of actions. The more sophisticated explanations of profit identified it as the reward for bearing risk. This cast profit in the role of a functional return similar to the relationship between wages and work effort. If risks are to be borne, compensation through profit must be paid. Knight is critical of this interpretation of the role of imperfect knowledge. His key point, and from the perspective of the writings of economists his most original, is that some risk is merely a forecastable cost of production. As such, risk is no different from any other cost, and competition can be counted upon to bring the price paid for risk-bearing services into equality (on the margin) with the cost of providing these services. No true profit can arise from this source. Profit requires a type of riskiness that is not forecastable. Knight calls this *uncertainty*. Thus, his argument is ordered as is the title of his book – from risk to uncertainty, and from uncertainty to profit.

For Knight, risk is a cost of production because it is insurable, and it is insurable because the probability of occurrence of the relevant contingencies, such as fire, are known to a high degree of predictability from past experience. The premium paid to insure against risk is simply a forecastable cost to the firm (which it may choose to avoid by self-insuring). Competition holds price to the level dictated by the unit value of this risk cost plus other production costs.

The uncertainty that, according to Knight, confronts many business decisions offers no possibility of being insured against because the relevant contingencies are unique. Historical frequencies do not exist, so the probability of occurrence of these contingencies is not known in the same sense that the probabilities of risky events are known. Uncertainty, therefore, cannot be converted to a forecastable cost of production that influences resource allocation in any usual sense. Profit becomes a pure *ex post residual* that derives from the unforecastable way in which these uncertainties resolve themselves.

Knight means by "uncertainty" complete absence of knowledge about the probability of occurrence:

> Uncertainty must be taken in a sense radically distinct from the familiar notion of Risk. . . . The essential fact is that "risk" means in some cases a quantity susceptible of measurement, while at other times it is something distinctly not of this character; and there are far-reaching and crucial differences in the bearings of the phenomenon depending on which of the two is really present and operating. . . . It will appear that a *measurable* uncertainty, or "risk" proper, as we shall use the term, is so far different from an *unmeasurable* one that it is not in effect an uncertainty at all. We shall accordingly restrict the term "uncertainty" to cases of the non-quantitative type. (Knight, 1965, pp. 19–20)

> The practical difference between the two categories, risk and uncertainty, is that in the former the distribution of the outcome in a group of instances is known (either through calculation *a priori*, as in the casting of a hypothetically fair die, or from statistics of past experience), while in the case of uncertainty this is not true, the reason being in general that it is impossible to form a group of instances, because the situation dealt with is in a high degree unique. (p. 233)

> Profit arises out of the inherent, absolute unpredictability of things, out of the sheer brute fact that the results of human activity cannot be anticipated and then only in so far as even a probability calculation in regard to them is impossible and meaningless. (p. 311)

The complete absence of objectively calculable probabilities is the meaning that Knight clearly wants to give to uncertainty, but at times he seems to waver, to write about reducing uncertainty by grouping events to form a larger sample – "even . . . true uncertainties show some tendency toward regularity when grouped on the basis of nearly any similarity or common element" (p. 239). Perhaps this inconsistency derives from the difficulty he must have perceived in developing a logical relationship between uncertainty and human behavior when his preferred definition of uncertainty deprives it of any rational motivating value.

In contrast to his use of uncertainty, Knight has much to say about how risk affects human behavior. For example, he describes risk as an important source of specialization of activity and of larger-size firms, for these help entrepreneurs acquire greater amounts of data upon which to calculate empirically based expectations about future events. He thus anticipates later writings about the impact of learning on cost.

His treatment of uncertainty seems to place it outside human calculation and control. Behavior is difficult to understand if it is not directed consciously and "rationally" toward goals that are attainable in principle. People cannot act toward Knight's uncertainty on a calculated, reasoned basis, yet they act *as if* they have calculated the chances of good and bad outcomes. Knight reconciles this appearance of rationality with its impossibility by another ad hoc assertion of "human nature." According to Knight, people may make "judgments" or form "opinions" about how likely an event is, but these are based on the *psychology* of a person, on his optimism or pessimism about the future, not on statistical or theoretical calculation. Knight thus stakes an early claim for a subjectivist, Bayesian, approach to decision problems:

> The problem of the human attitude toward uncertainty . . . is as beset with difficulties as that of uncertainty itself. Not merely is the human reaction to situations of this character apt to be erratic and extremely various from one individual to another, but the "normal" reaction is subject to well-recognized deviations from the conduct which sound logic would dictate. (p. 235)

The most important instance of his ad hoc resolution of this dilemma arises when Knight attempts to assess entrepreneurial activity in the face of uncertainty:

the profit-seeking business man . . . contracts for productive services in advance, on a basis of what he *expects* to be able to make by their use. . . . The conditions . . . under which entrepreneurs as a group will realize a positive profit is that they *underestimate* the prospects of their business relatively to their dispositions to venture. If, on the contrary, they *overestimate* their prospects (considering the degree of conviction necessary to move their wills), they will in the aggregate suffer loss, and if they estimate correctly on the whole, neither will occur. If the estimates are a matter of pure chance it would seem that the variations in the two directions would be equal, the average correct, and the general level of pure profit zero. . . . The question of fact is thus whether entrepreneurs as a class receive on the average more or less than the normal competitive rate of return. . . . The writer is strongly of the opinion that business as a whole suffers a loss. The main facts in the psychology of the case are familiar. . . . The behavior of men in lotteries and gambling games is the most striking fact. Adam Smith pointed out the tendency of human nature to exaggerate the value of a small chance of large winnings. . . . It is certainly true that . . . most men have an irrationally high confidence in their own good fortune. . . . Moreover, there is little doubt that business men represent mainly the class of men of whom these things are most strikingly true; they are not the critical and hesitant individuals, but rather those with restless energy, buoyant optimism, and large faith in things generally and themselves in particular. (pp. 363–6).

The impact of uncertainty on human behavior is to cause entrepreneurs to overinvest and bear losses, but this conclusion derives not from an analysis of logical, motivated action, nor even from careful examination of measured profits. It comes from the most casual of presumptions about the psychology of entrepreneurs – excessive optimism. It can be said without exaggeration that, unlike Knight's analysis of how risk affects behavior, the behavioral implications that he associates with uncertainty may be considered (perhaps dismissed) as armchair psychology. As a consequence, the sole role played by uncertainty in *Risk, Uncertainty, and Profit* is to identify pure profit as a residual deriving from the unforecastable games that "nature" plays with us: "pure profit is theoretically unimputable, in the sense in which the competitive system . . . imputes product value to agencies concerned in production (pp. 308–9).

Knight seems to have worked his thoughts into a bind. True profit requires true uncertainty; true uncertainty cannot be a cost of production; therefore, uncertainty cannot influence the rationally based conditions of supply as do labor–leisure trade-offs or opportunity costs; rational behavior is neither influenced by nor does it influence uncertainty, but people do seem to react to uncertainty; therefore, their reactions must be emotional, not rational. This chain of reasoning, which I ascribe to Knight, makes it easy to understand why he goes out of his way to insist that only a small portion of human behavior can be judged to be motivated by rational calculation of the sort so emphasized in economics.

It also implies that true profit is functionless in guiding behavior unless one can attach a predictable irrational response (optimism or pessimism) to uncertainty. Knight must have been uncomfortable about his inability to have true profit serve a social function. His ad hoc introduction of an entrepreneurially optimistic emotional response to uncertainty can be seen as a way of allowing the prospect of true profit to serve the interests of others in the economic system. It does this by transferring wealth from entrepreneurs to others when the former overinvest in the face of uncertainty. By preferring an uncertain future to a certain one, entrepreneurs transfer some of their wealth to others, presumably through the lower product prices wrought by their optimism.

This entrepreneurial preference for bearing uncertainty is peculiarly inconsistent with Knight's judgment about entrepreneurial attitudes toward risk. Risk becomes simply a cost of production in Knight's scheme, because entrepreneurs can purchase insurance to cover risky events. But a ready supply of such insurance requires a steady demand for the service, and this implies risk aversion for at least a substantial number of entrepreneurs.

The uniqueness that is Knightian uncertainty provides no objective basis for calculating the probability of occurrence of a particular state of the world. Although Knight does not really probe deeply for a meaning of uncertainty, preferring instead simply to disassociate it from risk and from anything else that might be calculable, his concept of uncertainty deprives us of general agreement about what can be expected. Any guess is as believable as any other. But it can be argued that Knightian uncertainty really is risk, at least when it is associated with possible events (and not with abstract concepts such as are found in rules of logic and mathematics). To be qualitatively different from risky events, uncertain events cannot be expected, contemplated, or even intuited; they are the purest of all windfalls or surprises, *announced to unknowing minds only by actual occurrence*. To be capable of communication, to be interpretably imaginable, an event possibility must be anchored, however loosely, in experience, for it can be imagined only if something "similar" has occurred already. A cataclysmic crash between a comet and the earth can be imagined only because comets and collisions are both within our range of experience. In principle, this experience imbues "new" possibilities with the characteristics of *risk*.

An entrepreneur considers marketing an "entirely new" product line. Knight writes as if consumer reactions are uncertain, and as if the probability of their not liking the product line is beyond objective calculation. What is the meaning of "entirely new"? By agreement, we are dealing with a product aimed at consumers. There must therefore be a plentitude of records of successes and failures of past "entirely new" products. A frequency distribution by magnitude of success can be made from such data, and the probability of a loss of stipulated magnitude can be inferred. True, the fewer are the past events that can be agreed upon as the marketing of "entirely new" product lines, the smaller is our confidence in this inference; but is it possible for the acceptable set of past new products to be completely empty if we can meaningfully conceive of the object of the present gamble as a product? It is a product only because it bears some, possibly remote, resemblance to products of the past.

However, it is not my purpose to delve into the philosophical question of the possibility of anticipating a Knightian uncertain event. My point is that it is difficult to think of many (any?) business decisions, even important ones, that strictly meet Knight's definition of uncertainty. The historical basis upon which to calculate frequencies may be small in some cases; the question of which datum rightly belongs in this base may be difficult to resolve to everyone's satisfaction; and there may be dispute even about which data are "successes" and which are "failures." This implies greater *disagreement* about the best probability estimates than when experience is richer. It also implies that it is virtually impossible to state that a business decision is made under pure Knightian uncertainty conditions or that the return to the decision is Knightian pure profit. The acceptance of this view of business decisions brings into question the usefulness of Knightian uncertainty and profit, either for analytical or for political purposes. It is better to assume that all business conditions are made subject to risk, including moral hazard risks, but that there are different degrees of agreement about the best estimate of the risk involved. Knight oversimplifies when he simply dichotomizes future occurrences into categories of risk and uncertainty.

In particular, it is useful to divide risk into two subcategories: risks for which there is widespread agreement about the probability of occurrence, and risks for which there is widespread disagreement. Greater agreement makes it more likely that "conventional" insurance can be purchased to cover the risk; greater disagreement makes it more likely that the risk can be transferred to others only by finding someone willing to take the opposite side of a "bet." The easier it is for one party to accumulate a stake in many *similar* bets, the closer betting comes to conventional insurance wherein risk is reduced by holding a portfolio of such bets. The more difficult it is to take a position in many similar bets, the smaller is the possibility for reducing risk in this way, and the closer insurance comes to betting wherein differences in best estimates, and, *seemingly*, not reductions in risk, create the prospect for gains from exchange. "Seemingly" because we are dealing only with different methods of reducing risks: in method 1, the accumulation of many similar bets, someone has made the decision that his risk is lower because his calculations show that similar bets can be made; in method 2, someone has made the decision that his risk is lower because his calculations yield a smaller risk than those of the person with whom he bets. Finding someone willing to bet on the basis of a lower calculated risk is like finding someone with an insensitive nose to rid the park of skunks. Both methods yield reductions in risk, and both calculations may be in sufficient error to yield losses to the person accepting payment to bear this reduced risk.

There is an operational significance in distinguishing these two subcategories of risk. For cases in which there is widespread agreement about the magnitude of risk, it will be relatively cheap to find some company (someone) with whom to insure (bet). Such companies are easy to find because they can more cheaply maintain continuity of existence. They stand ready to continue doing business with regard to these "insurable" risks (e.g., fire, automobile, marine, etc., insurance) because the next case to seek insurance is enough like past cases, so there is no need for them to calculate anew their fee and the risk they bear, and there are enough such cases to reduce the price for accepting these risks to marketable levels. Cases closer to betting situations are those for which it is more likely that new evaluations of risk are required to form some judgments about prospects.

The importance of this lies only in the fact that a person who makes a calculation of lower risk in one case, and who would be willing to make an even bet with another person in regard to this risk, may in another case calculate a higher risk, and be unwilling to bet on the same terms. There is therefore greater difficulty finding someone with whom to "bet" (at easily known prices) than there is finding someone to "insure" with. The greater cost of searching for a betting partner implies that "self-insuring" should be more common the more disagreement there is about probability of occurrence.

Is there any reason to believe that profit is more likely to be competed out of existence when broad agreement about the prior probability of an event exists than when it does not? Are risks that are more likely to be insurable to be thought of as production costs while those that are less insurable are to be thought of as "non-costs" that give rise to pure windfalls?

Suppose we interpret general agreement about a probability to imply that the common calculation is close to the value-weighted true probability of occurrence. This is what Knight must mean if he is able to conclude that competition in reacting to this probability holds profit to zero. Investments will be made and plans will be formulated "correctly" by most people, and input and product prices must adjust so as to eliminate profit and loss.

If there is general disagreement about the correct probability to use, but if the value-weighted true probability is near the mean of the distribution of these different calculated probabilities, competition will again force the elimination of profit when gains and losses are averaged over all players. The profit of specific individuals, positive or negative, can persist for as long as these calculated probabilities remain unchanged by events. However, if persons invest "rationally" when there is broad agreement about probabilities, they should also revise probabilities rationally when transpiring events suggest that prior calculations can be improved. Over time, there should be convergence to agreement to the true probability of occurrence in this "thin experience case" also.

The difference that emerges between these two cases seems to be only that the profit or loss of specific individuals can persist for longer periods of *time* under conditions of disagreement. But why should we distinguish between "profit" that persists over time for some individuals but cancels out across individuals, and profit that is zero for each individual? In both cases, the event itself yields zero profit because appropriate investments and preparations have been or will be made *in total*.

It is only the case in which there is broad disagreement about probabilities, but in which the mean of calculated probabilities is not a good calculation of the probability of an event occurring, that the system may yield too much or too little investment. One example of this is Knight's belief that the optimism of entrepreneurs leads to their overinvestment in the face of uncertainty. But this could, in principle, be true of cases in which there is broad agreement also, as the emerging literature about speculative ''bubbles'' demonstrates. It is not the fact of broad agreement or disagreement that creates the possibility of over- or underinvestment: it is the existence of a biased average of probability estimates.

From this perspective, ''profit'' is imputable to purposeful human activity. *This activity is the attempt to make better calculations of the probability of risky events when information about these events is too slim to yield general agreement.* The attempt is unlikely to yield large profits or losses when there is general agreement about the relevant probability, that is, when the event is in principle insurable. The potential for gain and loss is much greater in the presence of disagreement.

In this latter case, the purpose of human activity is more aptly described as *experimenting* rather than risk-bearing, and it is even better described as *commercial experimenting*, for its purpose is to devise means by which to produce better products or to lower the cost of production. Profit, then, is the return to commercial experimentation, an activity that is carried on when generally disseminated in-depth knowledge is lacking. If past experiments are few, and knowledge is suspect, the return to experimenting can be significantly positive or negative for some time, even if, for a specific line of experiments, the return to experimenting ultimately moves toward zero.

If it were somehow possible to subtract from ''profit'' the return on capital employed in non-experimental tasks, the return on management employed in non-experimental coordination tasks, and the return to owners for self-insuring, the remaining profit or loss would be the return to owners for experimentation and for bearing pure windfalls from the unplanned outcome of Knightian uncertainty. The division between the return to experimentation and windfalls is an empirical issue, but my belief, as stated above, is that most of this return is attributable to experimentation. This is a functional return; taxing it will reduce the rate of commercial experimentation.

ADDENDUM ON KNIGHT'S THEORY OF THE FIRM

One of Knight's main contributions to the theory of the firm is opening this theory to scrutiny by depriving it of the ''black box'' status it occupies in traditional price theory. Knight seeks to understand why firms exist and what goes on inside them, asking questions that played no prior prominent role in discussions of the firm. With apologies to R. H. Coase, whose classic contribution to this subject came in 1937, it can be said without hesitation that Knight launched the modern theory of the firm in 1921. This contribution overshadows the details of how he answered his questions.

Knight's theory of the firm is not set out concisely because this theory is not really the subject of his book. The main respects in which he does discuss the firm are three: the existence, the size, and the organization of the firm. His loose discussion of the firm may be contrasted with his highly organized and detailed discussion of risk and uncertainty. The subject of the firm arises when his discussion of risk and uncertainty temporarily brings it to the surface.

His overriding approach to the firm, and that for which he is noted, is to view it as an institution for allocating risk efficiently between employees and entrepreneurial owners. As is so often the case in Knight's writings about social institutions, he makes the plausibility of his view hinge on an assumption or assertion about the nature of people. In this case, people who become entrepreneurs are by their nature less risk-averse than those who do not. It is therefore efficient for the former to act as insurers of the latter. A major reason for the existence of the firm is to achieve this risk realignment. The manner in which it does so, by paying a contracted wage to employees that is largely independent of profit variability and by compensating entrepreneurial owners with (variable) profit, gives rise to the industrial wage system:

> With human nature as we know it, it would be impracticable or very unusual for one man to guarantee to another a definite result of the latter's actions without being given power to direct his work. And on the other hand the second party would not place himself under the direction of the first without such a guarantee. . . . The result of this manifold specialization of function is enterprise and the wage system of industry. (Knight, 1965, pp. 270–1)

The weakness in the evidence supporting Knight's explanation of the locus of control over labor was commented upon by Coase (1937), who points to the fact that a large portion of jobs are done on contract by an independent firm which is paid a fixed fee; yet the purchaser has no control over the way this firm goes about delivering that which it has produced.

Knight's views on this issue may be criticized on other grounds also. Relying on "human nature as it is" solves the firm's organization problem by assertion. His argument is further strained by the absence of any real attempt to deal with differences between entrepreneurs and owners. The issue of how real entrepreneurs, as distinct from owners, are compensated is never faced clearly. Knight presumes that their compensation is profit. Nor does he reflect on the fact that those he judges not to be entrepreneurs but to be mere lenders of capital to the large corporation – its numerous holders of small numbers of shares – clearly are compensated by profit. But perhaps the most glaring gap in Knight's reasoning about efficient risk allocation is his failure to recognize that, by exacerbating swings in unemployment, fixed wages make worker incomes less stable than would be true if wages were correlated with profitability. It is implausible that workers motivated to avoid risk would ignore the connection between fixed wages and income instability. While it might be said in Knight's defense that only a minority of workers are laid off when business encounters poor times, and that the majority bear less risk as a result of fixed wages, Knight never introduces this consideration.

Although the problem of allocating risk efficiently dominates Knight's discussion of the firm, there is a second theme that occupies a less prominent place in his book. This is the problem of moral hazard, which he uses to discuss the internal organization problem of the firm. On this topic, he is both penetrating and prescient. He clearly anticipates that part of the modern theory of the firm now based on shirking or opportunistic behavior, and he explicitly recognizes the importance of organizing economic activity so as to reduce the conflicts in interest between owners and employees.

He never treats the attempt to resolve moral hazard problems as the centerpiece of his discussion of the firm, perhaps because his interest is mainly on those aspects of the firm that tie in with his broad theme of the importance of risk and uncertainty. He quickly turns to and emphasizes different issues raised by risk and uncertainty, especially the unpredictability and uninsurability of consequences that are by their nature uncertain. This emphasis seems to have prevented most students of business organization, including myself, from recognizing what Knight had to say about the connection between moral hazard and business organization.

Knight's discussion of moral hazard is full of insight, but it is also loose. He judges the corporation to be a higher form of organization than the partnership or single proprietorship because it handles the two problems of risk and moral hazard better:

> The superiority of the higher form of organization over the lower from this point of view consists both in the extension of the scope of operations to include a larger number of individual decisions, ventures, or "instances," and in the more effective unification of interest which reduces the moral hazard connected with the assumption by one person of the consequences of another person's decisions. . . . It is the special "risk" to which large amounts of capital loaned to a single enterpriser are subject which limits the scope of operations of this form of business unit by making it impossible to secure the necessary property resources. On the other hand, it is the inefficiency of organization, the failure to secure effective unity of interest, and the consequent large risk due to moral hazard when a partnership grows to considerable size, which in turn limit its extension to still larger magnitudes and bring about the substitution of the corporate form of organization. (p. 253)

For Knight, it is the fact that there are "special risks" of lending to a single proprietorship that keeps this business organization from acquiring the large amounts of capital necessary to grow to large size, and it is large size that reduces risk by facilitating the accumulation of greater experience and knowledge within one organization. One source of the superiority of the corporate organization is the greater ease with which it can become large enough to reduce risk by broadening and deepening the frequency of its exposure to business data. But he fails to make clear the nature of the special risks of lending to a single proprietorship, so we are left uncertain as to why this type of organization cannot become as large as the corporation. The looseness in the argument is apparent once it is recognized that the lender to a proprietorship or a partnership is not hampered in reclaiming his due by limited liability. Knight does recognize this:

> It must be emphasized that this type of organization actually reduces risks, and does not merely transfer them from one party to another, as might seem at first glance to be the case. . . . But it must be evident that the mere fact of limited liability only serves to transfer losses in excess of invested resources from the owners of the concern to its creditors; and if this were the only effect of incorporation, the loss in credit standing should offset the gain in security to the owners. (pp. 254–5)

The dilemma can be resolved by recognizing that it is the proprietor, not the lender, that bears special risks by growing large; these are the risks of having his personal fortune undiversified. The corporation, by allowing a large number of owners to diversify their portfolios, reduces their risks, not the lender's, and by doing so makes them more willing to borrow at any given interest rate. Apparently, the lender's difficulties with the limited liability of corporate owners are not so great as to swamp the willingness of these owners to borrow.

It is also unclear why the corporation is a better institution than the partnership for coping with moral hazard. It cannot be, as Knight indicates, that in the partnership one bears the consequences of another person's decisions, for this is even more of a problem in the corporation. In the partnership, profit-sharing attenuates at least some of the tendency by a partner to act in a manner that reduces the firm's profit. This attenuation grows weaker as the number of partners increases; but the corporation, with its thousands of profit-sharing shareholders and its limited liability, surely is not a better organization for coping with moral hazard.

That Knight's true interest lies not in the firm, but in the economic system, is revealed by the summary fashion in which he disposes of the problem of a separation between ownership and control in the corporation. He does this by confusing control over who shall be an employee with control over what this employee does:

> The first necessary step in understanding the distribution of control and responsibility in modern business is to grasp this fact: What we call "control" consists mainly of selecting some one else to do the "controlling." . . . There is an apparent separation of the functions of making decisions and taking the "risk" of error in decisions . . . where the man who makes decisions receives a fixed salary, taking no "risk," and those who take the risk and receive profits – the stockholders – make no decisions, exercise

no control. Yet a little examination in the light of the preceding discussion of knowledge and indirect responsibility will show that the separation is illusory; when control is accurately defined and located, the functions of making decisions and assuring the responsibility for their correctness will be found to be one and indivisible. (pp. 291–4)

REFERENCES

Coase, R. H. (1937). "The Nature of the Firm." *Economica*, 4.

Knight, F. H. (1965). *Risk, Uncertainty, and Profit*. New York: Harper and Row (first published 1921).

PART IV
Normative Issues

16
Social Responsibility in the Enterprise Economy

I wish to emphasize at the outset that this article does *not* present a general ethical system or a specific ethical code to guide business behavior. Too many philosophers and economists, good men and mediocre, have failed in their attempts to define even "the fair price," "the just wage," or "fair competition." My purpose is to describe the manner in which a free enterprise economy evaluates behavior, whatever the substantive content of such behavior may be, but with an emphasis on those aspects of particular relevance to the firm and the corporation. In the process of doing this, I hope to reveal the subtleties, complexities, and difficulties of judging the ethical properties of that behavior that businessmen may legally undertake in a free enterprise system.

The decision to analyze a free enterprise system, of course, in no way implies the absence of ethical problems in command economies, but these present a peculiar problem of analysis. The rigidly controlled society may keep its people on the straight and narrow path, but it cannot be deduced from their taking that path that they are righteous. Ethical behavior is revealed when a person who chooses a morally superior course of action could have easily elected to follow an inferior one. The command economy, by virtue of its restrictions on choice opportunities, strips observed behavior of ethical significance. The analysis of the free enterprise economy as that economic system to which we *should* aspire does impose a predetermined moral framework within which to work, for it implies that the good society limits the use of legal sanctions, expands the opportunities for choice by individuals, and, therefore, places the responsibility for behaving ethically on its citizens.

The resulting wide scope of individual choice opportunities in the free enterprise economy is exercised against the background of resource scarcity. Some choices can be exercised (as fully) only if others are not (as fully). It is important to have

This lecture, delivered at Southwestern University on October 18, 1977, inaugurated a quarterly lecture series at which scholars from diverse fields spoke on current issues in law and related subjects. Reprinted with permission from *Southwestern University Law Review*, 10, 1978.

a filter through which these choice opportunities can be sorted to remove their inconsistencies. The competitive profit and loss criterion is the primary filter of the free enterprise economy. I shall discuss the operation of this filter, which is not without its ethical consequences, primarily in the context of *on-going society engaged in its day-to-day business*. This is the most important context in which to understand its operation. Toward the end of this paper, I will discuss briefly the problem of special situations not confronted on a day-to-day basis.

I

The enterprise economy operates against the background of a legal structure that divides conceivable activities into two sets which, very roughly speaking, are non-overlapping: legal and illegal activites. The illegal activities are primarily the use of violence, fraud, and duress in one's dealings with others. One interpretation of why these are illegal is the belief that on a day-to-day basis the costs engendered by these activities considerably outweigh any benefits they might produce; here the legal system provides an initial barrier by which activities tend to be filtered out or made permissible. Another interpretation, not at all inconsistent with the first, is that these activities confound our ability to measure benefits and costs. An object taken by force is not as surely being put to its highest value use as an object acquired in a voluntary transaction. The prohibition of overt forms of coercion thus reinforces the credibility of the profit and loss system as a second filter that forestalls or eliminates those legal, but plausibly ethical, activities that would misplace resources by keeping them from their highest value use. The manner in which this filtering mechanism operates is important enough to merit brief explication.

One seller invents a new marketing technique that allows him to reach potential customers at lower cost than his competitors. The introduction of this technique yields beneficial effects for customers by allowing them to satisfy their demands at a lower price, but it also imposes harmful effects on the firms losing these customers. The non-collusive open market will allow the innovation to succeed only if customers are benefitted more than competitive sellers are harmed, for only if this is the case will these sellers be unwilling to reduce price enough to retain the patronage of their customers. This example, which portrays the success or failure of a new product, simplifies greatly the task of filtering actually performed by the profit and loss criterion. Most choice opportunities are not of this either/or variety, but rather, how much of this or that.

A large, complex society, in which millions of individuals confront many choice problems each day, imposes a severe burden on a filtering mechanism. Any practical method for filtering choice in such a situation cannot be inconsistent with human nature. The profit and loss system relies on perhaps the strongest component of that nature, self-interest. Catastrophe and war, a local emergency, or on-going deliberations may bring altruistic emotions to the surface, and in family life altruism may play a steadier part in motivating us, but both the transiency of national emergency and the limited field of family life argue against a social organization that relies on self-sacrifice. Adam Smith tells us in *The Wealth of Nations* that:

> It is not from the benevolence of the butcher, the brewer, or the baker, that we expect our dinner, but from their regard to their own interest. We address ourselves, not to their humanity but to their self-love, and never talk to them of our own necessities but of their advantages.[1]

It is not that we are motivated exclusively by self-interest, but that, in dealing with great masses of unfamiliar people, self-interest is the only persistently reliable motivation. Adam Smith puts it this way: "In civilized society [man] stands at all times in need of the cooperation and assistance of great multitudes, while his whole life is scarce sufficient to gain the friendship of a few persons."[2]

The net benefit criterion of the market place is not unrelated to how we seem to judge behavior outside the market place. A man in a boat who sights a floundering swimmer but makes no attempt at rescue is more likely to be thought socially irresponsible than a man on shore who is a poor swimmer. The expected cost to the boatsman of helping the swimmer is lower than it is for the man on the beach. The ethical calculus might yield a different opinion of the boatsman were he rushing a desperately ill man to shore.

I do not wish to claim equivalence between a proper ethical calculus and the profit and loss filter, only that the filtering criterion of the profit and loss system creates a prima facie case in terms of the net benefit criterion in support of those legal activities that survive the market test. The net benefit criterion assumes ethical properties if the purchase of freedom that it allows is highly valued.

II

Three arguments are used to rebut this prima facie case: paternalism, the distribution of wealth, and externalities. The paternalism argument asserts that neither the minor nor the mentally incompetent knows his self-interest, so that reliance on the market filter misleads in such a case. Let us accept the need for paternalism in such instances, hoping that the authorities do not think that we, one and all normal adults, are in need of such protection, for that is the thought behind the command society. I hasten to point out that acceptance of the appropriateness of exchange by non-institutionalized adults is not without its moral ramifications; the net benefit calculations of the profit and loss system reflect the tastes of consumers, and these tastes reflect the persuasive efforts of government, church, school, home, and Madison Avenue. A producer and consumer may agree to the sale of a book containing the sonnets of the immortal Bard, the ravings of Adolph Hitler, or a gallery of pornographic photos. A case can be made that the availability of some quantity of such goods serves useful and even ethical purposes, perhaps if only to keep us informed. But I assume that the moral society is also a free society, tolerant of a large variety of *privately* indulged tastes, and I hope that my colleagues when choosing between *Hamlet* on live stage and *Deep Throat* on the silver screen can repress their taste for popcorn.

The distribution of wealth argument quite simply states that, since the benefit and cost dimensions of activities in the market place depend on what people are willing to pay, they are legitimate measures of net gains only insofar as the underlying distribution of wealth is morally defensible. I take it that it is not part of the individual business corporation's social responsibility to be concerned about wealth distribution questions in the large, although, of course, it is concerned with the distribution of its receipts among shareholders, employees, creditors, and the Internal Revenue Service. Paternalism and wealth distribution problems deserve more attention in other contexts than ours, so let us turn to externalities.

If soot from many factories descends on a multitude of private residences, the harmful effects suffered by their residents may be real but individually small relative to the cost of searching out and negotiating with the relevant factory owners. Yet, it could well be that the total damage done summed over all homeowners exceeds the value to the factory owners of using cheaper soot-yielding fuels. This hypothetical case poses a situation in which it is difficult (costly) for factory owners to appropriate enough of the value to homeowners of reducing soot. The self-interest of factory owners and homeowners leads them to forgo the required market transactions. This is in contrast to a situation in which one factory's soot descends on one neighbor's house, in which case market negotiations would be cheap enough to yield a net gain from negotiated reduction in soot.

There is a temptation to conclude that cleaner air is in fact called for, but that is because I have presented a hypothetical situation in which we know that the sum of the gains to homeowners exceeds the cost to factory owners of producing cleaner air; possessed of this knowledge, we are inclined to charge that the factory owners are shirking their social responsibility. But such knowledge would be difficult to possess in a real situation if market transactions were too costly to undertake, for it is the operation of the market that filters out those activities yielding no net gain. Factory owners are behaving as responsibly as they do when they do not produce automobiles without brakes, for which there also is no effective demand.

There is widespread misunderstanding about the nature of costs and social responsibility in these problems. If a chemical company uses a stream to carry away waste materials, the water may become sufficiently polluted to kill off fish for several miles downstream. If this happened it would be correct to accuse the firm, or its customers, of imposing costs on prospective fishermen. But suppose that the firm were prohibited from using the stream, so that it was forced to find more costly ways to dispose of its wastes. With equal accuracy we could now say that fishing in this stream imposes costs on the firm and its customers. The cost problem must be viewed as analytically symmetrical; it is incorrect to suppose that harmful effects follow only if the stream is polluted. In the general case the moral problem must be viewed symmetrically for the same reason: it is not morally more wrong for consumers of the firm's product to impose harmful effects on fishermen than it is for fishermen to impose harmful effects on the consumers. The frequent imputation of immorality or of lack of social conscience on the part of those who pollute is no more appropriate than for those who seek to reduce pollution. I have purposely left the firm's product unidentified. Weapons for Israel? Milk for babies? Textbooks for students? Opinions will vary and will be far from unanimous as to what should be done with the stream in each of these cases, and this reveals the difficulty of viewing the situation as one of moral asymmetry.

The problem is not one of minimizing *pollution* but one of devising institutional arrangements that do a fairly good job of minimizing the *harmful effects* that necessarily flow from resource scarcity, in this instance the scarcity of streams. In some cases harmful effects can be minimized by reducing pollution, but in other cases an increase in pollution may be required. Clean air and water are not unlike other resources in that they should be used when the gain outweighs the cost.

Once the complexities and ambiguities of arriving at a correct position to such problems are recognized, it is clear not only that the charge of social irresponsibility runs a considerable risk of being irresponsible itself, but that there cannot be any great confidence that a governmental solution is sure to yield net gains. Even so, the externality problem at least offers a conceptual premise on which to hang government involvement. This much cannot be said for other important instances in which business management has been charged with social irresponsibility, such as in the attempt to forestall price increases by jawboning. It may seem incredible to the non-economist, but an increase in price can serve a useful function. The price increase may be necessary to earn revenues sufficient to pay for the use of inputs. If this is the case, the product cannot be produced in the same quantities without raising price, *unless we wish to resort to coercion and slavery to acquire inputs.*

A non-monopolistic price increase that yields revenue in excess of the amount required to cover cost serves the useful function of attracting resources into the industry. This type of price increase can come about only if the resources presently available to the industry are inadequate to meet the demand for the product. The price increase then auctions off or rations the limited supply to those who place the highest value on securing the commodity. This keeps the commodity from being used in unimportant ways until additional resources are attracted into the industry.

If the price were not raised, some other method of allocating limited supplies to consumers would have to be adopted. This could be first-come-first-served, only whites served, only blacks served, poor served first, etc. All these rationing schemes have different ethical implications, but they all suffer from the clear defect of not providing to resource owners incentives to move resources into the industry.

It is instructive to illustrate how low prices or a price decrease can result in serious resource misallocation. Overutilization of scarce resources arises because the use of the resource, usually owned by the government, is under-priced. Asking a zero price for the use of our lakes and streams has been a basic source of water pollution. Asking too low a price to remove timber from state forests has resulted in overcutting. The fact that freeways are free during rush hours results in bumper-to-bumper traffic. The failure to charge higher landing fees during the late afternoon hours results in congestion over major airfields.

President Carter has recently accused the oil companies of trying to rip off the public by seeking decontrol of energy prices. Clearly, unethical behavior is being charged. But would it be unethical to decontrol these prices? It is clear that there is much natural gas that can be recovered, but only at a higher cost than has been true for past recoveries. The more prices are held below such costs, the smaller will be the amount of additional natural gas secured, because the companies will not receive sufficient revenues to pay for the resources and risk required to do the job. There are three alternatives. Either we insist on holding down natural gas prices, fail to increase our stock of gas much, and fail to allocate what gas we have to its highest value uses; or we hold down natural gas prices and *compel* these inputs to be applied to the task of securing additional supplies; or we allow prices to rise, encourage additional recovery, and discourage the use of existing stocks. The free society, it seems to me, would *not* view the last alternative as clearly inferior in ethical substance to the others.

When OPEC successfully colluded to reduce its output of crude oil, the first response by government was to impose price ceilings on domestically produced crude oil and on refined products. Rationing of existing supplies of refined products then was accomplished in part by waiting in line, a price measured by the value of time and not clearly more ethical than paying a higher money price.

Refineries that relied on imported crude oil, however, could secure their supplies only at OPEC's price, not the controlled price at which domestic crude oil was forced to sell. These refineries complained that they were being treated unfairly relative to those refineries that had access to price-controlled domestic crude oil. In response to their complaint, the entitlement system was created. The effect was to force refineries using domestic crude to subsidize the importation of foreign crude by other refineries. This encouraged imports, thus supporting OPEC, and discouraged domestic crude production that was now subjected to the risk of present and future price control. And what was the net effect of all this on gasoline prices, which, in effect, had been decontrolled in the meantime? Since a considerable part of gasoline production necessarily derives from foreign crude, there was no way in which the price limit on domestic crude could keep the price of gasoline below what was necessary to pay for foreign crude. Therefore, the lid on domestic crude prices produced very little short-run effect on gasoline prices.

The net effect of the first attempt to limit the profits securable by producers of domestic crude oil was to transfer wealth from them to refiners who relied on imports and from these refiners to OPEC by subsidizing imports. The cartel was supported, domestic crude production was discouraged, and the price at the pump to buyers of gasoline was largely unaffected.

Carter's new plan, as near as I can tell, eliminates the subsidy to importing refiners by imposing a tax on crude oil produced domestically. The tax is to be set at a level such that, when it is added to the still controlled price of domestic crude, the price to refiners using domestic crude will equal that paid by import refiners, who must buy at world prices. The net effect of this is to transfer wealth from domestic crude producers to the US Treasury, to discourage the search for more domestic crude, and to leave gasoline prices largely unaffected in the short run but higher in the long run, because of the lack of incentive to find and secure more domestic crude oil. At least this plan does not subsidize OPEC; it may do better or worse, depending on the use to which the government puts its new tax revenue. But the new plan and the old do not strike me as morally superior to allowing all prices to clear the market.

III

Special attention is given to the large publicly held corporation in the literature on social responsibility. This is for two reasons: first, a belief that large corporations have great power for good or evil, unlike the small independent grocer; and second, a belief that shareholders do not control their corporations.

Power might be interpreted to mean monopoly. I do not believe that corporations, as a class of economic institutions, even large corporations, have great monopoly power. There is much evidence that they do not. But suppose they did. It is the monopolist who is more likely to respond to broader social objectives when confronted by mounting public opinion, for he has less fear of losing customers to a would-be rival who might not respond similarly. The cost imposed on one of several automobile companies when it installs emission controls, an act that raises the cost to buyers and reduces the auto's performance from their individual viewpoint, surely is greater, because of the business it loses to rivals who refrain from installing such equipment, than it would be if that company had no rivals.

True, a monopolist can also cater more easily to his own interests in the absence of social pressure to do otherwise, but let us examine what his interests might be. He might very well reduce output, thereby increasing price and profit; I have no difficulty believing that his self-interest would be served by such an action. However, the issue then is one of antitrust. Would he find it in his interest to use water, air, or other resources in ways that reduced their quality by more than a competitive industry might reduce their quality? I have difficulty imagining plausible circumstances in which he would. The monopolist has an interest in producing his chosen rate of output at as low a cost as is possible, for this maximizes his profits. In this respect his incentives are largely the same as those of a competitive firm; both can be expected to combine resources in similar fashion in order to achieve this low cost. There is no reason to expect the monopolist to reduce the quality of air or water per unit of output he produces any more than would a competitive firm. Moreover, since a monopoly generally will produce fewer units of output than would a competitive industry, we have reason to believe that those external costs associated with larger outputs are likely to be less than if the industry were organized competitively. Environmentalists might very well find it easier to live with monopolies than with competitive industries.

If power refers to size alone, not to monopoly, then, again, it is difficult to understand why the large publicly held corporation is likely to be less responsible socially than a small firm. If we imagine the wheat industry restructured into a thousand large farms rather than the tens of thousands that now exist, why should we expect the industry to behave any differently? If the demand for wheat falls, then both structures of the industry would yield the same reduction in employment, fertilizer use, and output, and both structures should combine inputs in the same way to produce that output that remains.

The only relevance of size that I can imagine is with respect to capricious behavior. A firm that is much larger than another, both being in the same industry, employs more people and sells to more customers. A decision made by the larger firm, therefore, affects more people than the same decision made by the smaller firm. With respect to self-interested profit-maximizing behavior, this fact is of no importance. If there is a 10 percent decline in the demand for the industry's product, then it makes little difference whether the resulting reduction in employment and output derives from many small firms or from a few large ones.

Suppose there is no decrease in demand but that, for some completely capricious and unexplainable reason, the large firm decides to hold its plant and equipment idle; that certainly would affect more people than would a similar decision by a smaller firm. Indeed, it might take ten smaller firms, each behaving in this peculiar fashion, to have the same effect. Such behavior imposes losses on the firm, and in a world motivated largely by self-interest we would not expect to observe such behavior. To my knowledge we have never observed such behavior. Moreover, if we are discussing inexplicable, capricious behavior, then we are discussing a psychic phenomenon, likely to occur with a given probability in any one chosen at random. If an industry structure containing ten firms is compared with a structure containing one hundred firms, there are ten times as many owners likely to succumb in the second case as in the first. The *expected* share of industry output likely to be affected by such aberrant behavior is the same in the two cases.

The issue frequently is put in the following way. Suppose there were only one monopoly firm producing a very important product, and suddenly it just decided to shut down, either capriciously or maliciously. To that the answer is obvious. If it threatened to shut down or did shut down when its product was thought to be essential, why, then, the government either would force it to open or would subsidize it to open – remember Lockheed and the Penn Central – and such government action is likely to be more effective than against an industry made up of thousands of firms, the owners or employees of which, for good or bad reason, decide to withhold from the market their goods and services.

In summary, while monopoly may reduce output and require the application of antitrust, neither monopoly nor large size presents problems especially germane to the question of social responsibility. What would we have large firms do in the name of social responsibility that we would not want of industries comprised of small firms?

Turning now to the issue of separation of ownership and control, I find it difficult to see a clear line to the problem of social responsibility. Control of the corporation may be important to shareholders when devising contractual arrangements with managements, but of what concern is this to third parties? We know that incentives exist to dovetail management and shareholder interests in the tying of managerial compensation to the company's performance, in the market value of management's reputation, and in the discipline of the capital markets, especially through the takeover.

But suppose there were no way to bring these interests into perfect alignment, as indeed there never is. Do we think the small investor so naive that he believes he will have a sizable voice in managing the corporation? He is a shareholder, not a manager, precisely because he seeks to avoid the problems of decision-making. Anyone investing in stock would be prepared to do so only if he could secure it at a large enough discount to offset the lack of correlation between managerial and shareholder interests, and anyone seeking to manage a corporation would be prepared to do so for a lower salary than if there were no separation of ownership and control. What manager would want to take a poll of shareholders every time he faces a decision? What shareholder would think he would be better off with such an arrangement? Lack of perfect correlation in interests does not imply that management gets the best of shareholders. If shareholders are willing to put funds into a large corporation, knowing that individually they will not be able to exercise control, and if they find that the price of stock relative to expected earnings in the absence of individual control is attractively low, why does an issue of social responsibility arise? We have no reason to believe that corporate management is more likely to use the corporation's assets in socially undesirable ways than they would be used if control were exercised by shareholders. Special rules might be desirable to insure that management acts in behalf of shareholders, but why should the corporation's assets be more subservient to the ethical demands of outsiders than are the assets of proprietorships?

The absence of logical analysis in discussions of the relationship between the separation of ownership and control and social responsibility leads me to believe that it is an artifact behind which the true objective lies, and that, quite simply, is to deliver control of corporate assets into the hands of outsiders. By asserting separation of ownership and control, these outsiders hope to create the belief that these assets do not legally or ethically belong to the shareholders or the management that controls them (*even though shareholders have voluntarily entrusted them to management's care*). Therefore, and here comes the non sequitur, it is legal and ethical to deliver the control of these assets to morally motivated outsiders! Those who desire to sit on corporate boards of directors as representatives of the public interest assure us that their control over the wealth of others will turn to socially productive purposes. I wonder what those purposes are, but not whose self-interest will be served.

NOTES

1 Smith (1937, p. 14).
2 Smith (1937, p. 14).

REFERENCE

Smith, Adam (1937). *An Inquiry into the Nature and Causes of the Wealth of Nations*. New York: Random House (first published 1776).

17
Ethics and Efficiency in Property Rights Systems

INTRODUCTION

Frank Knight, who was neither antagonistic toward capitalism nor one of its more romantic supporters, in some ways was one of its more interesting critics. Knight never seemed in much doubt about the superior capabilities of the capitalistic system to efficiently satisfy those wants and preferences expressed in the market by consumers, although he readily recognized the imperfection in all human institutions. But he was concerned about the kind of person who emerges from the competitive milieu of capitalism.

> Is emulation as a motive ethically good or base? Is success in any sort of *contest*, as such, a noble objective? . . . In America particularly, where competitive business, and its concomitant, the sporting view of life, have reached their fullest development, there have come to be two sorts of virtue. The greater virtue is to win. . . . The lesser virtue is to go out and die gracefully after having lost.[1]

The question raised here implicitly assumes that economic organization has a detectable impact on our basic psychological drives. There is room for reasonable doubt about the validity of this assumption. There is some evidence from modern socio-biology that our inner motivations derive from many centuries of evolution; that, short of direct genetic engineering or selective breeding, there is no way for this genetic endowment, and hence these inner drives, to be modified significantly by the choice of institutional environment; economic organization may have very little to do with competitive drive, altruistic sentiment, or the propensity to *ape*.

Be that as it may, it seems difficult or impossible to define, isolate, and measure true inner qualities, and so we are left with no basis other than human action, or the consequence thereof, by which to judge the ethical properties of alternative economic organizations. In this chapter I wish to critically examine some ethical questions about the private property rights system from the perspective of human

Originally published in *Time, Uncertainty and Disequilibrium*, edited by Mario Zizzo, Lexington, 1979.

action, an especially appropriate viewpoint since so much of Austrian economics centers on praxeology. Ethical judgments about economic organization, however, frequently rest on some unspecified, usually vague, concept of "justice" or "morality," often stated quite independently of an examination of the human action implied by that economic organization. "It is immoral to allow owners of factories to put smoke into other people's air," or, "it is immoral not to assess the person *causing* damages with the liability for those damages:" these are typical of the statements I have in mind. My first task is to expose the weakness of this religious or intuitive approach to moral problems. This could be done rather easily by attacking the overriding faith of socialists in the correctness of a holistic view of society, or in their belief that altering economic organization alters the inner qualities of man, but before this audience [of libertarians] I choose what for me is the more difficult task of attacking the simplistic faith of a few libertarians in their notion of the ethical superiority of particular private property arrangements. A target is needed. Walter Block, writing critically about work by R. H. Coase and me in a recent issue of the *Journal of Libertarian Studies* (Spring, 1977), has inadvertently volunteered.

THE ETHICAL SUPERIORITY OF PRIVATE PROPERTY RIGHTS

Block raises a substantive positive issue as well as a moral one about property rights systems. It is necessary to examine both if our perspective on ethical matters is to derive from the implied outcomes of alternative property rights assignments. The substantive issue has to do with whether or not the assignment of rights ownership will alter the mix of output when "bargaining transactions . . . are costless [and] changes in the distribution of wealth . . . can be ignored." Coase and I (with a proviso about "free-riders") say no; Block says yes. Block then presents some examples that appear to refute our analyses, but which really only violate our explicitly made assumption that there are no wealth effects on the demands for the commodities being discussed. We both recognize that there will be allocative effects when this assumption does not hold.

He considers a case involving "psychic income" wherein a smoke prevention device can be installed for $75,000 by a factory which, in the absence of such a device, will ruin a neighbor's flower bed because of smoke pollution. The flower bed is worth nothing to anyone else, but to the neighbor it is worth $100,000 because of sentimental value. The factory would not be willing to pay its neighbor more than $75,000, the cost of a smoke cleaning device, for his permission to pollute the air, so, if the neighbor has a right to a soot-free garden, the factory owner would elect to install the smoke-cleaning device rather than pay the $100,000 demanded by its neighbor. But if the factory owner has the right to use smoke-producing fuel, the neighbor, being so poor, would be unable (unwilling) to pay the factory owner the $75,000 required to install the smoke-cleaning device. With the first assignment of rights, there is a flower

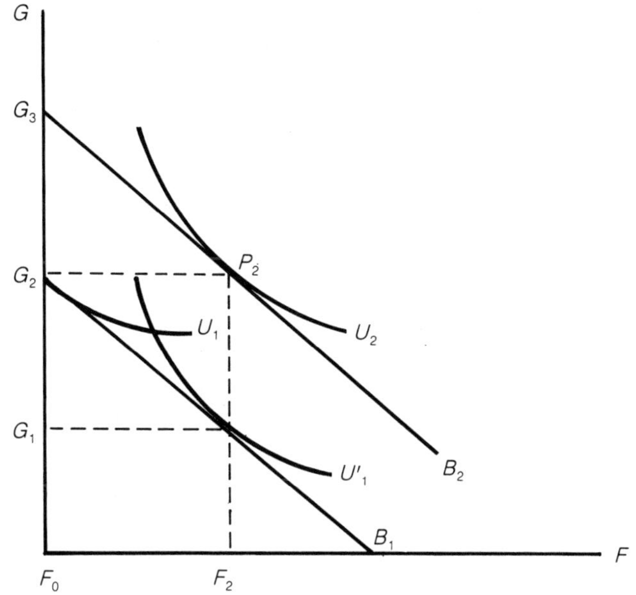

Figure 17.1 Rights Assignments and Income Effects

garden and no smoke (and there also is less factory output). With the second, there is smoke (more factory output) and no flower garden. The mix of output is contingent on the assignment of rights. True, but only because of the income effect, as can be seen with the aid of figure 17.1.

The horizontal axis of the figure measures quantity of flower garden, and the vertical axis, quantity of other goods. The indifference curves and budget lines picture the neighbor's situation in each of the rights assignment situations. If the neighbor has the right to soot-free air, he consumes P_2 containing F_2 of flowers and G_2 of other goods. But since he can sell the right to pollute the air for $75,000, he also can consume no flowers, F_0, and G_3 of other goods, where $G_3 - G_2$ equals $75,000 worth of other goods. He therefore confronts a budget line, B_2, that passes through P_2 and G_3.

The second rights assignment alters the budget line on which he can operate. Given his income and no right to soot-free air, he can consume G_2 of other goods and enjoy no flowers, or he can give up $75,000 of the other goods, consuming only G_1 of these, but increase his garden to F_2. The second rights assignment, therefore, has reduced his budget line to B_1. This alteration in income alters the mix of goods produced in Block's example because the indifference curve relevant to the new budget line is U_1; if it had been U'_1, he would have purchased the same quantity of flowers, F_2, as he enjoyed with the first rights assignment. The alteration in the mix of output reflects an implicit wealth effect on the demand for flowers, as can be seen easily if a compensating increase in income is given to the garden owner when the factory owner has the right to use smoke-producing fuel, and, therefore, is in no way acceptable as a refutation of Coase's analysis. An identical explanation lies behind the allocative difference Block sees between a "buy-him-in" voluntary army and a "let-him-buy-his-way-out" type of draft. In the Coase analysis, to assume no income effect is not to assert the unimportance of such an effect, but merely to keep the discussion within the Pigouvian traditional analysis of externality problems; that analysis was critical of the ability of competitive economic organization to produce efficient resource allocations quite aside from income distribution problems.

It is clear from the emotionalism of Block's discussion that he has strong ethical feelings as to how property rights *should* be defined in such cases. It is the gardener who should have the right to soot-free air, and the potential recruit who should have the right to his freedom. One is entitled to an explanation of why these assignments of property rights are ethically superior to their alternatives. A volunteer army undoubtedly has great intuitive appeal as superior even to a draft in which a person has the right to buy his way out, but the ownership by the gardener of the right to control the soot content of air does not. A general ethical resolution of the problem of property rights definitions cannot be supported by the definiteness of one's view about some intuitively easy case.

Tougher examples can be found easily. Consider the following analog to Block's gardening problem. Let there be an island that contains all the known stock of Austrian Pure Snow trees. The island is inhabited by a religious sect, the first to mix their sweat and blood with the island's soil, thus satisfying Rothbard's principle of "original ownership." They worship these trees as if they were God. Never would they let them be tampered with in any way. Unknown to anyone, these trees contain an ingredient that is a sure cure for cancer, and when this is discovered a question of the ownership of this ingredient, unavailable elsewhere, arises. The religious sect will in no way, for any compensation, allow that ingredient to be extracted. Is it "evil and vicious" to believe that it would be preferable for someone else to own the right to this ingredient, requiring instead that the religious sect purchase the inviolability of this ingredient? Might not "our most cherished and precious property rights" be still more cherished and precious if the private ownership of this new resource were not confined to those who own the rest of the island? Would the answer be much different if this ingredient not only was known to the island dwellers, but was precisely that part of the trees that they worshipped? Would the answer be different if the islanders were very poor?

The instrumental nature of property rights is made clear in this example. The multi-dimensionality of human want virtually guarantees that a sufficient alteration in the gains and losses of alternative definitions of property rights structures can dim the ethical aura that surrounds any specific structure. I do not believe that it is possible to defend effectively a particular property rights structure by appealing to some supposed overriding concern for freedom, or for equality, or for wealth, or for "original ownership." Lexicographic orderings crumble in the face of scarcity. The general constraint of scarcity imposes substitutability at the margin, even when one speaks of substituting alternative property rights definitions for present ones or for those that would derive from "original ownership."

Consider the problem of reconciling the demand to play tennis with the demand for peace and quiet. These often conflict, especially when there is a desire to play tennis at night on lighted courts. The conflict is similar to that of the factory owner and the gardener discussed by Block, both of whom wish to put air space to competing uses. Noise, like soot, can envelop a neighbor's home.

A private property rights system, in recognition of this conflict, may assign the right to determine nearby noise levels to those who would sleep or to those who would play tennis. *Both* rights assignments are equally private, and both seem equally productive of individual freedom. Neither exhibits any obvious ethical superiority over the other even when one's preferences are highly weighted in favor of individual freedom. The same can be said of a third alternative wherein the right to control noise levels during daytime hours belongs to those who would play tennis and during nighttime hours to those who would sleep.

The instrumental advantage of the third alternative can (but need not) be measured in terms of its consequences for resource allocation. The dollar value of benefits of assigning rights over noise levels during nighttime hours to would-be sleepers *plausibly* exceeds the dollar value of costs thereby imposed on would-be nighttime tennis players, so that, even if the cost to these parties of negotiating with each other were prohibitive, resources would tend to be utilized in an "efficient"[2] manner. Similarly, the assignment to tennis players during daytime hours of the right to control noise levels yields a dollar value of benefits that exceeds the dollar value of costs imposed on neighbors. The property rights system could be complicated further but not at zero cost; persons who are seriously ill might be allowed to control noise levels during daytime hours, while those who work at nighttime might not.

The fine-tuning is left largely to market negotiations. If a nighttime tennis player is willing to pay enough to his neighbor, his neighbor will give permission for tennis to be played. Once a private property rights system is defined, especially with respect to who owns the right to offer to sell specific entitlements to use resources, it can be expected that subsequent negotiations will *tend* to tolerate only efficient uses of scarce resources. If the cost of transacting were zero, and if there were no "free-rider" or "holdout" problems, any private rights system, once it is defined, will do this.

If there are significant transaction costs, then the choice of a private rights system will have direct consequences for resource allocation in addition to any indirect impact this choice may have through wealth distribution effects. To take an extreme case, suppose that the cost to neighbors of negotiating with each other is prohibitively high relative to the gains to be expected from such negotiations. No matter what the distribution of wealth, assume this remains true. If tennis players have the right to use tennis courts at night, they will play tennis even when the dollar value to them of doing so is less than the dollar value of sleep to their neighbors. Similarly, if would-be sleepers have the right to quiet all day, tennis players who would choose to play in daytime generally will be barred from an activity that they value more than their neighbors value quiet. Plausibly, when transaction costs are significant, a system of private rights that assigns entitlements to control nighttime noise levels to sleepers and daytime noise levels to tennis players would be ''superior'' to either of these simpler assignments if the objective is to achieve an efficient use of resources.

EFFICIENCY CONSIDERATIONS

Substitutability at the margin suggests that efficiency considerations may be relevant to the problem of choosing property rights definitions, and I will argue that this is the case, both normatively and positively. The instrumentalism of property rights systems can be recognized, although perhaps not completely, by employing the criterion of maximization of the real values of the resources whose uses are affected by the assignment of rights. I do not refer to simple maximization of recorded market value, which inappropriately reflects leisure/labor trade-offs, pecuniary/non-pecuniary trade-offs, and monopoly/competition trade-offs, but to the efficiency with which it is expected that resources will be deployed as a result of one rights assignment as compared with another.

This criterion undoubtedly will be suspect among both Austrian economists and libertarians, the first because it seems to imply that values are not subjective, that they can be measured objectively, and the second because it suggests that private property rights might not survive the efficiency criterion. Neither suspicion is completely unfounded; neither is completely warranted. I will turn to these issues below. But, first, let us eschew problems of state intervention in the exercise of rights, and also the pragmatic problem of just how certain information would be known and acted upon, confining attention for now to the question of which of two (or more) individuals should control the private right to use some resource – that is, to the problem typified by gardener and factory owner.

I wish to begin the analysis of this case assuming zero transaction cost and no income effects on the demands for cleaner air or for the product of the factory, but then to move quickly to more relevant assumptions. With these assumptions, the right to control the soot content of the air will have no impact on the quantity of soot, flowers, or the factory's output, since the contesting parties will negotiate to the identical quantity of soot, that which is efficient, no matter who pays whom to reach this level of soot content. (If there are third parties affected by the soot content, they simply are brought into the negotiation.) The only aspect of the situation that can be affected by the choice of owner of the right to control soot content is the distribution of income (or wealth), since with one rights assignment – that in which the gardener controls soot content – the factory owner pays his neighbor for permission to put more soot into the air, while in the other case the neighbor pays the factory owner to take soot out of the air. It would seem awkward for libertarians to argue for the ethical superiority of one distribution of income over another when no issue of freedom or resource allocation is involved. Moreover, if income distribution were the desideratum, there would be no clear ruling on the merits of the *situation*, only on the merits of the relative incomes of the two parties standing before the court, or likely in the future to stand before the court. Nonetheless in such a hypothetical situation there is *only* the comparison of resulting income distribution to guide the ethical decision. In such a case, it might well be thought that the person denied control of soot content should receive a compensating increase in income, but more about this later.

Real situations will seldom fit this hypothetical case. Generally there will be transaction costs and also income effects on demands for commodities. But let us proceed a step at a time, assuming still that transaction cost is zero but that income effects are present. As in Block's example, an assignment of the right to control the soot level to the gardener, if we assume the preferences implied in that example, now yields more flowers and less soot (and less factory output) than does the alternative rights assignment. A choice between different mixes of output is now possible, but on what grounds is it to be made, since the efficient mix of output is itself dependent on the distribution of income? More flowers and less soot (and less factory output) maximizes the real value of resources when the neighboring gardener owns the right to control soot content, and more soot (and more factory output) and fewer flowers maximizes the real value of resources when the factory owner owns the right (always noting that third parties should be included in negotiations over soot content in the absence of transaction cost if they have any interest in the outcome). We seem to be back to the ethical superiority of alternative income distributions, although in this case the mix of output will not be invariant with respect to the rights assignment. Of course, if a compensating increase in income is granted to the person denied the right to control soot content, then the mix of output will be invariant with respect to the decision as to who owns the right.

This will not be the case if the cost of transacting is significant. To make the point as easily as is possible, let it be assumed that transaction cost is so high relative to the gains from exchange that no exchange between the interested parties will take place once the assignment of rights is made, but that the party denied ownership of the right receives a compensating increase in income. The assignment of rights affects the mix of goods for a reason other than income distribution. Assuming that full income compensation accompanies the decision about who should control the soot content of air, can a reasonable statement be made as to which output mix is superior, and hence about which rights assignment is to be preferred?

If the right to control soot content is acquired by the gardener, there will be no soot, less factory output, and more flowers than if the factory owner receives the right, because the party denied the right cannot (because of transaction cost) economically bring his preferences for altering soot content to bear on the decision of the party who acquired the right. Monopoly aside, why not assign the right to that party who would find it most valuable? The second party is made whole through income compensation (still to be discussed), and the required compensation would be less than would be required by the first party if it was the second who had received the right; moreover, the air is put to a higher value use with this rights assignment than with the reverse.

Questions about this criterion will surely arise in the minds of some readers. Does this violate the notion that values are subjective and unknowable to second parties? Does this involve interpersonal utility comparisons? My answer to these questions is that the criterion of efficiency assumes no more than does the criterion of the market place. For, after all, all that has been done is to auction off the right to the party who would have been the highest bidder (assuming no problems of monopoly are present). Suppose that the right to control soot content belonged to some original settler, who was himself indifferent as to the soot content of air; that he was soon joined by two neighbors, one a factory owner and the other a gardener; and that he offers to sell the right to control soot content to that neighbor submitting the highest bid. Assuming negligible transaction costs, the problem of the identity of the ultimate controller of air quality would be resolved in a manner identical to that implied above by the efficiency criterion. Why not adopt the criterion of the market place in those situations in which the question of ownership arises? It is not as if that question need not be answered. In one way or another, it must be answered before negotiations can take place; clearly, identifying the owner through legal processes merely reduces the cost of negotiating by making clear who must pay whom. Absent such a legal determination, other methods, possibly violent, such as in a range war, will be adopted to settle the question of ownership. If settlement is to be made through legal processes, some criterion must be used. Attempting to use the market's criterion of placing resources in their highest value use seems difficult to improve upon.

To adopt the criterion of the market place in the court room is *not* to assert that values are objective or that it is possible to compare utility across individuals. The method of the market and the method proposed here for the court both adopt the *convention* that willingness to pay serves well as a *substitute* for utility comparisons in the resolution of conflicts over the use of scarce resources.

The specification of the underlying private rights system ultimately defines who has the right to impose harmful effects on whom, or, more accurately, how to identify who has such a right. The imposition of costs is inescapable given that our desires to use resources often conflict. But even after a private property rights system is in place, it is incorrect to claim, as does Rothbard, that "the free market always benefits every participant, and it maximizes social utility *ex ante*." The maximization of "social" utility implies interpersonal comparisons of utility, a notion fraught with pitfalls and arbitrariness; but it is the idea that everyone benefits from free market activities that must be rejected, for it completely misinterprets the function and the operation of free markets. The market weighs and compares the beneficial *and* harmful effects, measured in the money that people are willing to pay, and filters out situations that would yield a net loss in this metric. The free market does not prohibit harmful effects. Indeed, a system that did, such as one based on the unanimity principle, would be so intolerably impractical (*inefficient*) that it would soon give way to other arrangements.

That harmful effects are borne through the operation of free markets can be illustrated clearly when a new product is marketed. However beneficial a new product is to consumers, its purchase imposes harmful effects on producers of the old product that it displaces. One seller invents a new marketing technique that allows him to reach potential customers at a lower cost than his competitors. The introduction of this technique yields beneficial effects for customers by allowing them to satisfy their demands at a lower price, but it also imposes harmful effects on the firms losing these customers. The open market will allow the innovation to succeed only if customers and new product producers, including the owners of inputs used to produce the new product, are benefitted more than competitive sellers are harmed. If the customers experience a gain worth $100 by shifting their trade to the innovator while the sellers they leave suffer a loss of only $80 as a result, then these sellers will be unwilling to cut prices sufficiently to hold their customers. Whereas, if these sellers suffer a loss of $150 if customers switch, they would be willing to cut prices sufficiently to retain patronage. The innovation succeeds only if the gains it confers, measured in dollars, exceed the cost it imposes.

It is this aspect of the private property rights system that is one of its great strengths. In the absence of individualized voluntarily given consent to a transfer of resources, it would seem difficult to know whether the transfer yields a net gain since such transfers also impose harmful effects. The net gain so measured, it is worth repeating, is an index based on willingness to pay, not on some global utility maximization. Since the market does not forbid activities that impose costs on some individuals, some such index is desirable. It is amazing how tolerant we are of such costs when they are embedded in a private property rights system in which willingness to pay is the index. Perhaps one of the more redeeming features of such a system is its apparent ability to attenuate the degree of group conflict that seems to infect those socialistic systems in which collective decisions on resource allocation and wealth distribution are made through democratic political institutions.

The definition of rights by the legal system, which precedes market negotiations, does not of course have the benefit of market-revealed information when ownership decisions are made, and so any prescription that courts adopt the efficiency criterion is likely to find its application blunt and susceptible to error. The fact that efficiency considerations should perhaps influence the choice of private property rights systems therefore should not be misinterpreted to endorse frequent involuntary reassignment of such rights. It is precisely because it is so difficult to know what the underlying efficiency considerations are that it is useful to allow transactions in the free market to fine-tune the ownership and use of resources. Frequent involuntary reassignment would destroy confidence in the longevity of property rights, and all long-run consequences of resource use would tend to be neglected, at least in a world of uncertainty and positive transaction cost. Efficiency calls for a high degree of stability in property rights definitions, but it does not necessarily forbid all involuntary reassignment, especially when high exchange cost or free-rider type problems reduce the efficacy of allocations through the market.

Should compensation actually be paid? The producer of a new product receives the right to offer it for sale to all potential buyers; producers of rival old products are denied the right to the trade of their customers, and these producers therefore suffer an uncontemplated loss. (There is good reason for this rights assignment. It would be too costly to ascertain who is harmed by how much, or who would be harmed by how much, when a new product is to be introduced.) The payment of compensation to losers is itself a question of instrumentalism. If all losers in conflicts of rights were compensated, everyone would have an incentive to contend all rights determinations, whether or not they are at all likely to be accorded the right by courts. A "moral hazard" problem arises that will be worth bearing only in certain cases.

The choice criterion proposed by Rothbard, that "everyman has the absolute right of property in his own self and the previously unowned natural resources which he finds, transforms by his own labor, and then gives or exchanges with others," is hopelessly superficial and vague.[4] How would such a criterion be applied to the conflict over decibel levels between would-be tennis players and sleepers? One person desires to exercise his rights in himself by playing tennis, the other by sleeping, and the exercise of these rights conflicts. What does it mean to say "everyman has the absolute right of property in his own self?" It certainly cannot mean that everyone has the right to use his person as he pleases, for the very question of defining private property rights is that of determining what can and what cannot be done by one's self. When the use of one's self comes into conflict with someone else's use of himself, both cannot continue to exercise absolute property rights in themselves. The question is what are the property rights one has, not whether he can exercise those that he has. The uncritical substitution of words for analysis in much property rights literature merely postpones the careful attention that this complex question deserves.

The above discussion does *not* address the institutional problem of how to implement property rights systems, nor does it defend absolutely any particular criterion for defining property rights; but I did hope to demonstrate that (1) conceptually there are an infinite number of alternative private property systems; (2) one can conceive of better or worse private property arrangements; (3) the instrumental impact of a system on efficiency has a significant role to play in any such ranking; and (4) until this or other choice criteria are made explicit, there is no way to determine which definition of private rights is best, that is, whether the gardener or the factory owner should control the soot content of the surrounding air.

PRIVATE PROPERTY RIGHTS AND EFFICIENCY CONSIDERATIONS

I have attempted to argue for the relevance of efficiency to definitions of better rights systems within the confines of private property rights systems. In fact, we frequently encounter notions of fairness, equity, and justice that seem derivative from efficiency considerations. These notions are particularly conspicuous for situations in which transaction cost is likely to be high, and, therefore, in which rights assignment clearly has efficiency implications.

In a rear-end collision involving two cars, there is a prima facie case that the driver of the second car is liable. Could this be "because" in the general case the driver of the second car can avoid such accidents more *cheaply* than the driver of the first car? This rule of law is especially applicable at the slow speeds of city traffic, but for high speed expressways it is not applied so rigorously; the driver of a second car has a more difficult time avoiding rear-end collisions at expressway speeds, and we often observe minimum speed limits on expressways.

If the owner of a factory considers locating next to an existing laundry, and the owner of that laundry protests in court that soot from the factory will raise the cost of laundering, the factory owner is more likely to be held liable for damages than if it is the laundry that contemplates locating next to an existing factory. Although the reason for this difference in treatment might be ascribed to Rothbard's notion that every man has the absolute right of property in the previously unowned natural resources which he finds, it is more likely traceable to the generally correct judgment that he who has not yet located his business can move his business to another location at less cost than he who has already fixed his assets into a particular location.

The very notions of fault and accident seem inextricably tied to the cost of avoiding damaging interactions. A person is more likely to be held at "fault" when he could have avoided a damaging interaction with another person at relatively little cost to himself; and he is more likely to be held the innocent victim of an "accident" in which no one is at fault when neither party could have avoided the interaction at relatively low cost. Comparative negligence, in which both parties bear part of the damages of a costly interaction, seems associated with situations in which both parties could have contributed to the avoidance of the interaction at relatively little cost.

The idea of causation is also difficult to separate from the notion of the cost of avoiding damaging interactions. A boat is moored to a dock. A storm arises in which the dock is damaged by the boat. The boat owner is held liable for damages "because the boat caused the damages by striking the dock." However, all motion is relative, and it could equally be thought that the dock struck the boat, and it would probably be the dock owner that is held liable if the accident took place during gentle breezes and if the dock was rotten for want of proper maintenance. In the latter case, it is the dock owner who could have prevented the damaging interaction at least cost, and it is likely to be he, or his dock, that is viewed as "causing" the accident.

The last clear chance rule, which would hold a railroad liable upon striking a trespasser if the engineer did not attempt to warn the victim, would seem to violate the notion of efficiency. Since the trespasser could avoid the accident at less cost than the railroad, it would seem that efficiency would call for liability to rest on the trespasser even if the railroad made no attempt to warn. But that is a superficial view of the problem. The accident itself is very likely to kill the trespasser, a condition in which it would be difficult in any case to make the victim whole again, so there is much deterrent already in the situation, although undoubtedly some additional deterrent could be purchased by never holding the railroad liable. If, because of deafness, drunkenness, or daydreaming, the trespasser is nonetheless wandering carelessly on the tracks, then it is unlikely that this dangerous situation would have been otherwise even in the absence of the last clear chance rule of liability. After all, with the last clear chance rule, the railroad could easily escape liability by making sure that its engineer blew the whistle and applied the brakes. The trespasser, therefore, can be but little encouraged by the uncertain probability of his estate being enriched by his carelessness. Recognizing that not much deterrent is lost by the last clear chance rule, the law weighs the likelihood of saving a man's life, and the value of doing so, as sufficiently great to warrant holding the railroad liable if it fails to take the last clear chance at warning the trespasser.

The legal rules of thumb we adopt, and even our use of such words as "fault" and "accident," seem to reflect basic efficiency considerations. Efficiency seems to be not merely one of many criteria underlying our notions of ethically correct definitions of private property rights, but an extremely important one. It is difficult even to describe unambiguously any other criterion for determining what is ethical.

In some situations, such as in the development of common-law precedents, a conscious choice of assignment of private property rights is being made; but, although I have discussed this and several other matters as if such choices were straightforward and simple, I do not mean to miscalculate the difficulty of the problem, to suggest that mistakes are not made, or to underestimate the complexity of the real institutions used to resolve the problem. Just how a preferred system of property rights is to be achieved is an important matter about which we know little. There is reason to believe that a series of common-law-type decisions will tend to converge on efficient definitions of rights because a legal decision that generates inefficiency is more likely to set in motion a stream of appeals and new cases designed to upset that decision than would be the case had the decision been correct from the viewpoint of efficiency. ''Losers'' generally have more to gain from upsetting a decision than ''winners'' have in defending that decision when it has produced an inefficient allocation of resources, and just the reverse when it has produced an efficient allocation. This is particularly true when the damages are largely confined to the contesting parties, as would be true with regard to a conflict between neighbors over noise levels, or the bearing of collision damages as between drivers of the two involved cars, or the conflict between a factory and a laundry over nearby air quality. For such problems, common-law legal processes seem capable of converging on precedents and property rights definitions that tend to solve conflicts over resource use efficiently. In such cases, we are essentially dealing with problems for which the resolution can be found within the confines of alternative definitions of private property rights.

PRIVATE *v.* COMMUNAL PROPERTY RIGHTS

However, when the gains or costs associated with particular interactions are not confined to a few parties, but instead are spread thinly over large numbers of individuals, then ''high'' transaction costs and ''free-rider'' problems may be serious, even when utilizing the best of private property rights definitions, and some attenuation of private rights may be rationalized to achieve a more efficient solution to resource allocation problems. The traditional examples of providing national defense, national foreign policy, and cleaner air come to mind.

To rationalize a role for the state in this way, of course, does not insure that the state will confine its attention to such matters or even that it will improve the situation when it does. So much of the requisite information, let alone the motivation, is lacking precisely because private-property-based markets can function only with difficulty when such problems are serious. High transaction costs and free-rider problems sometimes can be resolved by substituting private rights for communal property rights arrangements, that is, those in which there is an individual right of use but not a right to exclude others from use. The conversion of a freeway to a tollway would be an example. But this is practical only when the cost of excluding nonpayers is not too high. When dealing with national defense and air pollution problems this does not seem to be the case, and when it is not, a rationalization for action by the state in the name of efficiency becomes available.

My point is not to argue on behalf of or against state intervention in such cases, but to call attention to the ethical distinctions that seem to exist in principle between state intervention in these cases and in other cases where high transaction costs or free-rider problems to not exist.

Where it is difficult to see how costs and benefits can be internalized at practical cost, as would be true with regard to air pollution in any private property rights system that I have been able to envisage, government intervention may be thought to be clumsy, costly, and misdirected, but it is seldom thought to be unethical. Similarly, the opposition to the government's use of defense forces may be based on its involvement in an immoral war or its use of an immoral draft, but it is seldom based on the immorality of the principle of using the government to provide for the "common" defense. But when a government confiscates property rights that could have been obtained through the market, as with condemnation proceedings, the military draft, or the nullification of gold clauses during the recession of the 1930s, there is more than a hint of belief that an unethical theft of rights has been perpetuated.

The problem of obtaining accurate measures of benefits and costs is not restricted to free-rider–externality problems. Especially in the case of young children, but possibly also in that of serious mental cases, the state intervenes to invalidate individual actions. The usual argument in such cases is paternalism pure and simple. The intervention is required if the interests of particularly incompetent groups are to be served.

It is difficult to resist an appeal to paternalism in some cases, while it is easy in others. The danger latent in the "paternalism" rationalization no doubt is great. The issue is whether a person should always have the right to act for himself when it is believed that he is incompetent to judge the costs and benefits of his actions. On what basis is the line drawn beyond which an ethical system of property rights no longer endorses coerced denial of normal contracting rights? Clearly, the greater the reliance on paternalism, the more extensive the use of coercion and the more likely it will infringe on the decisions of those who are in the best position to judge their own interests. But it is not clear from this line of reasoning that there should be no paternalism, or how far paternalism may be carried while yet not reducing the ability of the economic organization to deliver the net gains possible through free choice.

A possible way out of this quandary is offered by modern biology. The innate propensities of man, especially when he deals with day-to-day problems of living, may not allow for a very great supply of effort or inclination to aid others. A genetic endowment producing large amounts of such helping in individual behavior, it is thought by some modern biologists, would be (and presumably was) competed out of existence by genetic varieties that confined altruism close to home. A generally altruistic genetic endowment must succumb to genetic free-riders who take without giving. The selfish genetic endowment tends to displace the altruistic genetic endowment on which it rides free,[5] but it does not displace altruism completely. Biologists have found that limited amounts of such aid, even in the absence of reciprocity, confer survival ability to genetic endowments. To a large extent altruism is limited to kinship relations. Genetic endowments have greater survival ability if they encourage the helping of others when it can be expected that by doing so the survival power of that genetic endowment is enhanced. A person who willingly sacrifices himself to save two siblings, eight cousins, and so forth, who but for his sacrifice would surely die, increases the probability that "his" genes, independently of which body contains them, will survive, because "his" genes also exist, with descending probability, in the bodies of siblings, cousins, and so forth. The arithmetic of genetic inheritance guarantees that relationships more distant than uncles, aunts, and first cousins are not reliable sources of paternalistic care. Similarly, a culture generous only to its own will be more resistant to free-loading and to its displacement by free-loading cultures. (There are special situations, particularly in the insect world, for which this need not be true.)

Although these findings of socio-biology are still quite speculative and subject to debate, their implication for the problem at hand is direct and dramatic. Reliable paternalistic feelings between strangers are largely ruled out by evolutionary processes. It is unlikely that net gains from exchange can be enlarged by coerced intervention in the name of paternalism if the trustee is not closely related to his charge or if there is difficulty in setting up an incentive system that more or less makes the trustee's interests coincide with those of his charge, in which case we are no longer dealing with altruistic behavior. Paternalism is, in fact, largely limited by natural selection to intra-family relationships. Altruistic behavior toward offspring or siblings is not an anomaly in nature, and in some circumstances it may be relied upon to improve the gains from exchange, but its reliability for doing so diminishes rapidly once the coerced interaction is determined outside the immediate family of the person coerced. Adam Smith puts it neatly in his famous statement about benevolence and in his less well known one about friendship that follows closely on the first.[6]

> It is not from the benevolence of the butcher, the brewer, or the baker, that we expect our dinner, but from their regard to their own interest. We address ourselves, not to their humanity but to their self-love, and never talk to them of our own necessities but of their advantages.

> In civilized society [man] stands at all times in need of the cooperation and assistance of great multitudes, while his whole life is scarce sufficient to gain the friendship of a few persons.[7]

The limits to paternalism based on benevolence, however, do not arise only from an abhorrence of coercion; since coercion is a cost much like other costs, there is a practical inability of paternalism to deliver benefits above its cost except within narrow circles.

More fundamental than the problem of paternalism is that of competition itself. There are a multitude of methods for competing, ranging from a brick through a rival's place of business to a reduction in price to the introduction of a superior product. All these impose harmful effects on rivals, but not all are viewed as equally ethical. The distinction along the ethical dimension between alternative methods of competing is peculiar to the social sciences and the humanist philosophers. Biologists in their analyses of life make no such distinction. There is only competition and natural selection of the fittest, and although biologists may distinguish descriptively one form of competition from another, they do not do so ethically.

The ethics of competition is a viable subject for students of social organization precisely because we view our situation as one where we can choose to encourage or discourage particular forms of competition. This element of volition in choosing among social organizations is not a view that biologists bring to their subject, although it is not a view that is precluded by natural selection theory. The property rights system is in large part a set of definitions and rules of behavior that specify which forms of competition are approved and encouraged and which are not.

I believe there is a strong correlation between the efficiency consequences of various forms of competition and the degree to which they are judged to be proper or ethical. Competition via violence is generally frowned upon, partly because toleration of violent competition would obscure an assessment of underlying net benefit calculations. The thief who steals an automobile does not necessarily value it more than its original possessor, but the person who purchases it does. Competition via "voluntary" negotiations, as in the case of product innovation discussed above, is more likely to yield an increase in the real wealth of a society than is competition via violent "involuntary" methods, precisely because the former offers a superior technique for weighing benefits and costs, as these are measured in the market, and for filtering out net loss situations.

Methods of competing are not always easy to judge from the viewpoint of efficiency. Competition via patent procurement or by "predatory" tactics are unclearly evaluated because it is not obvious whether such forms of competition are likely to yield more gains than costs. Competition designed and executed solely to secure monopoly would be easy to frown upon if it could be detected and if it were not generally the case that it usually fails and, in the process, as with Schumpeter's "creative destruction," yields gains that greatly exceed cost. The securing of monopoly through legislated protection, however, seems much less likely to yield these gains than the securing of monopoly through superior products. It is difficult for me to see how to distinguish these two sources of negatively sloped demand curves other than by judging their likely contributions to real wealth, and it is only when judging that ethical considerations become relevant.

The general favoring of private rights of action when these can be expected to yield more accurate assessments of benefits and costs is revealed by our willingness to intervene when such expectations are not present. Competition between auto firms to reduce automobile exhaust emissions is not likely to succeed since emission controls impair the privately enjoyed services of an automobile to its owner and also raise the cost of obtaining these services. No amount of rivalry between automobile producers is likely to yield an efficient amount of smog control. A producer who incurs the cost of devising emission controls will only lose customers to his rivals if he places these controls on his automobiles. Competition based on usual notions of private rights is an ill-designed institution by which to foist private costs on consumers even if the collective benefits so obtained are greater than these costs. Intervention by the state is not viewed as unethical in such cases.

CONCLUSION

The legal and market implications of efficient resource allocation are no less arbitrary normatively than the preferences and tastes of the population of decision-makers upon which they rest. People are willing to pay for what they *want*. The ethical weight accorded efficiency in property rights assignments is thus dependent on the ethical properties of prevailing tastes and preferences unless freedom of choice occupies the lead position in a lexicographic ordering of such preferences. An uneasy feeling of arbitrariness is inevitable when basing normative prescriptions on efficiency (but no more so than when other criteria are proposed). This is so only as our preferences and tastes are thought to be arbitrary. In a scientific sense, they are not arbitrary but, rather, are explainable by variations in income and relative prices. Such explanation has just begun,[8] but, for example, there undoubtedly is much consistency across time and geography in the types of wants that arise out of higher income.

Although these regularities are not without use when adopting efficiency as a normative criterion, they do not themselves provide ethical justification. Such justification cannot be provided from outside, as by divine revelation, and, in a real sense, it must be as arbitrary as is our history. But that history cannot be completely arbitrary. We have survived. Preferences, tastes, and other life-style perspectives that seriously impair the survival capability of individuals cannot themselves easily survive. Competitive preferences and life-style views, whether these are held within or outside a particular social organization, provide competition for any set of existing preferences. Life-styles that promote survival come to be viewed as ethical, and those that fail in this respect come to be viewed as in poor taste, if not as unethical. Our present preferences and tastes must reflect in large part their survival promoting capabilities. (Such capabilities, of course, may not be good enough to insure survival.) Is there much doubt that a life-style of law and order within an extensive framework of individual choice has arisen from the constraints imposed by survivability? No large society today finds itself in a much different situation in these respects; it is in the details, some of which are no doubt important, that differences are found. In a loose and general way our life-styles, preferences, and ethical beliefs are not arbitrary but are the product of thousands of centuries of biological and cultural evolution.

There is, of course, error. An efficient social organization, that is, one with a high probability of survival, never reduces error or experiment to zero. Moreover, what has survival capability in one environment, or century, may not do so well in another. A command social structure is likely to do better in small tribal societies than in large complex societies. War and peace are likely to bring forth different ethical precepts. A society of plenty can tolerate more altruism toward special hardship cases than can a society of poverty. We are bound to view the proper resolution of legal problems from the perspective of what presently seems efficient, whether or not efficiency is explicitly applied. Our genetic and cultural endowment contains elements of ethical preference that have survived dramatically different environments. It undoubtedly contains some ethical preferences not well suited to present conditions, but then the present is not long with us.

I began this essay in disagreement with Knight. I now end it in similar fashion.

> It seems to the writer almost superfluous to deny the appropriateness of the term "ethics" to any such [biological] conception. The conditions of survival are merely the laws of biology. It may well be the part of prudence to act in accordance with them, assuming that one *wants* to survive, but it can hardly be associated with the notions of right or duty, and if these have no meaning beyond prudence, the whole realm of ethics is illusory. Ethics deals with the problem of choosing between different kinds of life, and assumes that there is a real choice between different kinds, or else there is no such thing as ethics.[9]

Those who do not *want* to survive generally have not, and neither has their genetic stock, so that most of us, under the usual conditions in which we find ourselves, do want to survive. To say that survival has brought with it (or inculcated) a general view of the good life (that style of living that has survived with us) is not to say that choice is ruled out. The ability to choose, or our lack of reliance on instinct, has itself promoted survival and has in turn been promoted by survival. Evolutionary forces do not equate to determinism, nor are evolutionary forces necessarily the only ones at work. We can exercise choice over the ethics by which to guide our lives, but it does not follow that all such choices are equally likely to survive and prosper. The competition between ethical criteria is meaningful because our condition and environment changes, but in that competition it is the set of ethics that survives and prospers that will identify what is efficient and what is not. If the environment does not change frequently or drastically, the set of tastes and preferences that emerge will have some guiding merit. A criterion of efficiency merely proposes that this merit not be ignored when choosing among alternative property rights systems.

This does not mean abandoning efforts to alter preferences or ethical beliefs. Today's mainstream beliefs may have lagged behind today's conditions or they may be poorly attuned to tomorrow's. However, the debate over ethics can be carried out at many levels. Those who value freedom highly would seem to be wasteful of their efforts and of those of others to issue a call to debate where no substantial issue of freedom is involved; the choice between alternative private property definitions would seem a case in point. Here there is no conflict between efficiency (even narrowly defined) and freedom. And there are ample instances where *both* freedom and efficiency can be served by debate, as in arguing for deregulation. Here the criterion of efficiency reinforces the appeal of freedom. Where freedom and efficiency seem to clash, as where paternalism, free-riders, and hold-out problems seem important, those who delight in pressing the cause of freedom hopefully serve some purpose other than diverting efforts from where the competition between ethical beliefs is most easily won for freedom.

NOTES

1 Knight (1935, p. 66).
2 The meaning I attach to ''efficiency'' is clarified later in this chapter.
3 Rothbard (1970, p. 11).
4 Rothbard (1970, p. 1).
5 For a discussion of the growing interface between economics and biology, see Hirshleifer (1977, 1–52).
6 See R. H. Coase's excellent discussion of ''Adam Smith's View of Man'' (Coase, 1976, pp. 529–46).
7 Smith (1937, p. 14).
8 Stigler and Becker (1977, 76–90).
9 Knight (1935, p. 71).

REFERENCES

Coase, R. H. (1976). ''Adam Smith's View of Man.'' *Journal of Law and Economics*, 19.
Hirshleifer, J. (1977). ''Economics from a Biological Viewpoint.'' *Journal of Law and Economics*, 20.

Knight, F. H. (1935). *The Ethics of Competition*. New York: Harper Brothers.
Rothbard, M. N. (1970). *Power and Market*. Menlo Park, Cal.: Institute for Humane Studies.
Smith, Adam (1937). *The Wealth of Nations*. New York: Random House.
Stigler, G. J. and Becker, G. S. (1977). "De Gustibus Non Est Disputandum." *American Economic Review*, 67.

18
The Meaning of Freedom

FREEDOM AS YOU WILL?

To be free is to be ''unrestricted,'' but the restrictions from which being free might spare us are so varied that it would be surprising if there were a single, proper meaning to freedom. England's parliament won its freedom in 1689 by reducing the restrictions that could be applied to it by English kings. In 1776, English colonies in America won their freedom from restrictions to which they were subjected by England; John Adams interpreted the freedom won as freedom of the colonies from English tyranny, but Thomas Jefferson interpreted the freedom won as freedom from the restrictions of any government, even that which was to govern the United States. Rousseau, about the same time, spoke of being free as a condition in which the restrictions of civilization are absent. For abolitionists, freedom meant the release of slaves from restrictions imposed by owners. Socialists interpret being free as the absence of restrictions stemming from poverty, while Hayek interprets being free as the absence the restrictions stemming from private or public coercion.

For some libertarians, a free society bars restrictions that others may place on the use of legitimate private rights, counting among such restrictions not only state-imposed limitations but also privately imposed limitations, such as the ''invasion'' of private air space with smoke and soot from distant private factories. Defining legitimacy, of course, is part of the problem of defining freedom. For conservatives, a free society bars prostitution, narcotics consumption, and commerce on Sunday, because they view such activities in the same way as libertarians view smoke and soot, as restrictions on rights to which they are legitimately entitled. Loyal citizens of the USSR are conservatives in the extreme in this respect, for they wish to protect their legitimate rights from all sorts of ''anti-social,'' or is it anti-state, behavior. Notions of legitimate rights are as varied as are the origins of restrictions to such rights, and the costs of reducing restrictions are as varied as the shades of meanings that different peoples seem to attach to freedom. This casual empirical observation seems at odds with the belief of intellects that freedom can be given a precise meaning. The object of this chapter is to demonstrate that economists, at least, have not been able to substantiate their belief in an objective meaning of freedom.

FREEDOM AS THE INVERSE OF COERCION

One important conception attempts to base the meaning of freedom on the absence of coercion. Hayek's (1960) important work on *The Constitution of Liberty* does this, and it may be taken as a convenient vehicle to launch this inquiry. Hayek begins chapter 1, "We are concerned in this book with the condition of men in which coercion of some by others is reduced as much as is possible in society. This state we shall describe . . . as a state of liberty or freedom" (p. 11). He thus begins with the proposition that freedom and coercion are inversely correlated. His search for the concept of freedom turns into a search for the meaning of and the minimal amount of coercion. Coercion "occurs when one man's actions are made to serve another man's will, not for his own but for the other's purpose (p. 133). Although a person has a choice of whether or not to act when threatened by coercion, his mind is made someone else's tool "because the alternatives before [him] have been so manipulated that the conduct the coercer wants . . . becomes . . . the least painful [to choose]." Now, it will be clear upon reflection that all methods of guiding the use of scarce resources are necessarily coercive at base. The enforcement of private rights, state rights, and long held traditions involves a significant amount of actual or implied coercion to maintain respect for the allocative rules of the game. Hayek desires to distinguish his notion of coercion from other methods of resolving scarcity-created problems, and so he is forced into a discussion that identifies coercion by two conditions: the quantitative significance of the coercion and the personal nature of its source. Both conditions require Hayek to rely on highly subjective judgments, the importance of which are signified by the following passage:

> Coercion should be carefully distinguished from the conditions or terms on which our fellow men are willing to render us services or benefits. . . . If a hostess will invite me to her parties only if I conform to certain standards of conduct and dress, or my neighbor converses with me only if I observe conventional manners, this is certainly not coercion. Nor can it be legitimately called "coercion" if a producer or dealer refuses to supply me with what I want except at his price. This is certainly true in a competitive market, where I can turn to somebody else if the terms of the first offer do not suit me; and it is normally not less true when I have a monopolist. If, for instance, I would very much like to be painted by a famous artist and if he refuses to paint me for less than a very high fee, it would clearly be absurd to say that I am coerced. The same is true of any other commodity or service that I can do without. So long as the services of a particular person are not crucial to my existence or the preservation of what I most value, the conditions he exacts for rendering these services cannot properly be called

''coercion'' . . . [U]nless a monopolist is in a position to withhold an indispensable supply, he cannot exercise coercion. (pp. 135–6)

Hayek's attempts to distinguish his notion of coercion from ''the terms on which our fellow men are willing to render us services'' signifies an effort to associate coercion with costs whose source is not in the *impersonal* workings of the market but in the *personal* decisions of men. The ability to exercise such decisions would seem to imply the possession of ''power''. Indeed, Hayek's use of coercion as an inverse index of freedom implicitly brings power into the definition of freedom. The ability to coerce is an expression of the possession of power. The monopolist can raise price above the cost of supplying goods because he alone possesses the power to control supply. Thus, the freedom of some (here, the buyers) is limited by the power of others (the monopolists). The correlation between coercion and power is revealed in Hayek's examples of true coercion:

A monopolist could exercise true coercion, however, if he were, say, the owner of a spring in an oasis. Let us say that other persons settled there on the assumption that water would always be available at a reasonable price and then found . . . that they had no choice but to do whatever the owner of the spring demanded of them if they were to survive; here would be a clear case of coercion. (p. 136)

Here Hayek runs into an apparent inconsistency, for when he faces the issue directly he denies the relationship between freedom and power:

Once this identification of freedom with power is admitted, there is no limit to the sophisms by which the attractions of the word ''liberty'' can be used to support measures which destroy individual liberty. . . . It has been with the help of this equivocation that the notion of collective power over circumstances has been substituted for that of individual liberty, and that in totalitarian states liberty has been suppressed in the name of liberty. (p. 16)

Had Hayek recognized this inconsistency, he would have taken greater care in stating his position. A sympathetic interpretation of what Hayek has in mind when he seeks to disassociate freedom and power is to disassociate freedom and wealth. He would assert that wealth, which may or may not be associated with power, has nothing to do with freedom; that Crusoe and Friday stranded on a resource-poor island are as free as if stranded on a resource-rich island.

It is true that wealth and power are not identical, or, at least, that confusion is created by attempts to link them. Wealthy persons may be unable to impose costs (the evidence of power) on others because their wealth does not represent monopoly. They face competition from a variety of substitutable persons and options. The possession of power increases the wealth of its possessor, but the possession of wealth does not in itself increase the ability of a person to limit the scope of action enjoyed by others. Coercion may be directly correlated with power and inversely with freedom; yet, because power is not necessarily correlated with wealth, freedom bears no necessary relationship to wealth.

The interrelationship, or lack thereof, between freedom and wealth is not so simple as the above interpretation of Hayek would have it. Buyers are coerced because the monopolist's power enables him to *impoverish* them to a noticeable degree. They are made less free by the desire to avoid (the threat of) impoverishment. The power to reduce the real wealth of others is the power to coerce, and the power to coerce others is the power to secure acquiescence from them. Therefore, to resolve Hayek's apparent inconsistency while still maintaining a degree of independence between freedom and wealth, we would need to treat sources of poverty differently. Poverty that emanates from impersonal circumstances would have little to do with freedom, from Hayek's perspective. The threat to property posed by accidental fire would be an example. Poverty emanating from the personal actions of others, such as the ability of the owner of the spring to raise the price of water, referred to by Hayek, constitutes a loss of freedom for nearby residents.

This distinction has a rationale. Precautions against fire may be taken to reduce the threat of fire from accidental sources, but costs incurred to do so cannot be linked sensibly to the interest of someone who seeks *acquiescence* from those so threatened. Costs may also be borne to diminish *someone's* threat to burn the property of others; in this case, costs can be linked to his demands for acquiescence. Absent his interest in acquiescence, these actions would not affect the probability of fire. Do we want to accept this rationale? Stigler (1978) expresses dissatisfaction with such distinctions and proposes instead to define freedom as real wealth.

FREEDOM AS WEALTH

Stigler asks, What purpose is served by Hayek's attempt to distinguish personally imposed costs from those that are determined impersonally? Costs restrict freedom by restricting the degree to which persons can achieve their goals. Behavior responds similarly to costs without regard to their source. Does an increase in the price of timber arising from the creation of a timber monopoly lead to substantively different behavior by timber purchasers from an identical price increase arising from naturally caused forest fires?

True, faced by *given* identical price increases, demanders of timber would be expected to economize identically. Yet the price increase is avoided by different actions in one case from those in the other, and in this sense behavior does differ: investing in anti-monopoly legislation is appropriate in one case, investing in fire protection in the other. Surely Stigler would accede to this, but he would press the issue more deeply. The threat of a price rise emanates from many sources – accidental fires, insect infestation, drought, monopolization, and so on. Each of these threats is moderated or avoided by different actions. The cost of reducing the threat of monopoly may be no higher, and may be lower, than the cost of installing lightning rods, spraying insecticide, or piping in water. We make no distinctions between the differences in the responses to different naturally caused costs. Why put the human who pursues a monopoly return beyond the pale of nature but not the insect who seeks gratification of a large appetite?

The essential equivalence of costs leads Stigler to argue for defining freedom as real wealth. The greater a person's real wealth, the more numerous the choices available to him. It is the scope of choice, the richness of the opportunities enjoyed by a person, that measure his freedom of action. For Stigler, Crusoe and Friday on a resource-meager island *are* less free than on a resource-rich island. Man's choice is restricted by all sorts of constraints. Why delimit a subset of these, to be identified as coercive, when discussing his freedom of action?

If coercion is to play a role in the economist's vocabulary, Stigler would apply it to all costs, irrespective of their sources. If a person may be coerced by *someone's* threat to build a wall between him and the ocean, it is because this act raises the cost to him of exercising options that he values, such as direct access to the sea or to a clear view. His opportunity set, and from Stigler's perspective his freedom, is affected in much the same way if the winds of "nature" blow a large hill of sand between him and the ocean. If the cost to him of preventing construction of the wall is the same as that of leveling the hill of sand, his freedom of action is affected identically even though the measures required to eliminate these obstacles may differ. What difference does it make to him if he pays *someone* to forgo building a wall or to commence construction of wind deflectors that disperse sand? Hayek, of course, would not approve a measure of freedom based on the richness of opportunities faced. He would reject the equivalence of all costs in restricting freedom. Freedom for Hayek is a question of *social relationships*.

Glasner's (1982) support of Hayek takes the view that the proper definition of freedom is to be found in the specification and content of property rights. "Fluctuations in wealth that . . . do not arise from violations of private rights will not constitute an infringement of liberty any more than a natural disaster that destroyed someone's property could be said to have constituted an infringement of his liberty" (p. 229). However, Glasner fails to describe the private rights system he has in mind. To do so is no small problem. Nonetheless, it is a necessary task before Glasner's objections to Stigler's real wealth standard can be judged. The private rights system appropriate to a state of liberty may be what is required to lead a society to maximize the wealth of its citizens. Although real wealth is affected by circumstances outside the private rights system, the private rights system that maximizes freedom nonetheless may also maximize real wealth to the degree that outside circumstances allow. The possible equivalence of the private rights and real wealth standards of freedom can be rejected only if state action, which may be presumed to be inconsistent with the exercise of private rights, reduces freedom while it maximizes wealth.

FREEDOM AS PROPERTY RIGHTS

We must begin somewhere, and a good beginning is to conceive of the freedom of the individual quite simply as the absence of personal or social restraints on his behavior. Crusoe (absent Friday) is a free man according to this definition, although he is confined to his island by physical circumstances. The smaller and the poorer the island, the less happy he may be, but not the less free. This definition of freedom sees all limitations on a person's freedom as emanating from individual or collective actions of others. (Are restrictions imposed on Crusoe's actions by insects and birds, who compete with him for terrain and food, limitations on his freedom?)

It is important to note that it is the freedom of an individual that has been defined, not the freedom(s) of individuals interacting in a society. Failure to keep these domains of freedom conceptually distinct is a source of confusion. They are fused, and confused, in the commonly used notion that freedom is the unrestricted right of an individual to act, provided his actions do not violate the rights of others. The confusion is to presume that a definition of freedom appropriate to an individual is also appropriate and meaningful to a society of individuals.

Extending the definition of freedom to a society of individuals is not straightforward. Individuals necessarily impinge on each other because resources are scarce. Unrestricted action for some can be purchased at the cost of severe limitations on the actions of others. The degree of freedom enjoyed by Crusoe can remain unaffected by Friday's arrival if Crusoe is judged to be able to treat Friday as just another insect. Whatever ability Friday possesses to act without Crusoe's agreement in the use of scarce resources comes at the cost of constraining Crusoe's ability to act. Our definition of individual freedom is inadequate to describe the freedom of a society of persons.

Ruling out interpersonal comparisons of freedoms gained and lost, we may begin by basing the freedom of a society of persons on two conditions: (1) all rights to act are private, which means not to be interfered with by the state, and (2) all persons enjoy the same rights. Such rights may include the right to veto actions of others. Call these conditions the universality and symmetry of private rights, and, for brevity, denote a society satisfying them as *privatized*. For most proposers of this approach to freedom, the right to act does not imply the ability to act. A cripple may have the right to walk but be unable to, and he may have the right to purchase an operation that would allow him to walk but be too poor to do so. Failure of ability is compatible with privatization. It must be, because in many (but not all) situations it is inevitable.

The connection between freedom and privatization may be examined in two contexts to reveal how easy it is to be lured into glossing over substantial problems by presuming that privatization has clear meaning. The first context assumes that privatization is implemented costlessly; this assumption underlies many discussions of privatization without the awareness of the discussants. The second context recognizes the cost of privatization.

A model of a social organization that is consistent with costless privatization is perfect decentralization (competition). In this model, all rights are simply assumed to be private, symmetric, known, and respected. No problems of defining and enforcing private rights arise. Each person in the perfectly decentralized economy is a Crusoe whose interactions with others are guided by impersonally set prices and whose domain of action is determined by his (acknowledged by others) wealth. The trade-offs available to him are determined by the non-collusive aggregate of wants and preferences, the given state of technology, and the relative abundance of resources.

Coercion in Hayek's sense is absent in this model since no one controls price or any other parameter of choice. Perfect decentralization also satisfies Stigler's real-wealth maximization criterion. Neither of these results flows from privatization alone, but both are consequences of the assumptions that underlie perfect decentralization. These assumptions assume diseconomies of scale (and, hence, dispersed ownership of substitutable resources), full information, zero transaction cost, and, implicitly, costless privatization. The implied dispersal of these rights deprives any one of the ability to impose costs on others. Zero information and transaction costs imply real-wealth maximization. Given its assumptions, perfect decentralization simultaneously satisfies the concepts of freedom employed by various writers. Coercion is absent, real wealth is maximized, and rights are private. Perfect decentralization seems very much like a leading candidate for modeling the state of liberty.

Its capacity for playing this role depends very much on the assumptions that underlie it. Weaken the assumption that private rights are freely known and respected, and ambiguities immediately cloud the relationship between privatization and freedom. How private is a private rights system that is less than completely enforceable? A private right to one's wealth is compromised by a positive probability of its being stolen. The positive probability that others will violate rights undermines privateness. The conception of a society of free men that is readily grasped under the conditions of perfect decentralization becomes elusive when decentralization is imperfect. How secure must private rights be for us to conclude that we are dealing with a society of free persons? How should such security be produced? These questions lie at the heart of the difficulty of defining a *society* of free persons because of the potential trade-offs they imply, trade-offs that would be unnecessary if privatization could be defined and secured costlessly.

A society of free men can be conceived of as permitting state activity that defines and enforces private rights. Persons are less free than in perfect decentralization because the state must command resources and use coercion to do its job. It may require the ability to invade rights of privacy to do its job effectively. Persons are more free than if state action were barred because the privacy that remains to individuals on average may be more effectively enforced through state action than through purely private enforcement. The state as "night watchman," whose sole activity is to preserve and enforce private rights, has wide appeal as a definition of a society of free persons.

Alternatively, a society of free persons can be conceived of as relying strictly on private means to define and enforce rights. Presumably, this definition implies private rights to act violently toward others in defense of one's rights. Anarchy is the result, causing well-known problems of competitive enforcement of rights, or, if another assumption of perfect decentralization – diseconomies of scale – is rejected, causing monopolization of the power to privatize.

The dilemma posed by these alternative systems for privatization is striking. The use of the state to enforce private rights may yield more secure rights than complete reliance on private enforcement. In this sense, freedom is enhanced by the use of the state. Yet, because pure private enforcement leaves individuals *free* to determine which private rights to secure, and how much security to purchase, freedom is enhanced by excluding the use of the state. A ranking on the scale of freedom provided by these two systems cannot escape interpersonal comparisons of freedoms gained and freedoms lost, and this ranking is reckoned differently by libertarians who favor anarchy and by fellow libertarians who favor a night watchman role for the state.

There is, however, an important problem that both alternatives fail to resolve: that of defining a state of liberty in a regime of scarce resources. Given that there are costs of improving the reliability of private rights, what degree of certainty in the exercise of private rights characterizes this state? Complete certainty in the exercise of private rights is impossibly costly, so every person's chosen level of security (whether secured privately or through the state) will fall far short of fully secure rights. Indeed, each person will consider what *other goals* must be sacrificed to improve the reliability of his private rights. Suppose that persons who populate a society place a very low value on improving the reliability of private rights and a very high value on other goals. Is the state of liberty appropriately characterized by the level of privatization chosen in this society? What values must a people attach to freedom before their chosen degree of privatization meets the requirements of a state of liberty? Defining the state of liberty in terms of private rights (defended privately or by the state) offers no answer to this question. The problem extends beyond that of defining the state of liberty to that of ranking the degree of liberty. As between two privatized societies, in both of which persons are *free* to choose the degree of security they confer on their rights, is that society freer in which greater levels of security are purchased? And if the night watchman state is employed? The connection between privatization and freedom, which can be given fairly clear meaning in the context of perfect decentralization, becomes opaque in the face of positive costs of privatization. Full privatization is not attainable in the face of positive implementation costs, and the degree of privatization that is attainable by persons *free* to choose is that which privatizes only to the degree that they judge *efficient*.

THE RELEVANCE AND IRRELEVANCE OF EFFICIENCY

Efficiency is related but not identical to real wealth. Indeed, toward the end of his paper, Stigler slips from real wealth to efficiency as a measure of freedom, but he seems to do so without noting that he is using different standards. Economics proceeds on the pesumption that a society begins its task of economizing from an endowed resource base. This base is difficult to define and measure because its outward characteristics are malleable. The malleability creates the possibility of economizing, but it would be foolish to presume the malleability of resources removes the gap that separates poor and rich societies. Efficiency, however, pertains to social organization, not to the resource base. Differences in real wealth whose source is in endowed resources have little to do with social organization. Interpreting freedom as efficiency (Moore, 1969) preserves the relevance of opportunity sets, as Stigler desires, but only insofar as social organization, not endowed resources, creates these opportunities, and this is as Hayek might desire. A society that has lowered costs to the fullest extent possible may be said to have achieved a state of freedom because it has expanded opportunities *as much as elemental resource endowments allow*.

However, so encompassing are efficiency and real wealth that both really define freedom as utility when it comes to individual behavior. The forsaking of nominal wealth to enjoy more leisure is real-wealth-maximizing and efficient only if the increment to utility gained through additional leisure exceeds the utility lost through the sacrifice of nominal wealth. Anything that one does to maximize utility also maximizes his freedom. This disallows a concept of freedom that permits individuals to substitute between freedom and other goals, because freedom is measured by the degree to which all other goals are efficiently pursued. At the level of social interaction, Pareto efficiency, which can be consistent with many different social organizations, not all of which seem equally rich in freedom, becomes the state of liberty.

This characteristic of an efficiency index of freedom is counter-intuitive. Exhortations that freedom remains only to those who make the needed sacrifice implies substitutability between freedom and other goals. A measure of freedom that treats freedom as utility makes it difficult to conceive of two societies experiencing different degrees of freedom. A world presumed to be guided by rational decisions does not easily accommodate inefficiency. Two societies built upon identical resource bases and manned by rational populations may differ in organization and in realized results because of differences in *tastes* or in *expectations*, but not in efficiency (see in volume II of this book, "The Social Variable in Economic Analysis"). That which some call inefficiency is merely an expression of disagreement with prevailing opinions and the policies these bring about. The claim of inefficiency cannot be taken as the fact. Efficient societies are likely to house viable demands for the services of (peaceful) dissenters, because different opinions entertain and provide food for thought. The assertion that there is inefficiency when there is dissent is not the fact. Rational behavior combined with the efficiency criterion of freedom requires all societies to exist in a state of freedom.

To claim irrationality is to assert that goals or objectives are not being pursued efficiently, and therefore that freedom is compromised. If there were some way to certify the validity of this claim for specific individuals, they could be *coerced* into behavior that is believed to be efficient. The difficulty is obvious. If efficiency indexes freedom, then, as the remedy to irrational (inefficient) behavior, so does coercion!

It would seem better to conceive of freedom, however we choose to define it, as one of many possible goals. Then, social organizations, all of which may be presumed to be efficient, need not be presumed to offer the same degree of freedom. We may then speak about an efficient amount of freedom but not about the state of freedom or the "truly" free society. A freer society is "better", or is Pareto-optimal in utility, only under specific conditions of tastes and costs. Under other conditions, a less free society is "better."

However, although blackboard demonstrations of trade-offs between freedom and other goals are easy enough to use, they lack sufficient substance to be a tool of empirical inquiry. Only grossly different societies permit a confident claim that one is freer than the other. Measurement of the degree to which a society is free is no simple matter. It is not possible to use the fraction of a society's resources committed to maintaining privatization as a positive index of freedom because this reflects the degree to which privatization is under attack as well as a society's demand for freedom, and, given the potential productivity of the state as night watchman, it is not possible to use the fraction of resources claimed by the state as an inverse index of privatization. Huge military expenditures can be counted as payments in defense of freedom or of privatization.

Undoubtedly, the degree of privatization is an important index of freedom, but how does one judge the degree of freedom in societies that secure different private rights in different degree? The problem of measurement is compounded still more by the multiplicity of assets subject to private rights. One person decides to use resources to police his private rights in his automobile more carefully (or a night watchman state invests more in the anti-auto-theft division of its police force). Another person (or night watchman state) chooses instead to spend more on immunization from communicable diseases. Since the privatized society seeks to protect private rights in one's body as well as in one's automobile, in which case have rights become more privatized?

The question of which rights of action are consistent with a free society and which are not becomes a question of values when interpersonal comparisons are important. Should the externality claims of those opposed to smoke in the air be legitimized while the externality claims of those opposed to Sunday commerce or "victimless" crimes are not? The debate over what constitutes the free society tends to cloak this value core of the disagreement. Coercion and freedom become inextricably involved in judgments about fair or proper prices, and, ultimately, about ethically acceptable methods by which wealth may be acquired. Judgments about freedom require a prior agreement about the higher ethic that is to used to validate certain desires while rejecting others. Knight, in *Freedom and Reform*, says this clearly:

> We say that the victim of a highwayman is coerced, not because the character of his choice between the alternatives presented is different from any other choice, but because we think the robber does "wrong" in making the alternatives what they are. (Knight, 1982, p. 16)

> Under "perfect competition" it is theoretically true that the income share paid to the individual who furnishes any unit of productive service is equal in market value to the share of the social product causally imputable to that unit of productive service as its contribution to the total. But is there anything ethical about these equivalences? In order to give them ethical significance, two assumptions have got to be made. . . . In the first place, the ethical claim of the owner of any productive service to its contribution to product can be no better than his ethical claim to the "ownership" of the service itself. . . . In the second place, . . . the value-scale on which products and contributions are measured is itself a reflection of the existing distribution of ultimate purchasing power. (p. 10)

The debate about freedom has taken place as if a constitution of liberty could be written on the basis of abstract principles relating to coercion, private property, and so forth. In this vein, Knight's essentially negative opinion may be contrasted with Hayek's optimism. Knight seems to me to have the better of the debate. Scarcity implies cost, and cost implies subjective values, and not everyone shares a common set of values. It is therefore possible for different persons to disagree as to whether a course of action promotes or diminishes freedom, and, certainly, to disagree about whether it is "worth" its "cost." Agreement on the *proper* methods of competing, the *proper* scope of limiting competitive imitation, and the *proper* methods by which to acquire wealth is required before it can be concluded that a particular institutional change is desirable, let alone promotive of freedom.

The debate on freedom is first of all a debate on ethics. Principles of freedom, if they exist, are not to be found in purely political or economic considerations. Nor can they be defined in terms of some abstract notion of coercion. They are the province of ethics. As Knight clearly states, "freedom" is itself an ethical category. It should be noted, without bias, that so are "'fair," "equitable," and "compassion." Economists recognize the lack of objectivity in these notions, but they seem less aware of the subjectivity inherent in "freedom."

Debate about policy, about what should be done, is in important ways a debate about which ethical positions are best. Judgments of "best" can be influenced by economists, by demonstrating the consequences likely to flow from different policies; but when economists argue on behalf of some consequences and against others, when they claim this is the path to freedom and that is not, they do so partly on the basis of ethical notions that cannot be derived from economics alone. This does not demean the policy position of economists; it merely calls to our attention the broader standards to be applied when judging such pronouncements.

REFERENCES

Glasner, D. (1982). "On the Difference Between Wealth and Liberty." *International Review of Law and Economics*, 2.

Hayek, F. A. (1980). *The Constitution of Liberty*. Chicago: University Press.

Knight, F. H. (1982). *Freedom and Reform*. Indianapolis: Liberty Press.

Moore, G. (1969). "An Economic Analysis of the Concept of Freedom." *Journal of Political Economy*, 77.

Stigler, J. (1978). "Wealth and Possibly Liberty." *Journal of Legal Studies*, 2.

Index

Index compiled by Meg Davies